THE IRISH SAINTS

Short biographies of the principal Irish saints from the time of St. Patrick to that of St. Laurence O'Toole

by

DAPHNE D. C. POCHIN MOULD, B.Sc., Ph.D.

DUBLIN
CLONMORE AND REYNOLDS LTD.

LONDON
BURNS AND OATES LTD.

First Published 1964

MADE AND PRINTED IN THE REPUBLIC OF IRELAND BY
CAHILL & CO., LTD., DUBLIN FOR CLONMORE & REYNOLDS
LTD. NIHIL OBSTAT : JEREMIAH O'SULLIVAN, D.D., CENSOR
DEPUTATUS. IMPRIMATUR: ✠ CORNELIUS EPISCOPUS
CORCAGIENSIS ET ROSSENSIS. JANUARY 6TH, 1962.

CONTENTS

		Page
	Introduction	1
1.	Abban of Killabban, March 16	14
2.	Abban of Moyarney, October 27	14
3.	Adamnan (Eunan), September 23	15
	Aedan of Ferns. See Maedoc	
4.	Aed Mac Bricc, November 10	22
	Aengus the Culdee. See Oengus	
5.	Aidan of Lindisfarne, August 31	25
6.	Ailbe, September 12 (Revised date, 13)	28
7.	Albert, January 8	30
8.	Asicus/Asic/Tassach, April 27 (Revised date, 29)	30
9.	Athracht/Attracta, August 11	31
10.	Benen/Benignus, November 9	32
11.	Berchert of Tullylease, February 18	33
12.	Brendan of Birr, November 29	35
13.	Brendan of Clonfert, May 16	36
14.	Brigit (Brigid), February 1	41
15.	Buite/Boecius, December 7	48
16.	Caimin of Inis Cealtra, March 24	50
17.	Cainnech/Canice/Kenneth, October 11	52
18.	Carthach/Carthage/Mo Chuta/Mo Chuda, May 14	57
19.	Cathal/Catald of Taranto, May 10 (Revised date, Maach 8)	61
20.	Cellach mac Aodh (Celsus), April 7	62
21.	Ciaran (Kyran) of Clonmacnois, September 9	71
22.	Ciaran (Kieran) of Saighir, March 5	76
23.	Coemgen/Kevin, of Glendalough, June 3	79
24.	Colman of Cloyne, November 24 (Revised date, 26)	84
25.	Colman of Dromore, June 7	85
26.	Colman Elo, September 26	86
27.	Colman of Lindisfarne, August 8 (Feb. 18)	89
28.	Colman MacDuach, October 29	91
29.	Colmcille (Columba), June 9	93
30.	Columban (Columbanus), November 23 (Revised date, 20)	105
31.	Comgall, May 10 (Revised date, 12)	125
32.	Conleth/Conlaid/Conlaed, May 3	132
33.	Cronan of Roscrea, April 28	132
34.	Cuthbert, March 20	134

Page

35. Damhnat of Tedavnet, June 13. Under Dympna   146
     Darerca. See Monenna.
36. David, March 1   135
37. Declan, July 24   137
38. Diarmaid/Dermot, January 10   142
39. Donard/Domangort, March 24   143
40. Donat (Donatus) of Fiesole, October 22   143
41. Dympna of Gheel, May 15   146
     Edan. See Maedoc
42. Enda/Eanna, March 21   147
43. Eogan (Eugene), August 23   149
     Eunan. See Adamnan
44. Fachtna/Fachanan, August 14   149
45. Faithlenn. Mentioned under Finan Cam.   158
     Fanahan. See Findchu
46. Fechin, January 20   151
47. Felim, August 9   154
48. Ferghil (Virgil/Virgilius), November 27   154
49. Fiacre of Breuil, August 30   156
50. Fiacre of Ullard, February 8   156
51. Finan Cam., April 7   158
52. Finan Lobur, March 16   159
53. Finbar of Cork, September 25   160
54. Findchu/Fanahan of Brigown, November 25   164
55. Finian of Clonard, December 12   165
56. Finian of Moville, September 10   169
57. Fintan of Clonenagh, February 17   171
58. Fintan/Findan of Rheinau, November 15   173
59. Fintan/Munnu of Taghmon, October 21   174
60. Flannan of Killaloe, December 18   177
61. Foillan/Faelan/Feuillan, October 31. Under Fursa   181
62. Fridian/Frediano/Frigidian of Lucca, March 20   180
63. Fridolin, March 6   181
64. Fursa/Fursey, January 16   181
65. Gall, October 16   186
66. Gerald of Mayo, March 13   191
67. Gobnet, February 11   192
     Hugh Mac Bricc. See Aed Mac Bricc
68. Ibar (Ivor), April 23   195
69. Ita/Ide, January 15   196

70. Jarlath, June 6   199
     Kenneth. See Cainnech
     Kevin. See Coemgen
     Kieran. See Ciaran of Saighir
71. Kilian of Aubigny, November 13   200
72. Kilian of Würzburg, July 8   200
     Kyran. See Ciaran of Clonmacnois
73. Laserian/Laisren of Leighlin, April 18   203
     Laserian of Devenish. See Molaise
     Lelia. See Liadhain
74. Liadhain (Lelia), August 11   204
75. Livinus, November 12   204
76. Lorcan Ua Tuathail (Laurence), November 14
     (Revised date, 13)   205
77. Macartan of Clogher, March 24   213
78. Mac Creiche—see under Caimin   50
79. Mac Nisse of Connor, September 3   214
80. Maedoc/Aedan/Mogue of Ferns, January 31
     (Revised date, 30)   214
81. Mael Maedoc (Malachy), November 3   219
82. Maelruain of Tallaght, July 7   228
83. Maelrubha (Malrubius), April 21   241
     Malachy. See Mael Maedoc
84. Mel (Maol), February 6   245
85. Mobi, October 12   245
86. Mochaoi of Nendrum, June 23   246
87. Mochua of Timahoe, December 24   248
88. Mochua of Balla, March 30. Under the above.
     Mo Cchuda/Mo Chuta. See Carthach
     Mogue/Moedhóg/Moeog. See Maedoc
89. Molagga, January 20   249
90. Molaise of Devenish, September 12   250
91. Molaise of Inismurray, August 12   252
     Molaise of Leighlin. See Laserian
92. Moling, June 17   252
93. Molua of Clonfertmulloe, August 4   257
94. Moluag of Lismore (Scotland), June 25   259
95. Monenna (Darerca) of Slieve Gullion, July 6   261
96. Under the above, Darerca of Valentia, March 22
97. Munchin, January 2   263

Page

98. Muredach, August 12 (Revised date, 13)   264
  Munnu. See Fintan (Munnu)
99. Nathy, August 9   265
100. Nessan, July 25   265
101. Ninian, September 16   265
102. Oengus "the Culdee", March 11. Under Maelruain   228
103. Olan of Aghabulloge, September 5. Under Finbar, Cork   160
104. Oran/Odrán/Odhrán/Otteran, October 27   270
105. Patrick, March 17   272
106. Ruadhan, April 15   280
107. Rumold/Rombaut, July 3   281
108. Rupert/Rudbert, March 27   282
109. Samthann, December 19   282
110. Senach   284
111. Senan, March 8   285
112. Sinach (Sionach) Mac Dara, September 28   288
  Tassach. See Asicus
113. Tigernach, April 4 (5)   289
114. Ultan, May 1. Under Fursa   181
  Virgil/Virgilius. See Ferghil

Litanies of Irish Saints   290

1. The litany of saints in the liturgy of the Mass in the Stowe Missal. c. 800.

2. The two litanies of Irish saints in the Book of Leinster. Translated from the Irish original, by Charles Plummer. ('Irish Litanies', London 1925, Henry Bradshaw Society).

3. An invocation of Irish women saints from the same source. Cf. the litany mentioned in the account of St. Moling.

Irish Preaching   300

A sermon of an Irish saint. The 13th of the set of sermons of St. Columban that have survived. Perhaps preached at Milan in 613. It is closely connected with the Eucharistic material in the Antiphonary of Bangor, and is almost a commentary on the last but one verse of the *Sancti venite* : —

> The heavenly bread,
> He gives to the hungry.
> From the living fountain
> To those who thirst.

Translation by D. D. C. Pochin Mould.

Bibliography   303
Index   309

DEDICATION

ALL THE SAINTS OF IRELAND

Á rí nóib not-guídiu
is íar scís fom-ruirmius
ro bithbeó it pardus
lasin slóg doruirmius!

In rígrad doruirmius,
ol is loim de romuir,
cechae co cléir chredail
robet ocomm chobuir!

O Holy King, I ask you;
it is after fatigue I have laid me down:
may I be for ever in your paradise
with the host I have reckoned.

The kingfolk I have reckoned—and
it is only a sip from an ocean—
each of them with a devout train,
may they be helping me!
(Martyrology of Oengus)

TO THE READER:—

" Books (Courteous Reader) may rightly be compared to Gardens; wherein, let the painful Gardiner express never so much care and deligent endeavour; yet among the very fairest, sweetest and freshest Flowers, as also Plants of precious vertue; ill favouring and stinking Weeds, fit for no use but the fire or muck hill, will spring and sprout up. So fareth it with Books of the very best quality, let the Author be never so indulgent, and the Printer vigilant: yet both may miss of their aim, by the escape of Errors and Mistakes, either in sense or matter, through want of wary Correction. If then the best Books cannot be free from this common infirmity; blame not this then, of far lighter Argument, wherein thy courtesie may help us both: His blame, in acknowledging his more sufficiency, than to write so gross and absurdly: and thine, in pardoning unwilling Errors committed, which thy Judgment finding, thy Pen can as easily Correct ".

(from a 17th century English version of
the " Decameron " of Giovanni Boccaccio).

THE 1963 REVISION OF THE IRISH CALENDAR

In 1963, as part of the general liturgical reform in the Church, a revised Irish Calendar was issued, in which saints mistakenly thought to be Irish, are dropped, and some of the dates changed on which the feasts of Irish saints are to be celebrated.

The new dates of feasts are given below:— but it is important to remember that in most cases the old date is the historically important one, under which references to the saint will be found in Martyrologies and calendars.

Ailbe, September 13
Asicus, April 29
Catald, March 8
Colman of Cloyne, November 26
Columban, November 20
Comgall, May 12
Fachanan of Kilfenora, December 20
Lorcan Ua Tuathail (Laurence), November 13
Maedoc (Aedan) of Ferns, January 30
Muredach, August 13

ACKNOWLEDGMENTS

A book of this sort is necessarily a compilation; it rests upon the work of very many different scholars and writers. Again, I have gathered the material over the years, and thanks are due to the many people who have helped in that gathering, both in the world of books and at the actual places frequented by the early saints.

I have also to thank the Franciscan Fathers, Killiney, for permission to make use of unpublished material collected by the late Father Felim O Briain, O.F.M.; Dr. Ludwig Bieler, and his publishers, Messrs. Longmans, Green & Co. Ltd. and the Newman Press, Westminster, Maryland, for permission to use extracts from his translation of the works of St. Patrick; Professor Aubrey Gwynn, S.J., and the ' Irish Ecclesiastical Record ' for permission to quote his translation of a letter of Gregory VII; the Royal Irish Academy for permission to make use of translations that have been published in its " Proceedings " and in " Eriu "; the Henry Bradshaw Society for the permission to use translations from their editions of the Martyrology of Oengus, the Irish Litanies, and their other volumes dealing with Irish material.

NOTE

In the matter of references to published literature dealing with the Irish saints; general references, and publications with collections of ' Lives ', are listed in the Bibliography at the end of the work. Specific books and papers dealing with particular saints are, however, given after each individual account.

CLASSIFIED GUIDE

References to the following subjects under the following saints :—

Monastic Rules
Ailbe
Carthach
Ciaran Clonmacnois
Columban
Comgall
Maelruain
Molua

Liturgy
Buite (musical instruments)
Carthach
Mael Maedoc
Colman Ela
Columban
Comgall
Fintan Rheinau
Fintan Munnu
Fursa
Maelruain
Moling
Patrick

Literary Works
Adamnan
Buite (for Flann)
Colmcille
Donat
Fachtna
Finian Clonard
Maelruain
Patrick

Pre-Patrician Saints
Abban
Ailbe
Ciaran Saighir
Declan
Ibar

English in Ireland
Gerald
Berchert
Cf. Colman Lindisfarne

Irish Saints Abroad
Aidan
Brendan of Clonfert
Cainnech
Cathal
Colman Ela
Colman Lindisfarne
Colmcille
Comgall
Donat
Columban
Fiacre
Ferghil
Fintan Rheinau
Fursa
Gall
Kilian of Aubigny
Kilian of Würzburg
Maelrubha
Moluag

Irish Art
Aidan
Berchert
Brendan of Birr
Buite
Caimin
Colmcille
Maelruain
Moling

Bogus Irishmen
Albert
Fridian
Fridolin
Dympna
Livinus
Rumold
Rupert

Mountain Pilgrimages
Aed mac Bricc
Brendan of Clonfert
Donard
Patrick

INTRODUCTION

The Irish Saints

IRELAND is unique among nations at the present time in that she has the privilege of celebrating a feast of all her native saints. Each November 6th, the feast of all the saints of Ireland pays a liturgical tribute to the ancient title, Insula Sanctorum, Island of Saints, and asks the intercession of every Irishman in heaven from those first Christian enthusiasts of the 5th century to those, perhaps as much unknown, in the obituary columns of the day's papers. The full tally of what St. Oengus called the " kingfolk around the king above the clouds " remains unknown to us, but the known names and histories are sufficient to justify the ancient brag. Furthermore, the apostolic quality of Irish Christianity, from its first massive achievements in the 6th century to contemporary expressions like the Columban Fathers or the Medical Missionaries, has helped build up the legendary concept of an island of saints. Unfortunately the legends, more especially about the earlier Irish saints, have come to obscure the reality of their achievement. There is a real need to return to the authentic sources, to the truth as far as we can find it out, about the Irish saints, and hacking down the jungle growth of pious hagiography, arrive at a critical and considered assessment of the meaning of Insula Sanctorum.

The biographies included in this book are only concerned with the first centuries of Irish holiness, from the introduction of Christianity to the period of Lorcan Ua Tuathail and the Anglo-Norman invasion. Ireland, of course, continued to breed saints after this early period of the Celtic Church came to an end. Her conversion had been a bloodless affair, and the drama of her Age of Martyrs came late in her history, in the 16th and 17th centuries. If the period of the Celtic saints and that of the Age of Irish Martyrs provide the most obvious basis for the belief in the island of saints, it is necessary also to recall those other names which remind us of the presence of holiness at all times, Blessed Thaddeus MacCarthy against a tangle of 15th century chicanery, Matt Talbot in a Dublin tenement, John McGuinness in the contemporary Irish Civil Service.

1

The First Preaching

It seems most probable that Christianity became known in Ireland through that country's southern ports and overseas trade sometime during the first half of the 5th century. In Wales, the archaeological evidence indicates that the substantial foundation of the Church in that country came, not from early Romano-British converts but from immigrant Gallo-Roman Christians. The strong tradition of " pre-Patrician " Irish saints in the south of Ireland—Ciaran of Saighir, Ailbe of Emly, Abban, Ibar and Declan, with the stories of their visits to Rome and to Wales, is not unreasonable. It is a natural part of the ordinary comings and goings between the south of Ireland, Wales and the Continent. By the year 431, there were sufficient numbers of Christians in Ireland to have papal notice taken of them. In that year, " To the Irish believing in Christ, Palladius, ordained by Pope Celestine, is sent as their first bishop ". Leaving aside the problems of what became of this Palladius and the Patrician controversy, the Irish Annals record the arrival of Patrick in the following year 432. The traditional account concentrates Patrick's activity in the north of Ireland, leaving the south to the existing apostolate of contemporary but Irish born saints. Patrick's achievement was not merely one of evangelisation but also of organisation; from his time it is no longer a matter of small pockets of believers but of an organised Church covering the whole island.

The country into which the Faith was introduced in this fashion lay outside the confines and influence of the Roman Empire. Essentially a rural civilisation whose wealth was counted in cattle, its cultural roots ran back unbroken to prehistory. Living was hard but traditional learning and art flourished. The country was subdivided into a series of small states, ultimately owing a more or less effective allegiance to an *ard ri,* high king. The method employed by Patrick, and later by men like Columban abroad, was to approach the local ruler in the first place and gain, if not his conversion, his permission for an apostolate in his territory. There are, according to an estimate of the late Canon Power, some two thousand ancient parishes (as distinct from modern reorganisation thereof) in Ireland and it may be that they go back to the 5th and 6th centuries, marking ancient, perhaps even prehistoric, political boundaries. The barony represents the smallest political unit, the tuath. A bishop's diocese covered a wider area and corresponded to a larger grouping; diocesan boundaries were only fixed exactly later but the idea seems to have been a working reality from Patrician times on. Abroad, exact definition of diocese and parish grew slowly likewise. It is an anachronism to contrast the modern structure of the Church with that of ancient Ireland.

Overseas the first centres of Christianity had been in the towns, the bishop had his seat, later his cathedral, in the city. The literal meaning of the word pagan is countryman, peasant. In Ireland, there were no great cities and the local chief lived in his self-contained rath. Thus it was logical necessity that made the early Irish Church so largely monastic. The initial Patrician scattering of priests and bishops in important centres over the country would naturally lead to the development of monasteries if the Church were to expand and flourish. The big farmer or the chief had his dun or rath, its huts grouped within concentric walls between which cattle could be penned at night. Immediate needs were supplied by local artisans and craftsmen. The Celtic monastery is simply the self-contained dun in a religious context, the same massive walls enclosing little huts but now with the addition of oratories and standing crosses. Martin of Tours had been the first great innovator, in changing the pattern of monasticism from its mainly contemplative emphasis in the eastern deserts, to the uniting of the contemplative life with the apostolate. Martin's monks were, sometimes against their will, engaged in the apostolate, and it is notable that it was this monastic apostolate that brought about the first evangelisation of the French countryside. Irish monasteries followed the pattern set by Martin, and later to be followed by the friars, of being both centres of prayer and study and centres from which preachers and teachers went out both to supply local needs and on the long sea roads abroad, " exiles for the love of Christ ".

Martin of Tours, Ninian of Candida Casa in Scotland and David in Wales, all had a part in the birth and development of Irish monasticism. In the great expansion of monasticism in Ireland during the 6th century, two early and key figures appear to be St. Enda on the Aran Islands and St. Finian of Clonard in the Irish midlands. The love of God expressed by the total following of Christ of the monastic vocation led immediately to the desire to bring the same knowledge and love of God to all men. Accordingly the second half of the 6th century saw the beginning of the great Irish overseas apostolate, with men like Colmcille and Moluag leaving for Scotland, and Columban and Gall for Europe.

Meantime Irish sanctity and learning was attracting foreigners to Ireland, either as pilgrims and students for a temporary stay, or to

settle permanently like Gerald and Berchert. From the growth of
devotion to the great Irish monastic founders and saints we must date
back the still surviving traditional Irish pilgrimages and patterns.

Irish learning was of considerable richness and diversity for its
period. To the traditional secular learning of bard and brehon (lawyer)
was added that of Christian theology, the study of scripture, liturgy
and the writings of the Fathers. The knowledge of Latin also made
available for study the pagan classical writers, which Irishmen could
read and enjoy much as we do ourselves, without feeling the impact
and influence of a too live paganism which had turned some early
continental Christians away from classical studies. Irish paganism was
not that of the Latin classical authors, and they were able to approach
them with a simple critical appreciation, and in so doing help preserve
their texts for the future.

In passing, it may be observed that the secular bardic schools
continued to flourish alongside those of the monasteries, and that it
was the Church, represented by Colmcille, who successfully defended
the status of the bards at the Convention of Drumceatt in 575.

Although large tracts of Ireland were then heavily wooded, or very
marshy and boggy, communications seem to have been good. The
frequent references to the use of chariots by the saints imply good
roads. Sea travel to Britain and the Continent also was relatively easy.
Irish sailing curraghs probably reached (and in so doing, discovered)
Iceland sometime between 650 and 750. On the other hand, it was
a long journey and a route not without dangers and interruptions, to
Rome. The over-discussed question of the relations of the Church in
Celtic countries with Rome must be seen against the physical and
political realities of the time, and the overall much looser and
necessarily more autonomous organisation of the whole Church in
those centuries. In fact, not until the long halt of the Popes in Avignon
was there real opportunity to begin to build up the highly centralised
Church organisation we know today. The question of the method of
calculating the date of Easter, in which St. Colman of Lindisfarne
was involved at the Synod of Whitby in 664, aroused strong feelings
as such things do, but in reality involved no more than arguing the
case for the most accurate calculation. Rome, Gaul and Ireland had
each used different methods in Columban's time. As early as the end
of the 2nd century, the same problem had been raised and settled
between the Eastern and Western parts of the Church, each of which
had been following a different usage. Columban's letters indicate

sufficiently that the Church in Ireland regarded herself as Catholic and not merely looked to Peter's successor as head of the universal Church but believed that the evangelisation of Ireland had been begun under papal initiative.

That periods of fervour are followed by reaction and relaxation is a normal experience of history; some such thing took place in Ireland after the first flowering of monasticism. Towards the end of the 8th century it was countered by a new reform movement, that of the Céili Dé, whose outlook and teaching is best known to us from that of Maelruain of Tallaght.

The Northmen

The first known Viking attack was made in 793 on Lindisfarne, the Northumbrian foundation of St. Aidan. Others quickly followed, Jarrow in 794, Lambay Island off Dublin in 795 and Iona in the same year, Inismurray off Sligo in 807. The Viking attacks which ranged all over Europe were a combination of private adventuring, commercial enterprise and colonisations. In Ireland, the Northmen began their permanent settlements around the year 832, and these grew into the first real cities to exist in Ireland—Dublin, Limerick, Waterford and so on. Clontarf in 1014 seems to have been the final blow to the Northmen's expansion and prestige in Ireland.

While it is true that the Northmen's attacks did very considerable damage and kept men for long periods on the same sort of nervous stretch as the bomber raids of World War II, it would be wrong to overestimate this side of the story. That the big monasteries were worth raiding over and over again (Clonmacnois 10 times, Armagh 9, Kells 5, Glendalough 4, Lismore 6, Kildare 16) shows that their powers of recovery were sufficient to make this worth while. The obits of scribe and *fer legínn* (master of the monastic school or college) continue to be recorded regularly in the Annals in the same period and suggest the presence of large scriptoria and centres of study at the bigger monasteries. The obits of scribes—presumably the " head of the department "—as recorded, suggest that around the year 825, the numerous small scriptoria of many monasteries gave place to larger and fewer units, virtually in commercial production of manuscripts, at the bigger monasteries. Thus one should remember that while the Vikings raided Armagh 8 times between 830 and 943, the obits of her scribes are recorded with equal regularity from 808 to 893 and her masters of the schools from 879. It is possible that some of the Irish manuscripts found on the continent were not taken there to escape Viking attacks but were ordinary commercial exports from the big scriptoria!

Then again Norse ideas mingled with and cross-fertilised those of Celtic art. The 10th century saw the peak of achievement in the sculpting of high crosses. The great high cross at Clonmacnois is dated 914 and one at Monasterboice, 923. The Cross of Cong, that supreme achievement of Irish metalwork made in 1123, shows both Celtic interlace and Norse worm-dragon ornament. Moreover the Northmen were gradually becoming Christian. That Scandinavian and Celt came to live amicably together often enough is indicated by a recently discovered rune on Beginish Island off Valencia in Kerry, where according to the inscription a man of an Irish name set up the stone and a Norseman carved the rune.

11th Century Reform

On the other hand, there was a further period of relaxation in the Irish Church and there was need of new reform and reorganisation in the 11th century. All through that century the Annals record visits to Rome by Irish leaders on pilgrimage and suggest that there must have been fairly close contact between Rome and Ireland over this period. Owing to the writing of the life of Maol Maedoc (Malachy) by St. Bernard, the man who came at the very end of the reform is far better known than others of probably greater stature who had begun the work which Malachy helped complete. In particular, one may mention Malachy's immediate predecessor at Armagh, Cellach (Celsus), together with the first papal Legate in Ireland, Maolmuire Ó Dunáin, the bishop of Meath, who presided at the first synod of Cashel in 1101.

From Maol Maedoc's time dates the first introduction of continental religious Orders to Ireland, the Canons Regular of St. Augustine and the Cistercians. How church life would have developed from then on in an undisturbed Ireland is anybody's guess, for the whole picture was violently changed by the Anglo-Norman landings in 1170. The career of Lorcan Ua Tuathail (Laurence O Toole) is a kind of commentary on the transition from the Gaelic/Norse Ireland to one in which the Anglo-Norman incomers would always exercise a more or less powerful control and influence.

The Record Of The Past

The most vital witness to the achievement and existence of the early Irish saints is their present day cult, both liturgical and popular. An Irish supplement to the Roman breviary and missal was first approved in 1741, since when it has received repeated revisions and additions. In 1960 it contained 59 Irish or supposedly Irish saints. The popular cult is represented by surviving pilgrimages and patterns in honour of Irish saints, both at home and on the continent. That Irish clerics celebrate Mass and Office of Irish saints, and that Irish people claim spiritual help or physical cure from rounds paid in honour of Gobnet or Declan; that the ascent of Croagh Patrick each year draws crowds estimated in the 50,000's; is sufficient witness to the existence of the Irish saints and to their sanctity. It is the doctrine of the communion of saints in action in our own times.

The second most obvious relic of the past are the surviving ruins on Celtic monastic sites, churches, round towers, beehive cells, sculptured stones and crosses. They enable us to picture the physical background to the careers of the Irish saints. Furthermore, their very location tells us much—about the nature of ancient communications, the sort of land that was sought for agricultural use, or the island and hillside hermitages so beloved by many of the saints. That the furnishing of these now bleak looking little buildings was very splendid is suggested by the glittering ornamentation of the surviving pieces of Celtic Christian art.

To penetrate further into the spirit and outlook of the early saints, there are their surviving writings, in particular the Confession and Letter of Patrick, the collected works of Columban, Colmcille's poetry and the records of the teaching of Maelruain of Tallaght. With this go the surviving liturgical books, in particular the Antiphonary of Bangor (late 7th century), the Stowe Missal from Tallaght (late 8th century) and some prayers and hymns together with the early Martyrologies. The Celtic penitentials (handbooks for confessors listing sins and appropriate penances) also provide information about the outlook of the saints and the conditions under which they had to work.

There are also a number of collections of maxims of the spiritual life known as the ' Rules ' of various saints. They are usually named after early saints, though the collections themselves are considerably later as we now have them. However it is possible they do enshrine older traditional material.

Apart from Jonas' ' Columban ' and Adamnan's ' Colmcille ', the so-called 'Lives' of the Irish saints are of very little help to the serious biographer. In general they were written centuries after the time in which their subjects lived, and the setting may reflect the author's period rather than the saint's. They may have a basic foundation of genuine tradition, and tradition is not to be despised in a society in which a pride is taken in its oral preservation. But to this is added a rather standardised series of wonder and miracle themes, taken from Irish pagan sagas, from scripture and the ordinary common stock of pious hagiographers the world over. It is true, of course, that miracles probably do run to type and occur over and over again in the lives of different saints, heal the sick, raise the dead, cleanse the lepers, cast out evil spirits, and so on. It is well to remember that these 'Lives' were never meant to be scientific biography as we know it today; they were intended to propagate devotion to a saint, to point a moral, or on a more commercial level serve as publicity for particular shrines and centres of pilgrimage. Perhaps Standish O'Grady's remarks on the stories of trickery and the like in the 'Lives' are sufficient comment on much of this material:—" These episodes have all the appearance of broad caricatures drawn to raise a laugh, and perhaps the worst that can be said of them is that they are not in the taste of our day. . . . It is idle to suppose that the native Irish writers of remote times, whose general tone indubitably is that of gentlemen writing for gentlemen, knew no better than seriously to credit men like S. Columbkill and Adamnan, for instance, with conduct worthy of Til Eulenspiegel " (preface, " Silva Gadelica ", London, 1892).

Thus whilst scholars interested in hagiography do much interesting work in tracing the different extant versions of the 'Lives' back to earlier basic sources; or in finding out the first appearance and subsequent mutations of a miracle story; the reader in search of real facts about the early saints must only use the same material with extreme caution and an active critical sense.

The witness of placenames is important but needs careful handling. The idea of dedicating a church to a saint or to a mystery of faith was something that grew up slowly and gradually in the Church, and it was hardly general in Ireland until after the Anglo-Norman invasion. Churches were named in the Celtic Church after their founders, but this does not mean that every church site bearing the name of an early Irish saint was a personal foundation. It could equally be one made by another of his followers, from one of the group of monasteries he had founded, or yet again, a place to which his cult had spread in later times. But there is a quite definite record in placenames of personal foundations by the saints. These can be linked with the itineraries found in the ' Lives ', in which the saint travels over the country making a series of foundations. Often these may be quite genuine, but again they may stand for putting a history and a justification on the later territorial possessions of particular monasteries.

The idea of dedicating a church to a particular saint is linked with the idea of canonisation and the liturgical cult of the saints. The cult of the saints began very early in the Church, with the veneration of the martyrs. Originally there would be little distinction between the Mass for the dead said at the martyr's tomb and the Mass in honour of the martyr. The cult of the saints was originally local and the result of spontaneous popular veneration, to which the local representatives of the Church gave official approval by allowing its liturgical expression. Thus the great church of St. Peter's in Rome is built on what the evidence suggests was Peter's tomb, round which early devotion to Peter was concentrated. A cult of holy men and women not martyrs grew up naturally enough as time went on and the opportunity of dying for the Faith less frequent. Again popular veneration and the local bishop's approval of the cult was the yard-stick. None of the apostles or martyrs or fathers of the Church under-went the long formalities of present day canonisation processes, any more than did most of the Irish saints. But to be canonised by popular acclaim is an extremely stiff test, involving as it does a continued consensus of one's only too well informed neighbours' opinions! Canonisation was finally reserved to the Pope alone in 1159 (thus Maol Maedoc and Lorcan Ua Tuathail were the first Irishmen to be canonised by the Pope himself); the modern process of canonisation only goes back to that introduced by Urban VIII in 1625.

Irish Spirituality

In spite of the destruction of records, both by accident and by invaders, enough survives to give a fairly clear picture of the spiritual life and outlook of the early saints. Certain characteristics of early Irish Catholicism have remained until the present day, the vivid sense of the unseen world, devotion to the Mass, a penitential streak, and until the hedge schools gave place to the national ones, a rather marked and widespread desire of learning and knowledge.

There never seems to have been the divorce between the intellectual life and asceticism which has appeared at some other periods of the Church's history. The Irish saints combined the two with the same easy grace so that they could both enjoy the beauty of nature, seeing it the handiwork of the Lord, and yet be vividly aware of the transitoriness of the world. This life was a pilgrimage through fleeting things to the true life of heaven, and from early times there is evidence of the Irish love of pilgrimage, either for life on the foreign mission, or undertaken to some special shrine. This liking for pilgrimage is linked up with the symbol of life as a pilgrimage, with devotion to the saints and a desire to visit their tombs, and with penance. On the other hand, the penitential side of the Irish saints has been highly over-rated on account of the tall stories told of their ascetical feats in the ' Lives '. The reality, as revealed in the penances laid down by the penitentials and in sources like the documents from Maelruain's Tallaght, is much more within the reach of ordinary men. The basic items, as in the Church everywhere, are prayer, fasting and vigil. It is also necessary to recall that asceticism is a relative term; to be judged against the norm of contemporary life. In early Ireland living was decidedly rough by our modern standards. One suspects that the mainly vegetarian and moderate diet of Celtic monks was a healthier one than that of ordinary folk!

The basis of prayer was the official prayer of the Church, the Divine Office and the Mass. Surviving material from Comgall's Bangor, Maelruain's Tallaght and from the pen of Columban, give some idea of what the liturgy was like in early Ireland.

There is plentiful evidence of a deep devotion to the Mass and to the Blessed Sacrament. The *Sancti venite* hymn, sung during the giving of Communion at Bangor, is claimed as the oldest surviving Eucharistic hymn in western Europe, and it seems certain that its author was an Irishman. Another indication of devotion to the Mass comes from the penitentials, some of which have special sections devoted to all the possible accidents that might happen the consecrated species, and show the care normally lavished on them. Together with this love of the Mass went a stress on frequent Communion and Confession and the need to have a " soul friend ", a spiritual director. On the continent, the old system of public penance for serious faults had broken down by the time the Celtic missionaries arrived, and they seem to have done much to popularise and spread the idea of private confession *and* private penance, for both serious and small faults. The Celtic penitentials with their careful tariffing of sins with so many days or years of penance, together with the Irish idea of substitutions—a short sharp penance in place of a more prolonged, less severe one, also seem to have played a part in developing the Church's system of indulgences.

It is probably inaccurate to speak of a " Celtic " liturgy, for the liturgical forms in use in Ireland belonged to the general pattern of the western Latin rites. It is well to remember that full standardisation of the Latin rite only came about with the Council of Trent. The Offices were longer and more elaborate than they are today in the west, but had the same underlying basic pattern. We do not have a set of liturgical books covering the Divine Office in early Ireland, but the Stowe Missal from Tallaght provides a Mass text for the end of the 8th century. It includes a litany with a number of Irish saints in it (the present Latin rite has reduced the ancient litany to the Kyrie alone), and a further long list of Irish names are commemorated in the Canon itself. The suggestion is that the Irish Church did not have Masses and Offices of the saints scattered through the year as in the present rite, but held to the basic liturgical cycle (Christmas, Lent, Easter, Pentecost, etc.) together with a very full commemoration of its national saints whenever Mass was celebrated.

The psalms, then as now, formed the basis of the Divine Office, and were, in addition, the staple of private devotion. The 118th psalm, *Beati immaculati in via,* was specially beloved, partly one suspects on account of its length, but also for its very attractive content. Twelve ' Beati ' were counted the equivalent of saying the whole ' Three Fifties ' (the 150 psalms of the psalter), and so used in imposing penances on the many who knew the 118th psalm by heart but not the whole psalter. It is possible that this devotion to the " Three Fifties ", which often meant their daily recitation, is a source of the 150 Paters or Aves as a simpler substitute for the unlearned, and thus one root of the modern Rosary.

Hymns also formed part of the Office and some noble examples of Irish hymn writing in Latin have survived. The Antiphonary of Bangor contains a dozen Latin hymns. One should also mention Colman Mac Mur-chon's splendid invocation of St. Michael (*In Trinitate spes mea fixa non in omine*) and St. Cú-Chuimne's hymn to Our Lady (*Cantemus in omni die concinentes varie*). Colman appears to have been an abbot of St. Finian's foundation at Moville and to have died in 736; Cú-Chuimne, who died 747, apparently belonged to Iona.

Irish was used, not in the official liturgy, but to a considerable degree in private devotion, in poetry, litany and lorica. In the lorica form of prayer, of which Patrick's Breastplate is the best known, an ancient spell formula was employed to encircle oneself not with magic but with the power and help of the Lord. Long litanies were very popular, they invoke not merely the great names of the Church but all the unknown ones as well, virgins round Mary, monks around Antony and so forth. Then as still in Ireland, the supernatural and spiritual was very real; men had a positive sense of the help and the presence of Our Lady, the angels and the saints.

That the country had two learned languages appears in the curious and rather attractive blend in commentary and homily in which Irish and Latin are mixed, phrase against phrase as appears best to fit the context.

The Irish seem to have turned their attention to overseas missionary work almost as soon as the country had been fully converted. The love of God meant the urge to bring Him to all men. It also meant the desire to be alone with the Beloved, and hermitages (marked by the placenames, *desert*, to this day) were sought amongst the woods and on the heights and on the islands. This hermit ideal was not an alternative to the apostolate but its immediate source of spiritual power; the great apostles like Columban and Colmcille are recorded seeking and retiring to such solitary spots as a part of the pattern of their public activities. The legend of the voyage of Brendan sets him first upon the mountain top from which he sees the vision of the Land of Promise. Again, the Irish monks were nearer to the inspiration of the desert fathers than we; in the desert communal monastic life had grown from that of the solitary hermits and their more difficult vocation. Eastern monasticism to this day sees the monk retiring to a hermitage as the crown of his spiritual achievement. Frequent mention of anchorites seems linked with the growth of the Céili Dé movement, but it is likely that they were hardly anchorites in the sense we would understand it today. They probably remained in close touch with a nearby monastery.

Nobody reading the sins detailed in the penitentials or the accounts of the lives of the Irish saints can suppose that Ireland was ever universally a land of saints and scholars. Men remained much what they usually are, good, bad and indifferent. Yet against this ordinary background of humanity, Irish monks and saints did set a standard of holiness which evoked the legend of the land of saints. They did achieve an integration of science and sanctity, of learning and holiness, of apostolate and contemplation, which remains a valid headline and example for us today. *Vive in Christo, ut Christus in te,* Columban urged, " live in Christ that Christ may live in you ", and in so far as we can trace the history of the early saints, this is the essential goal and theme of their lives. It is an attempt to turn wholly to God and to integrate the whole of life into a pattern ordered by His love. Columban, in a sermon and in phrases which remind one a little of St. John of the Cross, described something of this thirst for God. His words can well stand for the longing of the whole litany of less well documented Irish saints.

For Columban said : " How beautiful is that spring of living water, which never goes dry, water springing up into eternal life. Lord, you yourself are that fountain, always to be longed for, always to be drunk. Lord Christ, give us always this water that it may be in us a fountain of living water, springing up into eternal life. Yes, I know I'm asking a lot. But King of Glory, you know how to give great things and have made great promises. There is nothing that is greater than you, and you have given yourself to us, who gave yourself for us. So we ask that we may know what we love, for we are asking nothing less than yourself to be given to us. For you are our all, our life, our light, our health, our food, our drink, our God. Our Jesus, inspire our hearts with that breath of your Spirit and wound our souls with your love, so that we all can say in truth, ' Show me he whom my soul has loved, for I am wounded by love '. Lord, I would like those wounds. For blessed indeed is a soul so wounded by love. It will seek the fountain, always drink, yet always thirst, for here to drink is to thirst the more. Thus it will seek in loving whilst it is healed in being wounded. May then the Physician of righteousness and health, our God and Lord Jesus Christ, wound our inmost souls with this healing wound, who is one with the Father and the Holy Spirit, world without end. Amen ".

(from Sermon 13)

ABBAN

of Cell Abbain — March 16
of Mag Arnaide — October 27

The surviving Latin and Irish ' Lives ' have fused into one, more or less confused, story, traditions about two different men. One of them, of Cell Abbain (Killabban) in Leix appears to belong to the 5th century and the " pre-Patrician " group. His mother, Caoinech, was said to be a sister of Ibar. Oengus in his Felire notes him at March 16th, ' Abban doss oir ainglech ' (Abban, angelic bush of gold) and makes him obviously distinct from the Abban at October 27th, Abban abb cain cliarach ' (fair, train-having abbot). The October 27th Abban of Mag Arnaide, Moyarney in Wexford, appears to belong to the later part of the 6th century, he may have died around 620. His mother, Mella, is said to have been a sister of St. Coemgen (Kevin) of Glendalough.

That Oengus describes the second Abban as an abbot would fit in with his later period, and with the possibility of the earlier Abban, not so described, belonging to the first period of Christianity in Ireland. The ' Lives ' give a long list of churches said to have been founded by their synthetic Abban; it has been suggested that the Connacht and Kerry series belong to the older Abban, those in Meath, Leinster and Cork to the younger one, but there would appear little possibility of arriving at the real facts of the case about these churches' founders.

Two little stories are suggestive of a tradition about the early days of the Faith in Ireland, the pagan king who challenged Abban to say how much of a gallan (standing stone) was below ground, and whose conversion followed Abban's accurate estimate being tested by excavation; and the other about the youth's vocation. Abban's parents opposed this, wishing him to succeed to the local kingship, and even went the length of imprisoning him in the hostages' pit.

According to the Irish version of the ' Life ', Abban was invoked against shipwreck, " no one who goes to sea in curragh or ship shall fail to return safe, if he recites thrice in the name of the Trinity:—

Curach Abain foran linn	The curragh of Abban on the water,
Is Muinnter fionn Abain ann	And the fair company of Abban in it."

ADAMNAN (EUNAN)

September 23

St. Adamnan's own personal fame has suffered a certain eclipse by that of the subject of his great biography, Colmcille. Like St. Thomas Aquinas, so with Adamnan, one thinks first of his literary achievement and only afterwards of the saint himself. Meantime the modifications of the sounds of his name have produced a variety of quite different looking end-products, in the Scottish calendar he is Adamnan, in Ireland under the modern form of Eunan. In Scotland the name is even to be found under the disguise of a St. Arnold's Seat in Forfar! The oldest spelling is *Adomnán* and the meaning is " great terror ".

He came of the same stock as Colmcille and was born, probably about 624, in Tir-Aedha (Tirhugh). Thus only 27 years separated the boy's birth from Colmcille's death. Adamnan's father was named Ronan and was 6th in descent from Conall Gulban; his mother was Ronnat of the Cinel Enna (Eogain). It is possible that the young man studied at Clonard, certainly he received an excellent education, the best then available. Later he crossed to his kinsman's great monastery of Iona and became a monk there under Abbot Seghine, who ruled from 623 to 652. Eventually Adamnan himself was elected abbot of Iona, which he governed from 679 until his death in 704. As abbot of the chief monastery of the Columban group, Adamnan naturally played an important part in affairs and made various journeys both to Northumbria (which had been evangelised from Iona) and to Ireland.

Adamnan had become friendly with a certain Northumbrian prince named Aldfrith who was in exile in Ireland and Scotland. Aldfrith's brother, Ecgfrith, ruled Northumbria from 671 to 685, in which latter year Aldfrith gained the throne after Ecgfrith's defeat and death at Nechtan's Mere. During Ecgfrith's reign, some 60 Irishmen had been carried off from Meath in the course of a raid thereon. As soon as his friend Aldfrith was securely established, Adamnan went south to negotiate for the release of the Irish prisoners. Perhaps on this occasion, or a later one, Adamnan became converted to the Roman method of calculating the date of Easter which both Northumbria and the south of Ireland had already adopted. Adamnan threw all the weight of his position into trying to get it universally accepted but failed to persuade his own brethren of Iona.

It seems that he personally escorted the released prisoners back to Ireland in 686, returning at once to Iona afterwards. In 692, he is recorded as back in Ireland when the question of the exemption of the Leinster men from paying tribute to the high king was being discussed. He himself describes how he was held up by contrary winds on an island on his way to Iona from an Irish synod, when he particularly wished to be back on the island to celebrate the feast of Colmcille on June 9th. Adamnan was accustomed to use plain speaking to the aforesaid saint, Colmcille. " Are you really pleased that we should be storm stayed here, to keep your feast day amongst country people and not in your church," he prayed that night. " It would be easy enough for you to get a change of wind from the Lord and us to Iona in time for the festival Mass." Nights are very short indeed in Scotland in June and it was very early that the abbot and his monks rose to find such a sudden change of weather and scene that is a part of the splendour of the Western Isles. The sea lay mirror smooth, with the morning sun high-lighting island and hill. They hurried to their ships and as they took to the oars a south wind sprang up. The sails went up and the little fleet sped through the bright water, by 9 a.m. they had covered some thirty-five miles and were landing on Iona. At mid-day the abbot was in the church to celebrate the solemn Mass of Colmcille and his immediate successor, Baithene, whose feast falls on the same day. (Vita Columbae, Bk. II, ch. 45).

In view of his travels, it seems quite likely that a number of the churches in Scotland and Ireland which bear Adamnan's name are personal foundations. There is, for example, Adamnan's Croft on the main route from Iona to the east of Scotland through the Great Glen. It is in Glen Urquhart off Loch Ness. In Ireland, he is patron of Raphoe, southwest of Derry, though this seems to have been actually an earlier foundation by Colmcille. Raphoe today preserves two carved fragments of a cross base or a lintel, there is no trace of the round tower that stood there till early in the 17th century.

In Glen Lyon, in Scotland, there survived, right into our own times, a strong tradition of Adamnan halting the plague there. He set a limit to its ravages, the tradition told, by planting his crozier (Bachall) at Craigianie. This tradition is of interest in that it links up with Adamnan's own account of how, by the powerful aid of Colmcille, he and his party escaped catching the infection when they travelled through areas in which it was rife. (Vita Columbae, Bk. II, ch. 46). Adamnan says that all Europe except northern Scotland and the Picts and Scots had been twice devastated by plague during his lifetime, and he attributed their escape to Colmcille's prayers. Moreover he tells how when he went through infected areas to visit ' my friend, king Aldfrith ', though they walked through the shadow of death none of them died or even picked up any disease at all.

Adamnan was back in Ireland in 697, and may have remained there till his death. The Annals of Ulster record that in 697, " Adomnanus ad Hiberniam pergit et dedit legem innocentium populus ". This was the occasion of the promulgation of the famous " Cáin Adomnáin " at a synod held at Birr. It appears that previously women had been held on an equal footing with men by Irish law; now a change was made to give them special privileges. Thus murder by a woman was put on the same level as indeliberate homicide committed by a man. Moreover, penalties were decreed for the murder of women whether by an individual or a party of raiders, for violence of all sorts done to them, and it was forbidden to employ women in military operations. The Cáin however was not entirely concerned with the position of women; it legislated for other non-combatants, boys and clerics, and it set out to guarantee rights of sanctuary. It also defined the freedom of the Church. Raphoe preserved an old Irish tract on the Cáin and the assembly, which was divided into four parts. The first is an Introduction, written perhaps at the end of the 9th or in the early 10th century. Then follow details of the place of assembly and a fairly historical list of those present together with the fines granted Adamnan and his successors. The third section describes how an angel told Adamnan to make the law. The fourth part is the actual law as drafted at the assembly by its lawyers.

The Venerable Bede speaks of Adamnan as " a good and wise man, remarkably learned in Holy Scripture ", and went on to summarise Adamnan's account of the Holy Places in his history of the English Church and to use it as the basis of his own separate work on the topic. Adamnan's parade of a few scraps of Greek and Hebrew may however imply that he had simply picked up these items rather than that he had any detailed knowledge of either language. Certainly Adamnan's book on the Holy Places shows an intelligent interest in Greek and Hebrew names. Adamnan was a man of reasonably critical good sense, careful in handling his material, checking it against the information to be got in the Iona library which seems to have been a good one. He checked the eye witness accounts of the storm driven Arculf against what he already knew about the Holy Land and combined the traveller's account with information from his books. With the Life of Colmcille, he had grown up in the fulness of the tradition, with men who had known the saint, and he mentions on a number of occasions whom he got particular items from and how near they were to the incident described. A third work, on the Eclogues of Virgil, is sometimes claimed to be his, but the evidence seems very slight. The commentary is of interest however in showing that Ireland was maintaining the study of " grammar " in the ancient sense of the word, when it was dead in the rest of Europe and that they had available copies of ancient commentaries on Virgil. " The Vision of Adamnan " has no connection with the Iona Adamnan; it consists of a vision of the next world thought to be not later than the 10th century, together with an 11th century addition.

Adamnan's two great works then are the book on the Holy Places, *De Locis Sanctis,* and the biography of Colmcille, *Vita Sancti Columbae.* The book on the Holy Places was the earlier work and Adamnan gave a presentation copy to king Aldfrith on one of his visits to Northumbria. He probably wrote it in the period 683-6. His work on Colmcille was certainly written before 697 but probably not before 692.

The way in which Adamnan got the material for his first book was romantic in the extreme. A certain bishop named Arculf from Merovingian Gaul had gone on a prolonged pilgrimage to the Holy Land. He seems to have been there over the period 679-82, and appears to have been in Constantinople during the period of the Council condemning Monothelitism, that is 680-1. He may have returned to Rome with the papal delegates late in 681 or early in the next year. Continuing his journey, Arculf was storm driven northward and landed on the west coast of the British islands, eventually turning up in Iona. There Adamnan fastened on him eagerly and set about getting a full account of all his travels and experiences. Notes were taken down during the telling of the story, and when it came to descriptions of churches, Adamnan got Arculf to sketch plans of them on the waxed tablets used for note taking; these plans eventually went into the finished book. Jerusalem had fallen in 638, so Arculf had visited both Moslem and Byzantine countries. Adamnan was quite unimpressed it would seem by the descriptions of the great churches of these regions, Sancta Sophia in Constantinople is simply called the " very celebrated round stone church ", and he is rather superior about transportation. Possibly the Irish monasteries had large wooden buildings, of which they were proud, of which all trace is lost, and certainly they had good enough roads for wheeled transport to be a matter of course.

The most recent editor of Adamnan's book says that it made a real " contribution to the information previously available about the Holy Land ".

Adamnan was interested in questioning Arculf about the nature of the country over which he had travelled, the crops grown and so on. The Dead Sea brought up the question of the difference between salt crystallised out from sea water and rock salt:—Arculf had seen both, at the Dead Sea and at salt mines in Sicily. Rock salt, Adamnan thought, should be considered the " salt of the earth " of which Our Lord spoke. That pine wood used as fuel in Jerusalem should come to the city by camel back amused him. " Camels, I say, for in all Judea, as Arculf relates, wagons, or chariots even, are rarely found." Then too, a seaman himself living on an island, Adamnan was interested in the sea and to Arculf's story he added all he could find in reference books about the harbour of Alexandria, the dangers of its narrow mouth, its safety when you were once in it, and its lighthouse.

The relics seen by Arculf naturally included those of the Passion. There was the chalice, alleged to have been used at the Last Supper, the lance and the holy shroud, " which was placed over his head in the sepulchre " and was about 8 feet long. The tradition was that it owed its preservation to having been stolen by a believing Jew from the actual sepulchre and then for long handed down as an heirloom in his family. He mentions the finding of the True Cross, but as an aside to the story of the man raised to life by contact with it. In Sancta Sophia, the True Cross, or part of it, was preserved in a chest which contained three pieces of wood, the cross beam and the upright cut into two sections. It was only exposed for public veneration on the last three days of Holy Week; on Maundy Thursday the Emperor and the soldiers came to venerate and kiss it; on Good Friday, the royal ladies and all the other women; on Holy Saturday, the bishop and clergy.

Arculf visited a church of Our Lady in the valley of Josaphat in which he was shown her empty tomb. Adamnan, who like many in the west at this date, did not hold the doctrine of the Assumption, records " the empty stone sepulchre of the holy Mary, where she was once laid to rest. But how, or when, or by what persons her holy remains were removed from this sepulchre, or where she awaits the resurrection, no one, as it is said, can know for certain ". Bede is more cautious, in taking over the sentence, he leaves out the last half, from " where she awaits the resurrection ". It is curious that Arculf gathered no speculations on the fate of the body, which one would expect to find around a show piece of an empty tomb! Agnosticism on the fate of Mary's body was general at this period in the west. The feast on the 15th August was called the Dormition until the end of the 8th century. Adamnan died at the beginning of the 8th century, by its end, the Martyrology of Tallaght gives the present day title, Assumptio Mariae Virginis, to August 15th.

In Constantinople, Arculf heard a lot about the cult of a " confessor, George by name ", and Adamnan wrote up at length two rather amusing miracle stories about this George. It is ironic that the cult of George seems to have come to England from Irish sources. Adamnan is the first northern author to take him up, and it is in Northumbria, the area of Irish influence, that the English cult of George is first found, in the early 10th century Durham ritual. He was not really the national patron of England until the 14th century and Edward III.

Adamnan concludes his little book with the usual request for prayers, both for Arculf and himself—who had written up the former's experiences in spite of being " daily beset by laborious and almost insupportable ecclesiastical business from every quarter ".

In his book about Colmcille, Adamnan is writing of country that he knows intimately from living in it, and from a close contact through very fresh tradition, and through prayer, with the subject of the biography. Strictly speaking it is not biography in the modern sense, for its three books are not arranged chronologically but according to the subject matter of the incidents described. Book I is concerned with Colmcille's power of prophecy: Book II with his miracles and Book III with visions of angels and manifestations of heavenly light. Only at the beginning of the whole work and at the end does Adamnan use " straight " narrative. He starts with some notes about the saint's birth and his going to Scotland; at the end he tells the story of Colmcille's last days and death on Iona, justly famous as a gem of narrative writing.

The way in which his material came to him is indicated in a number of places. Thus the story about St. Fintan wishing to become a monk of Colmcille and the latter sending him back to Ireland to make a foundation of his own (Bk. I, ch. 2) comes from Oisseneus son of Ernan, an aged priest who had known Fintan and had the account from him direct. Virgno's seeing of Colmcille praying circled with heavenly light (Bk. III, ch. 19), came to Adamnan at one remove further, from Comman who had the story from his uncle—Virgno. Various people saw visions of angels and of brilliance on the night Colmcille died, and one of them, Ernene, described what he saw to young Adamnan. It sounds suspiciously like a very brilliant and for so far south, unusual, display of the Northern Lights!

There are attractive personal touches in the book. Adamnan tells of the effectiveness of Colmcille's intercession, when they pray to him for fine weather for transporting timber by sea, or to save it when a storm blows up on the way home. (Bk. II, ch. 45). Pine and oak were felled in the then extensive natural woods on the Scottish mainland, and towed by curragh to Iona for monastic building projects. Adamnan was obviously as much at home bringing home building material as in his library or on his various important missions! Again he vividly describes how a drought in Iona was ended by prayer to Colmcille, how they went in procession round their newly ploughed and sown fields carrying Colmcille's white tunic and the books he had written, taking in too the Hill of the Angels on which he had been seen with angels, and that the tunic was shaken out three times and the books read upon the aforesaid hillock. Rain followed immediately. Those who have seen a spring drought in the Western Isles will recognise at once the authenticity of Adamnan's description thereof! (Bk. II, ch. 44).

Adamnan's personal affection for Colmcille is one of his most attractive characteristics; it was an intimate familiar thing that did not hesitate almost to abuse the man when the seas roughened under the towing curraghs. " Indeed we thought you had some influence with God and would alleviate our toil! Are you enjoying getting us into this difficulty and delay?"

Adamnan combined in himself many of the finest notes of Celtic sanctity; this vivid sense of the communion of saints, a real scholarship that did not exclude other skills like seamanship or diplomacy, a love of learning that sought eagerly everywhere for new information.

Adamnan: *De Locis Sanctis*: Text and translation. Edited Denis Meehan. Dublin Institute for Advanced Studies, 1958.

Vita Sancti Columbae. A. O. Anderson and M. O. Anderson. *Adomnan's Life of Columba*, Edinburgh and London, 1961. Latin text and translation. There is a many times reprinted English version by W. Huyshe.

Cain Adomnain. Text and translation, edited Kuno Meyer in Anecdota Oxoniensia. Oxford 1905.

J. Ryan: *The Cain Adomnain* in the symposium *Studies in Early Irish Law*. R.I.A. Dublin, 1936.

The Canones Adomnani—rules on what food may or may not be eaten, have no connection with Adamnan other than their name.

Betha Adamnáin translated M. Joynt in *The Celtic Revue*, Oct. 15, 1908, pp. 97-107, is a highly coloured and legendary Irish account of Adamnan.

The Reliquary of Adamnan, Archivium Hibernicum. Vol. 4, 1915, pp. 199-214. L. Gwynn, text, translation and notes on the poem which describes the relics gathered by Adamnan and enclosed in one reliquary. It was brought by an envoy from Iona to Ireland as part of the effort to make peace between the Cinel Eogain and the Cinel Conaill after the battle between the two in 727. These two peoples had earlier agreed to keep the peace in honour of Adamnan, since they were respectively the races of his father and mother.

See also entries for COLMCILLE and AIDAN.

AED (AODH/HUGH) MAC BRICC

November 10

Aed (Aodh, Hugh) Mac Bricc died in 588 or 589, and today is chiefly of interest as the patron of one of Ireland's mountain pilgrimages, the now neglected *turas* of Sliab Liac in Donegal. Originally his fame seems to have depended on his powerful Ui Neill connections—he was descended from Conn of the Hundred Battles—and on his power to cure headache. Legend had it that he had relieved a man of a headache by transferring the pain to his own head. Aed is called in fact *sui liag*, master physician, and a lorica-like Latin hymn of 8th or perhaps even 7th century date invokes his aid against headache.

The Latin ' Life ', probably of 12th century date, tells a series of stories, most of them the stock in trade of hagiography, but nothing of Sliab Liac.

Whilst Aed's father, Bric or Bricc, was of the Ui Neill, his mother came from Munster. Apparently there was quite a family of boys for later Bishop Ilund (Iland) is described persuading Aed not to insist on his rights to a share of the family patrimony. Later Aed is ordained a bishop in Meath, and is described as founding monasteries in Meath and Munster. The traditions collected in the ' Life ' keep Aed fairly constantly on the move about the country. He visits Molaise at Devenish (and works a miracle by shifting a huge tree trunk with the leverage of prayer alone) and Rioc on Inishboffin in Lough Ree.

At the latter, the very common miracle story is told once again, of how Aed who never ate meat turns the hospitable Rioc's spread of meat into bread, fish and honey! It is quite likely however that Bishop Aed did visit many communities of women to direct and advise them; several stories about him relate to his visits to these small groups of religious women; at one, under the official direction of Ciaran of Clonmacnois (or better one would say under that of Clon-macnois, for Ciaran died young) he ate the dinner intended for Ciaran who was also expected. He also got the sisters out of the difficulty this involved them in, by duplicating the meal miraculously!

Here a miracle story is attached to what may well have happened, Aed's direction of nuns. Another story also is suggestive of real life in its background, the constructional engineer who travels the country building raths. Aed gets him a commission, the triple walled Rath Bailb. The man's payment is the fill of these three walls of cattle. Driving them away, the beasts took panic and galloped off in all directions, Aed recalled them by a miracle to their owner.

He is also connected in the tradition with the birth of Aed Slane. Mugain, a Munster woman and the wife of Diarmait Mac Cerbaill, king of Tara, is sterile, but after Aed had prayed for her, gives birth to Aed Slane.

Aed's principal church was Cell Air (Killare) in Co. Westmeath, on the road from Mullingar to Ballymore, close to the Hill of Ushnagh. In the Ordnance Survey letters of 1837, the fact that local devotion to Aed was dying out in Killare was reported, only the Irish speakers recalled that the patron of the place was *Easpog Aodh,* Bishop Aed. (Letter of Sept. 17, 1837). Again on October 11, 1837, O'Donovan noted at Rahugh (Ráth Aodha), " St. Aodh is generally called *easpog Aodh* ' bishop Hugh ' by the Irish speaking people throughout the country. His festival is still celebrated in this parish ". Rahugh appears in the Life. An angel tells Aed that he need not build a monastery there, as he is intending to do, as there is a local rich man who will give him an existing rath (dun). It appears that the Church did receive such gifts and the massive walls of Inismurray cashel are for instance very probably of secular, even pre-Christian origin.

Rahugh (Rath Hugh) is also in Co. Westmeath, but the great moun-tain of Slieve League (Sliab Liac) is in Donegal, rising in a tremendous face of precipices nearly two thousand feet above the sea in Donegal Bay. The mountain is 1,972 feet high in point of fact. From its summit there is one of those tremendous Irish panoramas of sea and mountain, the outlook reaching round by the limestone heights of Ben Bulbin and then across the bay to the Mayo heights. In clear weather, Croagh Patrick can be seen.

A broad, well-built pilgrim track ascends the gentler slopes of the mountain from Carrick and Teelin. Stational cairns are set along this track, and on the summit itself, in a sheltered fold of the ridge, back from the craggy drop to the sea, are the remains of a small hermitage. It is very ruinous and its details are not easy to make out. Large boulders invite the construction of shelters under or alongside them, and in fact this has been done. There is a ruined beehive hut of very large boulders and a wall that runs from it to some large boulders makes a semi-circular enclosure in front of the slope of the hill. Inside is a rectangular building in ruin. Outside is a well with a flake of rock with a Latin cross cut on it set in a cairn and here are the usual votive offerings of pennies, nails, rosary beads and the like. There is a second seepage or spring to the east, also with stone setting and cairn. On the ridge above this hermitage, on the actual crest of the mountain, are a large number of little cairns, some round, some like hut ruins. The full *turas* would have included prayers and rounds at all these points. It seems largely but not entirely abandoned at the present time. Bishop Aed is said to have gone to live as a hermit on Slieve League and this seems quite probable.

There was also devotion to him in Scotland if the identification of the saint of Kirkmabrick in Wigtown and Kirkcudbright with the Irish Aed is correct. He may even have visited Scotland himself.

In fact, Aed is one of the many Irish saints whose cult was widespread and who was obviously an outstanding personality, but of whom today little authentic history survives. It is, for instance, of interest that mention of his powers against headache and the hymn invoking his aid thereto is found in an 8th century ms at Karlsruhr —the Codex Augiensis 221 (cf. Mone, Lateinische Hymnendes Mittelaliers. Fribourg 1853-55, vol. 3 pp. 181-182). Oengus in his Felire gives Aed a whole verse to himself: —

Aed macc Bricc dend rígraid,	Aed son of Brecc of the kingfolk;
becc ná bu mó ecaib,	he was almost greater than death :
is ard isin mórflaith	he is high in the great kingdom,
in sab síl Chuinn chétaig.	the champion of the race of hundred-battled Conn.

The head of the crozier of Aed Mac Bricc was found in a lake at Loughrea, Co. Galway.

The 'Life' concludes with a curious little story intended to exalt Aed, and make him the object of admiration even of Colmcille. Aed had made a pact with one of his monks that they would both go to heaven together; as Aed lay dying the monk opted out on his side of the agreement. However a certain peasant, hearing what was doing, jumped at the opportunity! Colmcille in Iona knew miraculously of this happening and told the monks of the wonderful deed of holy bishop Aed who took a sinner to heaven who merited no place there.

See also for the other mountain pilgrimages, BRENDAN OF CLONFERT, DONARD and PATRICK.

Enrí O Muirgheasa: *The Holy Wells of Donegal*. Bealoideas, 1936.
S. H. O Grady. *Silva Gadelica*. I, 82-84. II, 88-91, prints an account of the Birth of Aed Slane from the Leabhar na huidhre (Book of the Dun Cow) in which both Bishop Aed and Finian of Moville are involved in a whole series of wonders, probably derived from pagan legend and saga.

AIDAN (AEDAN) OF LINDISFARNE

August 31

The first successful preaching of the gospel in the north of England, in pagan Northumbria, was in the Irish language. Paulinus indeed had come north and achieved the conversion of the king of Northumbria, Edwin, in 627. But at Hatfield, six years later, in 633, Edwin was killed and his men defeated by the pagan Penda of the Mercians and Cadwalla of Wales. Paulinus and Queen Ethelberga fled south to Kent and the north reverted to paganism. Earlier, in 617, Edwin had defeated and killed Ethelfrid of Bernicia in battle, and Ethelfrid's son, Oswald, had fled north and been hospitably received in Iona. Here his host was the same Virgno of whom Adamnan wrote, abbot Fergna, who had known Colmcille. Oswald was baptised and after Edwin's death, when he went south once more to claim his kingdom, determined to ask monks from Iona to evangelise it.

In 634, Oswald defeated the nominal Christian Cadwalla. He then, as soon as he was settled on the Northumbrian throne, wrote to Virgno's successor as abbot of Iona, Segéne (Seghine), the man who was also Adamnan's first abbot, and asked him to send a mission south.

Seghine sent one Corman, but he was quickly back in Iona saying that the Angles were impossible people and he could do nothing with them. Another Iona monk, Aidan, Irish born or of the Irish settled in western Scotland, then said that they should not give up so easily and that a different technique might be more successful in winning them. Accordingly Aidan was consecrated bishop and set off south. He made his headquarters on the tidal island of Lindisfarne from which he made rapid progress in evangelising the country. The king, an Irish speaker, often acted as interpreter for Aidan. The bishop travelled on foot except when there was real need for haste, and this mode of getting about the country must have helped him make friendly contact with all sorts of people. Bede, our chief source for Aidan's career, cannot speak too highly of him—always excepting of course his method of calculating the date of Easter! Aidan and his monks devoted themselves to prayer and meditation, reading the scriptures and learning the psalms by heart. He introduced the custom of fasting on Wednesdays and Fridays which was followed in Ireland —and indeed is still marked by the Irish names of these days, first and second fasts (dia Céadaoin and dia hAoine—day of the first fast (Wednesday) and of the fast (Friday). Aidan too gave alms liberally, he ransomed those who had been wrongfully sold into slavery, and of the latter educated a number for the priesthood.

Penda meantime was still very much alive and Oswald was killed in a battle against him in 642. Oswald seems to have been a good man, and was venerated as a saint and a martyr. His kingdom was now divided into two parts, northern Bernicia falling to Oswald's brother, Oswy, and Oswin ruling southern Deira. This arrangement was hardly likely to last and in fact Oswin was killed by Oswy in 651.

Oswin was very friendly with Aidan. Bede tells how Oswin gave Aidan a magnificent horse fully equipped for the road with harness and trappings. Aidan shortly afterwards met a beggar on the road and gave him the horse, furniture and all. The king was not unnaturally hurt at this and going into dinner with the saint asked him why he could not have given the beggar a less valuable beast, which Oswin would willingly have supplied. Aidan was quite unrepentant: " Is that foal of a mare more dear to you than the Son of God?" said he. The bishop sat down at the table and the king stood warming himself by the fire. Suddenly he moved over to Aidan and knelt at his feet. " I'll not speak of this again," he said, " nor set up to judge what or how much of our money you give to the poor ". They sat down to eat, the king cheerful enough now, but Aidan wept. Oswin did not speak Irish, and another priest of Aidan's party used that language to ask the reason of his tears. Aidan answered that he had never known so humble a king and he felt sure he would die soon. And indeed so it fell out. Aidan himself only survived Oswin by twelve days.

It was at the king's fortress of Bamborough (that Bede had no idea of what the place was like is evident from his calling it a " city ") that Aidan died, in the chapel there. The date was August 31, 651. Aidan had been bishop at Lindisfarne since 635. His successors were Irishmen, Finan, then in 661, Colman. The latter went back first to Iona and then to Ireland after the synod of Whitby in 664. Lindisfarne was a fully Irish monastery until Whitby, long after, it radiated Irish influences and was a centre in which Irish artistic inspiration mingled with that of the native Angles and that from Continental sources. The influence of Irish artists can be seen in the pages of the Book of Lindisfarne nor was it a one-sided contribution, for the Lindisfarne bird is on the Tara brooch. As well there are from Lindisfarne and Hartlepool (another foundation of Aidan) a series of early grave slabs with Irish affinities (Clonmacnois resembles them). Their like are found nowhere else in Northumbria.

Meantime Aidan's personal influence must have been far reaching through the men he trained for the priesthood. Eata, abbot of Melrose, who received St. Cuthbert there, was one of Aidan's students. Aidan's immediate successor at Lindisfarne, Finan, sent a missionary party of four priests to the English Midlands in 653. Further, Colman's return to Ireland seems to have encouraged Englishmen to go and settle there permanently.

See also: COLMCILLE, ADAMNAN, COLMAN OF LINDISFARNE, GERALD OF MAYO, BERCHERT OF TULLYLEASE.

Bede's History is the basic source for Aidan—Bk. 3, ch. 3, 5, 14, 15, 16, 17.

J. Ryan, S.J.: *Irish Missionary Work in Scotland and England*, pp. 96-102 in *The Miracle of Ireland*, Dublin, 1959.

C. R. Peers: *The Inscribed and Sculptured Stones of Lindisfarne*. Archaeologia vol. 74 (1923-4) pp. 255-70.

For the artistic tradition and influence of Lindisfarne—F. Henry in her *Irish Art in the Early Christian Period* (London, 1940) and pp. 29-38 in *Early Christian Art* (Dublin, 1954). Also article in Studies, 1948, pp. 267-279 on *Irish Culture in the 7th Century*. Cf. Carl Nordenfalk, *Before the Book of Durrow*, Acta Archaeologica. Copenhagen, 1947, pp. 141-174.

Charles A. Bolton: *Centenary of St. Aidan. Irish Apostle to the Anglo-Saxons.* I.E.R. August, 1951, pp. 105-110.

AILBE
September 12

Ailbe of Imleach Iubhair, Emly, in Co. Tipperary, is one of the pre-Patrician saints, so-called. Unfortunately the surviving ' Lives ' are of little value, amalgams of the usual miracle stories put together, at earliest, in the 12th century. Nor does the version we have seem to come from local Emly tradition or from an earlier text. But the idea behind its thesis may be true—that Ailbe was one of the first great saints in the south. He is represented as being born into pagan Ireland, baptised by a visiting Christian missionary priest, going to Rome to study (under bishop Hilary—? for Pope Hilarius, 461—68), then returning to a fairly wide ranging apostolate over Ireland. An angel shows him "the place of his resurrection ", Emly and here he had his principal church and died and was buried. Emly was the principal church of ancient Munster until its fame was eclipsed by that of Cashel to the east of it. At Emly, the bulk of the early part of the Annals of Inisfallen seems to have been compiled. For what it may be worth, they record Ailbe's death in 528.

The story brings Ailbe into contact with Patrick at Cashel, making him submit to Patrick and so establish Patrick's control over Emly and Ailbe's claims over Munster. Here too he is brought into contact with the older Ibar. He is also alleged to have petitioned king Aengus at Cashel for a grant of Aran to Enda.

Emly is three miles from Hospital on the road to Tipperary, a little rise of ground from the level Tipperary plain. To visit it in wet weather and see the floods out in the surrounding fields is to realise it was an island, probably grown with yew trees, rising from lake and marsh in Ailbe's time. There survives a cross, some 4½ feet high, with a solid ring marked by sunken panels, in the graveyard, and the well of Ailbe, with fine-cut stone masonry for its deep shaft. Ailbe's day is celebrated with a special Mass, but the custom of making rounds in the graveyard is dying out. O'Hanlon printed a sketch of the mediaeval church ruin here before it was pulled down for a Protestant church in 1825. There are still some fragments of old cut stone ornaments to be seen on the site. The burning of Ailbe's bell at Emly is recorded in the Annals in 1123. The ' Life ' mentions a cross of the angels, where Ailbe used to speak with angels, at Emly. It no longer survives but is evidence of the usual series of high crosses at such sites.

That the Irish saints were friendly with wild animals is shown from authentic sources like Jonas' biography of Columban. Added to this is a whole series of animal stories, a literary tradition of considerable beauty if not of any historical value. The story about Ailbe and the wolves is worth telling in this connection. He is said to have been born in a region of Munster called Cliu (apparently N.E. Co. Limerick) of a clandestine liaison between a servant girl called Sanclit and a certain Olcnais or Olcon. Fearing the wrath of the girl's master king Cronan, Olcon fled before the child was born, and the king in fact ordered that the baby be killed. However the servants told to do this simply abandoned it under a stone by a wolf's lair. The wolf carried it into her den and suckled the child with her own cubs. Some time afterwards, a good man called Lochan saw the child playing among the cubs and carried it home. The wolf followed Lochan in distress and would not leave him until she was assured of the child's welfare. Even then, she went back mournfully to her cave. Lochan gave the child to some Britons who lived in the area to rear, they called him Ailbe from his being found under a rock (*ail*-rock: *beo*-living). Irish traditional stories delight to find such explanations for names.

In Ailbe's old age, the people of Cliach decided to have a great wolf hunt to exterminate these animals. One wolf ran straight to Ailbe. Said he to her: " Don't be frightened, your cubs will come safe to you as well. I was suckled among you in infancy, so it is right you should come to me in my old age. I'll give you bread every day and nobody shall hurt you." So the wolf came and ate its meal in front of Ailbe every day and nobody touched her nor she them.

Ailbe, like Brendan of Clonfert, has also a voyage legend, but much less highly elaborated than Brendan's. In the Ailbe legend, he walks out over the sea from Corcumruadh in Clare to a magic boat and sails away. When he returns, he carries a branch bearing fruit, apparently from the Land of Promise.

The text of the Rule of Ailbe does not go back, of course, to the saint's time, but is quite likely representative of the ancient tradition of Emly. Its title is " Riagol Ailbi Imlecha oc Tinchosc Eogain mic Sarain " —Eogan was abbot of Cluain Coelain in Tipperary. The Rule consists of 56 verses in Irish, including maxims for priests and monks and some details of the Divine Office, and about food and rules of enclosure. The verses include:—

7. Let him be steady; let him not be restless; let him be wise, learned,

pious; let him be vigilant; let him not be reproachful; let him be a slave; let him be humble, kindly.

16. Let him be constant at prayer; his canonical hours let him not forget them; his mind let him bow it down without insolence or contentions.

25. A genuflection thrice, earnestly, after going in past the altar-rail, without frivolity and without excitement, going into the presence of the king of angels.

39a. A person who goes on a visit to servants of God (Céili Dé), the best thing he sees, let it be that he learns.

41. A clean house for the guests and a big fire, washing and bathing for them, and a couch without sorrow.

Joseph O Neill: *The Rule of Ailbe of Emly*. Eriu III, 1907, pp. 92-115.

ALBERT (Adalbert)
January 8

St. Albert, who has enjoyed an entirely undeserved period as patron of the diocese of Cashel, is a shadowy figure, an Englishman said to have been a friend and companion of St. Erhard at Ratisbon. But the earliest sources for Erhard make no mention of Albert. Dr. John Hennig has shown how the literary tradition of Irish sanctity was linked up with news of the new diocesan organisation developing in Ireland by continental authors. The 12th century legend of Albert is perhaps by an Irishman from Munster, then living at Ratisbon, and anxious to exalt the new metropolitan see of Cashel by making his hero its archbishop.

J. Hennig. *St. Albert, patron of Cashel*. Mediaeval Studies. Dec. 1945, pp. 21-39.

ASICUS (ASIC/TASSACH)
April 27

Asicus and Tassach are doubtfully identified as the same person, Patrick's expert craftsman in metalwork, as well as a priest in the saint's train. Patrick is said to have founded a church at Elphin and left Asicus in charge of it. Tassach is associated with Raholp in Co. Down. Here is a very old but over-enthusiastically restored ruined church standing within a rath. It is probably one of the oldest surviving churches in the Six Counties, for its walls are cemented in primitive fashion with yellow clay, just as are those of the Nendrum school house and Ninian's Candida Casa. Tassach is said in the Patrick tradition to have given Patrick the Last Sacraments.

A curious legend, possibly based on the flight of Antony into the desert, connects Asicus with Slieve League. Either a lie was told of him or he told a lie by sheer accident. Of this he was so ashamed that he fled from his monastery to live as a hermit for seven years on Slieve League and on Rathlin O'Byrne Island just off the coast in the same area. At the end of this period his retreat was discovered by his monks but their attempt to bring him home failed, for he died on the way at Raith Cungai, Racoon near Ballintra.

ATHRACHT (ATTRACTA)

August 11

St. Athracht (Attracta) is one of the many Irish saints to whom devotion has remained a live thing, but of whom nothing is known historically. A certain Augustine Magraidin, an Augustinian Canon of the Island of Saints, Lough Ree, wrote up such traditions as did survive in his day, he died in 1405. Unfortunately he was the kind of man to merit his description by O'Rourke in his " History of Sligo ", " one of the most uncritical and credulous of writers ". He apparently had no hesitation in making Athracht receive the veil from Patrick as well as bringing her into contact with 6th century St. Nathy and a 7th century king of Connacht!

We may assume that she flourished in the 6th or early 7th century. Local tradition claims she had great powers of curing the sick, and in some versions, that she made use of herbs medicinally. Her monastery was famous for its hospitality to travellers and lay on a main road. Some sort of a hospice flourished there for a long while afterwards. Lord Kingston is listed in the Quit and Crown Rents Book of 1692 as " Tenant of the Hospital or Religious House called Termon Killeraght ".

Athracht's settlement seems to have been at ancient Coolavin (Greagraighe) and her church was known as Cell-Saile. She is patron of the parish of Killaraght. There are some other Killaraghts (Church

of Athracht) in the country, in the parishes of Coolavin and Kilmac-
teige for example; a Cloghan Araght at Lough Gara and wells of
Athracht (Toberaraght) in the parishes of Kilturra, Drumrat, Kilbeagh
and near Tubbercurry in the diocese of Achonry. Attracta or Atty has
persisted as a baptismal name in the saint's part of the country.

St. Attracta's cross was formerly preserved in the diocese of Achonry.
Its hereditary keepers, the Ó Mochains, seem to have taken it on a
round of different centres for veneration, and one supposes, dues, at
stated intervals.

T. O'Rourke: *The History of Sligo,* vol 2, pp. 366-378.

BENEN (BENIGNUS)
November 9

Just as Asicus is described as Patrick's metal worker so Benen is
called his psalm-singer. Patrick's train is represented in the legend as a
more or less self-contained unit and indeed it probably had to be
versatile. Benen is also called Patrick's best loved disciple; he must
have been a good example of a fine type of young Irishman who was
at once attracted by Patrick's preaching and threw in his lot with him.
The rapidity with which an efficient Irish born clergy came into being
is indicated by Benen's career, for, accepting the traditional account,
he succeeded Patrick at Armagh, where he died in 467 (Annals of
Ulster; 468 in those of Clonmacnois and Inisfallen).

Unfortunately the legends included in the 'Life' of Benen are
not of much historical value. Benen came of the race of Oillil Olom,
his father being named Sescnan and his mother Sodelb. He was very
young when he joined himself to Patrick, the first or one of the first
of Patrick's Irish followers. His name, with that of Auxilius, Patricius,
Secundinus, is attached to one of the Canons of Armagh—saying that
difficult questions be referred first to Armagh and if not settled there
to Rome. This Canon, however, has been the subject of controversy;
Benen's name might have been added on the occasion of its reissue,
for he is hardly likely to have signed with Patrick, or it may simply
be a question of a later Canon to which these names were attached to
give it special status.

Benen is said to have evangelised in Clare and Kerry and he is

regarded as the patron of Connacht. His name is preserved in Kil-
bannon in the diocese of Tuam. On the Aran Islands is the well
preserved, massive, little stone church called Temple Benen. It resembles that on St. MacDara's Island, also in Galway Bay and both
may be as old as c. 700. Temple Benen on Inishmore in Aran is beautifully situated on the rocky ridge of the island overlooking the bay
beside which St. Enda founded his great monastery.

An Irish poem in praise of Benen is put in the mouth of Patrick
in the Irish Life of Benen, which, although much later than the period
of either saint, represents their traditional relationship. One verse
runs : —

Is e mo dalta blaith Benen,	Benen is my dear fosterling,
miadh go nglaine.	Respected, pure.
Is me ronalt,	I taught him
Is he mo mac gáire	He is a good son to me.

The principal source for Benen is P. Grosjean, S.J. in *Acta Sanctorum*, vol. IV,
November, pp. 145-188. Brussels, 1925.
This includes the text of the *Betha Beineoin Deiscipuil Patraicc* in Irish together
with a translation into Latin.

BERCHERT OF TULLYLEASE
February 18

Tullylease is in north Cork, some two miles southwest of Dromcolliher. It is in upland country, the eastern end of the ridge of the
Mullaghereirk mountains, but quite good farm land. Here at the old
church tucked into a sheltered hollow near two spring wells, the people
still honour the memory of St. " Ben " on February 18th, paying
rounds at the wells and church, together with a special Mass and later
afternoon devotions in the modern church nearby.

St. Berchert (Berectus/Berikert and in contemporary Tullylease,
Benjamin) was one of a considerable number of saintly Englishmen
who came to make their home in Ireland. St. Gerald, who came to
settle in Mayo, is said to have had three brothers, Balan, Berchert and
Hucbrittain. Yet it is difficult to identify the Berchert brother of St.
Gerald with that of Tullylease if the latter is the same man recorded by
the Four Masters. Gerald died in 732. In 839, the Four Masters record
that Berichter of Tulach-leis died on December 6th. A theory of two

Bercherts, one with Gerald and one later on, has been advanced by Padraig Lionárd, C.S.Sp. This has the support of the fact that the pattern day, February 18th, is not the day of Berchert's death as recorded by the Four Masters.

At Tullylease there are a number of beautifully carved cross frag-- ments. One great slab with an elaborate cross, still held in great veneration locally as the saint's tombstone, is inscribed:— QUI CUM QUAE HUNC TITULU LEGERIT ORET PRO BERECHTUINE. The lettering is a beautiful Irish script; the cross design closely resembles the decoration of the Lindisfarne gospels (c. 700). The suggestion of this and the other carved stones is of a monastic centre at Tullylease which preserved a strong tradition of its founder's and perhaps many of its monks' native land. They may have had a library of manuscripts written and illuminated in England or in Ireland in the English tradition, and these designs provided the skilled artists in stone with their inspiration.

It seems probable that the great inscribed stone did mark the founder's grave (it is now preserved on the wall of the ruined church) and perhaps the resemblance of its design to the Lindisfarne gospels is the safest way of dating Berchert. It is possible that the Four Masters put him too late, and allowing for a time lag and in addition for the persistence of a local artistic tradition, we could put Berchert's *floruit* as the 2nd half of the 8th century.

At Tullylease, the remains include the two wells, Our Lady's and " St. Ben's ", Tobar Berecheart. Beside the latter when the ground was being prepared for a new Calvary group, the walls of a rectangu- lar drystone hut were discovered. It is possible they may be ancient, like the round hut at Ballyvourney of St. Gobnet. Nearby is a large bullaun with a hole through its base—tradition tells of a deer who milked herself into this bullaun every day while the church was build- ing, so providing the workers with milk. But one day, one of them spied on her, and in her annoyance she kicked a hole through the basin stone and was never seen again! There are a number of other local legends of no historical value about St. Berchert, but of the real man's career nothing seems known.

He is significant as one of the English monks to come to Ireland, in this case contributing to the artistic as well as to the religious culture in this country. As an English born saint, he is also of interest as being still the object of a considerable local devotion. His name and cult is found elsewhere in the south, Kilberrihert, Knocktemple (near

Freemount): Kilberrihert near Aghabulloge in the Macroom district:
Kilberrihert, Truaghanacmy, Kerry: and Kilberrihert in the Glen of
Aherlow.

See also AIDAN OF LINDISFARNE, COLMAN OF LINDISFARNE,
GERALD OF MAYO.

James Grove White: *Historical and Topographical Notes etc. on Buttevant,
Castletownroche, Doneraile, Mallow etc.*, Cork, 1925. Vol. IV includes a
full account of Tullylease.

In the Journal of the Cork Historical and Archaeological Society:—
1938 H. G. Leask: *Tullylease, Co. Cork. Its church and monuments*, pp. 101-8.
J. Ryan, S.J.: *Ecclesiastical Relations between Ireland and England in the
Seventh and Eighth Centuries*, pp. 109-112.
1953 Padraig Lionárd, C.S.Sp. *A Reconsideration of the Dating of the Slab
of St. Berichter at Tullylease, Co. Cork*, pp. 12-13.

BRENDAN OF BIRR

November 29

Rígféil Brénainn Biroir,
fris mbruchta leir lébenn.
Ba cáin mind már nualann,
cenn find fáithe nÉrenn.

The royal feast of Brendan of
  Birr,
against whom bursts the surface
  of the sea.
He was a fair diadem, noble!
The white chief of Ireland's
  prophets.
     (Martyrology of Oengus)

Brendan of Birr's fame has been eclipsed by his better known and
better documented contemporary, Brendan of Clonfert. Both of them
were friends of Colmcille, all three had studied at Clonard. Brendan
of Birr's eminence is indicated, even if we now have little information
about him, by his title of chief of the prophets of Ireland. Nothing
survives of his monastery at Birr, except a holy well of Brendan.

Adamnan relates how at a certain synod at Teltown in Meath,
Brendan of Birr rose politely and kissed Colmcille on his arrival. As
the assembly was convened to excommunicate Colmcille, the others
were somewhat indignant with Brendan. He explained he had seen a
pillar of fire going before Colmcille and angels, and defended him
against the synod's unjust sentence. What Colmcille had actually done

is not known, except that Adamnan says it was some quite venial offence; Brendan's intervention at any rate ended the excommunication. (Adamnan, Vita Columbae, Bk. III, ch. 3). When Brendan of Birr died in 573, according to the Annals of Inisfallen (A. Ulster, 565, 572), Colmcille was in Iona, but saw a vision of angels coming down from heaven to meet the soul of Brendan. Accordingly he hurriedly ordered a special Mass for the birthday (into heaven) of Brendan. (Adamnan, Bk. III, ch. 11).

From Birr comes the great gospel book of MacRegnol of Birr. The latter died in 820, he was bishop, abbot and expert scribe of Birr. The text of these gospels is Jerome's; it was taken to England and a word for word Anglo-Saxon translation added line by line by two English monks Farman and Owun. It seems they belonged to the monastery of Harewood on the marches of the kingdom of Mercia and Northumbria.

S. Hemphill: *The Gospels of MacRegnold of Birr: A Study in Celtic Illumination.* P.R.I.A. 29 C (1911-12) pp. 1-10. This paper also includes a list of the abbots and bishops of Birr culled from the Four Masters.

BRENDAN OF CLONFERT
May 16

St. Brendan of Clonfert was both a hillsman and a seaman, in the one man met the two great traditions of the mountaineer and the sailor and we sense a personality moulded and cleansed by the experience of the heights, and the solitudes and tempests of the waste of seas. But it is essential to distinguish between the historical Brendan and the hero of the "Voyage". That Brendan did sail small boats to adventurous landfalls is true and because it was true it made him a suitable person around which to weave the later romance, which took this Kerryman's name and fame, best-seller fashion, over all Europe.

The dates of the historical Brendan as given by the Annals of Inisfallen, which as a Munster document are likely to have been the best informed, are: Birth 486: foundation of Cluain Ferta Brénainn (Clonfert) 561: death of Brendan 578. Brendan was the son of Findlug of the people called Ciarraige Luachra. Their territory lay on either shore of Tralee Bay. (In connection with the ancient geography of this part of Kerry it is worth noting that there has since been considerable land erosion by the sea). Brendan was born at Annagh on the flat marshy land below the Slieve Mish mountains on the south shore of Tralee Bay. (The tradition that he was born on the north shore at or near Fenit has been shown by D. A. Reidy to have been based on a mis-reading of a manuscript). He was baptised by a local bishop named Erc, of whom nothing else is known except what is told in the account of Brendan. He may have lived near the still much frequented Tobar na Molt or at nearby Ardfert. Tobar na Molt is the traditional place of Brendan's baptism and modern tradition claims that the name refers to three wethers which sprang from the well to pay Brendan's baptismal fees! But more likely this translation, " Wethers' Well " is a late gloss on a forgotten word and it may in fact be the " Well of the Psalms " (Old Irish, *Moltai*—psalms/hymns).

Fosterage was the normal Irish custom and young Brendan is claimed to have been sent as a small boy to St. Ita of Killeedy. The Annals of Inisfallen put Ita's death in 570, and it is possible that they were too near contemporaries for Ita to have had the rearing of Brendan. From Ita, or perhaps some other religious woman, young Brendan went on to higher studies first with bishop Erc, then at Clonard and also, it is claimed with Jarlath of Tuam. Erc is said to have ordained Brendan priest.

From then on, Brendan, tough and active, combined the building up of two large monasteries in the south of Ireland with far ranging, for those times, travels by sea. Ardfert (Ardfert Brendan) was probably already a religious foundation which Brendan took over. It was in his own " calf country ", about five miles north west of Tralee. Ardfert, where still stand the shells of the great cathedral and two chapels—the round tower fell in 1771, is an attractive place. From the ruins, one looks across fertile land to the dunes at the sea edge and beyond that to Mount Brandon. But the ruins themselves are set upon a knob of rock, so that from the eastern side, they appear spectacularly grouped against the skyline like a less elevated version of the Rock of Cashel. To sail around Kerry Head and up Shannon would be very much in character with Brendan and his second great abbey was on low lying country, west of Shannon, between Shannonbridge and Banagher. This was a new foundation on land gifted by a king of Connacht, Aed son of Echaid. Today it is still famous for the wonderful Romanesque west door of its church, all that is left to mark the site of the monastery of Clonfert.

Across Tralee Bay from Ardfert, and about twenty miles down the

Dingle peninsula from Annagh, is the 3,127 foot Mount Brandon, the highest ground in Ireland outside the Killarney Reeks. The " Voyage " legend puts Brendan praying and fasting on the mountain top before he sees the vision of the Land of Promise and sets out to seek it. It would be entirely in keeping with the spirit of the Celtic monks, quite apart from the " Voyage " story, for Brendan to have had a hermitage on the summit of this most beautiful of Irish mountains, Cnoc Breanainn.

On the summit of Cnoc Breanainn is a ruined beehive vaulted oratory, Teampaillín Breanain and traces of beehive cells. They are placed beside Tobar Bréanainn, the only spring well on the whole ridge. From either side, from Cloghane on the east, and Ballybrack on the west, pilgrim trails lead up the mountain for this is one of the great mountain pilgrimages of Ireland. The annual pilgrimage has lately been revived. The tracks up are called Cosán na naomh, road of the saints (saints in the Pauline sense meaning the Christian community). West of Brandon is Kilmalkedar (Cill Maol-chéadair) with a well and a stone built beehive oratory both named after Brendan, but the real monastery of Brendan under Brandon may have been on the eastern side at Cloghane. Cloghane itself is paróiste Bréanainn and other place names there suggest a monastery, e.g. Poll a'Mhainistir and Gort an bhrathar. The latter name suggests, however, the later orders of friars. The monks of Brendan there make a last appearance in history in 1207 when they asked and received letters of protection from king John. The early Christian settlement of the Cloghane area is further attested by two ancient cilleens (ceallurach in local speech) at Faha just above Cloghane and on the pilgrim route up Brandon. One has an early cross pillar with a Greek cross in a circle on either face. Again the now fallen cross pillar on the Brandon ridge at Arraglen is further evidence for the antiquity of the remains on the summit and the likelihood of their real connection with St. Brendan. It has a Greek cross in a circle on one face and a Chi Rho on the other, with, in Ogam letters, the inscription " Ronan the Priest son of Comgall ". Its resemblance to a Romano-British monument at Kirkmadrine in Scotland is striking and provides tangible evidence of the links between Whithorn and Ireland which we also know from the literary sources.

One is not surprised to find other Brendan sites in the same area on islands, the ruined Teampall Bréanainn on Inis Tuaisceart of the Blasket group, and on Valencia island stands a crude stone cross beside Tobar olla Bhreanain. A tradition of Brendan baptising and anointing two dying pagans explains the name as the well of Brendan's anointing, forgetting the other meaning of *olla,* a penitential station, which is its sense here.

Brendan's name is associated with Inisdadroum (Island of the Two Ridges—*inis da dromand* of the ' Lives ') in the mouth of the Fergus river and further north with the famous Inisglora off the Mullet peninsula. On this island there is a ruined cashel, three churches, three cells, various *leachts,* crosses and stations, but the ancient wooden statue of Brendan long venerated there has been lost.

It is certain that Brendan visited Scotland and sailed amongst the islands of the Hebrides. He may even have reached Orkney and Shetland. Adamnan (Book III, ch. 17) describes him at the ' Mass of the Saints ' on Hinba—usually identified with the Garvellach islands in the Firth of Lorne. Here, while Colmcille celebrated Mass in the presence of Sts. Brendan, Cormac Ua Liathain (another saint explorer and seaman), Comgall and Cainnech, Brendan saw a brilliant light over Colmcille's head at the Consecration. This light persisted till the end of the Mass.

That Brendan really did visit western Scotland means that many of the church sites there bearing his name may be personal foundations. On the Garvellach islands themselves is Cùil Bhrianainn, Brendan's retreat. There are church sites called Cill Bhrianainn in Lorn, Mull and Islay and in the Outer Isles others of his on Barra and St. Kilda. He was also patron of Boyndie in Banff, and of the island of Bute. Butemen were at one time called " Brandans ".

It is also very possible that Brendan visited Wales (here a church and a mount Brandon near Bristol may be noted) and he might also have travelled to Brittany.

The Odyssey of the Irish Church

The story of Brendan as we now have it comes into two versions. In the *Vita Brendani,* the voyage is worked into the whole history of the saint and is divided into two journeys, an unsuccessful one in curraghs and a successful one in wooden ships. The use of the latter was advised by St. Ita who told Brendan that no ship for whose construction blood had been shed (the curraghs were skin covered) could reach the Land of Promise. In the *Navigatio Brendani* the story begins straight away with the voyage which is told in continuous narrative as a single journey. It was this last version that became a mediaeval best seller. Translations were made into Norman French, Old French, Middle English, Flemish, Dutch, German, Provençal, Italian and Norse. Brendan's Island continued to appear on maps up to the 18th century.

Thus Brendan's fame, which extends over most of Europe, was spread partly by Irish monks bringing devotion to him with them, but more especially by the " Voyage " romance. Today, most of the studies of Brendan relate to the literary history of the " Voyage " and not to the man himself, and they are therefore not noted here. Nor has the actual story of the " Voyage " really anything to do with the saint. It is still enjoyable reading, if you suspend belief and accept this ancient literary tradition which corresponds in some sense to our modern " science fiction ". Pagan and Christian sources were drawn on for the incidents to make each island and adventure more wonderful than the last.

The Book of Leinster lists the stories that a *file* should know and they include eight *Immrama*. These Immrama were voyage romances in which the hero goes out to seek adventure, and had originated in pagan Ireland. Brendan's is a Christianised version to which are added " otherworld " incidents of the type of the " Vision " literature (Fursa's vision is the oldest surviving, the most famous that of Patrick's Purgatory). Brendan sets out to find the " Land of Promise ", the earthly paradise, led by the hope that somewhere Eden, unstained by Adam's sin, could still be found, its meadows bright with the flowers of paradise. The journey, in which the Easter Mass is celebrated on the back of a whale, is linked to some extent with the liturgical year, and the meetings with hermits and monks on lonely islands are, of course, based on the fact that such people really existed. Other incidents suggest a knowledge of both icebergs and volcanoes, and it is worth recalling that the Irish probably did make landfall on Iceland in mid-7th century. But in reality it is idle to try and make a real Brendan itinerary out of what is an enjoyable but fictional romance, written in the early 10th century by an Irishman resident abroad.

D. A. Reidy: *St. Brendan in History and Literature.* Address to the Library Association of Ireland at Killarney, September, 1948. In this Dean Reidy gave a very full bibliography.

Denis O Donoghue's *Brendaniana* (Dublin, 1893) contains some useful bits of local information and a description of the Mount Brandon pilgrimage of 1863, when the crowd was put at 20,000.

Carl Selmer: *Navigatio Sancti Brendani Abbatis.* University of Notre Dame Press, Indiana, 1959. The critical edition of the *Voyage.*

H. S. Crawford: *The Romanesque Doorway at Clonfert*. J.R.S.A.I. vol. 42, (1912) pp. 1-7, and cf. M. Duignan *Clonfert Cathedral. A note* in J. Galway Arch. and Hist. Soc. vol. 29 (1954/5), p. 29.

The R.S.A.I. Handbook (Dublin, 1905) covering the northern, western and southern islands and coast of Ireland describes some of the other Brendan church sites.

George A. Little: *Brendan the Navigator* (Dublin, 1945) contains much useful information and represents a recent attempt at the impossible task of turning the fictional *Voyage* into a history of Brendan.

BRIGIT (BRIGID)
February 1

Brigit bán, balc núalann,	Brigit, the fair, strong, praise-worthy,
Cenn cáid caillech n-Érenn.	Chaste head of Erin's nuns.
	(Martyrology of Oengus)

" Nowhere more than in the *Vitae* of Brigit is the unsatisfactory nature of Irish hagiographical remains apparent." This was the conclusion of the late Fr. Felim O Briain, O.F.M., after a detailed study of what one might well call the problem of Brigit. The would-be biographer is faced with a mountain of material on Brigit's cult, liturgical and popular, and an exceedingly small molehill of facts about her. The extent of the cult suggests that we have to do with one of the really great saints of the Church, who has been able to make her presence felt in spite of the lack of the normal human assistance of a proper historical record! Did something happen in Kildare resembling the spate of miracles after the death of St. Teresa of Lisieux? How did the foundress of a small and apparently insignificant Irish community jump to a position of European fame? Of course, the powerful interest of the kings of Leinster helped to promote the cult, but it seems highly doubtful that the most zealous publicist of Brigit could have made her so famous without some genuine supernatural reality behind it all. Even now, in Ireland, when the oral tradition is dying fast, it is fairly easy to come on truthful traditions going back well over a century. In Brigit's time, oral tradition was in its full strength, and it is the more amazing that her first formal biographer, writing perhaps not more than 140 years after her death, belonging to the same part of Ireland, should, to quote Fr. Felim, " know scarcely anything of the saint whose life he set out to portray ".

Yet, though we may trace the different incidents in the ' Life ' of Brigit to their respective sources, and show that they do not belong to historical fact at all, it seems unlikely that an entirely false picture of Brigit could have been foisted on the sisters and monks and people of Kildare. Whatever stories were told of her, one feels they were being told too near the saint's own time for them to have been completely out of character. We must, I think, accept the spirit of the legends and reading between the lines arrive at some sort of impression of Brigit of Ireland.

Brigit was born about 452 or 456 and died in 524. Her mother was a Christian slave, named Broicsech, her father, Broicsech's pagan master, Dubthach, earlier spelled Duptoch or Dubtoch. The child was named Brigit; which when Irish softened *t* to *d*, was later to be generally spelled Brigid. She belonged to a Fotharta sept of Uí Falge, her people were of the alien, tax-paying class called *for-tuatha* in contrast to the Leinster nobility, the *saer-clanda*. Brigit was born and reared somewhere quite near Kildare and the royal dun of Ailenn. What is described as a " strong local tradition " puts her birthplace near Uinmeras between Rathangan and Monasterevin, about 5 miles north-west of Kildare. (The idea that Faughart on the borders of Louth with Armagh was Brigit's birthplace is entirely without foundation; likewise her death or burial at Downpatrick).

The picture we get is of yet another bastard child of a slave growing up on the Kildare plains, helping her mother with the cattle, herding them, milking them and making butter. This particular child was beautiful and attractive enough for Dubthach to take an interest in her. The obvious thing would have been to have made a match for her, and it says much for Brigit's strength of character and powers of persuasion that she succeeded in gaining her freedom to take the veil. It was not very easy, even for a highly born woman, to choose virginity in the early days of the Faith in Ireland. St. Patrick describes the situation in his " Confession " : —

" A blessed Irishwoman of noble birth, beautiful, full-grown, whom I had baptised, came to us after some days for a particular reason : she told us that she had received a message from a messenger of God, and he admonished her to be a virgin of Christ and draw near to God. Thanks be to God, on the sixth day after this she most laudably and eagerly chose what all virgins of Christ do. Not that their fathers agree with them; no—they often even suffer persecution and undeserved reproaches from their parents; and yet their number is ever increasing . . . But greatest is the suffering of those women who live in slavery. All the time they have to endure terror and threats. But the Lord gave His grace to many of His maidens; for, though they are forbidden to do so, they follow Him bravely."

Brigit, being Brigit, got her way, and with some other girl companions, set off to bishop MacCaille before whom they vowed virginity. A later tradition says that the bishop was Mel and that they made a temporary home at Ardagh under Mel's patronage, but soon moved to Kildare. Here Brigit settled on a little rise of ground on the Curragh (the position is such that its surviving round tower still stands up as a prominent landmark from all around). It is said that the plot was granted to her by the king of Leinster. It was called Cell-Dara, the church of the oak.

To imagine Brigit and her companions living like modern nuns would be completely at variance both with the history of monasticism and with the spirit of the Brigit legends. From the earliest period, the Church had had men and women who lived lives of prayer and penance, vowed totally to God, but fully organised monastic establishments and rules only came into being by gradual stages. Mel gave Brigit the veil of the dedicated virgin. Brigit was neither the enclosed contemplative of modern times nor a forerunner of a member of secular institute. She wore a dress that marked her consecration to God, she lived a life in community with other like minded women, of prayer and penance, but her apostolate was essentially a mobile and roving one. Our impression is of Brigit in her chariot, Brigit with her cattle on the Curragh talking to a passing student, Brigit arriving when she was most needed. The women would, of course, have had their little farm and been self supporting, and the cows were a constant pre-occupation. For hospitality and liberal alms giving the little community soon became well known. Brigit too had some medical skill and was able to do a good deal for the local sick people. It seems very likely that she, and other Irish Christian women, played a vital part in evangelising Ireland, for a woman may penetrate where a man cannot. There is perhaps more than a little truth in the story of the pagan chief who told Brigit that he had refused baptism from Patrick but was willing to believe Brigit.

Again, there is the story that goes with the old custom of plaiting rush crosses for St. Brigit's feast day. The designs, which include the triskele, may go back to very ancient and pre-Christian origins. However the experience of actually making the different forms of Brigit cross shows that the three legged triskele is the easiest to do, and it may well be no pagan symbol but the lazy man's version of the cross! The legend about the crosses does suggest a real form of apostolate. Brigit, so the tale goes, was nursing a dying pagan chieftain, and sitting beside his bed was idly plaiting rushes off the floor into a cross. He asked her what she was doing, and her explanation made him ask for baptism.

There seems no reason to suppose that Brigit's apostolate extended very far from Kildare. Both for the community's needs and the apostolate, a priest was attached to the group, and Brigit succeeded in getting a certain hermit called Conleth to leave his solitude and settle at Kildare. The double monastery of men and women religious, rich and famous, all this came after Brigit's death. During her life, the place probably remained small and was only of local importance. Yet Ireland would never be quite the same place again after Brigit, who set a headline for Irish women, and men too. They called her the " Mary of the Gael ", seeing in Brigit a vivid likeness to Mary personally together with a mystical likeness in her bringing of Christ to Ireland. (St. Gregory the Great commenting on Our Lord's rather cryptic remark in St. Matthew 12, explains that we are mothers of the Lord in preaching, if by our words we bring to birth the love of God in our neighbour). Men saw her too as the leader and patron of all the consecrated virgins of Ireland. " Blessing of the patron Brigit with the virgins of Ireland about her," sang Colman Mac Ui Cluasaig, lector of Cork (early 9th century).

For Brigit, there is real truth in the formal panegyric that concludes her ' Life ' in the Book of Lismore. " She was abstinent, she was innocent, she was prayerful, she was patient: she was glad in God's commandments: she was firm, she was humble, she was forgiving, she was loving: she was a consecrated casket for keeping Christ's Body and His Blood: she was a temple of God. Her heart and her mind were a throne of rest for the Holy Ghost."

Ní car Brigit, a rather long hymn by St. Broccán Cloín to be found in the Irish ' Liber Hymnorum ' seems to be a versification of miracle stories current in Leinster, and to be a little earlier than Cogitosus' prose biography. The latter used the same *corpus* of traditions, but is not directly dependent on the hymn, and added to them a variety of literary borrowings from various sources including St. Gregory. Fr. Felim O Briain made a considerable effort to identify this Cogitosus, author not only of the first formal biography of Brigit to survive but of the first biography of any Irish saint. He calls himself 'Cogitosus nepos Aedo' which indicates he belonged to an Uí Aido sept. This would place his people in Leinster, of a race that gave monks and abbots to Kildare. The literal translation of 'Cogitosus' into Irish would give the rather rare name, Toimdenach. It is thus likely that Cogitosus may have been a monk of Kildare who became abbot of nearby Monasterevin (Mainister-Emín) which honoured a person of this name as a saint. Toimdenach's (or Cogitosus') style suggests he may also have been the author of the pseudo-Augustinian "De Mirabilibus Sacrae Scripturae". This was composed in 655, and is a more polished work than the Brigit 'Life', which may therefore be the earlier book.

Cogitosus is very valuable for his account of the elaborately decorated church at Kildare, with the jewelled shrines of Brigit and Conleth, the only surviving account we have for an Irish church of this period. In 833, Kildare was attacked by Cellach Mac Brain, the king of Leinster, and then in 836, it was sacked by the Vikings. The latter are not likely to have left much behind them of the splendid shrines of Brigit and Conleth, and we may assume that little enough survived of the bodies they contained. It is not very likely that the skull of Brigit venerated in a church near Lisbon is genuine. The fragment of an Irish "shag-rug" cloak venerated at Bruges in Belgium as St. Brigit's mantle is of interest as an example of the Irish method of weaving cloth so as to look like natural fleece. This shaggy cloth can be traced back to at least the Danish Bronze Age and was still being woven in Ireland in Elizabethan times.

Most of the other alleged St. Brigits are probably simply duplications and confusions of the great Brigit of Kildare. Churches of St. Brigit, which cannot be personal foundations, are very numerous in Ireland, Scotland and Wales. Kilbride is a very common place name; the Welsh Llansantffraid means the same thing, Church of Brigit. But Irish monks carried the devotion to Brigit all over Europe, and the way in which it spread is sufficiently indicated by the fact that there is an Office of St. Brigit in more than two hundred manuscript breviaries.

Manuscript copies of 'Lives' of Brigit are still common in continental libraries. Translations were made into various languages, Old French, English (a 13th century metrical version exists) and German, for example. Brigit is patron not only of farming and farmers but also of learning and poets. That her feast day comes at the beginning of spring has helped get it into proverbial lore about the turn of the year. Then too some pre-Christian customs would readily have been assimilated to this saint who was patron of the land and whose feast day came at the start of the spring work.

It would be a very long list that attempted to note all the different forms of the Brigit cult over Europe. In Ireland there is the plaiting of the rush crosses on Brigit's eve, to be blessed at Mass on her day and put in house or byre to ensure its safety for the year. Martin Martin, writing of the Western Islands of Scotland in c. 1695, describes another custom for St. Brigit's day. " The mistress and servants of each family take a sheaf of oats and dress it up in women's apparel, put it in a large basket, and lay a wooden club by it, and this they call Briid's bed; and then the mistress and servants cry three times, Briid is come, Briid is welcome. This they do just before going to bed, and when they rise in the morning they look among the ashes, expecting to see the impression of Briid's club there; which if they do, they reckon it a true presage of a good crop and prosperous year, and the contrary they take as an ill omen." An Irish custom was the carrying of a doll representing Brigit from house to house by young girls.

An interesting early example of devotion to St. Brigit comes from St. Gallen in Switzerland, whose Codex Sangallensis is full of Irish *marginalia*. The writers were obviously devoted especially to Brigit, calling on her 14 times as against Patrick 5 times, despite the fact that part of the work was done by a Maelpatric! The invocations may be a simple " Sancta brigita " or longer calls for help, " Sancta brigita adiuva scriptorem istius artis ".

Brigit appears as a beautiful woman in the traditional Gaelic prayers and hymns of the Scottish Western Isles. From South Uist comes a blessing to be said over the cattle as they are being driven out to pasture in the morning : —

> Comraig Dhia agus Chalum Chille,
> Bhith m'ar timchioll a fabh 's a tilleadh,
> Agus Banachaig nam basa-min-gheal,
> Bride nan or-chiabh donn!

(The protection of God and Colmcille, encompass your going and coming; and about you be the milkmaid of the smooth white palms Brigit of the clustering, golden brown, hair).

In Tipperary an old salutation linked Brigit with Mary : — Brid agus Muire dhuit. A prayer for Brigit's protection to be said twice daily was known both in Scotland and Ireland : —

A Bhríd Uí Dhubhthaigh Dhoinn	Brigit, daughter of Dubthach Donn
A bheireann an long ó phort go port,	Who guides the ship from shore to shore,
Cuiream sinn féin faoid choimirce	We put ourselves under your protection
Ós leat féin an oíche anocht:	For this night belongs to you:
Ó anocht go bliain ó anocht	From tonight till tonight next year
Agus anocht féin amháin le Dia.	And this night itself through God's will.

In the Black Book of Carmarthen (12th century) there is a Welsh invocation: " Sanffreid suynade ni undeith "—St. Brigit bless us on our journey.

The above are, of course, only a few examples of prayers to St. Brigit. The Irish " Liber Hymnorum " contains two Latin and two Irish hymns in her honour. A hymn in Irish to her attributed to various authors including Ultan of Ard Breccain (d. 656) begins with a couple of lines which indeed sum up one's impression of this great woman about whom so little is known:—

" Brigit, ever excellent woman, golden sparkling flame, lead us to the eternal kingdom, the dazzling resplendent sun."

Felim O Briain, O.F.M.: Unpublished ms. notes for a book on *St. Brigit, Her Life and Legend,* the property of the Franciscan Fathers, Killiney. See also the same author's article on *Brigide* in the *Dictionnaire d'Histoire et des Geographie Ecclesiastiques,* and *The Hagiography of Leinster* pp. 454-464 in Féil-Sgríbhinn Eóin Mhic Néill.

Mario Esposito: *On the Earliest Latin Life of St. Brigid of Kildare.* P.R.I.A., 30 C (1912) pp. 307-326. Additional material by the same author in Hermathena vol. 45 (1930) and 49 (1935).

M. A. O'Brien: *The Old Irish Life of St. Brigit,* Irish Historical Studies: I. Text, Sept., 1938. II. Introduction and notes. Sept., 1939.

A. Carmichael: Gaelic hymns and prayers invoking Brigit in *Carmina Gadelica.* Vol. I, pp. 165-174. Gives a detailed description of Scottish Island customs for St. Brigit's day.

For St. Brigit's crosses and photographs of the different types, T. H. Mason, *St. Brigid's Crosses,* J.R.S.A.I., 1945, pp. 160-66, and T. G. F. Paterson in Ulster Journal of Archaeology, vol. 8 (1945), pp. 43-49, *Brigid's Crosses in County Armagh.*

H. F. McClintock: *The Mantle of St. Brigid at Bruges.* J.R.S.A.I., vol. 66, (1936), pp. 32-40.

Another interesting relic, or rather shrine for one, connected with Brigit, is the shrine of *St. Brigid's shoe,* now in the National Museum, Dublin.

As with Patrick and Colmcille, many writers have attempted a biography of Brigit, using for basis the *corpus* of legends. E.g. Alice Curtayne's *St. Brigid.*

BUITE OF MONASTERBOICE (BOECIUS)

December 7

ó Mainister máinig	From treasurous Monaster (boice)
féil bán Buiti búadaig.	The bright feast of victorious Buite.

(Martyrology of Oengus)

St. Buite died, so says the tradition, on the day that Colmcille was born, December 7, 521. His foundation, Monasterboice, in Co. Louth, a little north of Drogheda and just west of the main Dublin-Belfast road, must therefore belong to the earliest series of Irish monasteries. The site is still of importance today with its magnificent high crosses, and its round tower rising, even in ruin, about 100 feet. Unfortunately the Latin ' Life ', a compilation of two separate texts, is late and practically worthless. We may get this much out of it, that the *Italia* to which Buite went to study under a St. Tilianus, is a scribal error for *Walia,* and that where the young man really went was to St. Teilo of Llandaf in *Wales* (see, Nicholson, Z.C.P. vi. p. 447). He is said to have come back to Ireland via Scotland, in which country he raised a king of the Picts to life. This was Nechtan Morbet who ruled from c. 457 to 481; he made a present of the dun in which the miracle took place to Buite, who built a church there. It is possible that Buite is commemorated in the Scottish place names, Kirkbuddo (Forfar) and Carbuddo. Buite returned to Ireland and eventually made the foundation at Monasterboice. This was his home country, for he appears to have been born quite nearby, his people were of the Cianachta Breg of Louth. His father's name was Bronach. There seems no reason why a young Irishman living near the east coast should not have taken ship to Wales to study and see something of the world, and then have sailed back to found a monastery near his home.

Monasterboice in the 1890's yielded evidence of pre-Christian use of the site when gravediggers unearthed a stone cist containing a cinerary urn and a polished axe head.

Between 759 and 1122 (after which the place seems to have been eclipsed by nearby Mellifont), the Annals record the names of 22 abbots of Monasterboice. Of these, Muiredach son of Domnall, who died 27 November 923 (Annals Ulster) was not only abbot but " high steward " of the southern Ui Neill and steward also of Armagh from the Fews Mountains to Leinster, as well as " chief counsellor " of the people of Bregia. He had become abbot in 887, and was responsible for the start of one of the high crosses of Monasterboice, claimed as the finest specimen still extant, a rarity in that it can be dated. At the base of the shaft is an inscription OR DO MUIREDACH LASNDERNAD IN CHROS (A prayer for Muiredach under whose auspices the cross was made). The lettering is arranged around and between two cats, one licking a kitten, the other eating a bird. The Irish monks, as witness various stories in the legends, and the famous *Pangur Ban* lyric, were fond of cats, and one wonders if these two on the high cross represent the abbot's own particular pets.

Muiredach's cross is very well preserved, and its details can be made out easily. It has a Last Judgment and a Crucifixion, a scene thought to be St. Thomas putting his hand into Our Lord's side, the Epiphany, Moses striking the rock, St. Antony and St. Paul in the desert, to mention only a few of its panels. In the Last Judgment scene, the choir of the blessed is led by a harper (with a bird perched on the harp —perhaps to inspire the melody?), and a man with a long straight trumpet, the third figure appears to be singing from a book. This is suggestive of the sort of musical accompaniment that would be possible for the liturgy in Ireland in the 10th century.

The second great high cross of Monasterboice is much more weathered. It is 21½ feet high, of three separate pieces of stone joined, not a single solid slab. One side has the Crucifixion with Christ bound to the cross by ropes; the other has the Ascension, with Christ and the eleven Apostles, all armed:—the Church Militant.

Monasterboice has two cross inscribed grave slabs, one bearing the words OR DU RUARCAN (A prayer for Ruarcan); a sundial, marking the hours of Terce (9 a.m.), Sext (mid-day) and None (3 p.m.). In addition to the round tower there are two ruined churches.

One other name of which we know something comes from Monasterboice, its fer léginn, Flann, who died November 18, 1056. He was a historian, one of a number of Irish scholars who tried to make a synchronism of Irish and world history. Flann's verses, based on Eusebius' chronological tables, are still extant. The earliest known Irish synchronist was Abbot Sinlan of Bangor (died 609). The attempt, laudable in itself, was always bound to fail, in that the Irish traditions and history were not sufficiently documented to be fitted to world history and the effort only ended in their distortion.

Monasterboice round tower has had its floors and ladders restored, so that one may climb to its top, and look over the green fields of Meath and Louth, checkered by hedges, fading into a blue haze of distance.

R. A. S. MacAlister: *Muiredach, abbot of Monasterboice. His Life and Surroundings.* Dublin, 1914. *Monasterboice.* Dundalk, 1946.

CAIMIN OF INIS CEALTRA
March 24

The green, fertile island of Inis Cealtra in Lough Derg of the Shannon, on the great waterway through the heart of Ireland, is one of the most important Celtic church sites in the country, with its great collection of early carved grave slabs, its ruined churches, hermitage and round tower. Sometime before O'Donovan described it in the Ordnance Survey letters of 1839, its great pilgrimage had been given up, as O'Donovan tells on account of riotous behaviour. Unfortunately very little is known of its founders, and what there is, is contradictory.

One version makes the founder MacCreiche (also of Cill Mic Creithe, Kilmacreehy in Clare, near Liscannor) give the island to Colum Mac Crimthainn (died 549, Annals of Ulster). This Colum is also associated with St. Fintan of Clonenagh who is said to have been one of his followers, and with Terryglass (Tir dá glas) on the eastern shore of Lough Derg. Nadcaem, Colum's successor as abbot, is said to have buried Colum at Terryglass.

But a quite different tradition says the founder was St. Caimin, half-brother of Guaire Aidhne, king of Connacht. This St. Caimin died in 654 (Annals of Inisfallen); he was descended from the king of Leinster, Enna Cennselach, and his mother, Cuman, was also Guaire's mother.

To add to the general confusion, there is a certain Stellan of Terryglass and Inis Cealtra, who is mentioned in a letter of 640 from the Pope to the Irish clergy about the date of Easter.

The surviving 'Life' of MacCreiche is of the stuff of pure fairy tale, but interesting in that it gives a description of the little anchorite's cell on Inis Cealtra or something very like it. " This was the size of the structure, viz, four stones: to wit, a stone at the back, a stone at either side, and a stone in front." MacCreiche used to spend Lent there fasting. The Inis Cealtra cell measures 10 ft. x 8½ ft., divided into two tiny chambers by two inclined monoliths. It has been suggested that the story of MacCreiche giving the monastery to Colum was invented to justify the ownership of the place by the Laigin sept of Uí Crimthennain later on.

The ' Life ' of Colum has the rather pretty story of Nadcaem asking Colum why the birds did not fly from him as they did from other men. The saint answered, " Why should birds fly from a bird (i.e. Colum—a dove)? For just as a bird flies, my soul never ceases to fly up to heaven ".

The island is still marked by very ancient banks, perhaps the same field divisions that were in use when the monastery existed. There is a great collection of early grave slabs, like those of Clonmacnois, of which 110 have been recorded. There is a series of ancient churches, some standing within their own enclosures. St. Michael's, very properly, is on the highest ridge; here tradition tells sick people were brought in hope of a cure, for Michael as well as being a warrior angel, was earlier regarded as a healing one. St. Caimin's was originally a simple early church to which a Romanesque chancel was later added. The place suffered much from Viking attacks and the reconstruction work, for which Brian of Clontarf fame was probably responsible, may have included this addition to St. Caimin's, as well as the building of the round tower. The other churches are Teampull na bhFear nGonta (of the Wounded Men), St. Brigit's and St. Mary's. Two sundials are among the remains on the island.

Higher up Shannon, at Clonmacnois, the pattern is still held and the traditional prayers said at each church and at the holy well. Clonmacnois is a very long round, even in its " short " version; Inis Cealtra was considerably longer, and it is worth quoting what the Ordnance men were able to save of its details. Its end, O'Donovan tells, was due to some " ill behaved young rascals " making a habit of carrying off girls from the assembly to provide themselves with " fresh consorts for the ensuing year ". T. O'Conor collected what he could of the then recently suppressed pattern in 1838 (Vol. 2 of the Galway Ordnance Survey Letters). He failed to get details of the prayers said at each station. The pattern was held on the Friday, Saturday and Monday of Whitsun weekend.

" The station commenced at Lady's Well; and the performers went round the extremity of the island one mile in circuit, seven times, equal seven miles. The short rounds were commenced at a station monument (a little mound of earth and stones) lying 35 yards to the west of the round tower. They went round this monument seven times and proceeded through the door on the west gable of St. Caimin's church and as far as the altar in St. Colum's chapel. They went that length seven times from the monument just mentioned, and at the commencement of every seven times of these; they went round the monument itself seven times. They went round St. Caimin's church 14 times; the tower and all the churches around it being included in the rounds.

They went round a station monument at the end of St. Caimin's Church, either the one (a little mound of earth) immediately at the south west corner or the one (also a little mound of earth) within a few yards of the north-west corner of it. They also went seven times round Gáraidh Mhichéail, St. Michael's Garden; and seven times round the bank of earth about St. Michael's Church, and seven times round a large flagstone lying at it, on which stone they finally (i.e. having gone round it the seven times) impressed kisses. They went seven times round St. Mary's Church and seven times round the baptism church (St. Brigit's). They finished at the well and drank of its water."

A splendidly written and decorated fragment of the 118th psalm, probably from a magnificent late 11th or 12th century manuscript psalter, preserved in the Franciscan Library, Killiney, is known as St. Caimin's Psalter and ascribed to him by tradition. Of course, it is far too late for Caimin, but it may have originated on Inis Cealtra, which would account for the ascription.

R. A. S. MacAlister: *The History and Antiquities of Iniscealtra*. P.R.I.A., vol. 33 C (1916-17) pp. 93-174. Fully illustrated.

Betha Meic Creiche: In *Miscellanea Hagiographica Hibernica,* edited C. Plummer. Brussels, 1925.

M. Esposito: *On the So-Called Psalter of St. Caimin*, P.R.I.A., 32 C (1914-16), pp. 78-88.

CAINNECH (CANICE/KENNETH) OF AGHABOE

October 11

Cainnech Mocu Dalon of Achadh Bó in Laois is one of the most attractive personalities of the early Irish church. In popularity, he ranks only second to the devotion attaching to Patrick, Brigit and Colmcille. Founder and/or patron of a large number of churches in

Ireland and Scotland, his cult was also known on the continent. Thus he is invoked in the litanies of the 9th century Pontifical of Basle; in a psalter of Rheims of the 10th century; at Reichenau a calendar copied by an Irish scribe in the 9th century includes his name.

Friend and contemporary of Colmcille, he appears in several incidents in Adamnan's 'Life'. In addition, there are three much later Latin 'Lives' of Cainnech, all stemming from a common original. The nearest to the source seems to be the version contained in the Codex Salmanticensis, a charming piece of hagiographical writing whose miracles seem based on an authentic background of Irish life.

The Annals of Ulster give two dates for Cainnech's birth, 521 and 527, and for his death 599 and 600. The Annals of Inisfallen say he died in 603. His father, Laitech Luerd (but also given as Lughaidh Leithdearg) was a bard. His mother was named Mella or Meld. They lived in the barony of Keenaght in Derry and here the child was born, but a move soon afterwards meant that he was reared in Chemnughe (or Keenbuge) in Ui Mic Uais. This may be represented by one of the places called Tamnach in Co. Derry. They were quite poor people, in fact the 'Lives' go the length of saying they did not even own one cow when the child was born and a cow arrives miraculously to provide the child with milk. Later Cainnech appears herding the cattle, the other lad with him plays at war, making spears and shields, but young Cainnech builds little churches. He studied at Clonard of St. Finian and Glasnevin of St. Mobi, and made intimate friends there, it seems most likely, with Colmcille. When the plague broke up the community at Glasnevin, Cainnech went across seas to Wales to St. Docc, Cadoc of Llancarvan. Returning to Ireland, he embarked on a far ranging apostolate, founding churches and monasteries both in the north and south of Ireland and crossing the sea to Scotland to visit his friend Colmcille and work in that country.

In Ireland, his principal church was the Cow Field, Achadh Bó (Aghaboe) in Laois. The site is now marked by the ruin of a later Dominican priory. Possibly a little bronze figure of a cleric, $5\frac{1}{4}$ inches high, found in the graveyard there, came from the shrine of St. Cainnech, which was destroyed in 1346. Kilkenny, probably a personal foundation though only a very small affair, later came to prominence with the Anglo-Normans. It seems that Ciaran's Saighir was replaced by Aghaboe as the chief church of Ossory and then Aghaboe in its turn by Kilkenny. Cainnech seems to have been on very friendly terms with the king of Ossory, Colman son of Feradach (d. 601).

In the north of Ireland, Cainnech had the church of Drumahose in Derry. There was also Clúain Bronig in Offaly near Birr in the south. The saint seems to have inherited his father's temperament; if he was a cleric, he was also a poet, a quieter, gentler type than his great friend Colmcille, with a liking to escape into the solitudes of the woods and islands, where the birds cheeped at tide mark or the deer moved softly between the trees to the lake shore to drink. The stories in the ' Lives ' take us to a number of islands; Ibdone or Inis Ubdain (King's Island, Limerick) from which he expels the mice for nibbling his shoes, and the Bird Island, probably Hebridean, where the birds make so much noise on a Sunday that the saint orders them to be silent till after Matins on Monday. He was also to be found fasting and praying on the then lake island in Lough Cree, Monahincha. There it was that he copied the four gospels and these were, when the ' Life ' of the Codex Salmanticensis was written, still in existence, the *Glas Kannechi*. Sometimes he slipped away and his monks did not know where he had gone to; one tale makes them discover him by following a youth whom Cainnech was teaching. The boy would come to him at night and Cainnech used to write out the psalms for him on wax tablets:—the scribbling block of those days.

Cainnech was a moving preacher. Comgall who asked him to preach one Sunday, said that often enough the people wept when hearing the word of God but never as they did at Cainnech's word. On another occasion in Iona, Colmcille asked who had taught him his interpretation of scripture. Cainnech said, " When I was in the island at Lough Cree by the mountain Smoir in Ireland, the Son of the Virgin, the Lord Jesus came to me and read the gospel with me and taught me this sense (interpretation) of it ".

In Scotland, Cainnech visited Iona quite often to judge by the tone of Adamnan's account, and the island has a church dedicated to him and a graveyard (Cill Chainnich and Cladh Chainnich). But he also had his own island close to Colmcille's, that most beautiful and fertile Inchkenneth in Loch na Keal, a sea inlet of the Island of Mull. Here on the green turf back from the little cliffs is still the shell of an old chapel, a slender standing cross and a collection of the later mediaeval carved grave slabs so typical of the western highlands and islands. Johnson and Boswell spent a night on Inchkenneth in 1773, Boswell, in a fit of piety, going out at night to pray to Colmcille beside the little chapel kneeling at the cross. Returning he took fright at the thought of ghosts, fell into a hollow and sprained his right foot. Dr. Johnson recorded that in the chapel on one side of the altar " is a bas relief of the blessed Virgin, and by it lies a little bell; which, though cracked, and without a clapper, has remained there for ages, guarded only by the venerableness of the place ". Both bell and sculpture have now disappeared.

Other churches of Cainnech in Scotland, where of course he is known as Kenneth, the original reason for the popularity of that Scots name, are, Kilchennich in Tiree; under Beinn Ruigh Choinnich (mountain of Kenneth's shieling) at Lochboisdale in South Uist; on Coll and Colonsay. On the mainland, there are foundations in Kintyre, along the Great Glen where the parish of Laggan is his—Lagan Choinnich, and in Fife, where dispute has centred on what Cainnech's *reclés* at St. Andrew's amounted to, whether he was the first to found a chapel there, or whether it was simply a chapel dedicated to him there later on. Kilchenzie is a common form of Cill Choinnigh in Scotland.

A story relating to some church of Cainnech's in the Great Glen, meant to explain some splintered mountain top, tells how the church lay always in the shade of the hill, how the Lord offered to move it and indeed the hill began to shift with a rumble and shattering of rock, but Cainnech objected and the hill stood fast. The noise of the minor earthquakes that occasionally take place in the Great Glen is probably part of the background to this yarn and highland screes and crags the rest of it: " to be telling a story you must be putting a place in it or it will not sound true " as Neil Munro made his hero say in " Gilian the Dreamer ". Another story that also ' sounds true ' is of Cainnech crossing the Great Glen in winter and coming on a mother and child, the woman nearly dead of exposure and the child entirely so. Cainnech and his companions light a fire and revive both of them with warmth and food. The ' Life ' says the spot was afterwards marked by a big cross.

From Adamnan comes the story of Cainnech present at the " Mass of the Saints " on Hinba, probably the Garvellach (Bk. III, ch. 17), the occasion when Brendan of Clonfert saw the luminous pillar over Colmcille's head. Adamnan also tells how Colmcille, one day of storm and wind on Iona, told the monks to prepare for a guest, and get water ready for washing his feet. They objected that a landing was impossible but Colmcille said that Cainnech was on the road, travelling in the storm's wake. And soon after, he arrived, the wind dropping. They explained they had seen the storm ahead of them but had travelled safely behind it (Bk. I, ch. 4). Another time, this almost telepathic sympathy between the two men was manifested in a violent storm in which Colmcille's boat was caught (Bk. II, ch. 13). The rest of the party urged Colmcille to pray for them while they struggled with the tossing ship. Colmcille refused and went on helping with the ship, saying that today Cainnech would pray for them. Meantime Cainnech was in Aghaboe. It was 3 p.m. (None) and he was just sitting down to dine, one shoe kicked off. Suddenly he jumped up and ran to the church saying it was no time for them to be eating with Colmcille in danger on the sea. Of a sudden the storm ceased. Colmcille said, " I know now, Cainnech, that the Lord has listened to your prayer and your race to the church with the one shoe has helped us ".

Another time, Adamnan says (Bk. II, ch. 14), Cainnech forgot to take his bachall (crozier) with him from Iona, remembered he had left it behind when he was near Islay and went ashore there to pray. Meantime Colmcille had carried the staff into an oratory on Iona and spent a long time praying likewise. Cainnech went up from the beach and found his bachall on the short turf there. Adamnan says this happened in the district called Aithche in the island Oidecha, which Prof. Watson thought might be the islet Texa off south-eastern Islay.

When Colmcille went to Inverness to visit king Brude there, both Comgall and Cainnech went along with him. There is a story told of these three, one which in different forms is told very many times of the Irish saints. It rains and only Cainnech stays dry. The other two ask Cainnech why this should be, and he asks them in turn what they are thinking of. Colmcille says he is thinking of his monks in peril on the sea, Comgall about the harvest. Cainnech says then in explanation: " The Son of the Virgin knows that my mind is in heaven among the angels from the day I first turned it there, and I have never turned my attention back to worldly things ".

Other stories in the Cainnech ' Lives ' do reflect a real world, the prisoner of king Cormac in Uí Cennselaigh in Leinster whom Cainnech saves by a miracle from death by *gall cherd* or *gialcherd*— being thrown onto the point of spears, and the very pretty stories of nuns fostering children. One such was blind and dumb and deaf. Yet Cainnech finds the good women of Cluain Siscnan (Clonsast, Offaly) mourning the death of this lad. Cainnech restores the boy to life and full health, the boy then says he is named Emene, of the clan Duach and of noble parents who abandoned him by night when they realised his physical defects. Another time Cainnech calls to see his sister. She received him joyfully but Cainnech asks where is the little boy who used to wait on him and wash his feet and was always so pleased to see him. His sister put him off with the soft answer, not wishing to tell him Brecan was dead. Cainnech refused to eat however until the lad came, at which Brecan is, of course, miraculously restored to life and walks into the room.

The close friendship between Cainnech and Colmcille led, naturally enough, to the composition of verses in later times which were attributed to the two saints, Cainnech singing of Colmcille and Colmcille of Cainnech.

Vita Sti. Kannechi. Extra volume presented to the R.S.A.I. by the Marquis of Ormonde in 1853. The Codex Salmanticensis text. Limited edition of 100 copies.

CARTHACH (CARTHAGE/ MO CHUTA/ MO CHUDA)

May 14

" Seven hundred true monks who were hidden in Rathen before Mochuta went on his course of exile to Lesmór."

(Invocation in an early litany of Irish saints)

The surviving ' Lives ' of Carthach or Mo-Chuta both in Latin and Irish, all seem to depend on the Latin original which was written at Lismore in the 11th or 12th century. Mo-Chuta died in 639 according to the Annals of Inisfallen, those of Ulster say 637. In spite of the long interval between the subject's death and the biography, the account seems reasonably historical and links up well with Irish geography. Lismore, Carthach's last and greatest foundation, was one of the most outstanding of the later Irish monasteries. (See also for its subsequent history, the entries for Flannan, Cellach and Mael Maedoc).

Carthach came of royal blood and the Ciarraighe Luachra people. His father was rich, with two residences, one on the southern slopes of the Slieve Mish mountains in the Dingle peninsula, the other on the River Maine, not very far off from the first, both are in Co. Kerry. The lad used to herd his father's swine, an occupation that was usual enough even for a well born youth, and was also a frequent visitor at the dun of the local king. One day some clerics led by a bishop passed by, chanting the psalms, and the boy was so attracted by the liturgy that he went trotting after them to their monastery. " I have never heard anything so beautiful as this," he told the king afterwards. He set his heart on joining the monks and learning to take part in the Church's liturgy. So he went to the bishop and in due course was ordained priest. There is some doubt over Carthach's baptismal name, whether he was christened Carthach or Mo-Chuta. The bishop was also named Carthach and there is a possibility that the boy was Mo-Chuta and took Carthach as a religious name, but a different version makes Mo-Chuta the bishop's (Carthach senior) pet name for him.

Bishop Carthach was greatly impressed by young Carthach's holiness and scholarship, and recommended him highly to the local king. Mo-Chuta made a foundation of his own at Killtullach (Kiltallagh, between the Slieve Mish and the River Maine) in his home country but seems to have run into opposition from some of the already established foundations and the king advised his leaving the area, at least for the time being. Carthach therefore went north and spent a year, probably that of 594, at St. Comgall's monastery at Bangor. Then he returned to Kerry to make some further foundations, but was soon off again, visiting other famous monasteries and finally reaching that of Colman Elo at Lann Eala (Lynally, about 2 miles south west of Tullamore in Offaly). This place lies in the heart of the central plain of Ireland, level country, rising to heathery drumlin ridges to the south and beyond that to the Slieve Bloom hills. Colman Elo refused to receive Mo-Chuta as a monk at Lann Eala and told him to start on his own, at Rahan a couple of miles away. Rahan is five miles west of Tullamore, and where Mo-Chuta and his two companions built their first hutments, there still stands an ancient grey church on a little green rise in green meadows beside the grey river.

The Rahan foundation was probably made in 595, and it grew rapidly. Mo-Chuta maintained his southern connections and monasteries, and indeed is reported going south to bring the last sacraments to the dying king of his own Kerry homeland. He was also at Lismore. He was given a church by the Clanna Ruadhan once when travelling from Kerry back to Rahan by a devious route through Decies, and this may have been an existing chapel at Lismore.

The Rahan remains today are rather later than Mo-Chuta's time, belonging to the revival of the place after he left it, but are of extreme interest in that the church shows the two small sacristies, prothesis and diaconicon, characteristic of the eastern churches and eastern rites. One was for the reception of the offerings of the faithful, the other for the clergy's preparations. The same plan is found in 7th century Gaul; at Rahan it may have come from a direct eastern contact. The decoration of the chancel arch at Rahan with human heads and palmettes is of Armenian inspiration:—a 9th century litany of Irish saints lists the bishops of Cell Achid (Killeigh, 15 miles from Rahan) and mentions a certain Cerrui from Armenia. It seems that Rahan was most likely not entirely originated by Mo-Chuta but had already a small cell founded by a bishop Camelacus in the 5th century. Once again Mo-Chuta ran into opposition, the nature of which, in spite of the colourful stories in the ' Lives ', is not exactly known. Perhaps the most likely reason was that Rahan, centrally placed in Ireland, was a frontier monastery between north and south, caught between the opposition of the northern Ui Neill to the encroachments of the Munster Eoghanacht. Mo-Chuta, as a Munster man, was not exactly *persona grata*. He was anyway forcibly expelled, and he and his now large community of monks took the road south.

It is of interest that there were British monks at Rahan, who apparently did not like Mo-Chuta over much for two of them tried to murder him. Originally the Rahan community kept no draught animals and did all the work on the land themselves. At the beginning also, Mo-Chuta refused all gifts from local chieftains and people. Eventually he was prevailed on to keep stock on his land.

The ejected monks, and the patients from the leper colony Mo-Chuta had established, took the road with a long string of carts and made a leisurely progress, calling on the various important monasteries on the way, down to Lismore in Waterford. They held west of the Slieve Blooms, to visit Saighir and Roscrea, then east of the Devil's Bit and so to Cashel. From there they held due south, more or less on the line of the present main road to Cahir and came to Ardfinnan, from which by one of the Knockmealdown passes, they were within striking distance of Lismore. The ' Life ' makes a king of the Decies give Mo-Chuta the Lismore site when the party arrived at Ardfinnan, but Mo-Chuta certainly already knew of the place and it is possible he already owned it.

The date of the expulsion from Rahan and foundation at Lismore is given as 638 in the Annals of Inisfallen, 636 in those of Ulster.

As the walls of the new monastic *lios* were being thrown up, a holy woman called Caimell asked them what was doing. " Only a little *lios*," said Mo-Chuta. Thereupon she made the prophecy that would explain the name, not a little *lios* but a big one:—" Ní bá lios beag acht lios mór ". A very similar story is told of Moluag's Lismore in Scotland.

Mo-Chuta was now an old man, and to escape the noise of the constructional work, sought out the quiet of a cave on the banks of the River Blackwater—Mo-Chuta's Inch. Here he lived as a hermit some 18 months, but when he felt death was near, had himself carried back to his monastery. There he died, beside a cross, that would be called thereafter, *Crux Migrationis,* because from there Mo-Chuta travelled to heaven. The year was 639 (Inisfallen) or 637 (AU).

Lismore grew and flourished. Like Rahan it had its leper colony nearby, probably dealing with a variety of skin diseases. Two miles south of Lismore are the remains of a small building called the *Lóistín,* possibly an ancient hospice attached to the monastery. The monastery itself lay on the south bank of the Blackwater, on the magnificent site now occupied by Lismore Castle. The castle gate lodge is sited on Carthach's holy well (that sometimes pointed out as his is Tobar na Céardchan, the Forge Well). Carthach himself, like Cellach of Armagh, was buried here in Reilig Muire (or Reilig na nEaspog) close to the castle entrance.

Nothing else survives of the ancient monastery except some inscribed cross slabs now preserved in the Protestant church. The pre-Reformation cathedral was virtually destroyed by the White Knight in Elizabethan times. The inscribed slabs bear names that may be correlated with Lismore personalities known from other sources. They read:— 1. BENDACHT FOR ANNAM COLGEN (a blessing on the soul of Colgen—d. 850.). 2. SUIBNE M̄. CONHUIDIR (Sweeney son of Cu Odhir, anchorite and abbot of Lismore, d. 878). 3. BENDACHT FOR AN̄ MARTAN (a blessing on the soul of Martin:—abbot Lismore, d. 878). 4. ÓR DO DONNCHAD (a prayer for Donnchadh—a Donnchadh O Bric was assassinated in the cathedral in 1034). 5. ÓR DO CORMAC P . . . (a prayer for Cormac P . . . a bishop Cormac Mac Cullenan was killed by his own people in 918).

The Crozier of Lismore in its elaborate shrine made in 1113 at the order of Mac Aedhogain, the then bishop of Lismore, probably is

Carthach's own bachall. The crozier was discovered in a walled-up passage in Lismore Castle in 1814 together with the so-called " Book of Lismore ". This 15th century ms. was compiled from the lost Book of Monasterboice and other ms. for Finghin Mac Carthaigh Riabhach and his wife Catherine.

" The Rule of St. Carthach " is at least as old as the early 9th century, and may contain much earlier precepts rewritten then. It consists of a long series of precepts, in Irish, addressed to different classes of people, bishops, abbots, priests, confessors, monks, culdees, kings, together with others about the ten commandments and on the order of meals and fasting. The bishop, to whom all are obedient, is himself to be obedient to Christ. He is exhorted " Be just in juris-diction, over laity, and clergy, be attentive to preaching, be gracious, be kind ". The abbot is told that he must love the souls of all as he loves his own soul, his job is to increase every good and banish every evil. " Continual preaching of the gospel to instruct all, offering of the body of the Great God on the holy altar." Priests must be indus-trious and learned. To confessors :— " If you are the soul friend of any one, do not ask his name, be not a blind man guiding the blind, do not leave him in neglect." The section for monks lists the vices they should be free of and the virtues they should possess. Kings are warned that it is through the falsehood of princes that every truth is broken and every peace violated between clergy and laity.

The spirit of the Rule is summed up in its first precept : " It is the way to the kingdom of the Prince—noble is its virtue, love of God with the whole soul, with heart and deed."

Life of Mo Chuda. Irish text, edited and translated by P. Power. Irish Texts Society, 1914.
The Rule of St. Carthage. Irish text and literal translation. *Mac Eclaise.* I.E.R. Jan./June, 1910, vol. 27, pp. 495-517.

CATHAL (CATALD) OF TARANTO

May 10

" San Cataldo " of Taranto in southern Italy is the object of a very widespread cult (extended over all Italy, Sicily, Malta and even into France) which according to Dr. Hennig is " one of the remotest ramifications of the continental tradition of the Irish saints."

The wealth of legends about Cathal, including his being bishop of Taranto, may be all safely discarded. His cult only goes back to the discovery of his relics in 1071 and the miracles that followed. With the body was a small cross, of the sort that could have been fixed on the head of a pastoral staff, of Irish workmanship of the 7th or 8th century. It is inscribed *Cathaldus Rachau*, and it is possible that the place name is a later addition. Attempts have been made to locate " Rachau " in Ireland—for example at Rachaa near Shanrahan, Clogheen, Co. Tipperary. Dr. Hennig, however, thinks it is simply a continental's idea of what an Irish place name should sound like!

San Cataldo is invoked against drought, tempest, plague, all manner of dangers on land and sea and public as well as personal calamities and troubles. Benedictine and Norman influence helped spread the cult in the late 12th century. Cathal is one of the saints to be painted on the pillars of the basilica of the Nativity at Bethlehem. His liturgical cult goes back to the second half of the 11th century—following the discovery of the relics.

All we may say with certainty is that the cross indicates an Irishman, probably on pilgrimage to the Holy Land, who died in Taranto either going or coming; he may have been a bishop (of " Rachau "). This is assuming that the name on the cross is that of its owner, for of course, it might have passed to other hands!

J. Hennig: *Cathaldus Rachav*. Mediaeval Studies. 1946, pp. 217-244.

CELLACH MAC AODH (CELSUS)

April 7

" Aodh is leading bishop in Ireland: he has studied the written word and his study has been ample; Aodh practises no base deceits; his talk is pleasant when men drink."

Aodh Úa Foirreidh was bishop of Armagh from 1032 to 1056. The verse quoted comes from a long Irish panegyric that may have been intended for chanting in the bishop's presence. Reading it, whilst realising that formal panegyrics are not necessarily the whole truth or even a part of it, one's impression is of a cultivated community, well intentioned and organised, at least knowing what it ought to be doing, what its leaders should be and do, even if the methods by which they had reached their positions seemed strange to men outside of Ireland. Here indeed is what a bishop ought to be, set out for Aodh's praise, a reproach if he was not " a son of grace unwearied on journey ", " a good ridgepole supporting a sound community ", " a nail through the ehart of Antichrist ", " the sage of western Europe ", " a moorland stag beneath the yoke of Christ ", " preacher of the gospel among the people ".

Aodh was bishop of Armagh; the rights of Patrick's successor, the comarb, went to its abbot, who, by the then established hereditary succession, might be a layman. Armagh's abbots at this period came of the clann Shíonaigh, descendants of one Síonach whose son Dubh dá Leithe had died as abbot of Armagh back in 793. In Aodh's time, the ruling representative was one Amhalghaidh: " Youthful Amhalghaidh is Ireland's abbot, around whom marauding steeds go foraging over the dew. . . . That man is a branch from the wood of Paradise," sings our anonymous bard. Amhalghaidh was married with a family, his great grandson would be St. Cellach Mac Aodh (Celsus), reformer and patron of St. Mael Maedoc (Malachy).

Round bishop and comarb, the other officials of the church at Armagh come to life in brief flashes in the poem. Eachnartach, " oeconomus "; the anchorite Dubhthach (" a righteous austere man "); Cumascach, " head of a thousand poor ". We meet the master of the schools at Armagh, Úa Bileóige, who died in 1046 " an angel who wrote a book beside the cross. The revered and venerable ancient is skilled in the radiantly-complete grace producing scripture ". Then there is Duilighéan, the priest of Armagh, and Mac Gille Chíaran, its guest master: — " Is there any man more generous by repute than the master of the house of Christ's guests?" And Flann, historian of Monasterboice, might be on a visit to Armagh: — " Flann from sweet voiced Buite's great abbey, slow is the glance of the eye in his gentle head."

Certainly 11th century Ireland had need of reform, still felt the effect of the long struggle with the Northmen. Yet it would be entirely wrong to take St. Bernard's picture of the country at its face value, a passionate French reformer who had never set foot in Ireland. It so chanced that the saint who came at the end of the effort for reform in Ireland was an intimate friend of Bernard. Mael Maedoc died in Bernard's arms and had the good fortune to be written up by him. None of the other leaders had such good fortune in the way of a biographer, and to see both Cellach and Mael Maedoc in their true

setting, it is necessary to piece together surviving entries from the
Annals, or to try to discover what kind of influence Irish monks
abroad were having on the contemporary world. It is noteworthy that
in 10th century Central Europe, the very places where new reforms
were being initiated in the Church, were those where Irish monks
and hermits were at work. They were to be found associated with
Otto the Great who revived the (German) Empire in 962. Otto's
brother, Bruno, became archbishop of Cologne in 953 and had had for
tutor, an Irishman named Israel, to whom he always paid high tribute.
Irish monks were favoured in this part of Europe, there were Irish
monasteries at Metz, Toul, Verdun and Cologne, for instance. The
monastery of Waulsort on the Meuse, whose church was dedicated
to St. Patrick, was reserved by Otto I in 946 for *peregrini* from Ireland.
As long as the abbey had Irish monks, its abbot was to be Irish. This
charter was granted at the request of the bishops of Mainz and Liège,
and countersigned by Bruno. In the poem quoted above, the anchorite
Dubthach was a Scot by birth; here in the previous century, another
Scot who had studied at Armagh and then gone abroad, succeeded
to the abbacy at Waulsort. His name was Cadroe, and his fame soon
spread abroad so that he was asked by its bishop to come to Metz in
953 to promote reform there. Cadroe died 6 March, 977. Metz was
one centre of reform, the diocese of Toul another in which Irish
influence was strong. St. Gerard, bishop of Toul from 963 to 994,
favoured both Irish and Greek monks, each maintaining their distinctive liturgy :—" it was their custom to assemble daily in his (Gerard's)
chapel, at different altars, where they offered praise and supplication
to God after the manner of their fathers ".

Later on, when Henry II succeeded in 1002, the Cluniac reform was
favoured in this part of Europe and there is some indication of conflict between its milder rule and the more ascetic Irish ones.

Then again, all through the 11th century, it can be shown that
Ireland was in contact with the new intellectual and religious life
stirring in Europe, more particularly with that in France but possibly
also with Spain. The entries in the Annals record a series of royal
pilgrimages to Rome, beginning with one in 1026 :— " Mael Ruanaid
Ua Maíl Doraid, king of the North, went on his pilgrimage to Cluain
Ferta Brenainn, and proceeded from there to Í Coluim Chille, and
thence to Rome."   (Annals of Inisfallen).

Mael Ruanaid died in Rome the following year, 1027. The next
year 1028, Sitric, king of the Dublin Norse, went to Rome in company

with the king of Bregia and Meath. Other royal pilgrimages follow in the years 1030, 1034, 1042, 1051 and 1064, after which the sequence is broken perhaps because of complications in crossing England after the Norman conquest of 1066. But less eminent men would still have been able to travel freely to Italy. Of monks abroad, there is record, for example, of the death of the abbot of Cork in Rome in 1036:—
" Cellach Ua Selbaig, comarb of Barre, one who had made a pilgrimage to Rome, and chief anchorite of Ireland, rested in Christ."

(Annals of Inisfallen).

Obviously then Ireland and Rome were during the 11th century quite well informed about each other. By the century's end it seems that the Irish had a little monastery of their own in Rome. The Annals of Inisfallen record in 1095 the death of Eogan, head of the Irish monks in Rome, " Eogan cend manach na Gaedel í Roim ". In a late 11th or early 12th century Roman ms., a list of Irish names locates this Irish colony on the Palatine Hill (S. Maria in Palladio).

And though the Annals for 11th century Ireland record battles and destruction often enough, these events are not the whole story, any more than headlined crime in the modern daily paper. The spirit of the Irish church can be seen in its church building, the reconstructional work with which Brian, who died at Clontarf in 1014, was so often concerned, the springing up of the splendour of Irish Romanesque. " In the 11th and 12th centuries, such Irish church builders as kings Brian Boru, Turlough O Connor and Cormac of Munster were building churches unsurpassed in beauty by any contemporary ecclesiastical structures in Europe." (H. C. Lawlor in " Ulster: Its Archaeology and Antiquities ", Belfast 1928). It was Turlough O Connor who commissioned the making of the Cross of Cong in 1123.

Over in England, it seems that the English church, whilst not in the forefront of the new intellectual and spiritual life of the continent, was by no means decadent or in very serious need of reform. It seems rather that the Normans attempted a propaganda line to denigrate the church of the country that they had taken by force, in order to gain Papal approval for their presence in England. Nor should we accept uncritically the attitude of Lanfranc and Anselm with regard to Ireland without remembering its political background.

Both Lanfranc and St. Anselm came from the great abbey of Bec, in the Cluny tradition though not actually one of its monasteries. Lanfranc, aged nearly 70, was consecrated archbishop of Canterbury on August 29, 1070. He worked in close liaison with William the

Conqueror and hoped to make Canterbury not merely the primatial see of all England but of Scotland and Ireland as well. In the case of Ireland, he had a certain footing in that the first bishops of the Norse in Dublin had gone to Canterbury for their episcopal consecration. In 1074, when the new bishop elect of Dublin arrived in Canterbury, Lanfranc got him to make the following oath:— " I Patrick, who have been chosen to rule Dublin, the capital city of Ireland, do hand to you, my reverend father Lanfranc, Primate of the British Isles and Archbishop of the holy Church of Canterbury, this charter of my profession, and I promise that I shall obey you and your successors in all things which pertain to the Christian religion."

Now Dublin certainly was not then the capital of Ireland, and since the Irish monks do not seem to have been working in Norman territories, it seems unlikely that the latter knew much about the Irish church. In fact, Lanfranc did retract his extensive claims in the rather shorter formula to which the next bishop of Dublin, Donatus, subscribed in 1085. On May 28th, 1089, Lanfranc died; his successor was St. Anselm, who also got acts of submission from bishops elect of the Northmen's Irish cities, from Samuel, fourth bishop of Dublin in 1095, and from Malchus, the first bishop of Waterford in 1096.

Both Lanfranc and Anselm were in correspondence with Irish as well as Scandinavian leaders. It was in 1074 that Lanfranc wrote his famous letter to the high king of Ireland, Toirdelbach Ua Briain. The latter was actually overlord of Dublin. In his letter, Lanfranc charged the Irish with simony (a common fault all over Europe at this period!), with various matrimonial abuses—which appear to have been the result of the survival of the older and more flexible pre-Christian Irish marriage laws, and with other lesser breaches of discipline, administering baptism without consecrated chrism and the consecration of a bishop by a single bishop. Finally he urged the king to summon a council to initiate the work of reform. St. Anselm wrote two letters to the contemporary high king, Muirchertach Ua Briain, and four to the Irish bishops. These letters do not, so far as we know, seem to have been resented, and they would have had their due effect, but they did not initiate the movement for reform which had been in existence in Ireland for some fifty years before the Lanfranc letter of 1074. Moreover the letter which Pope Gregory VII sent to Ireland —perhaps in 1076—makes no mention of any English claim on Ireland, or that England should be approached for advice, and simply supposes direct and independent contact between Ireland and Rome. The authenticity of this letter has been challenged, but it seems genuine enough now that Prof. A. Gwynn has shown that the place of origin given in the ms. is Marino (near the present Castel Gandolfo) and not Sutri, where it was argued the Pope could not have been on the given date. Professor Gwynn further suggests that the little Irish monastery on the Palatine Hill may have been established as a result of this letter.

Gregory VII's letter reads as follows:— (Prof. Gwynn's translation).

" Bishop Gregory, servant of the servants of God, to Terdelvachus, noble king of Ireland, and to the Archbishops, Bishops, Abbots, Lords and all Christians dwelling in Ireland: health and apostolic benediction.

The doctrine of the Lord Jesus has shone forth over the whole world, since He who has gone forth as a bridegroom from His bridal chamber has set His tabernacle in the sun, and there is none that can hide himself from His heat. His authority has founded Holy Church on a solid rock, and He has entrusted His rights to Blessed Peter, whose venerable name is from the Rock. He has also placed His Church over all kingdoms of this world, and has subjected to her rule principalities and powers and all that appears to be lofty in this world, thus fulfilling the words of Isaias: And the children of them that afflicted you shall come bowing down before you, and they shall worship the steps of your feet. Wherefore the whole world owes obedience and reverence to Blessed Peter and to his Vicars, among whom Divine Providence has decreed that my lot should be numbered. Be mindful ever devoutly to revere and obey the Holy Roman Church. We exhort you, as our most dear children, to practise justice; to keep and love the peace of the Catholic Church; and loving her, to clasp her to you in the embrace of charity. But if any matters have arisen among you that seem to need our help, be prompt and ready to inform us of them; and with God's help, you shall obtain what you have justly asked.

Given at Sutri (interlined Marino), on the sixth day before the Kalends of March."

Before the interruption of such work by the Anglo-Norman invasion in 1170, the Irish Church had held three reforming synods. The first of these was that of Cashel in 1101, the second Rath Breasail in 1111, and the third, Kells, in 1152, in which the present four archdioceses of Armagh, Cashel, Dublin and Tuam came into being, and the *pallia* were conferred.

The reform (like, it would also appear, the renaissance of Irish architecture) seems to have been initiated in the southern half of Ireland. The synod of Cashel may not in fact be unconnected with the gift of the Rock of Cashel to the Church.

There is an historical tract on the family of the O'Briens, called the Senchas Síl Bhriain, and in this is a brief account of this first synod of Cashel in 1101. It tells how:—

"The foremost men and chief counsellors busied with holding of this council were: Ireland's high king, Muirchertach mór, and Diarmuid his brother, king of Munster; Maol Muire Ó Dunáin, chief legate, chief bishop and chief senior of the island of Ireland with authority from the Pope himself; together with many bishops and clerks of Ireland. All these, both king and bishop, with laics, clerics and the learned, pronounced their curse on all and every one that should resist this statute or enactment, down to the world's final end and the very judgment."

The points dealt with at this synod were:—

1. Against simony, and more especially the activities of ex-laymen and ex-clerics in this matter.
2. That the Church pay no tribute to king or chief.
3. That no layman be an erenagh in Ireland (hereditary ruler of a church and its possessions):—the abuse of lay control of churches and church appointments was indeed to be found everywhere as well as in Ireland.
4. That two erenaghs should not be over the same church unless it was situated on a border march.
5. No erenagh to be married.
6. Sanctuary not to be granted to murderers who had killed with treachery or among their own kith and kin.
7. That the share of a cleric or a poet should not be given to a layman.
8. Concerning marriage and its prohibited degrees.

This Cashel synod's decrees most likely were only for the south of Ireland; Rath Breasail made the reform a national affair ten years later.

This account from the Senchas Síl Bhriain shows that Giolla Easpuig (Gilbert) of Limerick, the legate who presided at Rath Breasail, was not the first legate to be appointed for Ireland by the Pope. That honour went to Ó Dunáin, who had been appointed legate by Pope Paschal II, and who when he died at Clonard in 1117, seems to have been an accepted leader of the reform. We know very little about him, yet it is essential to understanding Cellach and Mal Maedoc to realise that there were men of his stature already active in Ireland. He and Cellach must have been well known to each other.

It seems quite possible that Ó Dunáin began his religious life at Clonard. He appears first in a charter that was copied into the Book of Kells. The date of this would be between 1087 and 1094, Ó Dunáin is titled "senior of Leithe Cuind." He also signed a letter to St. Anselm, together with Muirchertach O Briain and a group of Irish bishops. This letter of 1096 was concerned with the Church of Waterford. Here Ó Dunáin signs after Bishop Domnall Ui h-Enna, who seems to have been another reform leader. When Domnall died in 1098, Ó Dunáin seems to have taken his place as an accepted leader of reform. It seems probable enough that Ó Dunáin went to Rome, discussed Irish affairs with the Pope, and was personally appointed legate for Ireland by Paschal II. That might have been in 1100, the year before the Cashel synod. It would seem that Ó Dunáin was resident legate in Ireland, until he was replaced, perhaps on account of old age, by Giolla Easpuig (Gilbert) for the Rath Breasail gathering ten years later. Noting Ó Dunáin's death in 1117, the Annals of Inisfallen call him ". a master in piety and wisdom ".

These are the slight surviving indications of the men and the spirit that were active in Ireland when young Mael Maedoc (Malachy) was a boy, and Cellach of the Ui Sinaich found himself comarb of Patrick on the death of abbot Domnall in 1105. Cellach was Domnall's grand nephew, and had been born in 1080. It was an instance where the much abused hereditary succession was going to work very effectively, for Cellach was a man for whom the new spirit of reform was a call to action. He would be no lay comarb; at once he set on foot moves for his ordination, which took place on the 23rd September (St. Adamnan's day) the same year. The Inisfallen Annals have an amusing instance that year of Irish imports:—1105 " Domnall, comarb of Patrick died. In the same year, a camel, an animal of remarkable size, was brought from the king of Alba to Muirchertach Ua Briain ". Shortly afterwards, the bishop of Armagh, Caincomruc Ua Baighill, also died, and Cellach now took the obvious opportunity of joining the office of bishop and abbot. Sometime during Cellach's circuit of Munster in 1106, " by direction of the men of Ireland " (Annals Ulster) he was consecrated bishop—most probably by Ó Dunáin.

Cellach as comarb of Patrick made various circuits of Ireland, they were an occasion for collecting the dues appointed to be paid to the comarb, as well as opportunity to find out what was going on over the country and assert the position of Armagh. He seems as well to have acted as mediator in various disputes between the different Irish kinglets. He presided at the famous reforming Synod of Rath Breasail in IIII (or IIIO), in which the reforms of the earlier Cashel gathering were made nation-wide, and the country divided into formal dioceses with two archbishoprics.

It was Cellach who " discovered " young Mael Maedoc (Malachy) in Armagh and made him his vicar there. In 1120, Cellach went on visitation in Munster, the next year the bishop of Dublin died, and Cellach moved very fast to get an Irish bishop chosen. He was asked to do this by the Irish part of Dublin. Meantime the Norse had sent their candidate, Gréine, to Canterbury for consecration. Cellach however moved too fast for Gréine, who was unable to take possession of the see of Dublin. This ended the dependence of Dublin on Canterbury.

Cellach was again in Munster, when he fell sick and died, at Ardpatrick on April 1st, 1129. As he had requested, the body was taken for burial to Lismore, where the funeral took place on April 4th, 1129. The Inisfallen Annals note it was an exceptionally hot dry year and many cattle died. Cellach, though his own appointment had been by hereditary succession, obviously did not want the system to continue. Dying, he named Malachy as his successor. But tradition dies hard, and on the 5th April, Domnall's son, Muirchertach, was named comarb of Patrick.

St. Bernard calls Cellach " a good and devout man ". Except for the entries in the Annals, of circuits, peace making and the man's death, we know very little of him, though the strong suspicion arises that he was a greater man than Mael Maedoc.

See also MAEL MAEDOC (MALACHY).

Aubrey Gwynn, S.J.: In I.E.R. *Lanfranc and the Irish Church* (June, 1941, pp. 481-500; July, 1941, pp. 1-15). *Pope Gregory VII and the Irish Church* (August, 1941, pp. 97-109). *St. Anselm and the Irish Church,* (January, 1942, pp. 1-14). *The Origins of the Diocese of Waterford,* (April, 1942, pp. 289-296). *Bishop Samuel of Dublin,* (August, 1942, pp. 81-88). *Origins of the See of Dublin,* (January, 1941, pp. 40-55, February, 1941, pp. 97-112). *Papal Legates in Ireland during the 12th century,* (June, 1944, pp. 361-370). *The First Synod of Cashel,* (August, 1945, pp. 81-92, February, 1946, pp. 109-122).

Ireland and the Continent in the 11th Century. Irish Historical Studies, March, 1953, pp. 193-216.

Gregory VII as modern scholars see him. Studies, 1950, pp. 40-50.

Irish Monks and the Cluniac Reform. Studies, 1940, pp. 409-430.

The First Bishops of Dublin. Reportorium Novum, vol. 1, 1955, pp. 1-26.

Felim O Briain, O.F.M.: *Irish Missionaries and Mediaeval Church reform,* pp. 228-254. *Miscellanea Historica Alberti De Meyer,* Louvain, 1946.

Gerard Murphy: *A poem in praise of Aodh Ua Foirreaidh,* pp. 140-164. *Measgra Mhichil Uí Chléirigh,* Dublin, 1944.

CIARAN (KYRAN) OF CLONMACNOIS

September 9

Mór líth línass crícha,	Great the festival that fills countries,
crothass longa lúatha,	that shakes swift ships, (the festival)
Maicc in tsáir tar rígh,	of the wright's son beyond kings,
féil cháin Chíaráin Chlúana.	the fair feast of Ciaran of Cluain.

(Martyrology of Oengus)

Clonmacnois of St. Ciaran is still a name to conjure with. To sail up the broad and silvery Shannon, and of a sudden, see ahead the grey clustered ruins of the ancient monastic " city " grouped as dramatically on the green esker ridge as the Rock of Cashel's buildings, is one of the great moments of the Irish scene. Here the south to north water-way of Shannon is crossed by the east to west route of the Esker Riada across Central Ireland. Clonmacnois, by situation alone, was well placed to become what it did, one of the greatest of the Irish monasteries and centres of learning. It survived Viking raids, plunder-ing in various Irish wars, the coming of the Anglo-Normans (who burned 105 houses there in 1179), and the end only came at the Re-formation, when the English soldiers at Athlone came and pillaged the place in 1552. Clonmacnois is still a place of pilgrimage, with official annual commemorations by both the Church of Ireland and the Catholic Church. The latter celebrates the traditional pattern on the Sunday following the saint's day, with outdoor Mass and special sermon, after which the crowds make the long traditional " round " at holy well, and churches in honour of God and Ciaran.

The material in the various recensions of the ' Life ' of Ciaran, both Latin and Irish, all appear to go back to some Clonmacnois original which may not have been later than the 9th century in date. They appear to be substantially true, and include as well some mention of the relics of Ciaran still preserved (in the 9th century) at Clonmacnois. The birth of Ciaran is noted in the Annals at various dates in the second decade of the 6th century, the earliest being 511. The chronology of Ciaran has been a matter of some debate, the following scheme suggested by Dr. McNamee, seems reasonably probable:— 512. Birth. Baptised by the deacon Diarmait. 524. Fostered by Diarmait. 529. Goes to Clonard. Thereafter to St. Ninnid in Inis Muighe Samh (Inismacsaint) L. Erne, to Aran (534), to Senan on Scattery (541) and Iseal Chiarain. 541, after these visits, founds Inis Ainghin. 545, January 25th. Founds Clonmacnois. 9 September of the same year, dies at Clonmacnois aged 33 years, 7 months.

Ciaran mac an t-Saeir, Ciaran, the Carpenter's son, came of a very ordinary family, his father being a travelling craftsman, a carpenter and chariot maker. The modern tinkers are the ultimate descendants of the highly skilled craftsmen who once went from one place to another over Ireland, wherever their services were required. His father was called Beoit—" son of Olchan of the Latharna (whence modern Larne) of Mag Molt of the Ulaid ", a part of the kingdom of Dál n-Araide; perhaps on one of his journeys seeking work he had met Ciaran's mother who came from the opposite end of Ireland. She was Darerca, daughter of Ercan, of the Ciarraighe of Irluachra (S.E. Kerry). They lived first in the Ui Neill country until the local king imposed such high taxes that they moved to Connacht and made their headquarters near Raith Cremthainn (probably near Rathcroghan) in Mag Ai, the central plain of Roscommon. Connacht thus regards Ciaran as one of its patrons. He was born and reared at Rath Cremthainn, one of quite a large family. The genealogies give their names, Ciaran (the oldest spelling is Cérán or Quérán) and his brothers, Cronan, Donnan, Luachaill, Odhran, together with his three sisters, Lughbec, Patt and Raithbeo.

Ciaran appears in the ' Lives ' as an attractive, kind-hearted boy, whose generosity and pranks often irritated his mother. Men apparently were not allowed in the house when dye was being made, and there is an entertaining tale of all the series of curses young Ciaran put on the dye when Darerca tried to stop him watching the operation! Ciaran, like other Irish saints, is the hero of animal stories, he raises a dead horse to life, feeds a newly born calf of Darerca's herd to a hungry wolf and then avoids the natural wrath of his mother by restoring the whole calf from the licked bones! Legend apart he did herd the family cattle on the sunny, grassy plains of Roscommon, studying his lessons as he did so. The story adds by way of miracle that he and his tutor were able to converse with each other over great intervening distances, and that Ciaran had a pet fox which carried his exercises to his teacher, until such time as the animal started chewing the leather satchel in which they were packed.

When Ciaran was older, he went to study with St. Finian at Clonard, taking with him a cow to supply himself with milk. This is likely to be a quite genuine custom, each student bringing his own supplies, just as Scottish university students used to bring bolls of oatmeal and barrels of salt herring from home to their college lodgings. Ciaran's " Dun Cow " was an excellent milker and supplied many more beside himself. Her skin was one of Clonmacnois' relics, and it was said that whoever died lying on it would not go to hell.

The story of Ciaran's gospel book is unique in Irish hagiography and would seem to represent a genuine incident, though it is told in differing versions. The most probable seems to be that in which Ciaran is reading his copy of St. Matthew and has just got to the words, " Omnia quaecumque vultis ut faciant homines vobis, ita et vos faciatis illis " (All that you would like men to do to you, go and do to them), when in comes " Ninnid, the Squinting from the lochs of Erne ". " I have no book," says he, " would you lend me yours?" So Ciaran gave his copy to Ninnid, and in the subsequent class, of course, only knew the first part of the gospel they were then studying. The students started a joke about " Ciaran Half-Matthew ". Finian, who had a very high opinion of young Ciaran, stopped them. " Not Ciaran Half-Matthew," said he, " But Ciaran Half-Ireland, for Ciaran will have the half of the country and the rest of us the other half." Clonmacnois did come to be second only to Armagh and its standing probably gave rise to the legends of the jealousy of the saints of Ireland against Ciaran.

After Clonard, Ciaran went to visit other famous Irish monasteries. He went westward to Aran of St. Enda, and there the two saints are said to have had a vision of a fruitful tree in the middle of Ireland, " sheltering the island of Ireland, and its fruit was going over the sea that was around the island outside, and the birds of the air were coming and taking of its fruit ", an attractive symbol of what Clonmacnois would be, with its international reputation and foreign students. Ciaran was ordained priest on Aran, and then went to visit Senan on Scattery in Shannon mouth. On that day, he met a beggar and gave him his cloak, arriving on Scattery simply in his tunic. Senan met him with a spare cloak over his arm, and said teasingly, " Is it not shameful for a priest to travel without a cowl?" " Mercy on us," answered Ciaran, " God will have pity on my nakedness, there is a cloak for me under the covering of my senior." " Mercy on us " seems to have been Ciaran's pet exclamation, just as Patrick's was, " Thanks be to God ".

After Scattery, Ciaran visited two of his brothers, Luachaill and Odhran, who were also monks and were living at a place called Isel or Iseal. This place has not been identified, though Liam Cox has argued it might be Twyford in Westmeath, two miles from Lough Ree. (Journal Ardagh and Clonmacnois Antiquarian Soc: 1951 pp. 52-65). This site is marked by the fine Bealin high cross. Ciaran remained with his brothers a little while until they grew tired of his excessive alms-giving and asked him to leave. He then set off to make a foundation of his own, choosing Inis Aingin (Hare Island) in Lough Ree, one of the Shannon lakes. The island lies close inshore, just north of Athlone where the lake begins to widen out. Ciaran remained there some time and the miracle stories reflect real life. Ciaran's book, in its leather satchel, is accidentally dropped from a boat. In the summer drought it is recovered unharmed, when a cow going down to drink catches the strap of the satchel on her hoof. Here too Ciaran received a young man called Angus or Oenna, whom he educated and forecast would be his successor as abbot, to the surprise of the monks who thought very little of the youth. Ciaran finally handed over Inis Aingin to a certain St. Donnan, and sailed down Shannon to found Clúan Moccu Nois (Meadow of the Sons of Nois, Clonmacnois) on what was then called the height of the well, Ard Tiprait. This was to be Ciaran's permanent settlement and " the place of his resurrection " as the Irish saying went.

The founding party at Clonmacnois consisted of Ciaran and the following monks:—Angus (Oenna), MacNisse, Cael-Cholum, Mo-Beoic, Mo-Lioc, Lugna maccu Moga Laim and Colman mac Nuin. Ciaran himself worked at setting the corner posts of the wooden oratory in the ground (helped according to the Irish ' Life ' by Diarmait mac Cerbheil, but the latter's dates do not fit in very well with this story). But Ciaran only lived to see the first small wooden and wattle buildings go up. They reached Clonmacnois on January 25th, and on September 9th of the same year (545) Ciaran was dead. As the Irish Life puts it:—" The soul of Ciaran was not more than seven months in this town, before he went to heaven on the ninth day of September ".

The dying Ciaran asked to be carried out from the little church and laid on the grass on the higher ground. He looked up to the wide skies of the Irish Midlands. " Awful is this road upward," said he. " But not for you," replied the small group of monks. " I do not know of any of the commandments of the Lord that I have broken " went on Ciaran, " but even David son of Jesse and Paul the apostle were in dread of this road." He was leaning against a stone and the monks tried to move it. "Don't," said Ciaran, " put it under my shoulder. Qui enim perseveraverit usque in finem, hic salvus erit " (He who perseveres to the end, will be saved). And so Ciaran died, on the green turf of Clonmacnois under the wide sky and beside the silver river. Out of that beginning grew one of the most renowned of the Irish monasteries. The two round towers, the ruined chapels, the high crosses and the great collection of early inscribed grave slabs, still bear witness to the size and importance of Ciaran's monastery. Here were written the Annals of Clonmacnois and those of Tigernach, and the Lebor na hUidre. The enshrined Crozier of Ciaran is still in existence, also the so-called " crozier of the abbots of Clonmacnois " whose history is unknown. The Annals mention the loss of Ciaran's crozier in Lough Gara in 930 and its subsequent recovery; they also refer to the shrine of the Hand of Ciaran being profaned and to the carrying of the shrine of Ciaran after raiders in 1155 to ensure their defeat.

The high cross erected by Flann Sinna, high king, is another, like that of Monasterboice, which can be dated, for it bears his name, and we know he died in 915.

Clonmacnois, like Iona, is fortunate in that a complete list of its abbots has survived. Whereas at Iona, founder's kin were well to the fore; at Clonmacnois, this did not hold. Nor was the monastery ever regarded as the property of any state or great family, and its abbots and monks included many men of low social status. Since we only have abbatial lists in full detail from Armagh, Iona and Clonmacnois this evidence from the last named is of importance in showing that one should not jump to the conclusion that hereditary successions were always observed at the great Irish monasteries.

" Choirs lasting, melodious, around Ciaran, if you should mention him; with the victorious tumult of great Clonmacnois ".

(From the Prologue to the Martyrology of Oengus)

The Latin and Irish Lives of Ciaran. Translated by R. A. S. MacAlister, London, 1921.

R. A. S. MacAlister. *The Memorial Slabs of Clonmacnois.* J.R.S.A.I. Extra volume, 1907-8, Dublin.

R. I. Best: *The graves of the Kings at Clonmacnois.* A poem in praise of the kings, listing their graves. Eriu II (1905) pp. 163-171.

Rule of Ciaran. Irish text only in Eriu (1905), pp. 227-8. (Riagul Chiarain). Edited J. Strachan.

J. Ryan, S.J.: *The Abbatial Succession at Clonmacnois,* pp. 490-507, Féil-Sgríbinn Eóin Mic Néill. Dublin, 1940.

J. McNamee. *The Chronology of the Life of St. Ciaran of Clonmacnois.* Journal of Ardagh and Clonmacnois Antiquarian Society, 1945, pp. 2-16.

There are a number of guide books and descriptions of the ruins at Clonmacnois.

CIARAN (KIERAN) OF SAIGHIR

March 5

" Deus, qui B. Kieranum pontificem ante alios sanctos in Hibernie insulam misisti . . ." (God, who sent your bishop, Ciaran, into Ireland before any other saint) these lines, the beginning of a collect for the feast, bear liturgical witness to the antiquity of Ciaran's title " first born of the saints of Ireland ". Sean Chiaran (Ciaran the Senior) was, it appears, one of the first apostles of the South of Ireland, and he belongs to the traditional group of the pre-Patrician saints.

Unfortunately, although the ' Lives ', both Latin and Irish, go back to an original written by a monk of Saighir, they tell little of the real Ciaran, being in fact an amalgam of animal stories, multiplication of food miracles and tales of the saint getting the better of various local magnates and kings.

The truth of the story seems to be that Ciaran was born in west Cork on the cliff-bound island of Cape Clear in Roaring Water Bay. Ciaran's father is said to have been an Ossory man, Lugna of the Dal Birn, who whilst making a circuit in the south fell in love and married a girl named Liadain. Ciaran was born, so the tradition has it, beside the White Strand on Clear (Finnthracht Cleire) and was reared on that island. (His first miracle was saving a fledgling carried off from its nest by a hawk, according to the legend). He grew up eager for knowledge of God, and took passage in a ship for the continent, " for there was neither baptism nor belief " in Ireland at this time. In Europe, he was baptised, and later ordained, the accounts make him a bishop before he comes back to Ireland. When he returned, he went to his father's country, Ossory, and settled at Saighir (Seirkieran) to the west of the Slieve Bloom mountains. Here he seems to have started as a solitary hermit, around whom disciples soon gathered. Saighir rose to being the great monastery of Ossory, until it was eclipsed by Aghaboe, and indeed, the bounds of the modern diocese of Ossory still follow those of the Osraighi people, Ciaran's ancient parouchia.

Cape Clear maintains devotion to Ciaran, paying rounds at his well on the feast day, and proudly pointing to the shell of the mediaeval church by the harbour calls it " the oldest church in Ireland ". If it is a personal foundation of Ciaran, the site is likely to be, like Saighir, one of the most ancient in Ireland. Cill Ciarain is placed on a flat plot of land at the foot of the glen that divides Cape Clear island into two halves; it is under the shelter of the high cliffs at the glen's mouth beside the main harbour. Tobar Ciarain, the blessed well, lies up the valley a little way; on the side of the road from the pier is Gallan Ciarain, a smooth and rounded pillar stone, with a small cross cut on it (? a pagan phallic symbol Christianised). The beach at the (North) harbour is known as Traigh Ciarain. From this island church there is a wonderful panorama of the mountains of west Cork and Kerry, the great line of hills of Beara.

The site at Saighir is very different, good fertile land, with the monastic site, now marked by a Protestant church, on a little hill. From this, the land falls to a wooded valley beyond which rise the broad shoulders of the Slieve Bloom hills, rising to 1754 feet in Arderin. Saighir is immediately south of Clareen, about 5 miles E.S.E. of Birr and 8 miles north of Roscrea. At the churchyard, there are some carved fragments from a mediaeval church and an immense high cross base on which is to be seen a much lichened hunting scene, as well as a scriptural series showing the help of God. The size of the base and the skill of its carving, suggest that here must have once stood one of the biggest and finest high crosses of Ireland. Nearby, the recently reconstructed road still carefully avoids Ciaran's bush, a ragged hawthorn hung with a few ribbons, rosaries and medals.

The ' Lives ' mention Ciaran's bell, Bardan Ciarain, as a famous relic at Saighir, it is now lost. The glosses on the Martyrology of

Oengus not only say that Ciaran took Saighir thirty years before Patrick but tell of another treasure of the monastery there. " Now Cairnech the Bald was the scribe of Ciaran of Saighir. 'Tis he that wrote the wonderful manuscript, namely ' Ciaran's Journey ', with its many various illuminations, and this book still remains at Saighir. And let everyone who shall study it give a blessing on the soul of Cairnech the Bald, and on my own soul." It would seem that Ciaran, perhaps naturally enough with his island background of Cliara, had like Brendan, a voyage legend attached to his name. A litany of Irish saints, mainly those who went on pilgrimages, invokes " The 15 men who went with Ciaran of Saighir ".

Ciaran's mother, Liadain, is said to have come with a group of virgins, to " serve God and Ciaran ", as the reputation of the Saighir monastery grew. Ciaran is represented as preaching over all the neighbouring country, as indeed he must have done. He is also described as living on bread and water, and going about dressed in the skins of wild animals.

From the Ciaran legend, as distinct from the facts, come some of the most attractive examples of the animal stories that are a feature of the literary tradition of the Irish saints, as they were to be later of St. Francis. (For true animal stories, see the entry for Columban). Here is the legend of the foundation of Saighir from the Irish Life (I). (Plummer's translation).

" When he (Ciaran) began to dig the cemetery (of Saighir) all by himself, he saw a wild boar coming towards him, which began to cut and root, and with this rooting it cut down the whole wood, and turned up the ground and levelled it. Afterwards he made a hut in which to stay whilst engaged in that great work, the wild animal cutting and dragging the timber for him until it was finished. God gave additional monks to Ciaran and he saw coming to them a wolf with a badger and a fox in his train, and they remained with him doing him duty and service.

Thus they remained for a long time in this service, till it befell that the fox's native character came uppermost in his mind, and he stole Ciaran's shoes and fled to his cave house. As soon as Ciaran missed them, he said to the other monks, to the wolf and to the badger: ' It is not fit practice for a monk,' said he, ' to plunder and steal: and go," said he to the badger, ' and bring him with you willingly or by force, that he may be reprimanded for it.' Then the badger set out and overtook the fox, and he bound him from his ear to his tail, and brought him with him by force. Ciaran said to him: ' Fast and do penance, for such ill conduct is no fit practice for a monk, and be sensible, and if you have any longings, God will give you as you shall desire.' He did as Ciaran bade, and remained under the same service as before, so that the name of God and of Ciaran was magnified thereby."

F. H. Gilling: *Ancient sculptured cross base at Seir-Kieran, Offaly*. p. 294, with plate, J.R.S.A.I., vol. 67 (1937).

P. Grosjean, S.J.: *Vita Sancti Ciarani, Episcopi de Saighir ex Codice Hagiographico Gothano*. Analecta Bollandiana, t. 59 (1941), pp. 217-271. This paper lists the versions of Ciaran's life, and edits the above text—in which Ciaran (or Pyran as he is called in Cornwall) is said to have left Saighir for Cornwall and died and been buried in that country. There does not seem to be any truth in this Cornish story, and it may be that the Cornish Pyran is another person altogether.

J.R.S.A.I., vol. 74 (1944). Plate 13, p. 123, is a fine aerial photo of Seirkieran.

COEMGEN (CAOIMHGHIN/KEVIN)

June 3

Míl Críst i crích nÉrenn,	A soldier of Christ into the border of Erin
ard na-ainm tar tuind trethan,	a high name over the sea's wave:
Cóemgen cáid cáin cathair,	Coemgen, the chaste, fair warrior,
i nGlinn dá lind lethan.	In the Glen of two broad lakes.
	(Martyrology of Oengus)

"The cemetery of the west of the world is multitudinous Glendalough" Oengus wrote in the Prologue to his Martyrology, and even today, the valley of the two lakes, Gleann da Locha, is probably the best known and most visited of the early Irish monastic sites. Here the extensive remains, round tower, churches, and crosses, are set off by the beauty of one of the dramatic ice-cut gorges of the Wicklow mountains, where the still water of the lakes is cradled between wooded slopes and sheer crags, above which rise the rounded moorland shoulders of the summit ridges. Coemgen, founder of Glendalough, died either in 618 or 622; two Latin and three Irish (one in verse)

'Lives' survive, but they do not tell us very much about the saint himself, though they give a fairly clear idea of his movements. They are in point of fact often more concerned to exalt Glendalough and its claims, a natural consequence of the very real importance and fame of the monastery and its founder.

Coemgen's father was named Caemlug and his mother was called Caemell; his family belonged to the Dál Messe Corb and were Leinster nobility. At one time, they had been the ruling house but were ousted from the kingship at the end of the 5th century. They lived west of the massive range of the Wicklow mountains, east of which was the then largely uninhabited coastal plain between the hills and the Irish Channel. This coastal strip has very few prehistoric remains and the place names indicate some early Christian hermitages such as were to be found situated in " desert " and unpeopled country.

Coemgen, who is said to have been baptised by a St. Cronan, went to Cell na Manach, now Kilnamanagh, about a mile north of modern Tallaght outside Dublin, for his monastic training. Three saints then had a monastery at Cell na Manach, Eogan (of Ardsratha), Lochan and Enna. There is a St. Kevin's well at Kilnamanagh.

From Cell na Manach, Coemgen sought a hermitage. The majority of the 'Lives' simply describe his going to Glendalough and remaining there, but one Latin version says that he was got back to Cell na Manach against his will by Eogan, Lochan and Enna, after his retreat had been discovered; that he later visited a hermit named Beonanus, and then the monastery of a Bishop Lugidus who ordained him priest. After this Coemgen founded the unidentified Cluain Duach and then returned to Glendalough.

The excellent condition of the Military Road over the heights of the Wicklow mountains gives an entirely false impression of their real nature. Before the roads were built, they were a waste of featureless, wet moorland, and Coemgen's road across them to look for a hermitage would have followed the great natural passes and not the modern route from Tallaght to Glendalough. He would go south down the west of the hills and turn up the Wicklow Gap Pass from Hollywood. Hollywood has St. Kevin's bed, chair and cave, and the 'Lives' set themselves to explain its name, Holy Wood. From it, through the Wicklow Gap to Glendalough, are still traces of the paved 'Kevin's Road', the great pilgrim route to Glendalough, with church ruins and cross inscribed stones along its line. Liam Price holds that the famous Labyrinth stone found on Lockstown Hill west of Hollywood on this route may quite well not be a pagan symbol stone at all but a Christian one, a pictorial impression of the difficulties of the pilgrimage of life.

" Coemgen crossed the summits with the angel," says the Metrical Life. He would come down on the further side of the hills, where the river from the Gap meets that from the branch valley of Glendalough, up which he made his way. It would be wild mountain country, wooded and with few people, though if the old caher (rath) at the foot of the Upper Lake was already inhabited, the place was not entirely deserted. Coemgen passed the small lower lake, the valley flat above it, the dun or caher if it was then there, and came to the crag circled upper lake. Coemgen chose a place to stop on the south side of the foot of the upper lake, Diseart Caoimhghin, and began to live there as a hermit. It is not surprising to find animal stories told of him in this remote retreat, including one of an otter that rescues his book when he let it fall down the steep rock into the lake.

Coemgen's cliff edge dwelling, usually approached by boat, is now marked by the remains of Teampull na Scellig (Church of the Rock) as well as by the cave called Kevin's Bed. ' Kevin's Bed ' is east of Teampull na Scellig, and is an artificial cave in the crags some thirty feet above the level of the lake. It was originally a Bronze Age rock tomb, of which another example is Kelly's Cave at Cong. Coemgen found out this old tomb and turned it into a hermitage. His retreat did not remain private, for his presence was discovered as a result of a cow straying from the herd of a " hundred cow " farmer named Dima. The Metrical Life calls Glendalough, a " glen without threshing floor or corn rick, only rugged rocks above it " :

> Coemgen was among stones,
> On the border of the lake on a bare bed,
> With his slender side on a stone,
> In his glen without a booth over him.

Once Coemgen was known to be there, disciples began to gather round him, and Teampull na Scellig was probably then constructed. It is on a flat bit of land about twenty feet up from the lake water, on the crag face, the foot of which is reached by boat. Here are the ruins of a small ancient church and a flat space on which the first few monks could have had huts of wood and thatch. But Teampull na Scellig is a very confined space, and the community overflowed off the crag face onto the gentler slopes at the lake foot above the dun.

Here is the ruin called Coemgen's cell, a beehive hut, and Reefert
Church. Reefert (probably Ríogh fheart, royal cemetery) church as
it stands is probably of 8th century date, but would be on the site of
an earlier structure. It was originally enclosed by a cashel wall and
there were other remains of buildings nearby which have now disappeared. It is to Reefert that one should apply the lines in one of the
Irish ' Lives ' (I in Plummer's edition). " For this cause (Coemgen's
power and merits) many kings and chiefs among the kings of Erin,
and of Britain, chose to be buried in Glendalough for love of God
and Coemgen. There are relics of the apostles hard by Coemgen's hut
to go with him to the judgment of doom in the presence of the Lord."
Tradition said the cemetery had been hallowed with earth brought
from Rome, and was said to be one of the four best burial places
(' Romes ') in Ireland. The great pilgrimage of Glendalough survived
almost to the present day, it is still recalled in living memory, but
is now extinct. The ' Lives ' attribute the origin of the pilgrimage
to Coemgen and are, of course, correct in the idea that it was centred
on devotion to him and that it would have been formally organised.
One of the Irish ' Lives ' (III in Plummer's edition) makes Coemgen
go to Rome and receive from the Pope, " authority for the establishment of a pilgrimage in Glendalough in perpetuity, and that the
indulgence and profit should be the same to any one who should
make seven pilgrimages to Glendalough as to one who should make
one pilgrimage to Rome ". The same account names the four great
pilgrimages of Ireland as the Cave of Patrick in Ulster (Patrick's
Purgatory), Croagh Patrick in Connacht, Inis na mBéo (Island of the
Living) in Munster, and Glendalough in Leinster.

It seems that the monastery in Coemgen's time remained entirely
concentrated at the foot of the Upper Lake. Mr. Liam Price's study
of the rather conflicting accounts of the angel telling Coemgen to
move down the valley to the lower lake site, indicates that the move
did not come until later on, and that the story was invented as a
convenient legend for the origin of the great ' city ' of Glendalough.
Coemgen and his monks would have remained at Reefert, and
Coemgen would have been buried there. Then as the fame of the place
grew, this site, like the earlier Teampull na Scellig, became too small,
and they shifted east, down the valley, to the lower lake. Later,
perhaps in the time of St. Lorcan O Tuathail, St. Saviour's Priory
was constructed still further east, between the lower lake and Laragh.

The impressive ruins of the great ' city ' of Glendalough, Kevin's church ('kitchen'), the cathedral, Our Lady's church, the round tower, are approached by the only gateway of a monastic cashel to survive in Ireland. To best appreciate the location of this great monastery one should go along the top of the crags above the Upper Lake and Teampull na Scellig and look down valley. From there, the round tower stands out boldly, and the whole little 'city' is seen to be grouped on a marked hillock of dry land which rises clear of the general marshy flats of the valley between the lakes and by the river.

At the head of the upper lake, is a level area representing silted up lake bed, and a deep gorge with immense boulder beds on its floors, beyond which one climbs out by an old track to the moors above. One miracle told of Coemgen seems to describe these boulder beds and their caves, how Coemgen picked one in which to spend Lent, how an angel warned him that the rocks were about to fall and how Coemgen says that God willing, he means to spend all Lent there. The rock fall is accordingly postponed until after Easter!

The 'Lives' have attractive incidents; the animal stories, and how Coemgen would supply sick people with "the things which sick and morbid folk had a desire for, such as blackberries in winter, apples on willow trees and would cause them to find habitually sprigs of sorrel growing on rocks in winter time". These stories may be based on a real tradition of special care for the sick at Glendalough.

An Irish litany of Irish saints in the Book of Leinster (no. I, of the two printed in the Henry Bradshaw Society's 'Irish Litanies') seems to have had special interest in Glendalough among other places. It invokes the saints of Cell na Manach, and "Forty saints in Glenn da Loch with Coemgen, noble priest", some of whom it then lists. They include a Frank, Affinis, and "Cellach the Saxon" who lived at Disert Cellaig southeast of Glendalough. The gloss in the Martyrology of Oengus explains (October 7th), "He was not English, but he came from the English to the Irish, because he was Irish".

See also LORCAN UA TUATHAIL.

Liam Price: *Glendalough: St. Kevin's Road,* pp. 244-271, Féil-sgribhínn Eóin Mhic Néill. Dublin 1940. *Rock Basins or 'bullauns' at Glendalough and elsewhere,* J.R.S.A.I., 1959, pp. 161-188.

H. G. Leask: *Glendalough, Co. Wicklow.* Official guide.

W. J. Hemp: *St. Kevin's Bed, Glendalough,* J.R.S.A.I., 1937, pp. 290-294.

P. Grosjean, S.J.: *Relations mutuelles des Vies Latines de S. Cáemgen de Glen dá Locha,* Analecta Bollandiana, t. 48 (1930), pp. 99-123.

COLMAN OF CLOYNE

November 24

Colman MacLenin (macc Lenéni rolaind—son of Lenine the vehement, says Oengus) was a late vocation to the priesthood, a man of the class called ex-laymen, *Ath-laech*. The Triad names the three ex-laymen of Ireland, Enna (Enda) of Aran, Mochamnoc of Inis Cealtra, and Colman MacLenin. He was a bard by profession, both a metrical Latin life of St. Senan and an Irish poem in praise of St. Brendan have both been attributed to his authorship.

The Annals of Inisfallen give the year 530 for Colman's birth and 606 for his death. He was 9th in descent from Mogh Nuadat, king of Munster, and was probably born and reared in Muskery, in West Cork. A dispute about succession, and the following inauguration at Cashel, at which Colman was carrying out his professional duties as bard, brought him into contact with St. Brendan of Clonfert. There is some doubt about the historicity of this whole incident, in the course of which Brendan is said to have advised Colman to give up poetry for the Church. It is certain however that Colman did become a monk and priest sometime in early manhood or early middle age. It is uncertain whether, as it is claimed, he first of all visited St. Jarlath at Tuam. The main field of his apostolate was in his native Co. Cork. There he had his principal foundation at Cloyne, but there was another important one at Kilmaclenine.

Kilmaclenine (Church of MacLenin—Cill Mac Lenin) lies on the high uplands between Mallow and Dromcolliher. The site is now marked by ruins in open fields, including part of a ruined church, but it was once quite an important place and was noted for its horse fair at least till 1775. With Cloyne and Coole, Kilmaclenine was one of the three seats of the Bishop of Cloyne.

At Cloyne, Colman's principal settlement, are the remains of an oratory, as well as the round tower beside the cathedral and there is also a holy well of Colman. A small bronze cross, probably from a cumdach (book shrine), was found in Cloyne cathedral. Records of

Cloyne only begin about 800, with a complete gap between that date and Colman's death.

The genealogies give Colman no less than six sisters and claim that they all had a reputation for sanctity. Late vocations and ex-laymen are mentioned at various times in Irish records, indeed the example of a saintly individual of this class who was reported to have done no good except that "on lying down and rising up he recounted the saints of the world, as is the custom of ex-laymen " inspired Oengus to write his Martyrology. As a class, they were evidently regarded as somewhat suspect by the first Synod of Cashel which specifically mentions them in its decree against simony. (See entry for Cellach).

" J. C.": *St. Colman of Cloyne,* J.C.H.A.S., 1910, pp. 132-142.

T. Olden. *Kilmaclenine,* J.C.H.A.S., 1898, pp. 165 et seq. Mostly concerned with the later history of the place.

COLMAN OF DROMORE

June 7

Very little is known of St. Colman (Mo-Cholmóc) of Druim Mór, Co. Down. He was born in Dal Araide in Ulster and seems to have spent his life more or less in the area of modern Co. Down. He seems to have studied under Caylan at Nendrum on Strangford Lough, and it may well be that St. MacNisse of Connor was the man who advised him to make his settlement at Dromore. It is possible that he had St. Finian of Moville as a pupil there. Dromore may have been founded c. 514. The surviving ' Life ' of the saint is a quite fabulous composition and of little help for the history of Colman.

He seems to have really been a famous man, and his cult was known in Scotland to which it was probably taken by emigrant Ulstermen. Thus he is supposed to be the saint of Inchmahome (Innis mo-Chol-máig) in the Lake of Menteith, and Kilmachalmaig in Bute may also be his. In Wales, Llangolman near Maencloghog and Capel Colman in the same district are thought to be churches of Colman of Dromore.

COLMAN ELO (EALA)

September 26

Colmán ó Laind Elo
la hógi alt légend,
conid hé, án núallan,
Ionhain már macc nÉrenn.

Colman from Lann Eala,
with perfection of his studies,
so that he is, splendid cry,
the great John of Ireland's sons.

(Martyrology of Oengus)

Colman moccu Sailni, of the Dál Sailne, son of Beogne, was born about the year 555 in Glen Fhichle, Glenelly, Co. Tyrone. His people had fled to this place because Meath, where they had been living, had been devastated by the Leinster men. Young Colman was educated first by a certain Coemen and then made a round of other monasteries, including Connor of MacNisse, after which he travelled south to Meath. Here he came on an assembly of lay and clerical leaders, Aed son of Ainmire (d. 598) ard rí, Aed Slane of the Ui Neill, Sts. Colmcille, Cainnech and many others. They welcomed Colman and Colmcille asked that he be given a good site for a monastery. Aed Slane, lord of Meath, then offered the Lann Eala site, which Colman accepted as the " place of his resurrection ". Colman died in 611 (Annals of Ulster) or 613 (Inisfallen), aged 56.

Lann Eala, modern Lynally, some three miles west of Tullamore in Offaly, is centrally placed in Ireland and was an important monastery. Mo-Chuta visited it before his foundation at nearby Rahan. Today there is no trace of the early foundation, only a featureless ruined church standing in an old graveyard around which stretch the level fields. Colman seems to have been very friendly with Colmcille and visited him in Scotland; indeed to have exercised a rather widespread apostolate with Lann Eala as the chief base of operations. The name is rather unusual, Lann being the same as Welsh *llan*, originally meaning an enclosure but later coming to be the general Welsh term for a monastery and its church. One wonders whether this name, much more usual in Welsh and Breton, may have come to Lynally with the British monks who feature both in the ' Lives ' of Mo-Chuta at Rahan and of Colman. In both ' Lives ' nearly the same tale—it could be copied from one to the other, is told of British monks who try to murder the founder, in the Colman version they were irritated by some triviality, " secundum irascibilem Brittonum naturam " (according to the irritable disposition of Britons) and one text adds a marginal note—' Britannorum colera '!

There exist three recensions of the Latin ' Life ' all apparently from a common source, and an Irish one, which is a curious composition of wonder stories and magical themes. It does tell, however, of Colman's going to Scotland, which we know to be true from Adamnan.

> ' I went on a journey eastwards
> To Cantire in Alba;
> And I took with me
> Without neglect Duinech and Cuined '

says a verse in the Irish ' Life ' which represents the two monks, Duinech and Cuined, as Colman's inseparable companions. (These verses inserted in prose ' Lives ' repeat the information in a kind of easily remembered shorthand, to help the memory to learn the full story).

It seems from Adamnan that Colman visited Scotland on several occasions. One time he was caught in the dangerous tide race and whirlpools of Corrie Bhrecan. Colmcille in Iona knew of this and said that the Lord had let Colman into this danger, not to drown him but to make him pray more earnestly. Colman's ship arrived safely in Iona. (Bk. I, ch. 5). In one version of the ' Life ', this incident takes place when Colman is thinking of working permanently overseas, but Colmcille tells him to go back to Ireland to feed his flock there with the word of doctrine and of grace. The granting of Lynally follows after this. Adamnan tells of a later visit when Colmcille got a fair wind in the morning for Baithene going to Tiree, and another in the afternoon in the opposite direction for Colman going back to Ireland. After he had gone, Colmcille said he would never see him again. The year was in fact 595, in which Colmcille died. (Bk. II, ch. 15).

In Ireland, Colman is represented as preaching at Clonmacnois—so effectively that the day was always remembered afterwards as that of the preaching of Colman Elo. Another story tells of his getting lost in Connacht, and how the saint told the party to sing the 118th psalm, ' Beati immaculati in via ' (Blessed are the undefiled in the way, who walk in the law of the Lord). As they do this, they pick up the right road again, and moreover come on a house whose hospitable owner puts them up for the night. In return, Colman works a miraculous cure of the man's deformed child.

The miracle stories include some life-like touches, the account of brewing beer at the monastery, and how Colman miraculously restored yeast that had gone dead, and another that goes well with the low lying land around Lynally. The monks built a hut in summer on a triangle of land between two streams. In winter, this was in great danger of floods, but Colman halts the waters by drawing a line round the building with his bachall. The latter was obviously the great relic in Lynally in later times and was taken on the tribute collecting circuits. The liturgy is represented by a story of Colman seeing Patrick standing amongst the monks when they were chanting the hymn to Patrick.

One day, Colman is said to have heard some soldiers shouting and laughing on the road back from some minor victory. He says one among them will be a monk, and points out a certain Tochnan. " Son," said Colman, " you are called to belong to God." Tochnan was willing enough but the captain of the party refused to let him go. Tochnan collapses to the horror of the captain, who then relents. Tochnan is, of course, duly restored to life by Colman, lives to a ripe old age and a reputation for sanctity, as a monk.

Colman and Mo-Chuta at Rahan are represented as intimate friends on frequent visiting terms. Colmcille's Durrow, only a few miles away, was another nearby important monastery; it appears in the Irish Life in the story of its monks pilfering some of the Roman earth that Colman had brought to hallow Lynally cemetery!

In Scotland, Colman's visit to Kintyre is still marked by Kilcol-manel (Cill Cholman Eala in Knapdale). He is also the saint of Col-monell in Ayr. These are likely to be personal foundations; according to the Irish Life, a local king made him a gift of a site in Kintyre.

The Irish Life puts some verses into Colman's mouth on the subject of how to recite the Divine Office : —

> When you shall recite your hours,
> And when you shall be in the womb of your mother (the Church)
> Recite them yourself leisurely to the congregation,
> If you will gain the profit of them.

Every verse of them that you recite,
Expound their texts minutely;
Speak in your own character exactly,
And fix on them your understanding;
You shall then receive (your request) from the king of the
    stars,
Whose protection is never ending.

COLMAN OF LINDISFARNE

August 8 (February 18)

Colmán epscop aille ó Inis Bó Finde, Colman, a praiseful bishop
from the island of the White Cow, is noted by Oengus at August 8th;
in Scotland, however, his feast is kept on February 18th. In 661, when
abbot Finan died, Colman succeeded him at Lindisfarne. Colman
was Irish and Lindisfarne then an Irish monastery. In 664 came the
Synod of Whitby and when the decision went against the method
followed by the Columban monasteries of calculating the date of
Easter, Colman resigned and returned to Ireland.

Since the whole of the liturgical year is geared to the date of Easter,
the different methods by which this key date could be calculated were
always the subject of controversy. It was an old problem in the Church,
the Alexandrian method had been widely adopted for the city had a
high reputation for mathematical and astronomical studies; Rome
however had its own system and claimed an apostolic origin for it.
Britain had yet another system and this seems to have been that
followed in Ireland. The difficulties resulting from these different
systems were therefore widespread and of long standing. One Denis,
an Eastern monk resident in Rome, eventually drew up a new scheme,
based on the Alexandrine one. This was in 525; by the end of the
century Rome had adopted it. About 632, the south of Ireland accepted
it, but not the north nor western Scotland and the monasteries founded
therefrom. Accordingly, king Oswy called a synod, or more correctly
a royal council, to discuss and settle the question for the north of
England. Bede says that at the synod there were present the king and
his son, " Bishop Colman and his Scottish clerks, and Agilbert with
the priests Agatho and Wilfrid, James and Romanus were on their

side; but the Abbess Hilda and her followers were for the Scots, as was also the venerable Bishop Cedd, long before ordained by the Scots, as has been said above, and he was in that council a most careful interpreter for both parties ". St. Wilfrid argued for the authority of Rome and the king accepted what he said and ruled the new system be adopted. It was hardly a true synod, for the majority were against the change (two bishops against one). The form of the tonsure was also discussed, a triviality capable, as such things are, of rousing intense feelings. Not unnaturally Colman determined to go home, and a number of English monks to travel with him. Tuda, who had studied in Ireland and probably was Irish, but from the south of that country, succeeded Colman as bishop of Lindisfarne, and Eata from Melrose, a man trained by St. Aidan, became abbot. The Irish influence continued strong at Lindisfarne in spite of Colman's departure.

He went north to Iona and then back to Ireland, where the whole party settled on the island of Inishbofin off the coast of Connemara. Here an international dispute arose, for the English said the Irish went away all summer, leaving them the work to do, returning in winter to batten on the results of their labours. Possibly Bede's story is a garbled version of the custom of taking cattle to summer pastures (booleys/shielings). At any rate, Colman decided the question by letting the English party make a fresh start on its own at Mayo, Mayo of the Saxons, for long famous as an English monastery in Ireland. The best known name connected with this place is that of St. Gerald, (q.v.).

St. Colman of Lindisfarne died in 672 (Annals Clonmacnois), or 674 (Four Masters) or 675 (Ulster).

On Caher Island near Inishbofin, two cross inscribed slabs in the early Christian monastic ruin there, have been compared with slabs from Lindisfarne and Hartlepool, and with a design in the Book of Lindisfarne, respectively. Their inspiration most likely came from Colman and his party. They are of 7th century date.

See also GERALD, BERCHERT OF TULLYLEASE, AIDAN OF LINDIS-
FARNE.

Bede. History. Account of Synod of Whitby. Bk. III, ch. 25. Of Colman going to Ireland and the foundation of Mayo, Bk. IV. ch. 4.

F. Henry. "The Antiquities of Caher Island, Co. Mayo." J.R.S.A.I. 1947, pp. 23-38.

COLMAN MACDUACH
October 29

Colman MacDuach of Kilmacduagh in Co. Clare, whose name is still invoked in traditional prayers (for an example see under Sinach MacDara) flourished in the 7th century. The legends bring him into close contact with Guaire the hospitable, king of Connacht, who died in 663 or 6, but it is possible that, if the genealogies of the saint are correct, he really lived some 50 years later than the king.

Colman, son of Duach and Rinagh, was born in the parish of Kiltartan, tradition pointing out Corker as the actual spot. A story, perhaps based on that of the Holy Innocents, says the mother had to conceal herself from the king who had heard a prophecy that her child would be greater than all Connacht's royal line. Colman anyway survived, and went to study on Aran, where he has two churches, claimed as personal foundations, on Inishmore. From there, he came back to the limestone karst country of the Burren in Clare, a short, direct sail from Aran, and sought a hermitage. The place he selected, where he lived a considerable time, with a lad for servant and companion, was Ceannaille, the Eagle's Rock, a little to the south of Kinvarra. It was then wooded country, of which Burren is now stripped, though its rocky clefts are thickly grown with hazel and hawthorn. Ceannaille rises a great rocky cliff, to the foot of which one walks across bare limestone pavement—in which are found all the brilliant flowers of Burren. At the cliff foot, the scrub wood conceals a ruined chapel and a well (Tobermacduach). There is a stone " altar " between the two at which rounds used to be paid, and cairns marking the route to the site from the public road. Colman lived in a cave in the cliff back from the chapel. He was, like most saintly hermits, not left there in peace, but discovered and induced to take up the active apostolate. (Perhaps the curious weathering of the limestone rock, like wheel tracks, inspired the wonder tale of the Flying Dishes, in which after his servant had complained of the poorness of their Easter fare, Colman magicked away king Guaire's banquet from Kinvarra, the king and court taking horse and chariot for it in amazed and hungry pursuit!)

Colman then made a monastic foundation on the good land that lies between the Burren Hills and Slieve Aughty, Cell Maic Duach, Kilmacduagh. It lies west of Gort and commands a wonderful view of the grey hills of Burren to which Colman later returned. Colman

is claimed to have been both first abbot and bishop of Kilmacduagh.
The place today is marked by an interesting series of ruins, a fine
round tower which leans some two feet out of the perpendicular, the
ruins of the cathedral (14th-15th century rebuilding) and of the church
of the Canons of St. Augustine. Two dolphins snapping at one another
are among the carvings on the capitals of the pillars of the chancel arch
in this second church. There is also a solidly built house which is
thought to have been that of the bishop.

St. Colman felt himself unworthy of his position at Kilmacduagh
and longed for the solitude of the hills. He therefore resigned, and
went back to the Burren, this time to Oughtmama (Breast of the Pass),
where he made another foundation and where he died. After his
death, his body was brought back to Kilmacduagh for burial. Oughtmama is different from Ceannaille, for it is an ideal site to develop
into a large monastic settlement, an oasis of good land in a hollow of
the hills. It lies on the flank of Turlough Hill just above Burren
village, and above too the later Cistercian foundation of Corcomroe
(' Sancta Maria de petra fertili,' or ' de viridi saxo ' 1182). Three ruined
churches still mark the site, the biggest, with nave and chancel in a
plain Romanesque style, has a holy water stoup on the side of which
two antlered stags are shown fighting. (At that time, they would have
roamed the Burren woods). There is also a small oratory with very
pointed gables, intact except for the roof, and another church of which
only a gable end remains. The place shows an interesting pattern of
older field divisions beneath the modern ones, perhaps these belong to
Seanbhaile Octmama—Oughtmama Old Town. Oughtmama seems
to have developed into an important monastery, the curious Litany or
spell invoking holy bishops in sevens, invokes the seven holy bishops
of Uthmana, and in the Leabhar Breac there is a mention of three
Colmans, sons of Lugaid, who belonged to Uchtmama.

The hereditary keepers of the crozier of St. Colman were O'Heynes,
from whom it was purchased by Dr. Petrie. An enquiry made in 1840
about the celebration of the feast of Colman in Kilmacduagh parish
—as a holiday of obligation—resulted in the information that it went
back to time immemorial, and had been a general diocesan holiday.
The vigil was kept as a strict fast and traditional tales told of the
awful fate that befell those who broke it.

J. Fahy: *The History and Antiquities of the diocese of Kilmacduagh,* 1893,
    pp. 48-114: 447-453.
*Illustrated Guide to the Northern, Western and Southern Islands and coast of
    Ireland,* R.S.A.I., Dublin, 1905, includes a full account of Oughtmama.

COLMCILLE (COLUMBA)

June 9

" Behold my servant: I will uphold him. My elect; my soul de-
lighteth in him. I have given my spirit upon him; he shall bring forth
judgment to the gentiles. He shall not cry, nor have respect to person;
neither shall his voice be heard abroad. The bruised reed he shall not
break, and smoking flax he shall not quench; he shall bring forth
judgment unto truth. He shall not be sad nor troublesome till he set
judgment in the earth; and the islands shall wait for his law."

(Isaias, ch. 42 from the epistle, feast of St. Colmcille in Scotland)

The extract from Isaias quoted above, which forms part of the
liturgy for Colmcille's feast in Scotland, could almost have been
written with the man himself in mind. Bold, courageous, outspoken,
a man born to rule and to command, Colmcille was also the " kind
Colmcille " of Scottish tradition, a man of helpfulness and sympathy.
Here compassion was no empty expression of regret, but linked to
ability, power and resourcefulness. He was the kind of person who did
not help a Lochaber beggar with a carelessly tossed coin, but got him
cut a stake from the wood, which the saint himself then fashioned
into a pike to catch wild animals and provide the man with a permanent supply of food. (Adamnan. Bk. II, ch. 37).

But as the object of a nation-wide cult both in Ireland and in Scotland, Colmcille, like Patrick and Brigit, has become surrounded by a
legend. Presented, as in Manus O Donnell's ' Betha Colaim Chille '
(1532) in which legend and history are skilfully mingled, it must be
admitted the tale makes excellent and racy reading. But the true story
of Colmcille is rather more scrappy and sparse, the man himself however more attractive in reality than in legend. Even things that one
took for granted like the famous copyright case with Finian of Moville
seem better set aside or labelled ' Not Proven '.

The authentic sources for the life and character of Colmcille are
his surviving poems, the ' Life ' of St. Adamnan (q.v.) and the
material remains, the sites of the famous Columban monasteries, Iona,
Kells, Durrow, Derry and the rest. Unlike those connected with many
other famous saints, the Columban monastic sites still preserve a great
series of material relics including the magnificent high crosses of Iona,
Durrow and Kells. Colmcille too is still the object of a live devotion

in various places and is invoked in traditional prayers, both in Ireland and in the old Gaelic invocations and hymns of the Scottish Highlands.

Colmcille was born on Thursday 7 December, 521 at Gartan in Donegal. Here a broad lake is cradled in green and fertile country lying just east of the rockier and heathery Donegal mountains. Colmcille came of royal blood, his father Phelim (Felim) MacFergus being great grandson of Niall of the Nine Hostages. Colmcille's mother was named Eithne, the child himself seems to have had two names, Colm (with the ' cille ' perhaps added later, Colm of the Church) and Crimthann (fox or wolf). He was baptised and fostered by a priest called Cruithnechan who lived quite near Gartan at Kilmacrenan. Some much later ruins mark this spot, on a green ridge of drier land rising from water meadows, a country of wood and field but with a distant prospect to the mountains. Colmcille had early determined to be a priest and a monk but he was also aware of his abilities as a poet and wished to cultivate these too. So his subsequent studies took him first to Finian of Moville, where he was ordained deacon, then to bardic studies with a bard called Gemman, and afterwards to Finian of Clonard, where he was ordained priest, and to Mobi at Glasnevin. At Moville, he would have come into contact with a scripture scholar who had trained at the Scottish monastery of Candida Casa, founded by Ninian. At Clonard, he not only got to know many of the other great saints of contemporary Ireland who were fellow students, but in its founder learned from a man who was one of the originators of the great expansion of Irish monasticism, and had studied in Wales. His stay at Glasnevin was short, for the place had to be abandoned on account of an outbreak of bubonic plague, in which Mobi himself died —in 544 or 5. Colmcille escaped the infection and returned to the north and his own people, the clan Niall. Here he was given, in 546, the little hill covered with oak wood which was always so dear to him ever after and would be known as Doire Choluim Chille (Colmcille's oakwood, modern Derry). This was his first monastic foundation of his own—nothing survives of it in the modern town of Derry.

From Derry, Colmcille began a widespread apostolate in Ireland, which would set a network of Columban monasteries over the countryside. Durrow, right in the centre of Ireland, $3\frac{1}{2}$ miles north of Tullamore, was founded before 588, in which year the Four Masters record the death of the chieftain who had given the site a few years earlier. The exact date of the foundation may lie between 553 and 563. At

Durrow there survive a series of early grave slabs and a magnificent high cross; Kells (Ceannanus Mor) has still four high crosses and seems most probably to be a personal foundation also. Swords, north of Dublin, not far from Glasnevin, is very doubtfully another, Moone of St. Colmcille in Co. Kildare, west of the Wicklow mountains, is important for yet another great high cross. Glencolumcille in Donegal, very likely a mountain hermitage site chosen by the saint, has still an annual, and very penitential pilgrimage on the saint's day, visiting its great series of early cross inscribed pillar stones set about its glen. Tory Island, with its T shaped cross, is also claimed for Colmcille and there is no reason why he should not have visited it. Aran likewise claims him as a visitor. One's impression is that this very active and energetic young man, who was also a poet and scholar and of good family—the old accounts say he could, had he wished, been *ard ri,* first of all ranged over Ireland and then looked about for further scope for his talents and for furthering the kingdom of God. He had quite likely already paid visits to Scotland to the struggling Irish colony of Dalriada. Accordingly this ' island soldier ' as Adamnan calls him, determined to go to their help, both in the religious and political fields, for Dalriada had to face both Pictish paganism and Pictish opposition to the settlement. He crossed to western Scotland, as many other Irish monks had done and were doing, contacted the king of Dalriada, and looked about for a suitable site for a monastery. In 563, he selected the island of Iona off the coast of the island of Mull; a place set on the seaways from Scotland to Ireland and about the Hebrides, close to the mouth of the Great Glen, the great west to east crossing of the mountains of Druim Albyn.

Adamnan merely refers to the battle of Cooldrevny as a well-known date, 561, two years before Colmcille left for Iona, and makes no mention of the famous legend of the stolen copy of Finian's gospel book. The cause of the battle, on the slopes of Ben Bulbin in Sligo, is said to have been not only because of the killing of the son of the king of Connacht, who was a hostage of the ard rí, and had sought Colmcille's protection, but because the high king, Diarmait, had ruled that Colmcille's copy belonged not to him but to the owner of the original text. (To every cow her calf, to every book its little book). Colmcille's people from Ulster and a force from Connacht defeated the high king, Diarmait macCerball, at Cooldrevny. Later on, Colmcille is said to have repented of his part in causing the battle and the slaughter of so many men and to have gone into exile in penance therefor. Quite apart from the pyschological difficulty, that a man of Colmcille's time and temperament would hardly have regarded his part in such an affair as a sin, the story, of which Adamnan makes no mention and which comes to us only in later traditions, would seem very difficult of proof. The battle undoubtedly took place, but the story about the book would appear much more likely to be one of those romantic legends that grew up around the great Columban relic of the O Donnells, to which they attributed so many of their military successes.

To identify Finnen of Druim Finn (Dromin, Co. Louth) with Finian of Moville, as owner of the book that Colmcille copied without permission, is to go directly contrary to Adamnan's evidence, in which Finian of Moville appears as Colmcille's very dear friend. (Bk. II, ch. 1, and Bk. III, ch. 4). The second mention when Finian was " by this time a very old man ", describes the saint seeing Colmcille accompanied by an angel and goes straight on to tell that it was at this time that Colmcille left for Scotland with twelve companions. These relations are hardly to be squared with the picture of the irate and jealous scholar!

The Cathach, a portion of the psalter, is, with its shrine, still in existence, and has been dated to the late 6th or early 7th century. It may well have been written by Colmcille, who spent much time and energy copying texts, but though it has been suggested that it shows some signs of a scribe working under pressure, its beautiful regular script could never be equated with the work of a man stealing a copy of a text and scribbling away in constant fear of detection! The later legend was that if this book in its shrine, " was borne thrice sunwise round the host of the clan of Conall when they go into battle, they come back safe in triumph " (Betha Choluim Chille). This is the reason of its name, Cathach, ' Battler '. We may, I think, explain the story thus:—the Cathach was the great relic of these people, they attributed victories to it and Colmcille, and they knew of the victory in the saint's lifetime, involving the saint's kinsmen at Cooldrevny. An elaborate legend could grow out of such material. But it may genuinely enshrine a strong tradition, even a certain fact, that in the mutilated psalter called the Cathach, we see and handle a text written by Colmcille himself.

Adamnan describes Colmcille at work writing. The Cathach certainly belongs to his period and even if not his, gives an idea of what kind of job he would produce out of his little hut on Iona. The capital letter at the beginning of each psalm is decorated with red dots, a form of decoration of Coptic origin used in the west only by Irish scribes at this period. Initials and text are by the same hand, and the book represents the earliest surviving example of Irish script. Carl Nordenfalk points out that it represents the first example of the decoration of the actual script and it would appear that this form of ornamentation originated in Ireland and then spread abroad through the Irish missionaries and their monasteries.

The political position in Scotland when Colmcille arrived was that the Irish colony of Dalriada in the west Highlands, with its capital at the rock of Dunadd, was struggling to maintain itself against the far more powerful and larger Pictish state (or possibly states, for all Pictland may not have been a single unit). Druim Albyn, the north-south backbone of the Highland hills, provided something of a natural frontier between the two peoples. The Picts spoke a language of the same Celtic family as Welsh and Breton; Colmcille used an interpreter when talking with Pictish speakers, Adamnan tells us. Dalriada was in some danger of being swallowed up by the Picts, and Colmcille's efforts in throwing himself into its political life and defence appear to have done much to re-establish its autonomy. Indeed we may look ahead from his work to the time when this small colony of " Scots " would give its name to the whole country as well as a king, Kenneth MacAlpin. The Pictish language vanished too, being replaced by Irish (Gaelic) in the Highlands, and eventually by a form of English in the south. It is evident that Colmcille worked only in Dalriada, though he travelled through the Great Glen to the Pictish king, Brude, at Inverness, and treated with him, probably partly on affairs of state and partly on religious matters. Comgall and Cainnech went with Colmcille on one visit, and it may be that Comgall then got permission for his monks, in particular Moluag of Lismore in Loch Linnhe, to work in Pictish territory east of Druim Albyn. Comgall is often described as himself an ' Irish Pict ' but the *Cruithni* of north eastern Ireland seem to have been of British descent and unrelated to the Scottish Picts. That the Bangor monk, Moluag, worked in Pictish territory, may perhaps not be so much a matter of race, as that he was less identified with the cause and aspirations of Dalriada than Colmcille. The area worked by Colmcille emerges quite clearly from the incidents related by Adamnan :—over a large part of Ireland; in Scotland, on Iona, Tiree, Skye and ' Hinba ' (probably the Garvellach islands) with the mainland peninsula of Ardnamurchan, the Lochaber district, and the Great Glen when travelling to negotiate with Brude. That is, quite simply, that he worked in the territory of the Irish settlers.

Nor, of course, was he the first Christian missionary in Scotland. Long before, Ninian's Candida Casa had been established in the south and probably sent its missions far north up the east coast. The Dalriada settlers were Christian. Moluag had come to Lismore a year before Colmcille to Iona, and Iona would seem to have had an already established little chapel of St. Oran. The curious legend of Oran being first to die on Iona is refuted by Adamnan's definite statement that the first monk to die of Colmcille's abbey there was Brito (Bk. III ch. 6), but the legend and the veneration in which Reilig Oran is held would point to it being the island's first little oratory.

The control that Colmcille had on the affairs of Dalriada is shown by the incident described by Adamnan about its royal succession. Conall MacComgall, who had been forced to acknowledge the Pictish king Brude as overlord, died in 574. Colmcille was on the island of Hinba when he got the news, and it fell to him to inaugurate the new king with the Church's blessing. His choice was Iogenan. But on three successive nights an angel with a book in which the form for the coronation was set out, appeared to Colmcille and the name in the book was Aidan, Iogenan's brother. Colmcille's stubborn resistance to this new idea indicates the authority he had in the matter. The angel struck him with a scourge, the mark of which, says Adamnan, he bore for life, and in the end Colmcille gave way. Aidan, nicknamed the False, was duly crowned, and made a good ruler. He was king of Dalriada from 574 until 606 the year in which he died. He asserted himself against the Picts and repudiated their overlordship. (Bk. III, ch. 5).

The following year, Colmcille, who governed the whole chain of Columban monasteries from Iona and kept in very close touch with them, returned to Ireland for Mórdáil Droma Ceta, the famous Convention of Drumceatt in Co. Derry. This gathering of clergy and kings had been called by the high king, Aedh MacAinmire, and would seem to have been a genuine national assembly though we cannot put too much trust in the details of the list of those present. Adamnan only tells of miraculous incidents that took place during this journey to Ireland (Bks. I, ch. 49 and 50, II, ch. 6) and does not tell of its actual business though he may have known people who had been at it. The traditional account of the agenda only goes back to the 10th century but seems reliable. This says there were three items, the release of a certain Scandlann, and the two great questions, the position of the bards and the position of the two Dalriadas, the mother state in Ireland and the daughter colony in Scotland. What obligations had Scots Dalriada to render to Ireland? It was decided that Irish Dalriada could be called on, as usual, to provide land forces for the Irish high king, but that Scottish Dalriada could only be asked for its fleet. With its close links with Ireland and the indented, island studded coast of its territory, Scots Dalriada was probably well supplied with ships.

Finally the position of the bards was dealt with. The position, with its privileges, of the bards in Irish society was being strongly attacked. It was suggested that the whole order and its claims and demands be done away with, perhaps the Irish laity felt that two learned orders, clerical and secular, were one too many! The Church, however, with Colmcille as its spokesman, took up the defence of this lay scholarship, and successfully negotiated both for their survival and adequate privileges. "Drum Ceat did much, therefore, to save the traditional learning that had been transmitted from generation to generation in Ireland since the earliest times " (J. Ryan, S.J.).

Adamnan's stories give a vivid picture of life on Iona. Voices shout across the narrow Sound for the ferry, the monks work on the little fields amongst the grey rocks, the little boats come and go, the liturgy is celebrated in the monastic church. There was constant coming and going, Cormac Ui Lethan on his adventurous voyages, Brendan of Clonfert (who seems likely to have founded the first church on the Garvellach islands with which Adamnan's Hinba is usually identified), Cainnech, Comgall. Colmcille was always receiving news of what was doing elsewhere in Scotland and in Ireland. On one visit to king Brude, he got permission for Cormac Ua Liathain to go and seek a hermitage in the Orkneys—the under king of the Orkneys whose good behaviour was guaranteed by hostages held by Brude, being then present at the latter's court. Adamnan says that Cormac in fact escaped death on the strength of this recommendation Colmcille obtained. (Bk. II, ch. 42). In the Irish ' Life ' of Colman Elo, Cormac appears as abbot of Colmcille's Irish monastery of Durrow.

Men came to Colmcille for confession and penance. Iona had an establishment on the neighbouring, very fertile, island of Tiree and this farm was one of the places to which penitents were sent to carry out the long terms of Celtic penance. Another was ' Hinba '. Both the gentleness and the detail of Celtic penance is well described in the touching story of Libran of the Rushfield (Bk. II, ch. 39). Libran arrived from Ireland and stayed in the guest house at Iona. After some days, Colmcille asked him in true Irish fashion, about his country and his relatives and family, and why he had come to Iona. Libran explained why he had come, and Colmcille then asked him if he was prepared to carry out their rules for penitents. Libran said he was, and kneeling at Colmcille's feet, confessed his sins and promised to fulfil the laws of penance. " Get up, and be seated," Colmcille told him. Then he told him he was to do seven years penance in Tiree, at the end of which he would come for his Easter communion to Iona. Libran asked next what he would do about a false oath he had made —he had killed a man, been saved from death by a nobleman paying his eric, blood money, and then promised to serve the latter all his life. Then he had decided to serve God rather than man and betaken himself to Iona. Colmcille decided to deal with this after the seven years penance was finished; he then sent Libran back to Ireland with a present of an ornamental sword as ransom from his broken oath. All went as Colmcille had told Libran it would, and he finally sailed back from Derry to become a monk in Colmcille's monastery on Tiree. He died, however, in Ireland, when on a visit to Durrow.

Colmcille liked people. Nobody seems to have been beneath his notice. Thus he told a certain Saxon lay brother of his vision of the angels meeting the soul of a certain poor woman when she died, and the same thing when her husband died the next year. They were very ordinary poor people but it appears outstanding examples of holiness in married life. (Bk. III, ch. 10). Another time, the saint was travelling through the Great Glen along Loch Ness-side, and as they came near Glen Urquhart, he urged the party to make haste. Colmcille said they must hurry to meet the angels who were waiting to carry to heaven the soul of a certain pagan of Glen Urquhart, called Emchath, who had lived a good life and now desired baptism. Colmcille indeed pushed ahead of his companions, found Emchath and baptised him before he died. Emchath's son, Virolec, and the whole household were also converted. This story is not only of interest as an example of the work of the angels but is almost identical with an account of our own times told by Father André Dupeyrat in his ' Mitsinari '. Here the scene is set on the jungle trails of the Papuan mountains, and Fr. Dupeyrat, to the surprise and annoyance of his companions, is suddenly and irresistibly urged to turn off the trail. He too came on a dying and abandoned pagan waiting for baptism. Father Joseph Bachelier, the leader of the party, said:—" So the angels have been taking a hand again. As soon as he saw me bending over him, he said, ' I have been waiting for you. . . Baptise me, so that I may go to God our Father ' . . . Poor old fellow! He's clearly sincere . . . I tell you, the angels must have led us here!"

Another story of great interest is the account of the blessing of the well, worshipped by the Picts as a divinity. It was regarded as poisonous and Colmcille's drinking of it after the blessing was expected to kill him. In fact, it had curative powers afterwards. This is likely to be a perfectly true account of the way that a pagan cult of wells and springs was Christianised. (Bk. II, ch. 11).

At the end of his account, Adamnan tells in detail of the last days of Colmcille. It is a story to be read in the original to appreciate its full beauty and Adamnan's narrative powers. The saint travels on a cart to make a last visit to the little fields of Iona where the monks are at the spring work. He blesses the remaining store of grain, enough he carefully notes, to last till harvest. As he leaves the granary and rests for a moment at a cross fixed in an old millstone, the old white horse, that carried the monastic milk churns, came up to him and nickering, laid its head on the saint's shoulder and began to weep. His attendant, Diarmait, would have driven it off, but the saint stopped him, pointing out how Diarmait, a rational man, did not know Colmcille's death was near but the horse did. He blessed the horse, and slowly climbed onto one of the rocky knolls overlooking the monastery and there stood, hands raised, and blessed it, " not only Irish people but rulers of foreign and barbarous nations will hold this place in honour," he said, " and the saints of other churches shall give it reverence " (i.e. the saints of other groups of Celtic monasteries, other than the Columban group of which it was the principal house).

He went back to his hut and went on transcribing a psalter. It was the beautiful psalm 33 that he had reached. " Divites eguerunt et esurierunt, inquirentes autem Dominum non minuentur omni bono," he wrote in the clear Irish script, " The rich have wanted, and have suffered hunger, but they that seek the Lord shall not be deprived of any good." He was at the foot of the page. " I must stop here," he said, " let Baithene finish it." Baithene, Colmcille's kinsman, had been governing the Tiree monastery and now succeeded Colm as abbot of Iona.

It was a Saturday night in June, and there was hardly any real dark. Colmcille was at the Office in the church and then went back to his hut, where he gave the community a final exhortation to have charity among themselves. The bell rang for the midnight Office and Colmcille, moving in the pale dusk of the Hebridean night, was the first into the church. He knelt before the altar, and Diarmait, hurrying after him, saw a blaze of light round Colmcille. The light vanished and Diarmait, half blinded, found the saint lying before the altar. The rest of the community were now at hand with lights, grouped round the dying abbot. Diarmait lifted his hand so that he could give them a final blessing. It was very early on the morning of June 9th, a Sunday, in 597. Even the elements seemed to mourn Colmcille's passing, for the islands were lashed with wind and rain, and the monks buried their abbot with all the would-be mourners from elsewhere storm stayed on the mainland.

Of the actual Celtic foundation on Iona, the grave slabs, the fine high cross of St. Martin, and the Romanesque oratory of Oran, are all later than Colmcille's time. Recent excavations (1956/7/8/9) on Tor Abb have laid bare what is thought to be the foundations of the little square hut of Colmcille, stone walled, with a thatched roof. A flagstone was perhaps the saint's bed, and three stones could have supported the table at which the saint wrote and read. Some evidence found suggests the Celtic monastery was on the same site as the later Benedictine one. There seems a probability that the Book of Kells was begun on Iona and then finished in Ireland where it was taken to escape the Viking attacks, to which Iona was much exposed.

Further insight into the personality of this born leader, poet and scholar and saint, comes from his surviving poetry, the long and complex, magnificent, *Altus Prosator,* and the shorter, *Noli Pater.* Both are in the Irish 'Liber Hymnorum', and one story in this collection connects the *Noli Pater* with the founding of Derry. There also exists a Gaelic poem very descriptive of Iona which may well be Colmcille's; there are many other poems ascribed to him but actually of later date. The alleged 'Prophecies' of Colmcille, like those of Mael Maedoc are, of course, wholly spurious.

The *Altus Prosator,* an alphabetical hymn (each verse begins with a successive letter of the alphabet) is a theocentric world picture, a statement of the writer's faith. Its first verse is a careful definition of the Trinity. Colmcille then tells of the creation of the angels, in order that the " goodness and majesty of the Trinity might not be inactive " but reflect something of itself in created beings. Then the fall of the angels is described; the creation of the material world, sea and water, the blades of grass, the twigs on the trees as well as sun and moon and birds and fish and animals, finally man. " As soon as the stars, the lights of the heavens were made, the angels praised the Lord of the vast mass for His wonderful work, the Builder of the heavens."

Colmcille next tells of the fall of man; then diverges to sing of the clouds and the rain and the sea and the crops. " By the divine power of the great God is suspended the globe of earth, and thereto is set the circle of the great deep, supported by the strong hand of Almighty God; promontories and rocks sustaining the same, with columns like to bars on solid foundations (was he looking across from Iona to Staffa?), immoveable like so many strengthened bases."

Below the earth is hell with its torments. The poet turns to the delights of paradise, and to Moses on the mountain, face to face with God; then to the Last Day, that " day of wrath and vengeance, of darkness and cloud ". " Trembling we shall be standing before the judgment seat of the Lord and shall give account of all our deeds." The dead rise at the archangel's trumpet, Christ returns, before Him shining " the most brilliant sign and standard of the Cross ". In conclusion, Colmcille returned to the praise of the Trinity and to the thought of heaven:—

Y mnorum cantionibus sedulo tinnientibus
tropodis sanctis milibus angelorum vernantibus
quatuorque plenissimis animalibus oculis
cum viginti felicibus quatuor senioribus
coronas admittentibus agni dei sub pedibus
laudatur tribus vicibus trinitas aeternalibus.

Z elus ignis furibundus consumet adversarios
nolentes Christum credere deo a patre venisse
nos vero evolabimus obviam ei protinus
et sic cum ipso erimus in diversis ordinibus
dignitatum pro meritis praemiorum perpetuis
permansuri in gloria a seculis in gloria.

Quis potest deo placere novissimo in tempore
variatis insignibus veritatis ordinibus
exceptis contemptoribus mundi praesentis istius.

(Literal translation:—" By chanting of hymns continually ringing out, by thousands of angels rejoicing in holy dances, and by the four living creatures full of eyes, with the four and twenty happy elders, casting down their crowns beneath the feet of the Lamb of God, the Trinity is praised with eternal threefold repetition.

The raging fury of fire shall consume the adversaries, unwilling to believe that Christ came from God the Father; but we shall fly forthwith up to meet Him, and so shall we be with Him in divers orders of dignities according to the everlasting merits of our rewards, to abide in glory for ever and ever.

Who can please God in the last time, when the glorious ordinances of truth are changed. Who but the despisers of this present world?")

See also ADAMNAN, CAINNECH, COMGALL, BRENDAN OF CLONFERT AND OF BIRR, FINIAN OF CLONARD AND OF MOVILLE, MOBI, ORAN.

Text of *Altus Prosator* (with literal translation) and of *Noli Pater* in the *Irish Liber Hymnorum,* H.B.S., London, 1898, I, pp. 62-89, II, pp. 23-28: 140-172.

Adamnan: *Vita Sancti Columbae.* Latin text, translation and notes. *Adomnan's Life of Columba.* Edited by A. O. and M. O. Anderson. Edinburgh, 1961. English translation by Wentworth Hysche, London, 1905, and many times reprinted.

W. Douglas Simpson: *The Historical Saint Columba,* Aberdeen, 1927.

Betha Colaim Chille. Compiled by Manus O Donnell in 1532. Irish text and translation edited by A. O'Kelleher and G. Schoepperle. University of Illinois, 1918. The fully fledged legend of Colmcille.

There are a number of Latin and Irish accounts of Colmcille as well as modern popular biographies, all using a mixture of fact and fancy.

H. J. Lawlor: *The Cathach of St. Columba,* P.R.I.A., 33 C (1916-7), pp. 241-443.

Carl Nordenfalk: *Before the Book of Durrow,* Acta Archaeologica, Copenhagen, 1947, pp. 141-174. Includes account of the Cathach.

J. Ryan, S.J.: *The Convention of Druimceatt,* J.R.S.A.I., vol. 76, 1946, pp. 35-55.

There is a very considerable literature on the relics from and remains at the principal Columban monasteries:—on the Book of Durrow, and the Book of Kells, and on the high crosses and buildings at the sites. A crozier survives from Kells and that claimed to be Colmcille's from Durrow. The following publications on this topic may be cited:—

T. H. Bryce and Frank Knight: *Report on a Survey of the Antiquities on Eileach an Naoimh.* Trans. Glasgow Arch. Soc. New series, vol. 8 (1927-34), pp. 62-102. This is probably Adamnan's *Hinba* though W. J. Watson did not subscribe to this identification.

Helen M. Roe: *The High Crosses of Kells,* Meath Archaeological and Historical Society, 1959.

Liam Price: *Glencolumbkille, Co. Donegal and its Early Christian Cross Slabs,* J.R.S.A.I., vol. 71, (1941), pp. 71-88.

J. Romilly Allen: *The Early Christian Monuments of Iona,* P.S.A.S., vol. 35, (1900-1901), pp. 79-93.

R. A. S. MacAlister: *An Inventory of the Ancient Monuments remaining on the Island of Iona.* P.S.A.S., vol. 48, (1913-14), pp. 421-430.

S. De Courcy Williams: *The Termon of Durrow,* J.R.S.A.I., vol. 29, (1899), pp. 44-51 and 219-232.

For Scots Gaelic traditional invocations of Colmcille, see A. Carmichael's *Carmina Gadelica.*

For an example of a breviary hymn to Colmcille see *Iesu Redemptor omnium* which is found in two or three 15th century Irish breviaries, text in *Pange Lingua,* (Breviary hymns of old uses, collected by Alan G. McDougall), London, 1916.

COLUMBAN (COLUMBANUS)

November 23

" Therefore let us concern ourselves with heavenly things, not human ones, and like pilgrims always sigh for our homeland, long for our homeland. It is the end of the road that travellers look for and desire, and because we are travellers and pilgrims through this world, it is the road's end, that is of our lives, that we should always be thinking about. For that road's end is our true homeland . . . Don't let us love the road rather than the land to which it leads, lest we lose our homeland altogether. For we have such a homeland that we ought to love it. So then, while we are on the road, as travellers, as pilgrims, as guests of the world, let us not get entangled with any earthly desires and lusts but fill our minds with heavenly and spiritual things: our theme song, ' When shall I come and appear before the face of my God?' "   St. Columban. Sermon 8.

" The influence of St. Columbanus rocked the conscience of Europe for nearly half a century around the turn of the year 600 : wherever he went there were veritable outbreaks of sanctity. A new spirit breathed upon the clergy, and the episcopate was visibly improved by him. His own foundation at Luxeuil, became a real nursery of bishops, and his distinctive stamp was impressed on many other communities, such as those of St. Wandrille at Fontenelle and St. Philibert at Jumièges. Through him, the custom of auricular confession, with private, fixed penances, was imposed on the whole of western Europe. As a contemporary aptly wrote, he ' hurled the fire of Christ wheresoever he could, without concerning himself with the blaze it caused '."

H. Daniel-Rops in " The Church in the Dark Ages "

Columban, who headed the first great Irish mission, *ob amorem Christi*, for the love of Christ, to Europe, is perhaps also Ireland's greatest missionary to date. Abroad, his influence was widespread and long lasting, not only in raising the standard of Christian living, but in forwarding secular studies as well. Thus Pius XI claimed that " the more experts study the most obscure problems of the Middle Ages, the clearer it becomes that the renaissance of Christian learning in France, Germany and Italy, is due to the work and zeal of St. Columban ".

It is fortunate therefore that Columban is our best documented Irish saint, a ' Life ' written by a contemporary, and a collection of the saint's writings, letters, sermons, poems, penitential and monastic rule. Jonas, Columban's biographer, entered Bobbio in Italy three years after Columban's death at that last foundation of his (Columban died November 23, 615). In 618 most of the Bobbio monks would have been intimate with Columban. Bertulf, the second successor of Columban as abbot, commissioned Jonas to write the founder's life. Jonas had first hand material from those who had known and worked with Columban, in particular St. Gall, to this he added a personal tour of France in 640 to gather material. The book was published in 643. Jonas was a careful and reasonably reliable historian, who noted names of people and places with accuracy. The miracles that he describes rest on first hand, or nearly first hand, evidence.

Jonas is naturally more vague about Columban's early life in Ireland, which he had never visited himself. Columban, writing to Pope Boniface (letter 5), describes what manner of land it was that gave him birth and training. " We Irish, living at the edge of the world, are followers of Sts. Peter and Paul, and of all the disciples who wrote the sacred canon inspired by the Holy Spirit. We accept nothing but the teaching of the apostles and evangelists. There has never been a heretic or a Judaizer or a schismatic amongst us. But we hold unbroken that Catholic Faith which we first received from you, the successors of the holy apostles." (Evidently Columban believed that the first mission sent to Ireland had come direct from the Pope and Rome).

Columban was born somewhere in Leinster, Jonas does not say where, nor who his parents were, nor the date. It is likely to have been about 543, if Columban's poem saying he had reached his 18th Olympiad, and extreme old age, was written at Bobbio, and is not a mere formal poetic turn of phrase. (An Olympiad might be either four or five years—making the saint 68/72 or 85/90: the four year period seems the most likely).

Columban was a well grown, very handsome and attractive youth, and though of a studious turn of mind, had all the local girls in love with him. Columban called to a local holy woman and asked her what he should do in this situation: she told him that his only safety lay in flight. She said she had been living a hermit life for 15 years, and " were it not that I am a weak woman, I should have crossed the seas, to find a more secluded retreat ". Columban's mother was heart broken at the idea of her son leaving home. Her tears and arguments were all in vain; she threw herself across the doorway—perhaps the low roofed entry to the family rath, but the young man clambered over her and headed down the road.

He made his way to the monastery of Sinell at Cleenish, Lough Erne, a man who had been trained at Finian's Clonard. By going to Sinell, Columban put himself in touch with the full stream of the Irish monastic tradition in its purest form. He remained a lay student and impressed Sinell with his ability. He began to write, a commentary on the psalms (that has not survived) and other little books and poems. Perhaps the *Carmen de Mundi Transitu,* the song on the transitoriness of the world, was one of them. The constant flux and change of the created world was an idea that bit deep into Columban's consciousness, he felt the very tears of things, the passing of all beauty including that of women, and turned his mind to the royal halls of heaven and the company of heaven, the unchanging and glorious life of heaven:—

Tunc dolor, tunc taedium,	Then sorrow, then weariness,
Tunc, labor delebitur,	Then work, will be at an end.
Tunc rex regum, rex mundus	Then the King of Kings, the
A mundis videbitur.	pure Lord
	Shall be seen by the clean of heart.

At Cleenish, Columban decided to become a monk but he did not enter Sinell's monastery, going instead to that of St. Comgall at Bangor on Belfast Lough. There, through Comgall's (q.v.) own attractive personality, young Columban came into contact with the adventurous missionary spirit of the best men out of Ireland, for Comgall knew Colmcille and Cainnech and Brendan of Clonfert, and had travelled in Scotland. It would be wrong to stress solely the asceticism of Bangor, and forget its great tradition of devotion to the Mass and the Blessed Sacrament, Comgall's stress on the need for spiritual direction and frequent confession, the apostolic outlook of the whole monastery. The song about the Rule of Bangor in the Anti-phonary of Bangor (written between 680 and 691) is suggestive in its symbolism of the virgin mother of its apostolic ideals:—

Virgo valde fecunda	A very fruitful virgin
Haec et mater intacta,	and a virgin mother,
Laeta ac tremebunda,	joyful and reverent,
Verbo Dei subacta.	submissive to the word of God.

The liturgy, with its day hours of Terce, Sext, None, and its night hours of Vespers, Vigils and Lauds, patterned the whole life, giving it direction and inspiration. Columban's own notes in his Rule about the liturgy probably are simply those of Bangor, the above ' Hours ' are those to which he refers, he does not mention Prime or Compline. The night offices lengthened for the long winter nights, shortened for the summer ones, so that the night ' Hours ' had a minimum of 48 psalms and a maximum of 99; the three day ' Hours ' included 9 psalms. Each psalm at night was followed by a prostration and a silent prayer. The Mass on Sundays and feast days, the Divine Office, study, and the essential work on the monastic lands, made up the day's round. There were crowds of students. Columban was ordained priest and appointed chief lecturer in the schools. His poetry, with its many classical echoes and allusions, shows that he had not only considerable theological training but a good acquaintance with the classical authors. He may have written the poems to Hunaldus and Sethus at Bangor, once more brooding on the transitoriness of life, the years revolve, season returns on season, but not youth to man. Yet his rather melancholy verses reflect also the spirit of Bangor :—" Quisquis amat Christum, sequitur vestigia Christi "—whoever loves Christ, follows in the track of Christ ".

Bangor on the sea, shipping coming and going from Scotland, Columban determined to be going himself, pilgrim for the love of Christ. Comgall, though he did not want him to leave, eventually consented, and Columban set off, with, says the tradition, twelve companions. Of these, St. Gall would be the most famous. Their route was via Britain and then to Brittany. Perhaps St. Columb in Cornwall and St. Coulomb on the Bay of St. Malo may mark their passage.

The Irish party set off on a roving apostolate over Gaul. " From 511 until 613, the Frankish lands were really nothing more than lists where brothers and cousins slaughtered one another " is M. Daniel-Rops' summing up of the situation in which the monks had to work. (" The Church in the Dark Ages "). Clovis' empire had been divided amongst his sons and the background to Columban's work is the complex history of these little states with their shifting frontiers. There were three main divisions, Neustria (Neuester Reich), Austrasia (Oster Reich) and Burgundy. A son of Clovis, Clothair who had died in 561, had ruled Neustria and some of his sons became the rulers of the whole area. Thus Gunthram (d. 593) had Burgundy, and Sigebert (d. 575) had Austrasia, where he was succeeded by his son Childebert II (d. 595). Chilperic (d. 584) ruled Neustria, and was succeeded by his son Clothair II. Gunthram's death put Childebert II in command of both Austrasia and Burgundy, when he died, his elder son, Theudebert, got Austrasia, and the younger, Theuderic, Burgundy. Jonas gives no date for the arrival of the Irish party but says that Sigebert received them favourably. He further says that Sigebert was ruling Austrasia and Burgundy. This has raised considerable chronological difficulty, for Jonas might have got either the name or the territory wrong. If the former, then it might have been Childebert who received them, and the date would be 590/1. On the other hand, this seems to leave insufficient time for Columban's work in Gaul, and J. O'Carroll has argued for an arrival in France in about 573 and that Sigebert really was the ruler who made them welcome. It seems certain that Columban had foundation charters for his monasteries and that Jonas would have seen these—it might be that Sigebert was there styled ' King of the Franks ' or by a similar title, and that Jonas concluded he had ruled the same territory as later kings.

These quarrelsome states and rulers lived in a permanent condition of violence and vice. Not that there were not good men, and monasteries too scattered over the country, but the overall picture was black; jealousy, lust and war could at any moment destroy the work of years. If the long years of penance laid by Columban in his Penitential read harshly to us, we need to remember the sins involved, and their frequency, murder, sodomy, fornication, magic, abortion, child murder, reverting to paganism, perjury. It needed a certain violence to recall men to a sense of having done wrong, to halt them repeating the same crime again and again. Beyond the actual area in which Columban first found himself there lay real pagan country, for it took about 400 years from the baptism of Clovis to make all Europe Christian.

But with all their faults, these Merovingian princes did recognise and respect sanctity when they saw it. Columban and his party soon attracted attention and were invited to Sigebert's court. The king took a liking for Columban and pressed him to stay in his territory, giving them the old Roman fort of Annegray, up in the woods on the slopes of the Vosges. (This Annegray site, has, very recently, been excavated and the Columban foundations laid bare). The Irish settled themselves in this ruin and began a somewhat precarious existence. Food was scarce enough, there was sometimes only the bark off the trees and herbs to be got; sometimes there was a windfall in the way of a gift from a friendly neighbour. Columban had a great power of attracting ' native ' vocations, and his monasteries were not Irish in the sense of being composed of only Irish monks. Very soon, the numbers at Anne-gray overflowed its resources, and another foundation was made at a second old Roman fort, Luxeuil, eight miles from Annegray. Taking the 573 date for Columban's arrival in Gaul, the Luxeuil monastery would have been founded in 590. Later still, three miles from Luxeuil, a third monastery was started at Fontaines. Round Columban gathered monks, students and crowds of ordinary folk who came to hear Columban's preaching, be cured of their diseases, get spiritual direction. Here it would seem he wrote his Rule and Penitential, writing down the tradition he had learned at Bangor and adapting it to local conditions.

At times, Columban would go off into the woods alone. Solitude was very dear to him. " You know I love the salvation of many and seclusion for myself," he wrote to his monks (Letter 4), " one for the progress of the Lord, that is, of His Church, the other for my own wishes." And for all his lamenting of the passing nature of created things, a sense of transitoriness which the violent world into which he had come must have emphasised still more, he also loved the wild creatures of wood and hill. " Understand, if you want to know the Creator, created things," he said in a sermon (no. 1). Natural beauty and the birds and beasts were for him the handiwork of God, a way in which to approach the Lord. Here Jonas is important, for his accounts of Columban and the animals come nearly first hand, and we have the facts about Irish saints and nature as against the legends. At Annegray he was walking in the woods meditating on scripture, and began to wonder whether he would rather suffer the attacks of men or beasts. He decided for the beasts, as it would involve no souls in sin! Just then a pack of wolves appeared; he stood quite still and they snuffled round him, then made off without harming him. The danger was not over, as a plundering band of Suevi were also on the road, but they missed seeing Columban.

He went far into the woods one day and found a cave formed by an overhanging rock. A bear had made it her home and was inside when Columban arrived. By some means or other, he got her to leave, and make a fresh den elsewhere, whilst Columban turned the cave into a hermitage. He used to go there on Sundays and the vigils of feast days, living on herbs and little wild apples. Domual, the lad who attended him, complained of the long carry for drinking water; at the saint's prayer, they got a fresh spring from the rock, a fountain still venerated today.

Chagnoald, who succeeded Domual as Columban's personal attendant and secretary, later to be bishop of Laon, used to tell Jonas about the wild animals and how they would obey Columban. When the saint went into the wilds to pray, Chagnoald said he often heard him call the wild animals; they came at his call and let him stroke them, they frisked round him " like little puppies around their master ". There was a squirrel that used to come down from the tops of the trees, it would jump onto Columban's shoulder or onto his outstretched hand as he went in or out of the cave.

Columban's monks worked hard on the land around their settlements to provide themselves with food. They also went fishing in the rivers, using both nets and fixed fish traps. Jonas tells various stories about this work, of cutting grain on " a good day for reaping with a gentle wind from the south ", and of a monk who slashed his finger nearly off. At Columban's touch, it healed at once and he went straight back to work. A similar miracle was worked on a head wound when the monks of Bobbio were felling and splitting timber in the woods and an onlooker was hit by a wedge springing out unexpectedly. Now and again they were on very short rations, but Columban said that if His people served the Lord rightly, they would never go hungry, and the situation always seems to have been saved in time, by one means or another.

The life was hard, but its hardness needs to be seen against the hardness of the times. Columban's ' Rule ', like all ' Rules ' of the earlier period of monasticism, is not a detailed set of regulations to govern the whole day's activities, but is rather a meditation on the virtues needed by the monk. Day by day routine was, of course, fixed, but by custom and the abbot on the spot. Columban laid down an excellent line of prudence and discretion in his Rule. True discretion demands a moderation, a temperance, in the use of life and in work, his ideal is a balance of mortification of the flesh with spiritual progress. " For," he wrote, " if abstinence is pushed beyond right measure, it becomes a vice and not a virtue; for virtue sustains and maintains many good things. So then, we must fast daily, but equally eat daily; in that eating however indulge the body poorly and sparingly; we must eat daily since we must progress daily, pray daily, work daily, study daily."

Columban's Rule is in the full tradition of the monastic ideal, stemming from the Desert Fathers, St. Martin and Irish monasteries. Its stress falls on absolute obedience, on the virtue of silence, of abstinence in food and drink, of poverty and chastity. The monk's treasure must be in heaven, not in material things or the desire thereof. Columban details three stages of monastic perfection, first, neither to own anything nor to desire to do so; second, to cleanse oneself of all vices; third, a most perfect and unceasing love of God and divine things. Chastity for the monk means purity of mind, what use is there, asks Columban, in being virgin in body if one is not virgin in mind? The monk's perfection, he wrote, is to live in community under the rule of one father, but in company with many others, so that the different virtues, humility, patience, etc., can be learned from the different individuals.

St. Benedict's Rule, originally one among many, eventually came to replace the other early codes, not only on account of its balanced moderation but because it was more detailed. It told the abbot how to govern, whilst an early Irish Rule told the individual monks how to be saints. Gaul, when Columban arrived, had its monasteries, and a variety of monastic Rules—of Martin of Tours, of Honoratus of Lérins, Caesarius of Arles. The Columban Rule became very popular and had a run of some two centuries in Gaul before it was replaced by the Benedictine Rule. The first appearance of real Benedictine influence in this part of Europe came in the mid-8th century, when Carloman, Duke of Austrasia, held meetings of bishops at Estinnes (743) and Soissons (745), after which he ordered the Benedictine Rule to be followed in monasteries. Later, in 802, Charlemagne held a council at Aachen, when the abbots and monks present decided to have the Benedictine Rule read and explained to them. At Luxeuil, the first mention of St. Benedict is in a brief of Innocent II, dated 1136.

Columban had a quite extraordinary influence on people, a mere meeting or a blessing was often enough to sow the seed of sanctity. Just as earlier on, Martin's monastery of Tours had been regarded as a place from which a good bishop could be got, so now, cities tried to obtain a bishop from a Columban house. M. Daniel-Rops may not exaggerate when he says that Columban's influence in Europe was so great that not until St. Bernard did another saint hold a comparable position. Columban's monks became monastic founders and/or bishops; women too were attracted by this Irish ideal of holiness. A list of monasteries, including those of women, which derive directly or indirectly from Columban, in Europe prior to 700, runs to some 94 names. There is also a quite considerable list of canonised saints who were connected with Columban one way or another.

The date of Easter was again a bone of contention, Ireland, Gaul and Rome each following different calculations. Columban wrote a letter (Letter 2) to a French synod about this matter, saying that he was sorry that they did not hold such gatherings more often, glad that the Easter question had provoked such a meeting. He tells them they should be moulded to Our Lord's pattern of the true shepherd, He who in preaching the beatitudes began with humility and worked up to martyrdom; a man is not only just by what he does, but by his suffering, martyrdom if need be, for the sake of justice. " Thus it is written that he who says he believes in Christ, ought to walk as Christ walked, poor and humble and always preaching truth despite persecution by men. Then again, they who wish to live truly in Christ shall suffer persecution, and faith without works is dead."

Where and when was this synod held? Those who date Columban's journey to Europe to 590, identify it with that held at Chalon in 603, but if the earlier date for his arrival is accepted, it probably was that of Mâcon held in 585, which was attended by some 50 bishops and did, in fact, deal with the Easter question. The latter seems the more likely occasion, for it was the only council to discuss the Easter question during Columban's time in Gaul.

Columban wrote at intervals to the Pope. Not only Easter but other difficulties harassed life at Luxeuil. The Irish rural economy, where abbot and monastery was the great unit in the Church, came up against the city, diocese and bishop, grouping of Gaul. Nor could

Columban keep silence over the vices of the times, more especially of the royal court, and his security was thereby in some danger.

He wrote accordingly to Pope Gregory the Great about these matters (Letter 1):—Easter and various difficulties of current ecclesiastical discipline. Bishops might ordain men for money, ought one to be in communion with them? Could men who had bought their priesthood or committed adultery whilst deacons, become bishops lawfully? That problem, whether a priest with such a past could accept consecration as a bishop, had been put to Columban in confession. Then, what was to be done about monks who left their monasteries without permission, either to relapse, or to live as hermits in search of greater perfection.

Columban goes on to say how much he would like to visit Rome and the Pope, and that he has read Gregory's book on Pastoral Care, how succinct yet packed with doctrine it is. He asks Gregory to send him his commentary on Ezechiel. " I have read six books of Jerome on him but he did not expound even half." " Send too the Song of Songs, from the point where it says, ' I will go to the mountain of myrrh and hill of frankincense ', to the end." He wants Gregory to explain the obscurities of Zacharias. He knows he is asking a lot, " but you have a lot and you know that from a little, a little can be lent, from a big store, much ". He asks the Pope's prayers, " but I don't think its necessary for me to pray for you, whom the Lord says should be received as coming in His Name ".

Gregory's sermons on Ezechiel were preached in 593 but not published until 601; there is a record of the Pope sending a copy of his ' Pastoral Care ' to the " priest Columbus " in 594, probably Columban. So that this letter was likely to have been written between 594 and 600, perhaps closest to the latter year. For in October of that year, Gregory wrote to the Abbot of Lérins, Conon, mentioning " our son, Columbus the priest "; he seems not to have answered Columban directly but rather commended his difficulties to the Abbot of Lérins.

In 607, Columban wrote again to Rome, leaving the name of the Pope blank for he had not yet had news of who had been elected to the vacancy. Once more he bewails that he cannot visit Rome personally, encloses a copy of the earlier letter to Gregory, to which he had received no answer, and asks for a decision and discussion of the points raised.

After Childebert's death in 595, his son Theuderic was ruling in Burgundy. He liked Columban and was proud to have such a man in his territory. His grandmother, Brunichild, however wished to be all powerful and encouraged Theuderic to keep a harem of concubines rather than introduce a lawful Queen and possible rival. Columban's outspoken reproaches made Brunichild hate him; he refused her request to bless the little family of bastard sons; and she determined to be rid of the saint. Theuderic swithered between the two, alternately frightened by one or the other into action. Columban's rigid rule of enclosure, that forbade free entry into the monastery, was made a cause of offence. Theuderic however was not so foolish as to wish to destroy the Columban monasteries; he only wanted to get the troublesome Irishman out of the way. He decided to send him back to Ireland. He told Columban that the saint might be hoping for martyrdom but he wasn't going to get it!

Columban was first exiled to Besancon. Here he miraculously released some prisoners, and then managed to slip back to Luxeuil. A second force was then sent to remove him, with the order that no Gaulish monks could go with him, only the Irish and those who had come from Brittany.

The route by which the exiles travelled to the sea was a very long one. They went by Besancon, Autun and Avallon to Auxerre. From there they went to Nevers, on the Loire, on which they took ship and sailed downstream for the port of Nantes. They made a halt at Orleans, where by royal edict, all the churches were shut against them and they had to bivouac on the river bank. Their food was running short and the Orleans people were far too afraid of the king to supply them. In the end, a stranger living in the city, a Syrian woman, came to their aid. Her husband, also Syrian, was blind; Columban restored his sight. A number of insane people came to be cured, and Orleans began to be impressed by Columban though they dared not show it openly.

At Tours, Columban was forbidden to visit the tomb of Martin. The boat itself drifted inshore to the right landing place and so the saint got his way. He spent the night in prayer at Martin's tomb; next day, the bishop, Leuparius, made him and his party welcome. Over a meal, the following conversation took place. Leuparius asked Columban why he was going back to Ireland. " That dog, Theuderic, has driven me from my brethren." Another guest, Chrodoald, whose wife was an aunt of Theuderic, muttered to himself, ' better to drink milk than wormwood.' " I see," said Columban, " you mean to keep your oath of loyalty to Theuderic." " I do." " If then you are bound in fealty to the king, you will be glad to act as messenger from me to him. Tell him that within three years he and his children will all perish and that his whole family will be uprooted by God." " Why do you say that?" " When God bids me speak, I cannot be silent."

This prophecy of Columban's was exactly fulfilled. Thus Theuderic's death in 613, fixes the date of Columban's exile from Luxeuil as in the year 610.

When Columban returned to the ship, he found that the party had been robbed of all their money. Thief and booty were discovered after Columban had prayed once more at Martin's tomb. The bishop gave them further supplies as well. Eventually they came to Nantes, and here they had a long delay. Once they gave away all their food to a poor man and were left fasting for three days until a woman called Procula came to their help. Columban remarked on the wonderful nature of God's love, letting us be in want, so that He could show His love in coming to our aid; allowing us to be tempted, so that we may draw closer to Him. After another woman had brought further gifts, the bishop of Nantes began to feel somewhat ashamed of himself for he had refused even to sell anything to the exiles. A boat trading with Ireland was eventually found, all went aboard but Columban who said he would follow them to the open sea in a small boat. The ship was driven ashore by a storm, almost immediately, and the captain, feeling the exiles were the cause, put them all ashore before refloating his vessel. No further attempts were made against them and Columban set off for the court of Clothair, king of Neustria.

Whilst they were waiting for a ship in Nantes, Columban wrote one of his most moving letters, to the monks left behind at his monasteries (Letter 4). Once again, he sets their vocation before them, warning that persecution comes not only from men but also from devils; against both they must take up the armour of God. They must dwell in unity and peace amongst themselves. He names Attala, formerly a monk at Lérins and later to succeed Columban at Bobbio, as prior. If Attala wants to come after Columban, then they should elect Waldelenus, to whom he now sends the kiss he failed to give him in the hurry of departure. Troubles, difficulties, are on every side, he tells his dearest Attala. There is danger in being hated, and danger in being loved. Columban has checked his tears in making this farewell, writing rather of essential duties, " the brave soldier does not weep in battle. Nor is it a new strange thing that has happened to us, but what we have preached every day . . . the true disciples of Christ Crucified should follow Him with the cross . . . that man is blessed who shares in (Christ's) passion and shame . . . therefore let us bear all adversities for the Truth's sake, that we may have a share in the passion of the Lord, for if we suffer with Him, we shall also reign with Him". So Columban urges them to persevere to the end, to trust in God not in themselves, to hold to the road to the city of the living God, in work, in humility of spirit, in study, in everything, remembering always that if you remove the battle, you also remove the crown of victory.

As Columban wrote, getting to the end of his parchment, the messenger came to say the ship was ready. He concluded hurriedly. " I wanted to say everything briefly, but I could not." If he is free again, he will make provision for them. He sends his blessing, that if God is with them, they may increase to thousands of thousands; finally asks their prayers that he may live to God.

Clothair received Columban and his party in very friendly fashion and bore patiently with the saint's lecturing him on the sins of the court. He wanted Columban to settle in his territory, but Columban refused, though he made a long stay. Meantime the brothers Theudebert and Theuderic were disputing over the boundaries of their kingdom, and both asked Clothair for help. Columban repeated his prophecy and advised the king to keep out of the quarrel, for " in three years, both kingdoms will be yours".

Perhaps because Columban still hankered to visit Rome, he decided to set off for Italy. With an escort from Clothair he crossed Theuderic's territory. His route was via Paris, Meaux and Ussy. At Meaux he blessed Burgundofara, the daughter of a nobleman and dedicated her to God, she became a nun (her feast is in the Roman Martyrology on April 3) and founded Faremoutiers. At Ussy Columban did the same by two boys, Ado (founder of Jouarre) and Dado (of Rebais in La Brie).

Theudebert welcomed Columban, and wanted him to settle in his kingdom too. Some Luxeuil monks now joined Columban and they all set off for a possible foundation at the ruined town of Bregenz. They went to Metz on the Moselle and took ship down the river to the junction with the Rhine, up which they then sailed. It was a long journey up river to Bregenz on Lake Constance; the rowers pulling against the current sang to lighten the tedium and keep in time. Columban picked up the refrain and turned it into a Latin rowing song, Virgilian in form, Christian in outlook.

En silvis caesa fluctu meat acta carina
Bicornis Hreni et pelagus perlabitur uncta.
Heia viri! nostrum reboans echo sonet heia!
Extollunt venti flatus, nocet horridus imber,
Sed vis apta virum superat sternitque procellam,
Heia viri! nostrum reboans echo sonet heia!
Nam caedunt nimbi studio, caeditque procella,
Cuncta domat nisus, labor improbus omnia vincit.
Heia viri! nostrum reboans echo sonet heia!
Durate et vosmet rebus servate secundis,
O passi graviora, dabit deus his quoque finem.
Heia viri! nostrum reboans echo sonet heia!
Sic inimicus agit invisus corda fatigans,
Ac male temptando quatit intima corda furore.
Vestra, viri, Christum memorans mens personet
    heia!
State animo fixi, hostisque spernite strofas,
Virtutum vosmet armis defendite rite.
Vestra, viri, Christum memorans mens personet
    heia!
Firma fides cuncta superat studiumque beatum,
Hostis et antiquus cedens sua spicula frangit.
Vestra, viri, Christum memorans mens personet
    heia!
Rex quoque virtutum, rerum fons, summa potestas,
Certanti spondet, vincenti praemia donat.
Vestra, viri, Christum memorans mens personet
    heia!

Poetry being form, sound and sense, is untranslatable. Columban's
Latin formality is merely stilted in a literal English version. The
following attempts to catch the spirit of his song, rather than its word
for word translation.

The galley, forest born, cleaves the stream,
The dark, unbroken waves of two horned Rhine.
Shout heia, lads, till echo rings again!
Wind driven squalls lash on us, dark as night,
But skill and courage yet can overcome.
Shout heia, lads till echo rings again!
Hold fast, for cloud and tempest pass at last
And brave endeavour claims the victory.

Shout heia, lads, till echo rings again.
Stand firm, and at the end, we shall succeed,
Worse sufferings, yes, but God commands the end.
Shout heia, lads, till echo rings again!
Just so, the unseen devils try to break our hearts
By evil temptings and despair's dark storms.
Hold then to Christ, lads, shout heia in your souls!
Stand fast, beat down the tricky foe's attacks,
With the bright weapons of the saints of God.
Hold then to Christ, lads, shout heia in your souls!
The rock of faith, desire of the Lord, will overcome
And break the lances of our ancient foe.
Hold then to Christ, lads, shout heia in your souls!
The Lord of hosts, Creator, almighty God,
Rewards His warriors with the victor's crown.
Hold then to Christ, lads, shout heia in your souls!

They now came into contact with real paganism and both Columban
and Gall were active, perhaps too violently, in attacking pagan
sacrifices and customs. The Bregenz site was not very suitable, and
Columban decided to go on. Before he left however Jonas tells a
story of a bear that came to take the apples that, so short were they of
food, were the sole source of supply for Columban when he had gone
off alone to a forest cave he had chosen as a hermitage. Chagnoald
saw the bear moving amongst the scrub, eating the apples and told
Columban, who then marked out the wood into two sections, one for
the bear and one for himself. The bear " as long as Columban was
in those parts " kept to his own half.

In 613 came news that both Theuderic and Theudebert had died
violent deaths, Columban's prophecy had been proved true. But
Columban had already, in the autumn of 612, crossed the Alps to Italy
and Milan. Gall remained behind.

The baptism of Clovis (c. 498/9) had been the turning point in the
preaching of the Catholic Faith in western Europe. But earlier, the
Arian version of Christianity had been accepted by a number of
barbarian races: Columban coming to Lombardy came to one such
people—who in fact did not become fully orthodox till after the
middle of the 7th century. And here one should note as well the part
that women played in the spread of the Faith, mixed marriages, if
one partner was of the stuff of a St. Monica, often had immensely

far reaching effects. Columban now came on one such, the Catholic princess Theodelinda who was married to the Arian Duke of Turin, Agilulf. The people loved their Queen, and her children were baptised and brought up as Catholics. Agilulf welcomed Columban, but he still hesitated to become a Catholic himself. Part of his excuse for delay was the controversy over the " Three Chapters " schism. The Emperor Justinian in a theological excursion of his in 543-4 had attempted to reconcile his Catholic and Monophysite subjects, in a document which condemned the writings of Theodore of Mopsuestia, Theodoret of Cyrrhus and Ibas of Edessa (whence the title " Three Chapters "). In 547, he had got the Pope, Virgilius, to Constantinople, and forced him to subscribe to the Emperor's solution. Although the Popes were not bound by a decision obtained in such fashion, much harm was done, and Columban found himself not merely up against Arianism, but two rival Catholic hierarchies created by the schism. That the Pope, Boniface IV, took no action, made people say he was really a Monophysite, who supported the condemned authors. This was the background to Columban's anxious letter to the Pope (no. 5) urging him to take immediate action to clarify the situation.

Columban began by apologising for his impertinence in writing to the Pope, but asks that the matter, not the status of the writer, be the thing considered. Like all genuine saints, Columban could not keep silent when he felt both Pope and Church were in need of outspoken criticism. He urged Boniface to be vigilant, to take a firm stand and give a bold lead, that the sheep might recognise their true shepherd and the wolves be destroyed. He urges the Pope to call a Council at which the various charges made against him could be refuted. Men, writes Columban, say that the Pope himself is favourable to heresy, he hoped it was not true, but if it were, the head of the Church would be turned into the tail. Once more he apologised for his outspoken remarks, perhaps offensive to ' pious ears ', but he points to the freedom of Irish custom. In Ireland, it is not a man's standing but his principles that count.

This very long letter, written in Milan in 613 at the request of the Lombard king and queen, is notable for the way it mingles criticism, suggestion for action, with an equally firm statement of loyalty and devotion to the see of Peter.

The editor of the critical edition of Columban's works (Dublin 1957) believes that the series of thirteen sermons that have come down to us, were preached in Milan at this time. They give a good idea of what sort of a preacher he was. They are not theologically or philosophically profound, indeed the audience would not have been capable of assimilating such matter. The first, naturally enough, is on the Trinity, and Columban was content to state the doctrine and say that it was to be believed, not argued over. The material is popular, dramatic in presentation, meant to move ordinary people to belief and good living and the love of God. In the troubled times they lived in, it is not surprising to find Columban always, indeed as ever, harping on the transitory nature of this life, how people run after the perishable goods of this earth and forget the true end of man, his real good, in eternity. How easy for a man to be fooled. Whoever would go willingly to death? And yet that is just what mankind does do (no. 3).

Love yourself rather than your property, Columban urged, what is your own but your soul, all else is lost at death. He was something of a " hell fire " preacher, pointing out the terrors of the Last Judgment (sermon 9). He did not leave it at that, but took his listeners on to teach them how to live rightly, how to live for Christ and in Christ. Thus sermon 10 leads on from the Judgment to this great theme. " Let us be Christ's, not our own, for we are not our own since we have been bought at a great price, an immense ransom, when the Lord is given for the slave, the King for the servant, God for man. And what ought we to do in return, when the Creator of the world died for us, His sinful creatures? Don't you think you ought to die to sin? Of course you should! Come on, now, let us die, die for life, since Life died for the dead in sin. Then we shall be able to say with Paul, I live, but not I, but Christ lives in me—He who died for me: that's the cry of the chosen. Nobody can die to himself unless Christ lives in him; if Christ is in you, you can't live to yourself. Live in Christ that Christ may live in you."

Columban sees life both as a battle, the Christian conflict, and as a journey through the world of change and perishable things to the true homeland of heaven. We change and move from the day of our birth to that of our death (nos. 6 & 7). Human life is fragile, passing, deceptive; those who love human life don't see it for what it is, they who do see it clearly, despise it. Mortal life is not true life but a way to true life (no. 5). Columban contrasts our readiness to work and suffer and struggle for objectives in this life with our lack of interest in eternal ones (no. 4). A man will work hard to be a musician or a doctor, with no certainty even of living till he graduates; should we not do the same for the certain rewards we can have in eternity?

These sermons, meant to shock and startle, would make the listeners aware, perhaps as never before, of the fleeting nature of the things they were so keen to have, sinful or otherwise. Columban now led them on toward God, the Fountain of Life, the Bread that came down from heaven. The same person is " Bread and Fountain, the only Son, our God, the Lord Christ, for Whom we ought always to hunger " (sermon 13). He is the eternal Fountain, the eternal Bread, " if you thirst drink of the fountain of life, if you are hungry eat the Bread of life. For they are blessed who hunger for this Bread and thirst for this Fountain ". There is a touch of St. John of the Cross in the prayer with which Columban finished this sermon, calling on God to wound our hearts with His love, his image of the soul wounded by such love seeking out the fountain to drink, and of the wound by which we are healed.

In another passage (sermon 12), Columban took up the theme of the servants, loins girded, lamps in their hands, waiting for their Lord's return, and links it with the whole symbolism of light and fire. It is a commentary almost on the Easter Candle of Holy Saturday night, it reminds us also of the hymn for the lighting of lamps in the Antiphonary of Bangor. Columban prays that the Lord will light the flame of His love in him. " I wish that I had that wood that would catch light at that fire, feed and maintain it, that fire that knows neither end nor increase. I wish that I were deserving enough that my lamp would always burn at night in the church of my Lord, that it would illuminate all who come into the house of God."

" I ask you Lord to give me in the name of Your Son, my God, Jesus Christ, that love that knows no end, that my lamp may catch light, never fail, set me aflame and give light to others. We ask you, Christ, our dearest Saviour, to light our lamps, that they may always burn in your Church and receive eternal light from You, the Eternal Light. So then, may the darkness of ourselves be illuminated and the darkness of the world driven from us. So I ask You, my Jesus, to give that light to my lamp, that in its light I may see the Holy of Holies in which You are, Eternal Priest of eternal things. And going into that great church of Yours, may I always see, look on and desire You alone, love You alone, my lamp alight and burning before You for ever."

Columban's stay in Milan was short for he was soon given an option on a site for a monastery well up in the hills on an important pass of the Apennines. There the river Trebbia, that same Trebbia beside which Hannibal had defeated the Romans, flows over a broad, bouldery course between steep, storm gutted hillsides. Here, at Bobbio, far up in the mountains, but yet a fertile, well watered spot, Columban took possession of a ruined church of St. Peter, itself on the site of an older Roman settlement. Here Columban spent his last years, writing perhaps that long poem to Fidolius, mentioning his extreme old age. Here amongst the mountains, parched in summer drought, or snow clad in winter, he made his last great foundation, " The Monte Cassino of the North " as it would later be styled from its importance. And here on November 23rd 615 he died, and was buried in the new church on the slope of the Italian hillside with its fields of grain and vines. To-day, the white tomb of the great Irish missionary in the crypt of the church, impressive in its restrained simplicity, still witnesses to the greatness of Columban and the long, successful pilgrimage of his life, " exile for the love of Christ ".

Even today, Bobbio has a certain sense of the greatness of its past, it still recalls and venerates its Irish saint. It was, immediately following Columban, a great centre of Irish influence and learning, gathering a valuable library (the surviving mss. are now divided between the Ambrosian library in Milan, the Vatican library and that of Turin). It came to have very extensive possessions and it was situated on a important pass:—both factors in making it influential and in spreading the cult of Columban. He was very widely venerated in Italy, 34 Italian parishes are dedicated to him. In the end, Bobbio became a Benedictine monastery which survived until its seizure by the French in 1800.

Columban wrote a letter (6) to his secretary, either Domual or Chagnoald, who had asked for further spiritual direction. Columban in giving it probably also gave a pen picture of himself, the sort of person he himself strove to be. In one long Latin sentence, which a translator must subdivide and paraphrase, he sets out his ideal:—

First we must overcome lust and pride, then " be helpful in humility and humble in authority, straightforward in faith, instructed in right living, exacting in your own affairs but not other people's. Be pure in friendship but suspicious where you suspect trickery. Be hard in easy times, easy in hard ones, versatile in easy circumstances but level headed in difficult ones, have joy in sorrow, sorrow in joy. Don't be afraid to disagree if need be, but agree about truth. Be hard amongst pleasant things, but gentle among bitter ones. Be strong in trials, but useless at quarrelling, slow to lose your temper, quick to learn, slow to speak as St. James advises, but just as quick to listen. So then make effective progress, don't look for revenge, be careful what you say, quick and efficient in your work. Love good folk but be rough with the dishonest; be gentle to the weak, firm with the stupid, correct to the proud, gentle to the poor. Always right living, chaste. modest and extremely patient. Don't ever be covetous, always be generous, in spirit if not in money. Be regular in fasting and vigils, correct in your duties, tenacious in studying. Stay unmoved in turmoil, joyful in suffering, bold in the cause of truth, but don't start quarrels. Be receptive to good, impregnable to evil, kindly in generosity, unwearied in love, always just, respect the good and help the poor. Don't forget the good things you have received, but do forget your past injuries. Don't love riches but a reasonable, moderate line; make your thoughts known. Obey your seniors, set the pace for your juniors, equal your equals, work with the good but not envying those who are better or ahead of you. Equally don't sneer at those who are behind and agree with those who call on you. If you're tired, don't give in. Weep and rejoice at one and the same time, for zeal and hope; have a fear for the end though making steady advance."

See also: COMGALL, GALL.

Sancti Columbani Opera: Edited and translated by G. M. S. Walker. Dublin Institute for Advanced Studies, 1957. With a bibliography of the immense literature on Columban to this date.

Jonas: Life of Columban in *Scriptores Rerum Merovingicarum* iv, (1902), edited B. Krusch and cf. J. Leclercq, Analecta Bollandiana, 1955, pp. 193-6.

Melanges Colombaniens: Paris, 1950. Papers given at the 1950 Luxeuil Congress, containing very detailed and extensive material relating to Columban, his cult, outstanding followers, and his influence.

James O Carroll: *Monastic Rules in Merovingian Gaul*. Studies. Winter, 1953, pp. 406-419. *The Chronology of St. Columban*. Irish Theological Quarterly, January, 1957, pp. 76-95.

Jean Laporte: *Le Penitential de Saint Columban*. Introduction and critical edition. Monumenta Christiana Selecta, 1960.

H. Daniel-Rops: *The Church in the Dark Ages*. English translation, London, 1959, gives a good idea of the background to Columban's apostolate in Europe.

D. D. C. Pochin Mould: *St. Columban and the Mass*. I.E.R., May, 1962, pp. 296-303.

Paola Collura: *Studi Paleografici: La Precaroline e la Carolina a Bobbio*. Milan, 1943. A study of the Bobbio manuscripts.

There are many popular biographies of Columban—e.g., that by James Wilson.

COMGALL

May 10

Benchuir bona regula,	Good the Rule of Bangor,
Recta, atque divina;	Correct and divine;
Stricta, sancta, sedula,	Strict, holy and constant,
Summa, justa ac mira.	Excellent, just and admirable.
Munther Benchuir beata,	Happy the family of Bangor,
Fide fundata certa,	Founded on a sure faith,
Spes salutis ornata,	Graced with the hope of
Caritate perfecta.	salvation,
	Made perfect in love.

(Antiphonary of Bangor)

Comgall, says the Martyrology of Donegal, " kindled in the hearts of men an unquenchable fire of the love of God". His monument is stamped on the history of Europe, for Comgall and his monastery of Bangor sent the party headed by Columban and Gall to the continent, and Moluag of Lismore and Maelrubha to Scotland.

Comgall was born in Dal Araide (roughly Antrim in N.E. Ulster) in the early 6th century, in 515 (Inisfallen Annals) or 516 or 520—the two dates given in the Annals of Ulster. He founded Bangor in 555 or 559 (Ulster), or 558 (Inisfallen), died in 602 (Ulster) or 605 (Inisfallen). These dates, which vary from one set of Annals to another by a few years, may be taken as approximately correct. He is said to have been aged 80 when he died. He was of the Cruithni, the so-called Irish " Picts ", who had nothing to do with those of Scotland; his father said to have been called Sedna, or Sethna, was of the free soldier class, and expected that his son would also embark on a military career. Like St. Martin, Comgall refused, though like St. Martin he does seem to have gone on one expedition, deputising for his elderly father, for the boy was a child of old age, but on a campaign that did not, in fact, materialise.

The sources for Comgall are the near contemporary mentions of him in Adamnan's ' Colmcille ' and Jonas' ' Columban,' and much later, from perhaps the 12th century, a Latin ' Life ' in two versions. One of these, the longer, seems from a now lost Irish original from Bangor; both give a reasonably phrased account of Comgall though they run into chronological difficulties in trying to bring him into contact with other famous Irish saints.

Comgall, free of his military obligations, studied first with a cleric, who amongst other failings, kept a mistress. When Comgall found he had no hope of reforming his teacher, he left him for one of the great monastic schools. The ' Life ' says that of St. Fintan of Clonenagh, a house of very ascetic reputation, but as Fintan died in 603, it would appear very improbable that this slightly younger contemporary would have been teacher of Comgall. He might have gone to Finian of Moville near his own home country. The account says that during this period Comgall was assailed with temptations against the monastic vocation, a general boredom and fed-up-ness, a longing for his home; that he told the abbot of the monastery, who prayed for him and put the demon to flight, and that Comgall himself went and prayed before one of the crosses set about the monastic precincts, and weeping, was filled with a great spiritual joy. After spending some time at this monastery, Comgall returned to his home, and was ordained priest by a Bishop Lugaid, of whom nothing else is known. Next Comgall made a foundation of his own on an island in Lough Erne, called Inis Cometa (Island of Guarding—Ely Island). Here his asceticism is said to have been the death of some of his companions. He was forced to mitigate the rule for other people if not for himself! (We may suspect this story in view of the discretion and prudence enjoined by Columban in his rule which must derive direct from Comgall, and be cautious that we are not dealing with a tale meant to justify later mitigations of primitive observance). Comgall is one of the many saints who is said to have prayed standing in water. Like Colmcille's, his hut at night was sometimes seen ablaze with a mysterious light.

Comgall wished to go abroad on the mission to Scotland, but Lugaid urged him to stay at home—to form apostles. Accordingly, he made the great foundation at Bangor on Lough Laoigh—now called Belfast Lough; a place beside the sea and the shipping routes to Britain, for Scots Dalriada, for the famous Candida Casa, and for the route to the Continent via Britain. Here by Comgall were formed men of the stuff of Columban and Moluag, and the missionary spirit and techniques of the Irish " exiles for the love of Christ " developed. The monastery, of which nothing now remains on the site, attracted numerous students; the old Litany of Irish saints speaks of the " four thousand

monks with the grace of God under the yoke of Comgall of Benchor''.
Perhaps there were not that many, but it may represent an idea of the
numbers of students who passed through Comgall's hands. Columban
was, for a time, professor in the monastic schools.

Comgall did not visit the Continent, but he did go to Scotland. He
and Cainnech travelled with Colmcille to visit King Brude in Inverness
according to the ' Life ', though Adamnan does not mention the other
two saints in his version of this incident. It is likely that Comgall went
to get Brude's permission for, or at least tolerance of, Bangor monks,
like Moluag, working in Pictish territory. Adamnan tells of Comgall
present at the " Mass of the Saints " on Hinba (Bk. III, ch. 17), and
of how Colmcille had a miraculous knowledge of the drowning of a
shipload of Comgall's monks in Belfast Lough. He called the
community on Iona together to pray for the monks, who with the
angels were trying to defend the soul of a stranger guest who was with
them, whom the demons were trying to carry to hell. With the
Iona monks' prayers, they were successful in saving the guest's soul as
well as their own (Bk. III, ch. 13). Adamnan also tells of Colmcille
having a conversation with Comgall on his way home from the
Convention of Drumceatt (Bk. I, ch. 49). On this occasion, Colmcille
made a prophecy of the battle that would take place in the area where
the two saints were resting together on their journey, between
Colmcille's kindred and Comgall's. This was the Battle of Dun
Cethirn in 629.

Comgall made a personal foundation in Scotland, on the fertile
island of Tiree in the Inner Hebrides. Here are level plains very
suitable for grain growing, so that the place was dotted with early
monastic foundations. Iona had a large farm there. Here a party of
Pictish raiders once attacked Comgall's monastery and carried off all
they could, including the monks. Comgall was working in the fields
and had with him one of the little house shaped chrismales, which
the Irish used for carrying the Blessed Sacrament. This object puzzled
the pagans, who thought it was Comgall's " God ", and let him alone
on account thereof. Comgall followed them to the shore and stormed
at them with such a violence of words that they gave up the whole
of their prey.

Finian of Moville, then a very old man, is recorded visiting Bangor.
He had to have a milk diet and Comgall's monks took no milk, so the
saint had to provide some specially by a miracle! In future, Comgall
allowed milk to the sick and elderly monks. When Finian died,

Comgall knew of it miraculously and asked the monks to pray for him when they assembled for Matins. The stories about the friendly association between Finian and Comgall may bear out the suggestion Comgall had been his student.

The 'Life' tells an interesting story of a hermit called Critan coming to Bangor so as to be present at the full liturgy of Easter. At the Easter Mass—this would be that of the Holy Saturday vigil, Critan saw Comgall surrounded by angels as he offered the Holy Sacrifice, a vision like that described by Chrysostom in his treatise on the Priesthood. Critan was very thirsty after the Lenten fast, and he thought the way to quench his thirst would be drink something that Comgall had already tasted. Comgall knew this instinctively and when the Mass had ended, took a drink and passed the vessel to Critan. This may be a reference to the ritual ablution, the drink given to the people after Communion when this was given in both kinds.

Comgall's long life of penance and austerity ended with a long and difficult illness that lasted all winter and on till Pentecost when the saint died. People said he had brought it on himself by his asceticism. Then a St. Meldan appeared to a monk named Colman in a dream and told him that Comgall's illness was because of Comgall's love of Christ, it was to add to his merits and increase his reward in heaven. Comgall insisted, it is said, on receiving the last sacraments from St. Fiacre of Airard (Ullard) on the river Barrow in Leinster. Fiacre is said to have taken an arm of Comgall back to Leinster, when the saint's body was enshrined at Bangor. The Annals record not only the plundering of Bangor by the Vikings in 822 but that they also desecrated the relics and shrine of Comgall preserved there.

Comgall, says Jonas, was " the outstanding ' Father of Monks ' in Ireland, and was known for his insistence on study and strict discipline". We may take it that the basic ideas on the monastic life in Columban's Rule and Penitential come direct from Comgall and Bangor. In one sermon, Columban quotes a not very original passage from the brilliant teaching of St. Faustas, who had taught him, and who Columban says is superior to him in age, merits and knowledge. The 9th century Martyrology of Notker says that Faustus was a Latin name used by Comgall. Faustus, or Comgall, then used to instance how a farmer had both to plough his field and clean it of weeds before he could grow a good crop. So we should cultivate the ground of our bodies with fasts and vigils but not forget to uproot vices. " Let us therefore set ourselves to uproot vices and to plant virtues; root out pride, plant humility, dig out anger and lay down patience, cut out envy and insert good will " (Sermon 2).

In the 9th century the library of Fulda had a copy in Latin of the Rule of Comgall. It is now lost. It was very likely similar to Columban's derivative therefrom, with his insistance that mortification is the greatest part of the monastic rule, that the monk should follow his superior's decisions and not his own, obey instantly and without complaint, keep silence even when he has suffered wrong. " Let him come tired out to bed, and sleep on his feet, and be made to get up before he has had his sleep out." There also exists a metrical " Rule " in Irish which in one text is attributed to Comgall. It may be as old as the 7th or 8th centuries. It repeats the ideas of Columban's prose in Irish idiom, the total love of God, need for spiritual direction (on which Comgall is said to have placed very considerable stress), on patience, humility, bearing injuries patiently. A literal version of some verses runs :—

2.   This is the essence of the Rule : love Christ, hate wealth; piety to you towards the King of the sun and smoothness towards men.

7.   These are your three rules, have nothing else dearer; patience and humility and the love of the Lord in your heart.

15. A devout sage to guide you, 'tis good to avoid punishment. Though great you think your firmness, be not under your own guidance.

17. Though great injuries come to you, do not lament thereat, because they are not more abundant than those of the King who sends them.

A little bronze bell was dug up in the graveyard of Bangor but the great relic of the place, indeed our oldest and most important witness to the liturgy of the early Irish church, is the Antiphonary of Bangor. This includes a hymn, " In memory of our abbots ", up to the one reigning at the time of composition, which dates the manuscript to the years 680-691, the period when Cronan ruled Bangor. Taken to Bobbio, the manuscript is now preserved in the Ambrosian Library in Milan. Strictly speaking it is not an antiphonary at all, for it contains a variety of items, hymns and prayers as well as antiphons, for the Divine Office. Columban's remarks on the Office, which would be the then use of Bangor, suppose six " hours ". There were three short day "hours ", Terce (9 a.m.), Sext (mid-day) and None (3 p.m.); and the three longer night Offices, Vespers at dusk, a midnight Vigil or Nocturn and a dawn Lauds. By the time the Bangor Antiphonary had been compiled, a century later, Prime (here called Secunda) and Compline had been added.

The Antiphonary is an important witness to the devotion of the early Irish church to the Mass and the Blessed Sacrament. The great hymn, " Sancti venite ", composed in Ireland and claimed as the oldest surviving Eucharistic hymn of the West, was to be sung when the priests came for Communion. (The Irish would follow the old use, which the Latin rite now only has on the last three days of Holy Week, though the Eastern rites still retain it, of a single Mass in the church, at which both clerics and laity communicate). There is also a set of antiphons for singing during the giving of Communion. One runs, " Gustate, et videte, Alleluia, quam suavis est Dominus, Alleluia " (Taste and see, how sweet is the Lord), and it is of perhaps more than coincidental interest that Columban used this very line of scripture in his moving sermon on God as Fountain of Life and the Bread which came down from heaven (sermon 13). " Look," said Columban, " where that fountain flows from, for it and the Bread that comes from heaven have the same source. It is our God, the only Son, the Lord Christ, who is both Bread and Fountain for Whom we ought always to hunger." The whole theme of this sermon links with the Bangor antiphons, " Hic est panis vivus, qui de coelo descendit. Alleluia. Qui manducat ex eo, vivet in aeternum. Alleluia " (This is the living bread that came from heaven. Who eats of it, lives for ever).

The importance of the Antiphonary of Bangor in all study of the early forms of the liturgy in Ireland and its spirit, is such that it appears worthwhile to list its contents here. It contains six Canticles, which are still a part of the Divine Office, the two of Moses ('Audite caeli' and 'Cantemus Domino'), the Benedictus, and the Song of the Three Children, the Te Deum and the Gloria in Excelsis. There are twelve metrical hymns. The first is in honour of Christ and is attributed to St. Hilary (' Ymnum dicat turba fidelium '); it is a summary in verse of the gospel story. The next is the hymn of the Apostles, (' Precamur Patrem ') also in honour of the Word made Flesh. Then there is the Sancti venite:—

Sancti venite	Come you who are holy,
Christi Corpus sumite,	Receive the Body of Christ,
Sanctum bibentes,	Drinking the holy Blood
Quo redempti, sanguinem.	by which you are redeemed.

So runs the first verse of this long and forthright statement of Catholic teaching on the Blessed Sacrament.

' Ignis creator igneus ' is the hymn for the blessing of the candle, perhaps a daily ceremony at dusk, but with marked affinity to the ideas of the " Exultet " for the lighting of the Easter candle. There is a hymn for the midnight Office, ' Mediae noctis tempus est', in which the angel who struck down Egypt's first born is recalled, the night in which Israel was saved by the blood of the lamb on the doorposts. We are the true Israel, who are preserved from the powers of darkness by the blood of the Lamb. Likewise the wise Virgins, waiting with their oil filled lamps for the Bridegroom's coming, are recalled.

There is a very beautiful hymn in honour of the martyrs " Sacratissimi Martyres summi Dei ", and a very fine invocation of Our Lord to be sung at Matins, (dawn) on Sundays. (' Spiritus divinae, Lucis gloriae, Respice in me, Domine ').

There follows St. Secundinus' hymn in honour of Patrick (' Audite omnes '), a long alphabetical hymn of fairly conventional praise in honour of Comgall (' Recordemur justitiae '), another on the same plan in praise of St. Camelacus (' Audite bonum exemplum '). Finally there are the two sets of verses, one in honour of the Rule of Bangor, quoted at the beginning of this account of Comgall (' Benchuir bona regula ') and the other in memory of the abbots of Bangor (' Sancta sanctorum opera ').

The book contains as well 69 prayers for the Canonical ' Hours ', some in verse, some in prose, 17 more for particular people or occasions, 70 antiphons, the Pater Noster and a version of the Creed. The latter is rather impressive in its repetition of the actual word, Credo, I believe :—" I believe in God the Father almighty . . . And I believe in Jesus Christ, His only Son, our Lord . . . And I believe in the Holy Spirit, God almighty, having one substance with the Father and the Son . . . I believe in life after death, and in eternal life in the glory of Christ. I believe all these things in God. Amen ".

Most of the prayers are addressed to Christ, possibly in reaction against the Arian heresy which denied His divinity. One prayer for the dawn office may stand for the spirit of Bangor, and for the spirit of Comgall :—

" Tu es spes et salus. Tu es vita et virtus. Tu es adjutor in tribulationibus. Tu es defensor animarum nostrarum, Deus Israel, in omnibus. Qui regnas, etc."

(" You (Christ) are our hope and salvation. You are our life and strength. You are our help in trouble. You are the defender of our

souls in everything, God of Israel. Who reigns with God the Father
in the unity of the Holy Spirit, world without end Amen.")

See also: COLUMBAN, GALL, MOLUAG, MAELRUBHA.
The Antiphonary of Bangor. Facsimile and transcript, 2 vols., H.B.S. London,
     1893.
Riagail Comhgaill Bendchair: An Old Irish Metrical Rule. Edited and translated,
     J. Strachan. Eriu I, (1904), pp. 191-208.
A. Gwynn: *The Irish Monastery of Bangor.* I.E.R. November, 1950, pp. 388-
     397.
P. Grosjean, S.J.: *S. Comgalli Vita Latina. Accedunt duae narrationes gadelicae.*
     Analecta Bollandiana, t. 52, (1934), pp. 343-356.

CONLETH (CONLAID/CONLAED)

May 3

'Bás Conláid cain áge', the death of Conleth, a fair pillar, as
Oengus styles him, took place in 520, or perhaps a little earlier, the
Inisfallen Annals put it at 516. Conleth—the oldest form of the name
is Conlaed, was the son of, so it is said, Cormac, of the Dál Méis
Corb, a sept of Crich Chualann (an area equivalent to the diocese of
Glendalough) in later times, but in Conleth's period living west of
the Wicklow mountains. Nothing is known of Conleth but what
emerges from the accounts of St. Brigit. Looking for a priest for her
community at Kildare, she persuaded Conleth, then living a hermit
life, to come to serve the sisters' needs. He is said to have been a
skilled metal worker. He was venerated as a great saint, and his
body enshrined alongside Brigit's in the great church at Kildare. It is
likely that we would be anticipating later developments at Kildare
in either styling him a bishop or an abbot of a male community there.

CRONAN OF ROSCREA

April 28

Cronan, of whom the 11th or 12th century recensions of a Latin
'Life' tells us very little, is associated with three interesting sites at
Roscrea, Co. Tipperary. Cronan's father, Odran, was a Munsterman
of Eile; his mother, Coemri, belonged to Clare and Connacht. Some

quarrel between the chief of Eile and Odran made the family move to Clare and there young Cronan grew up. The account claims that Coemri's two sisters each had a saint for a son as well, St. Mobi and St. Mochoinne, and that Mobi and Cronan were bosom friends. Mobi, it was claimed, was noted for his devotion to monastic observance; Cronan for his generosity and hospitality. Young Cronan may have visited Scattery Island, he is described as visiting Clonmacnois with Mobi.

Cronan made his first foundation at a place called Tullach Ruaidh (Tullyroe, Red Hill) a common enough name; another at Lus Mag (Lusmagh) near Banagher, which he gave away to some monks who were looking for a place to settle; finally he came to the Roscrea district. At this time, the flat, marshy fields around the mound of Monaincha, were covered with shallow water, Loch Cree, and Monaincha was an island. The lake and island also appear in the life of Cainnech. Cronan settled first at Sean Ross by the lakeside, a site marked by the shell of an old church at the present time. It was a wild and remote place and some travellers, looking for a night's shelter, failed to find it and had to camp out. This breach of hospitality upset Cronan very much and he moved his monastery immediately to a main road site at Roscrea. " I won't remain in a desert place, where the poor and travellers cannot find me easily," said he, " but I'll be on the public road where they can do so readily. And in that place (Roscrea) I'll serve my Lord, Christ, the King of kings."

However, Cronan, like Cainnech, made use of the island of Monaincha as a hermitage. It now has the most impressive of the Roscrea remains, a beautiful little Irish Romanesque Church, at which is preserved part of a cross on which is shown the figure of Christ, fully dressed. He is shown in the same fashion on the high cross in Roscrea town; on the other side of the cross is a figure held to be Cronan. Nearby is the Romanesque west front, all that remains of the old church in Roscrea, and a round tower. The Roscrea round tower has a slab with a ship and a cross carved on it, built into the masonry at the doorway. There used to be a big pilgrimage to Monaincha until the middle of the 18th century, when the proprietor of the land stopped it.

Cronan died in 665. From Roscrea comes the 7th-8th century ' Book of Dimma MacNathi ' with its mid-12th century shrine. Dimma died in 816 but three scribes worked on the book including the one whose name it bears. It is a text of the gospels, with a form for the visitation of the sick in a much later hand. There is also a monastic Rule, of Echtgus ua Cuanain of Ros Cre, a 9th century composition, which is attributed to one Cormac Mac Cuilen Dáin. It may either have come from Roscrea itself or from Monaincha. One precept is an interesting example of Irish devotion to the Blessed Sacrament:—

" A protection of the soul, an approach to heaven, a wonderful power, a fostering of purity, is the food which is after extinction of desire, Christ's body with the blood of Mary's Son."

One miracle told of Cronan is worth mentioning in that it reminds of the travelling professional scribes, contemporaries of the author of the ' Life '. Cronan asked one such to copy the whole Gospel. The man said he could only give a day's work:—so Cronan extended that day to one of forty days and nights and got the job finished!

Dermot F. Gleeson: *Roscrea*. Dublin, 1947.

H. G. Leask: *Monaincha,* description of the ruins. J.R.S.A.I., vol. 50, (1920).

J. Strachan: *Cormac's Rule*. Text and translation. Eriu II (1905), pp. 62-68.

CUTHBERT

March 20

Cuthbert (c. 634-687) was born in the south of Scotland, entered Melrose whose abbot had been trained by Aidan of Lindisfarne, to which island and that of Farne, Cuthbert's subsequent career would take him. He is mentioned in this book in that he represents a man belonging to the south of Scotland and north of England whose spirituality was formed and developed when Irish influence was at its height in that area. The earliest life (written between 699 and 705) from which Bede compiled most of his better known account, is a story reflecting much of the spirit of the Irish saints as it was taken up by the men amongst whom they worked.

Bertram Colgrave: *Two Lives of St. Cuthbert*. Cambridge, 1940. Texts and translation, with notes, of the anonymous *Life* by a monk of Lindisfarne and Bede's prose *Life*.

DAVID

March 1

Whilst historical accident seems to have been the reason why David was chosen, from a whole group of as eminent men, to be patron of Wales, he is the saint most often mentioned in the ' Lives ' as the Welsh ' contact ' of Irish saints. Indeed, St. David's, near the modern port of Fishguard in south-west Wales, was a most convenient landfall for Irish shipping. Moreover it was in a part of Wales in which a number of Irish from southern Ireland had settled permanently. It was a region in which both the Irish Gaelic form of Celtic and the Welsh were spoken.

Most of us are much less aware of this considerable Irish settlement in Wales than of that in Scotland. It would appear that although there may have been Christians in Wales at the end of the period of Roman rule in Britain, the main influx of the new Faith came from Gaulish immigrants, who arrived after the last legions pulled out of Wales in 383. Meantime the sea passage was a link rather than a barrier between Ireland and Wales, and from the 3rd to the 10th century there were Irish petty kings ruling in south-western Wales. They seem to have come from the Decies of Waterford, and to have kept in close touch with Ireland at least until the 8th century. There would thus seem to have been a close contact between Ireland, the Continent and Wales, and this would fit neatly into the strong tradition of pre-Patrician saints in the south of Ireland and with Declan, of Decies', contacts with Wales.

Ogam stones with Irish names, sometimes bilingual, Irish and Latin, still mark the area of Irish settlement in Wales. The headland of St. David's, the kingdom of Dyfed, was no isolated hermitage but a real ' hub of communications ' as E. G. Bowen styles it, with shipping routes linking it to southern Ireland, south-west England and to Brittany, and the old tracks leading inland onto the line of the Roman roads.

In the south of Wales, dedication evidence makes Dyfrig, Cadoc and Illtud, the chief saints of south-east Wales, and Dewi (David), Teilo and Padarn of south-west Wales. The first three are the earlier and the historical evidence for their work rather better than for the second. The ' Life ' of David is the earliest surviving life of a Welsh saint; of it, E. G. Bowen remarks that it " is so obviously legendary

in character that it cannot be relied on for a single historical fact ".
Its author, Rhygyvarch (Ricemarcus, 1057-99), was an interesting
person in his own right, belonging to the period when Welsh national
rights were struggling against Norman encroachment. He came of
a learned family, his father, Sulien, had been twice bishop of St.
David's, being brought back to the See after he had resigned from it.
Curiously, the home of this learned family was at a foundation of St.
Padarn, not of David, Llanbadarn.

David belonged to the 6th century but even the date of his death
is a matter of controversy. Perhaps the Annals of Inisfallen are not
far out with 589, though some have argued for 601. This would
appear to be much too late. He died on a Tuesday, the first of March.

David of Cille Muni (of the monastery of Mynyw) is recorded in
the Martyrology of Oengus (c. 800), and he is also mentioned in the
9th century ' Life of St. Paul Aurelian '. With Gildas and Docus, he is
mentioned in the curious document describing the " Three Orders "
of saints of Ireland. David is put in the second of these and it said that
Ireland got a Mass liturgy from " holy men of Britain ", David,
Gildas, Docus. But P. Grosjean, S.J. has lately shown that this " Catalogus Sanctorum Hiberniae " is late, perhaps 9th or even 10th century
(Analecta Bollandiana, " Edition et commentaire du ' Catalogus
Sanctorum Hiberniae secundum diversa tempora ' ou ' De tribus Or-
dinibus Sanctorum Hiberniae ' ". t. 73 (1955) pp 197-213 : 289-322).
We cannot therefore put too much reliance on this text.

For what it may be worth, the story of David as given by Rhygyvarch is that he was the son of a nun (Nun or Nonnita) who was
raped by a king, Sant, of Ceredigion (roughly modern Cardigan)
when he was travelling in Dyfed. Dewi Sant was Nun's only child,
and if this is true, the elaborate genealogies of his sister and her
descendants, must fall to the ground. Dewi was baptised by Aelvyw,
a bishop of the people of Mynyw—glossed Munster, and possibly
Ailbe. The boy was educated at Hen Vynyw (Vetus Rubus), which
has not been certainly located, and studied later with St. Paulinus.
Eventually he set out to make a series of foundations of his own,
finally coming to Tyd Dewi (Vallis Rosina), David's House, St.
David's. It is well placed for communications, with two creeks, Porth
Mawr and Porth Clais, on either side, giving anchorage for small
ships and outlet to sail in any direction. Rhygyvarch shows a strong
Irish interest in his story, bringing David into contact with Aedan
(Maedoc) of Ferns, Finbar of Cork and Modomnoc. He even goes

further and says a third part of Ireland was subject to David! He describes too the opposition of an Irish chief named Bwya to the settlement of St. David's—where Bwya lived. He takes David on a pilgrimage to Jerusalem as well, and makes him the hero of two Welsh synods convened against Pelagianism—but as it seems this heresy might well have been defunct in Britain by David's time, the very existence of these synods is in doubt.

Rhygyvarch gives details of David's monastic rule, its asceticism and round of work and prayer. He was David the Waterman, for he allowed only water to be drunk in his monastery. His foundation would seem to have marked a move toward greater asceticism in Welsh monasticism, and it is therefore important to note that Finian of Clonard, who had so great an influence on Irish monastic life, studied at Tyd Dewi.

David was never formally canonised, but papal recognition of an age old cult was given by Pope Calixtus II, when Welsh affairs were under discussion in Rome and the first Norman bishop of St. David's appointed. The Pope styled this bishop, Bernard, " episcopo de Sancti David " (May 25, 1123). The ' Life ' by Rhygyvarch seems to have marked the period at which the cult of David ceased to be local and spread over Wales and elsewhere.

A. W. Wade-Evans: *Life of St. David*. London, 1923.
D. Simon Evans: *Buched Dewi. The Life of St. David*. Cardiff, 1959.
E. G. Bowen: *The Settlements of the Celtic Saints in Wales*. Cardiff, 1954.
Melville Richards: *The Irish Settlements in South-West Wales*. J.R.S.A.I., 90, 1960, pp. 133-162. With list of Ogam inscriptions.
Nora K. Chadwick: *Intellectual Life in West Wales in the Last Days of the Celtic Church*, pp. 121-182 in *Studies in the Early British Church*. Cambridge, 1958. Background of Rhygyvarch.

DECLAN

July 24

Mad toich duit a Hére,	If you have a right, O Erin,
dot chobair cing báge,	to a champion of battle to aid you,
tathut cenn céit míle,	you have the head of a hundred thousands,
Declan Arde máre.	Declan of Ardmore.
	(Martyrology of Oengus)

" It is hardly too much to say that the Declan tradition in Waterford and Cork is a spiritual actuality, extraordinary and unique, even in a land which till recently paid special honour to its local saints." So wrote Canon Power in his edition of the Irish ' Life ' of Declan in 1914, recalling that earlier, in 1847, some 14,000 people had taken part in the Ardmore Pattern. Since 1951, the spectacular revival of interest in Declan's well at Toor has shown that this very early saint is still a force in the contemporary scene.

Declan is one of the pre-Patrician saints. The tradition, as it is phrased in the Irish ' Life ', gives a vivid impression of the ' Irish believing in Christ ' to whom the Pope eventually sent a bishop:—

" There were in Ireland before Patrick came thither, four holy bishops with their followers who evangelised and sowed the word of God there; these are the four:—Ailbe, Bishop Ibar, Declan and Ciaran. They drew multitudes from error to the faith of Christ, although it was Patrick who sowed the faith throughout Ireland and it is he who turned chiefs and kings of Ireland to the way of baptism, faith and sacrifice and everlasting judgment."

Shorn of its hagiographical trimmings, the basic story given in the Declan ' Life ' does indicate the way the Faith first filtered into Ireland. There were trade links with the continent, and close connections too with Wales, where archaeological evidence has shown that Christianity came in with Gallo-Roman emigrants. They would, of course, have brought not only the Faith, but monastic life as it was then lived in Gaul. Declan's own people of the Déisi of Waterford and others from elsewhere in southern Ireland, had already made settlements in Wales. This would be the background to the birth of Declan well before the coming of Patrick. He came of noble blood, his father was Erc MacTrein and his mother Deithin. The child was born when his parents were on a visit to Erc's brother, Dobhran. He lived on the high ground south of the Blackwater, between Cappoquin and Lismore, good agricultural land rising to gentle ridges. The actual site, in the townland of Drumroe, called Reiligin Deagláin or Cillín Déagláin, is now marked by a very insignificant ancient graveyard with traces of the foundations of a church, the whole closely planted with trees. It is just under 3 miles east of Lismore and a mile and a half south west of Cappoquin.

" A certain true Christian ", a priest named Colman, called to the place soon after Declan's birth and talked with sufficient pursuasiveness to the parents that they let him baptise the baby. Colman advised them on his upbringing and that they should send him to study with a

Christian scholar when he was seven years old. Meantime Dobhran was taking a keen interest in the whole affair and asked to have Declan to foster. So Declan lived with his uncle on the ridge above the Blackwater till he was seven, and then was sent to another Irish Christian, Dioma, " who had come at that time by God's design into Ireland having spent a long period abroad in acquiring learning ". Dioma built a small cell for himself and Declan to live and study in, another pupil, named Cairbre Mac Colmain, later to be a bishop, joined them as well.

Declan next decided to continue his studies abroad, which would be the obvious move at this early period for a young Irishman wishing to evangelise his own country. We may discount the story of a visit to Rome and meeting with Patrick as a hagiographical commonplace, but it is very probable that Declan did spend some time in continental Europe, and was there ordained a priest, if not a bishop as the ' Life ' claims. On the way back, he received his wonder working bell, the Duibhin Declain, that came down from heaven when Declan was celebrating Mass. This was the story attached to this famous relic of Ardmore—Canon Power believed it was not really a bell at all but a small cross inscribed bit of stone, an amulet last heard of in the middle of the 19th century. The bell, or a bell, is made the centre of the story about the founding of Ardmore. Declan was on a visit to Wales and St. David. The Welsh contact is very likely indeed, but David, of course, belongs to a later period. The bell was left behind when the Irish party left for home, but at Declan's prayer the bell came sailing after them on the boulder on which it had been set down. Then Declan said the bell and its rock ship would lead them to the place, " Where my city and my bishopric will be, whence I shall go to paradise, and there my resurrection will be ". It led them to the headland of Ardmore in Co. Waterford beside the long, sandy strand. The tradition makes Ardmore an island from which Declan drives back the sea by a miracle, so turning it into a headland. The island was Inis Aird na gCeaorac (High Sheep Island) and the headland formed from it was then called Aird Mór Déclain, the great headland of Declan. The sea is in point of fact encroaching at Ardmore, and the legend the very reverse of actuality. Declan's stone is still on the beach, a good example of a legend made of a geological fact, for it is an ice carried erratic of conglomerate resting on the strikingly different flagstones of the beach. To crawl under the boulder, through a hollow in the rocks of the beach, is an entertaining piece of agility attached to the traditional pattern. It is alleged both to be curative and possible only to those in a state of grace; it involves wallowing in a shallow rock pool.

Declan, from Ardmore, worked over Decies, roughly over the country covered by the dioceses of Lismore and Waterford. Patrick managed to gain royal co-operation or toleration for his mission, but this does not seem to have been forthcoming in the first days of the Christian mission in Ireland. There is the story of the king of Cashel refusing to be baptised by Declan (because his people were at enmity with Declan's), and waiting for Patrick's coming. Again, the king of the Deisi refused baptism, either from Declan or Patrick, and the story goes on to describe Declan engineering a revolt against the king, and his replacement with a nominee and relative of Declan's, Feargal MacCormac. Of the famous pre-Patrician saints, there was close friendship between Declan, Ailbe and Ibar, the two former being like brothers and hating to be away from each other. That, as the story has it, there was friction between these southern bishops and Patrick and the Patrician organisation of the Church, seems very probable. There could be difficulties in fitting these initial Christian " cells " into a new and national structure. Ailbe was looked on as head of the group and his submission to Patrick made the others follow suit. However, it was only later that Ibar accepted Patrick's leadership, for " it was displeasing to him that a foreigner should be patron of Ireland ".

The remains at Ardmore are extensive and well preserved. There is the fine round tower, nearly a hundred feet high, with its unique feature of external string courses marking the floor levels inside. Beside it is the cathedral, dating from the 10th century, with on its western front, a series of panels with scenes from scripture, now very much weathered. Nearby, is the much rebuilt Declan's House, " Beannachán "—from its peaked gables, an early oratory in which Declan is claimed to have been buried. This is the main monastic " city " of Declan, further out along the headland is " Diseart Declain ", Declan's hermitage, to which the saint is said to have retired in his old age. Here is the ruin of a large church beside a holy well on a sheltered little hollow from which the cliffs fall sheer to the sea. The Irish ' Life ' describes the place very well, " a small venerable cell which he had ordered to be built for him between the hill called Ardmore Declain and the sea, in a narrow place at the brink of the sea by which there flows down from the hill above a small shining stream about which are trees and bushes all round ". It says also that " Thence to the city (of Ardmore, the monastery) is a short mile and the reason why Declan used to go there (to Diseart Declain) was to avoid turmoil and noise so that he might be able to read and pray and fast there. Indeed it was not easy for him to stay even there because of the multitude of disciples and paupers and pilgrims and beggars who followed him thither. Declan was however generous and very sympathetic and on that account it is recorded by tradition that a great following (of poor, etc.), generally accompanied him ". When however Declan felt that death was near, he had himself brought back to the main monastic centre, where he actually died. His tomb in the Beannachán, and a skull found there and claimed to be his, which survived till the 17th century, were the original focal points of the pilgrimage. More recently, the centre of popular devotion has shifted from praying at the Beannachán to praying at the well at Diseart Declain. Here the pilgrim says 7 Paters and Aves kneeling at the well, goes three times round the ruined church deiseal (sunwise) saying five decades of the Rosary, and concludes at the well with another 7 Paters and Aves. The correct prayers for grovelling under the stone on the beach are said to be five Paters and Aves.

" Pattern Sunday ", the day the big crowd comes to make the rounds at the well is that nearest Declan's feast day. But Ardmore celebrates a whole Pattern Week, with a variety of events, whilst in the church, the Forty Hours devotions are held, beginning or ending on St. Declan's day. A plenary indulgence was attached to the Ardmore festival at the request of Dr. Sheehan (bishop of Waterford, 1891-1915) and the then parish priest of Ardmore, John Walsh (1884-1901).

Declan's clients still, in fact, find him " generous and very sympathetic." Not merely is there age old devotion centred on Ardmore itself, but since 1951, the crowds have gone to Toor Well. This insignificant spring in the moors, some ten miles from Ardmore, between Clashmore and Aglish, is connected by a tradition with Declan and was occasionally frequented for skin diseases. But the action of a grateful client, whose failing sight was greatly improved by the water, in donating a concrete setting, bathing place, oratory for Mass, and statues of Declan and Our Lady, has brought this small spring back into the public eye. Cures are claimed by a number of people, and an impressively large and devout crowd, either stringing through the gorse and heather in summer dresses on a fine day, or standing doggedly in pouring rain, gather for the annual Mass at the well on or near St. Declan's day. None of the alleged cures have been investigated, for they run on the lines, highly satisfactory to the sufferer, of " I was sick and now I am well ". Mostly, as at all Irish patterns and wells, it would be difficult to get full documentation of cures, but the overall impression is that they do, one way or another, take place.

Declan's position amongst the saints of Ireland is well summed up by the Irish verse put in the mouth of Patrick in the ' Life ': —
Ailbhe umhal: Patraicc Muman, mó gachrach,
Déclan, Patricc na nDéisi: na Déisi ag Declan gan brath.
(Humble Ailbe, the Patrick of Munster, greater than any saying, Declan, Patrick of the Deisi, the Decies to Declan for ever).

Life of St. Declan of Ardmore. Edited from the ms. in the Bibliotheque Royale, Brussels, with introduction and translation. P. Power. Irish Texts Society, London, 1914.

DIARMAID (DERMOT)

January 10

Diarmaid or Dermot, who flourished in the 6th century, was the founder of the monastery on the island of Inchcleraun (Inis Clothrann) in the northern half of Lough Ree. The island has an interesting series of six churches, the little oratory of Dermot, Teampull Diarmada, and Teampull Mor, the so-called Chancel Church, the Church of the Dead, the Women's Church and Teampull Clogas—which has a square tower. The place became a much sought after burial place, as well as a great centre of pilgrimage.

Unfortunately we know very little about Diarmaid. He is said to have been of royal blood, on both father's (Lughna of the Ui Fiachrach) and mother's (Deidi of the Ciannachta) side. He was a native of Connacht, but it must be taken as not proven whether or not he was the Diarmaid or Diarmait who fostered young Ciaran of Clonmacnois. Diarmaid is also said to have been very friendly with St. Senan. Neither the date of the foundation of the monastery on Inis Clothrann nor of Diarmaid's death is recorded. Colgan said that in his time there existed an ivory statue of Diarmaid on the island, buried first of all for safe keeping, it was now in the possession of a man whose name Colgan did not dare reveal for fear of the figure being sought for and destroyed. There is no further record of what became of it. It was most probably a small figure, if carved in ivory. (Cf. the ivory of Our Lady of Graces of Youghal, still in existence, venerated in the Dominican church in Cork, and only a few inches high).

DONARD

March 24

Donard (Domangard/Domangort/sometimes Latinised Dominic) is a shadowy individual, who, according to the Martyrology of Tallaght, died March 24, 506. He is of importance because he is the saint of one of the great mountain pilgrimages, the now extinct one of Slieve Donard in the Mournes. Near Newcastle, under the Mourne Mountains, are the remains of Donard's principal foundation at Maghera. Here a massive cashel wall, $9\frac{1}{2}$-$10\frac{1}{2}$ feet in thickness, encloses a very ruined church. There is, outside the cashel, the stump of a round tower. This was blown down in c. 1714, and was said to be of such good mason work that the whole tower lay on the ground like a gun barrel for a long time. From Maghera, one looks up to the rounded summit of Slieve Donard, highest of the Mourne mountains. On its top are two, now ruinous, prehistoric burial cairns, one at the top, at 2,796 feet; the other on the shoulder at 2,720 feet. Donard is said to have converted these chambered cairns into a hill top hermitage. The pilgrimage went up to them on July 25th, and there was very considerable devotion to Donard at one time, despite the lack of information about him.

For the other mountain pilgrimages see BRENDAN OF CLONFERT, AED MAC BRICC, PATRICK.

P. Grosjean, S.J.: *S. Domangort de Sliab Slainge*. Analecta Bollandiana, t. 61, (1943), pp. 106-7.

DONAT (DONATUS) OF FIESOLE

October 22

The nature of the work and the objectives of the Irish abroad necessarily changed as time went on, Europe became more Christian and church organisation improved. The roving apostolate of

Columban was the earlier type of Irish activity abroad; it was gradually replaced by that of Irishmen going overseas to study or to teach, or on a definite pilgrimage to some particular place and then straight back to Ireland. Charlemagne (d. 28 January 814) set himself to bring about an intellectual renaissance, and invited scholars of all nations to his court. There were a number of Irishmen among them, indeed Charlemagne's biographer complains that there were too many! Charlemagne's work in this field was rather to preserve intellectual culture than to break new ground. Although after his death, there was again anarchy and violence in Europe, made worse by the widespread Viking attacks, the intellectual renaissance continued for some 70 years, and indeed reached its peak after Charlemagne's time.

Donat (Donatus) left Ireland because of the attacks of evil men, most probably the Vikings, and went on a pilgrimage to Rome about the year 825. He is said to have studied at Inis Cealtra on the Shannon, which was well in the road of the Northmen's lines of attack. Returning from Rome, he and his companions had reached Fiesole, when they were halted by an excited crowd. The election of a new bishop was under discussion, and the arrival of the Irish party brought a sudden decision—the crowd acclaimed Donat as bishop.

Fiesole is a sudden little hill outside the city of Florence, which was then the lesser town. The river Arno, which flows through Florence, was known to the Vikings, and they had sailed up it and sacked Fiesole in 825, destroying all the archives belonging to the bishop. Europe was at this time menaced both by Islam and by the Northmen. Louis II, king of Italy from 844 to 875, was a strong ruler and capable of dealing with the Saracen menace, a religious man who was also a good ruler and in continual action against his enemies, eventually capturing the Saracen base of Bari.

Donat, in becoming bishop of Fiesole, was involved at once in all the political and military life of the times. He was obviously both a capable man of affairs and a scholar. We can fix the period of his episcopate fairly accurately—he is not the bishop of Fiesole named at the Roman Council of 826, nor that at the Council of Florence of 877. This fixes Donat's death as October 22, 876.

In c. 840, Donat is found at the head of his vassals, other Italian bishops doing likewise, in a military expedition led by young Louis, whose father, Lothair I, was then still alive and ruling the country. Later in 844, Donat was in Rome, when the Pope, Sergius II, crowned Louis king. At the same time, the bishop was one of those who adjudicated in a dispute between the bishops of Arezzo and Siena, the decision being given for Siena. In 861, Donat was in Rome at the Council Pope Nicholas I had convened against the archbishop of Ravenna. In 866, Donat was back again leading his men as part of the massive campaign of Louis against the Saracens in the south of Italy. During this campaign, Donat secured immunity for the territory of the bishop of Fiesole from royal control, the bishop furthermore to have the right to hold his own courts and impose his own taxes. Donat got confirmation of these rights from Charles the Bald at Piacenza in February 876.

But Donat was a man of letters and a scholar. In 825, Lothair in his Edict, *Constitutiones Olonnenses,* set about the work of reviving learning in Italy and set up schools in nine Italian cities. One was Florence, then just a small town, and Donat worked at the establishment of this new university as one might style it. He himself modelled his Latin verse on Virgil; other classical authors of which he makes mention in his writings are Democritus and Hesiod. He had great devotion to St. Brigit and wrote her biography both in verse and in prose. The verse account contains his much quoted " Credo " and a description of Ireland. To Donat's efforts is largely due the existence of devotion to St. Brigit in Italy, and the legend of an Irishwoman, named Brigit, dying at Opaco where she is venerated, is nothing more than a development of the Brigit of Kildare cult. Out of this grew a story of Andrew, a companion of Donat, getting his sister Brigit out to Italy. It is evident this lady never existed, and that the Opaco chapel is really connected with Brigit of Kildare. It celebrates the feast of St. Brigit on February 1st which helps eliminate the idea of a second Brigit.

Donat himself lived not on the actual height of Fiesole but on the site of the now secularised Badia Fiesolana. This is not far from Fra Angelico's church and priory of S. Domenico. In 1817, Donat's body was removed from this Badia Fiesolana to the present cathedral of Fiesole on the hill above. His head was preserved by the Confraternity of St. Donatus of ' Scotland ' (the old use of the name Scots) after the abbey had been secularised. They built themselves an oratory beside S. Domenico in 1792. Fiesole boys still often enough are named Dino, after Donat.

St. Donat is a well documented example of the kind of man produced by the Irish monasteries and schools in the 9th century, a person capable of holding the highest positions and directing affairs, as well as a competent, if not brilliant scholar and writer. Irish pilgrims must have been common in Italy, for Donat founded a hospice specially for them, under the invocation of his beloved Brigit, at Piacenza. He gave it in to the keeping of the Bobbio monks in 850. The church of St. Brigit at Piacenza still exists, with a new mosaic of Brigit and her sheep over its doorway.

Donat must be the only Irish saint whose self-composed epitaph has survived. It tells that he was Irish, that he served the kings of Italy for many years, the great Lothair and the good Louis, that he had been bishop 47 years, that he had taught grammar and poetry; finally he asks the passer-by who reads the inscription to pray for him that the Lord may grant him the kingdom of heaven.

> Hic ego Donatus, Scotorum sanguine cretus,
> solus in hoc tumulo, pulvere, verme, voror.
> Regibus Italicis servivi pluribus annis,
> Lothario magno, Ludovicoque bono,
> Octenis lustris septionis insuper annis,
> post Fesulana praesul in urbi fui,
> Grammata discipulis dictabam scripta libellis;
> schemmata mentrorum, dicta beata senum.
> Posco, viator, adis quisquis pro numere Christi,
> te, modo, non pigeat cernere busta mea,
> atque precare Deum, regis qui culmina caeli,
> ut mihi concedat regna beata sua.

DYMPNA OF GHEEL

May 15

DAMHNAT OF TEDAVNET

June 13

The biography of Dympna of Gheel compiled by Pierre, Canon of St. Aubert's church at Cambrai, is without any historical foundation. It may be dated to 1234-47, for it was written at the request of the Bishop of Cambrai, Guido de Lauduno, who occupied the see during those years. There was a long standing devotion to Dympna in Gheel near Antwerp and a number of oral legends about her. Dympna is most probably an archaic spelling of a common Germanic name, Thiemo or Dimo. That she came from Ireland may be rejected with reasonable certainty, and the whole romance of her father's incestuous love for her, with absolute certainty. She is invoked as patron of the insane, on the strength of this legend, which sees the father as possessed. Her cult is widespread at the present time in the U.S.A. and she is patron of mental hospitals both there and at Gheel.

Occasionally, attempts have been made to identify Dympna of Gheel with Damhnat of Tedavnet, an entirely different person. Very little is known of Damhnat of Sliabh Beagh, as she is also styled. It would seem certain that she lived and died at Tedavnet, her principal church, which she very likely founded. Her enshrined crozier, now in the National Museum in Dublin, was long preserved and venerated at Tedavnet, and oaths used to be sworn on it.

B. O'Daly: *St. Damhnat and St. Dimpna.* Journal, Co. Louth Archaeological Society. Vol. XI. 1948, pp. 243-251.
Maire MacDermot: *The Crosses of St. Dympna and St. Mel and 10th century Irish metal work.* P.R.I.A., 58 C 1957, pp. 167-195.

ENDA (EANNA)

March 21

Enda of Aran stands, a sort of western Pachomius, as the father of the great expansion of monasticism in Ireland. His monastery on the Aran Islands in Galway Bay is held by the tradition to have been the first of the large and influential Irish monasteries. To Enda, or at least to his monastery of Aran, came many others of the great monastic founders, Ciaran of Clonmacnois, Brendan of Clonfert, Colmcille. Enda himself may have died as early as 520, but the writers of the 'Lives' of the Irish saints were eager to bring their subjects into contact with so famous a man! The Annals give no date for Enda, and his 'Life' in Latin is a late compilation. A triad names him as one of the three great " ex-laymen " of Ireland, and it does seem that he was a late vocation.

He was the son of Ainmire, son of Ronan of the Cremthanns (Meath). In the 'Life' he is confused with a different Enda, son of

Conall Derc of Oriel. Young Enda was trained up as a soldier and succeeded to his father's little kingdom. His sister, Faenche, however was a nun, and when her brother wanted to marry one of the young women being educated at her convent, managed to turn his mind to a monastic vocation. After making a foundation of his own at Cell Aine (Killany, Ardee, Louth), Enda, again on his sister's advice, went abroad for further study to the famous Scottish monastery of Ninian, Rosnat, Candida Casa. Afterwards he returned to Ireland, sailing into the port of Drogheda (Inver Colptha) and making some foundations in the Boyne Valley, before, once more urged by Faenche, going on to Aran in the west. He is further said to have been granted these islands by King Angus mac Nadfraich of Cashel, who was killed in 490 or 91, a donation one may well suspect.

If this account is true, at least in outline, it is of great interest in showing how the Scottish Candida Casa of St. Ninian influenced this early and important Irish abbot. Aran too was well placed for the propagation of ideas, easy to reach by sea and set half way up the west coast of Ireland on the main sea ways. Meantime, the great east to west cross country route over central Ireland from the Dublin area, led down to the Atlantic at Galway, facing out to Aran. Aran would in those days have been regarded as a much more accessible and central place than it is now.

The three islands of ' Aran of the Saints ' are even yet dotted with ruined churches bearing the names of important early Irish saints.

St. Enda's monastery was on the largest of the Aran Islands, Inishmore, at Killeany. It was placed on good land, sheltered by the main ridge of the island and fronting a sandy beach on which curraghs can run ashore. At present, the sea is encroaching on the land here. The original group of churches here are said to have been Killenda, Teglach Enda (where the saint was buried), Teampull mac Longa, Teampull mic Canonn, St. Mary's and Temple Benan—which is on the bare rock of the ridge above. Part of Teglach Enda still stands, half buried in sand. There are some fragments of carved stones and the shaft of a noble high cross. There is also the stump of a round tower, which was blown down early in the 19th century—it had stood 80 feet high and had five floor levels inside.

At the northern end of the island are the so-called Seven Churches of Onaght. Kilmurvey has Teampull na Naomh and Teampull MacDuagh. In addition there are Teampull an Cheathrair Aluinn (of the Four Comely Saints), Teampull Assurnidhe and Mainistir Ciaran.

Inisheer has a Kilgobnet (Gobnet of Ballyvourney), a Teampull Choemhain (St. Cavan, alleged to have been a brother of Coemgen of Glendalough) and Kill na Seacht Inghean. On Inishmaan is Teampull Seacht MicRigh and Cilcananagh.

The extremely interesting series of remains on the Aran islands, both churches and stone forts, have been often described in both technical and popular accounts (e.g., T. J. Westropp's " Excursion to the Aran Islands ", J.R.S.A.I., vol. 25 (1895) pp. 250-278). Colgan gave a list of the churches as they were recorded by the archbishop of Tuam in 1645, before the Cromwellians ravaged the area in 1655; this list is most readily accessible in the extract printed by J. Fahey in his " History of the Diocese of Kilmacduagh " pp. 54-5.

EOGAN (EUGENE)

August 23

Very little is known of Eogan, the 6th century founder of Ardsratha (Ardstraw) near Strabane. His father, Cainnech, belonged to Leinster, his mother, Muindech, to Ulster. He is said to have been carried off to Britain by pirates, then gained his freedom and went to study at Candida Casa (Rosnat, Whithorn). From there he returned to Ireland and made a foundation at Cell na Manach, Kilnamanagh near Tallaght on the foothills of the Wicklow mountains. At this place, he appears in the accounts of Coemgen of Glendalough who was a student there. Eogan is also said to have been very friendly with Bishop Tigernach. His chief foundation was Ardstraw. It is possible that he is also the saint of Kirkcowan in Wigtownshire, Scotland, which would fit in well with the account of his stay at Whithorn in the same part of the country.

FACHTNA (FACHANAN)

August 14

Except that he was founder of the monastery of Ross Ailither, now Ross Carbery and flourished in the second half of the 6th century,

nothing is known about Fachtna with any certainty. Oengus calls him
' son of the wright ', the same title that Ciaran of Clonmacnois bears,
and says his father was Mongach. Fachtna was born somewhere in
west Cork, of the Corca Laighe, at an unidentified Tullach Teann
" in sight of the southern sea ". He is said to have been fostered by
Ita and to have studied with Finbar, though the latter statement
raises some chronological difficulties. He may have died about the
year 600. A story of the loss and miraculous restoration of his sight is
the theme of the present day Collect for his feast.

At Ross Carbery, Ross Ailither, Ross of the Pilgrims, two sites are
associated with Fachtna. On the ridge above the sea inlet is Teampull
Fachtnan, on the line of the old (not the modern) road to Cork. There
is a holy well below the ruin of an old church at this place, both are
still visited by a number of pilgrims on August 15th. Bishop Pococke,
writing from Ross Carbery, 21 July 1758, gives a curious little note
about this " chapel rebuilt by a Protestant, who made a vow on
recovery from sickness according to an inscription there concerning
which Chapel they have a legend relating to St. Fackman, as built
about his time ". Perhaps this little church site on the hill was Fachtna's
first settlement, and he later moved down to the main church site,
Teampull Mor Fachtnan, at which today is a ruined church and the
extensive graveyard of Ross Carbery. Ross Ailither developed into the
principal monastery of west Cork and had a famous school. It is
chiefly remembered for a metrical geography of the world written by
Airbertach mac Coisi-dobrain, the fer legínn. The work is a compilation drawn from classical sources, so that the author, who died in
1016, describes the world of the Roman Empire ! It divided the world
into Europe, Africa and Asia and mentions such things as petroleum
springs, elephants, tigers, Indian magnets and asbestos. The author
had at least one exciting adventure, being carried off in a Danish raid,
according to the Annals of Inisfallen, in the year 972 :— " The son
of Imar left Waterford and (then followed) the destruction of Ross of
the Pilgrims by the foreigners, and the taking prisoner of the Fer-
legind, i.e., Mac Cosse do brain and his ransoming by Brian at Scattery Island."

C. A. Webster : *The Diocese of Ross and its Ancient Churches.* P.R.I.A.,
    40 C (1931-2), pp. 255-295. With a picture of the 1661 seal of the Dean and
    Chapter of Ross, showing the ancient round tower, long since vanished.

Thomas Olden : *On the Geography of Ross Ailithir.* P.R.I.A., vol. II, 2nd
    series, (1879-1888), pp. 219-252. Irish text and translation.

FECHIN

January 20

A Man, abstinent, pleasant, charitable,
powerful, emaciated, just worded,
honest, pious, rich in sense,
godly, affectionate, discreet,
opportune, wise, prayerful,
skilful, righteous, holy-worded,
active (?), chaste, possessed of illuminated books,
to wit a man of a bright, summery life, an abbot and an anchorite,
fair-worded Fechin of Fore, from the delightful borders of Luigne,
from the loveable province of Connacht.

> (From the beginning of the Irish life of Fechin).

Fechin of Fore was born toward the end of the 6th century, died,
of the bubonic plague, in 664 or 5. There are two 'Lives' in Irish
and one in Latin of Fechin, but they are not very informative; the
three important sites connected with Fechin, Fore in Westmeath,
Cong (Cunga) in Mayo and High Island (Árd Oílean) in Galway,
are of very great interest.

Fechin was born in the west, at a place called Bile Fechin, which
has been tentatively identified with Bile, south of Ballysadare. His
father was named Cailcarn and his mother Lasair, he is said to have
studied at Achad Conairi (Achonry) with Nathy. Nathy urged him to
seek ordination so that he could " offer the King of heaven and
earth ". Fechin's first foundation after finishing his studies with Nathy
was at Fore in Westmeath. But he also made a foundation in his home
country, at Eas-dare (Ballysadare) and of his stay there, it is said that
in Lent he used to pray at midnight standing in the stream, and he
is also described " preaching to the tribes in front of the monastery ".
Then he also went into the far west, making a foundation at Cong
—Cunga Feichín, on Lough Corrib, and then going out to some of

the islands of Connemara. There is a well of Fechin on the northern-most pass over the Maamturk mountains, between Cong and Kyle-more and on the route to Omey and High Island; the way Fechin would have travelled to the latter places. Imaid Island, Omey, is a tidal island, that one may reach by walking across the sands at low tide; here Fechin had a church, now represented by a ruin half buried in the sand dunes of that low grassy islet. It is said that the people were then pagans, a doubtful statement at so late a period, perhaps they were merely neglected, and inevitably Fechin is brought into contact with the famous hospitable king of Connacht, Guaire. The latter saves the Omey community from famine, after two monks had already died, by sending a hundred men's supply of food and ale, and a cup, which was apparently a famous relic (Fechin's Cup) when the 1329 Irish Life was written, or rather translated from a Latin original. From Omey one looks out to sea to the islets, the spectacular rocks of Cruagh, and to cliff bound Árd Oílean, on which Fechin also made a foundation, of which there are still considerable remains. Colgan got his oldest manuscript of Fechin's ' Life ' from Árd Oílean.

Fore of St. Fechin lies in a countryside of extraordinary attractive-ness, little green valleys between sudden little green hills, with grey limestone bluffs. Between the hills lie reed edged, smooth surfaced, gleaming lakes. Fore is in one such little valley, the early site marked by church and high cross on the green hillside with a limestone crag above, and across the marshy floor of the valley, on the opposite side, are the extensive ruins of the later Benedictine Priory. Meantime, beside the present road still stand the old gateways of the town of Fore. Above the graveyard and main church of Fechin is a building called the Anchorites Cell. Part of it is a 19th century mausoleum, but it may be on the site of one of the early oratories of the monastery. The big church lower down is famous for its west doorway. It con-sists of an early rectangular church to which a chancel was added later, c. 1200. The west door has a massive lintel with a Greek cross inscribed in a circle on it. This type of cross over a door can be compared with similar examples in the East—e.g. in 6th century churches in Central Syria and Coptic ones in Egypt. It would appear to be one of the oldest surviving church buildings in Ireland, though it would be difficult to put an exact date on it. There is an old font preserved within the church. Outside a rather plain high cross stands in the graveyard.

At the roadside, below church and graveyard, a powerful spring, typical of limestone country, gushes up and flows down to the ruined mill buildings. There are many legends about Fechin's mill, and of how he got the water to turn it by sending his crozier burrowing through the hill to Lough Lene at the other side! With the beautiful expanse of that lake just back of the hill called Carraig Bhaile Fhobair, the idea behind the tale is easy enough to understand; it is possible that, as water levels change in limestone country, the spring did appear of a sudden.

The whole *termon* of Fechin at Fore was marked by crosses, of which the remains of some are still to be seen. 16 are marked on the Ordnance maps, and there are two in the graveyard at the Catholic church; they may be fairly late in certain cases, one being dated 1604, some are merely sockets or fragments. O'Donovan in the Ordnance Survey letters of 1837 was told that there were 14 crosses at Fore and that 13 more could be located, further that an old man called Conor Corrigan could point out yet another 6.

The mill, *muilean gan sruth,* mill without a stream, being fed direct from the spring (which indeed is supposed to have given the name to the place, Fobhar, spring), seems to have been used until about the middle of the 19th century.

The crozier of Fore 'Abbey', of brass and of Irish type, still exists. From Cong comes, of course, the 1123 Cross of Cong, which enshrined a fragment of the True Cross. The present remains at Cong itself all belong to the later foundation of Canons Regular of St. Augustine.

Árd Oílean may be reached by the, to us today, adventurous method of transferring from a larger boat to a dinghy, and then jumping onto the rocks at the right moment. Cliff bound, the island itself is green and fertile, with a spectacular panorama of the hills of Connemara. One end of it is occupied by the old monastic site, with three enclosing walls, one cutting off the monastic end of the island, one enclosing the monastic settlement within this outer defence as one might style it, and one enclosing the actual church. When Petrie was on the island in 1820, the remains seem to have been almost complete, but are now very ruined, and only one beehive cell is still virtually intact. Some ancient cross inscribed slabs are still to be seen; there was also a little mill fed by water from a small tarn. The monastic site is rather cunningly placed in a hollow, a veritable sun trap, and would thus have considerable shelter from the Atlantic gales.

The Latin 'Life' of Fechin includes two hymns for the Office on Fechin's feast day, as well as a short poem on the saint's miracles.

Fechin was also known in Scotland. His pet name was Mo Fhéca—
(Moéca—My Fechin), whence Lesmahagow—Lios Mo-Fhégu, Fechin's
enclosure. St. Vigeans in Forfar is perhaps named from the Latin
form of Fechin. Scotland also had a personal name—servant of Fechin
—Máel Fhéchín.

Life of St. Fechin of Fore. Edited and translated by Whitley Stokes. (Irish
    version of 1329). Revue Celtique. Vol 12, (1891), pp. 318-53.
H. G. Leask: Official guide to *Fore, Co Westmeath.*
R. A. S. MacAlister: *The Antiquities of Ard Oilean, Co. Galway.* J.R.S.A.I.,
    vol. 26, (1896), pp. 196-210.

FELIM

August 9

Of Felim (or Feidhlimidh, incorrectly Latinised Felix) virtually
nothing is known except that he existed. He appears to have flourished
in the 6th century, to have belonged to the district of Breiffne, to
have begun his religious life by retiring into the wilds as a hermit
near Kilmore. Later he founded a monastery at Kilmore, of which
diocese he is now patron. At one time a fair was held on his day,
that is on August 3rd, the date given in the Martyrologies of Tallaght
and Donegal. Thus in 1608, there is a record of " one fayre holden
at Kilmore yearly the third day of August being Saint Phelim's day ".
Father J. Brady has suggested (" Some Wells in the Parishes of Abbey-
lara and Granard ", Ardagh & Clonmacnois Antiquarian Society
journal, 1951, p. 86) that the townland and well of Toberfelim may
refer to the Felim of Kilmore.

FERGHIL (VIRGIL/VIRGILIUS)

November 27

Ferghil (Virgil) was an eminent Irish " exile for the love of Christ ",
who died as bishop of Salzburg, November 27, 784. He is one of the
few Irish saints to have been formally canonised, but he is not the
same person, as is so often stated, as the Ferghil, abbot of Aghaboe
(who died, Annals Ulster, 789). The Annals of Inisfallen record the
death of Scannlan, abbot of Aghaboe in 782, and this would most

likely be Ferghil of Aghaboe's immediate predecessor. Meantime Ferghil of Salzburg lived nearly forty years abroad.

On arrival on the continent, Ferghil found favour with Pippin the Short and spent some two years at his court. Pippin had been dealing with an insurrection in Bavaria. After this had been suppressed, he sent Ferghil on the difficult mission of going into that country with recommendations from Pippin to the defeated leader of the rising, Duke Odilo. Ferghil seems to have succeeded in his mission, so well indeed that Duke Odilo made him abbot of St. Peter's monastery as well as putting him in charge of the diocese of Salzburg. St. Peter's had been founded by St. Rupert, and its previous abbot, John, placed there by St. Boniface.

With St. Boniface, Ferghil came into acrimonious conflict. Boniface complained to the Pope about Ferghil's ideas on cosmology and on baptism, but we may suspect there were other reasons for his dislike. Irish ideas of the jurisdiction and powers of an abbot may well have come into conflict with Boniface's ones on those of a bishop and his diocese. Ferghil is mentioned in a couple of Papal letters and other documents, in a poem of Alcuin, and his epitaph states his Irish origin clearly. Unfortunately the ' Life ' tells nothing about his ideas on cosmology, and what these were we can only surmise from the papal replies to Boniface, a very third hand version. Pope Zacharias was a Greek and likely to have been well informed on Greek cosmological speculations, and not too easily worried by Boniface's complaints. He wrote to the latter however on May 1st, ? 748, saying that Ferghil would endanger his own and other people's salvation by holding his idea that there was under the world, another world and other men or sun or moon (quod alius mundus et alii homines sub terra sint seu sol et luna). If Ferghil really held these views, Boniface should call a council and excommunicate Ferghil. Ferghil has been held to have believed in a round world and the Antipodes, a more naughty suggestion is that he believed in an underground fairyland, that commonplace of folklore.

Boniface's opposition seems to have prevented Ferghil being made a bishop although he governed the diocese of Salzburg. Another Irishman, Dubdáchrích, was consecrated bishop and carried out the diocesan functions that only a bishop could do. He later became abbot of the monastery of St. Saviour in Chiemsee in Upper Bavaria, a foundation dedicated by Ferghil in 782. Sometime between 755 and 767, when Boniface was dead, Ferghil was consecrated bishop.

He left a great reputation of holiness and learning, and his work extended not only over Bavaria but to the Slavs in the Carinthian mountains. Virgil is still a common name in the Salzburg district. He is co-patron of the cathedral there. His formal canonisation took place in 1233. He is said to have brought relics of St. Brigit out to Salzburg.

The *Liber Confraternitatis S. Petri Salisburgensis* compiled at Ferghil's suggestion, contains a number of names of Irish saints, and has formed the basis of some speculations about Ferghil's Irish connections. It includes a list of dead bishops and abbots, beginning with Patrick, and then listing the abbots of Iona from Colmcille to ' Zslibdeni ' (Slebhine, 752-67). In the Iona list are two breaks for saints not of that monastery, Columban and Ciaran of Clonmacnois. It seems that there were two original lists, one of abbots of Iona, and one of names commemorated in the ' Memento ' of the Mass. Ferghil may have had some special interest in Iona, though we cannot jump to the conclusion he came from it. Père Grosjean, arguing from some litanies in the *Libellus precum* of Fleury, has speculated on Ferghil having been reared by St. Samthann in Ireland. Alcuin wrote a poem on the relics and altars of Salzburg, and the litanies, with their mention of Brigit, Ita and Samthann (written Samfdenna) recall Alcuin's work except for this last woman saint. She died 19 December 739, and so relics would not have been available in all likelihood so early for Salzburg, but it is possible that Ferghil could have known her and brought devotion to her to Europe.

P. Grosjean, S.J.: *Virgile de Salzburg en Irlande*. Analecta Bollandiana, t. 78 (1960), pp. 92-123.

FIACRE OF BREUIL
August 30

FIACRE OF ULLARD
February 8

Fiacre of Breuil was the object of an intense and widespread devotion in France, the long list of distinguished names who paid homage to him includes those of St. Vincent de Paul and of Bossuet. Fiacre was an Irishman who went abroad, where he sought a hermitage. Arriving in Normandy, he came eventually to St. Faro at Meaux. St. Faro (d. 672) seems to have been a patron of the Irish, having got St. Kilian (not the martyr) to settle at Aubigny, and he placed Fiacre at a hermitage named Broilum (Breuil). Here Fiacre settled down and remained until his death in c. 670.

We are very much better informed on the cult than on the saint, on the successive enshrinements and translations of the relics, of the famous people who came on pilgrimage to Fiacre's church. He is said to have been a successful horticulturist and is therefore the patron of the gardeners of France. He was also invoked for the cure of syphilis. A picture of the saint that hung over the hotel from which hackney carriages were first let out for hire, gave the French a name, *fiacre,* for the new cabs.

Where Fiacre came from in Ireland seems problematical. A genealogy, making him son of Colman, of the race of Conn of the Hundred Battles, does not take us very far, nor the supposition that he is the Fiacre of Kilfera on the Nore.

On the river Barrow, north of Graiguenamanagh at Ullard is an old church with a Romanesque doorway and a high cross. Not far off is a holy well still visited on February 8th. This Ullard (Irarda) site is connected with a different Fiacre from the hermit of France. Oengus eulogizes the " noble abbot of Irard " at February 8th, and this seems most probably modern Ullard. It was this Fiacre or Fiachra who brought the Last Sacraments to Comgall of Bangor (q.v.). He is later said to have taken an arm of Comgall back as a relic to Leinster.

Scotland venerated St. Fiacre, though as appears from the above, the name was borne by more than one eminent man, and one hesitates to dogmatise which of them was the object of Scots devotion. It may, of course, have been introduced to Scotland from France, with which country the Scots had long and close relations. There was a St. Fiackres Well at Nigg in Kincardine which caused the Kirk Session much trouble. The people of Aberdeen, they said, went " in ane supersitious maner for seiking health to thameselffis or bairnes " to this well. In 1630, Aberdeen Kirk Session:—" Margrat Davidson, spous to Andre Adam, was adjudget in ane unlaw of fyve poundis to be payed to the collector for directing hir nowriss with hir bairne to Sanct Fiackres Well, and weshing the bairne tharin for recoverie of hir health; and the said Margrat and hir nowriss were ordainit to acknowledge their offence before the Session for thair fault, and for leaveing ane offering in the well ". Despite this, people continued to visit the well until the beginning of the 19th century.

C. O'Meagher: *St. Fiacre de La Brie*. Proc. R.I.A. vol. 18, (1891-93), pp. 173-176. This gives a full account of the history of the cult of the saint and of popular expressions of devotion to him to the time at which the paper was written.

FINAN CAM OF KINNITTY

April 7

Fionan Cluana-Iraird 'sa cleire,	Finian of Clonard and his clerics,
Finan Faithlin air an Lein-loch,	Finan of Inisfallen on L. Leane,
Finan Locha-laoich, mo naomhsa,	Finan of L. Currane, my patron,
Do rug an phlaig Uibhrathac saoir leis.	who brought Iveragh safe from plague.

These lines from John O'Connell's " Dirge of Ireland " (c. 1660) indicate the possibilities of confusion between the many Irishmen bearing the name Fínán or Fionáin (white, fair haired). Nowhere is the confusion worse than in trying to distinguish between Finan Cam (of the squint) and Finan Lobur (the infirm, incorrectly and popularly " the leper "), or indeed in finding out anything historical about either of them.

Finan Cam came from Kerry, Corcu Duibne, his father was Mac-Cairge and his mother Becnat. His period is fixed approximately if it is true he was educated by Brendan of Clonfert. The latter is said to have directed him to make his own monastic foundation at Cenn Eitigh (Kinnitty) on the slopes of the Slieve Blooms. Here, at Castle Bernard, just outside the village of Kinnitty, is preserved a fine high cross, on which two figures have been interpreted as Brendan giving Finan the Kinnitty site.

Finan's Kerry connections have been hopelessly confused with Finan Lobur, and the 'Lives' relating to him are compilations of stock miracle and wonder tales. He is said to have gone as envoy of the people over a census and tax to Falbe Fland at Cashel. This king of Munster died in 637, which would make Finan a very old man if he had been trained by Brendan of Clonfert (d. 578).

Finan Cam seems probably connected with the interesting Church

Island on Lough Currane in Kerry, with its Romanesque church and series of crosses. The massive beehive cell at the far end of the island, now called St. Finan's Cell, has been suggested by Dr. F. Henry to be in reality a kiln for drying grain.

It seems that all the stories connecting Finan with Inisfallen, Lough Leane and with Skellig Michael, are to be discarded. The founder saint of Inisfallen seems definitely to have been St. Faithliu, later written Faithlenn, son of a king of West Munster, Aed Daman, who died c. 631. Inisfallen is, of course, most famous for its beauty, set amongst the lakes of Killarney, and for the Annals, " our main extant record of Munster mediaeval history ". But these Annals have Emly and Killaloe connections as well and only finally came to be kept and preserved on Inisfallen.

The gloss on the entry for Finan Cam in the Martyrology of Oengus records the curious tradition that " Finan Cam brought wheat into Ireland, i.e. the full of his shoe he brought. Declan brought the rye, i.e. the full of his shoe. Modomnoc brought bees, i.e. the full of his bell; and in one ship they were brought. Finan is entitled to true circuits, a measure of wheat for every household, the full of his brazen shoe : a tribute that no great saint had taken ". This recalls the shrine of Brigit's shoe in the National Museum, and makes one wonder whether at one time a shoe of Finan Cam was similarly enshrined and venerated, and carried on the due collecting circuits.

FINAN LOBUR

March 16

Finan Lobur has enjoyed immense popularity, but while the extent of his cult suggests the greatness of the man, virtually nothing is known of him. In Kerry, where the native St. Finan would seem certainly to have been Cam, popular devotion now connects the Finan sites with Lobur. The word ' Lobur ' means infirm, rather than " leper " as it is usually translated, and of course, the word " leprosy " in the past covered a variety of skin diseases.

Finan Lobur appears to have flourished in the second half of the 6th century. He came of the race of Oilill Ólum of Munster but appears to have been born in Leinster and to have worked there. He seems to be connected with Swords of Colmcille north of Dublin.

The Colmcille legend relates that " a church was builded there by
Colmcille (at Swords). And that is Swords of Colmcille today. And
Colmcille left a good man of his household to succeed him there,
even Finan the Leper. And there he left the missal that himself had
copied " (*Betha Coluimb Chille*).

Again, it is possible that Finan may have had some connections with
the other Inisfallen, Ireland's Eye, and that this led to connecting a
St. Finan with the Kerry Inisfallen.

Finan Lobur may well have worked in Scotland, more especially
if he was an associate of Colmcille. There was considerable devotion
to him there. The Martyrology of Aberdeen commemorates him on
March 18th. Dunlichity in Scotland had a much venerated wooden
statue of Finan. In 1643, the Presbytery of Inverness, hearing that
" there was in the Paroch of Dunlichitie ane Idolatrous Image called
St. Finane, keepit in a private house obscurely " sought it out and
burned it at the Market Cross of Inverness.

Eilean Fhionain in Loch Shiel in Moidart has a ruined chapel on
whose altar a little celtic bell, claimed to be Finan's, has been long
preserved. Like other west Highland church sites, it has a series of
interesting later carved slabs and crosses, and was an ancient burial
place of Clan Ranald. The placename, again commemorating Finan,
at the head of the loch, is however far better known:—Glenfinnan,
where Prince Charles raised his standard in 1745.

Other Scottish placenames of Finan include Cill Fhionain
(Kilennan) in Islay, Cill Fhionain on Loch Ness at Abriachan and
Seipeil Fhionain at Foynesfield, Nairn. There was also a fair that
took place in March or April at Migvie in Marr under the title of
Finzean's Fair.

In Wales, there is a Llanffinan in Anglesey. Most likely this is a
different Finan, neither Cam nor Lobur.   ,

FINBAR OF CORK

September 25

La líth ind fir sercaig	The feast of the loveable man,
féil Barri ó Chorcaig.	The feast of Barr from Cork.

St. Finbar (Findbarr/Barr) is a saint of the Lee valley in Munster,
his monastery formed the nucleus out of which the city of Cork grew,

he is claimed to have been its first bishop. His death has been variously ascribed to c. 610, 620 or 630. He definitely belongs to the second half of the 6th century. There are some six versions of his ' Life ' in Latin including the texts used for the lessons at Matins on his feast day; there are two, not very different, recensions of his ' Life ' in Irish. The Latin accounts tend to be brief, make no mention of his stay at Gougane Barra; the Irish versions are full of place names and local colour. Whilst a general impression of the man's attractive personality remains, little enough is told about him. What does emerge is a substantially true account of his movements and work.

Finbar's father, Amargin, was the illegitimate son of a nobleman. He came of the Ui Bruin Ratha of West Connacht, but migrated south from the country of his birth to the country between Bandon and the River Bride in West Cork. Here lived the people from whom the O'Mahony sept claims its descent; Amargin became their chief metal worker. He fell in love with a bondwoman of the local king, Tighernach, of Raithleann, and was secretly married to her. When the king, who also desired the woman, discovered this, he first threatened her with death but was eventually, the ' Lives ' claim by a miracle, pacified. A child was born to the couple and named Lochan or Loan. Later, as he grew up and had a shock of fair hair, he got another name, Finbar, " Fair crest ".

Until comparatively recently all memory of where Finbar was born was lost, except it was known to be somewhere near Bandon. But one man's intimate local knowledge was able to place an Irish poem which described the various raths located around that in which Finbar was born. This fixed the site at Garranes (Lisnacaheragh), at 525 feet above the sea on the ridge between the Bride (a tributary of the Lee) and the Bandon river. Here is the great enclosure of Raithleann, with its three concentric banks and ditches, in fertile country and close to the old cross country route over the ridge. From these heights one may see a view ranging from the Knockmealdowns and Galtees in the east, to the Killarney mountains in the west. The identification by means of the poem received startling confirmation when the rath was excavated, and found to have been a metal workers' site—the central date for its occupation was put at around 500 A.D. Here were made beautiful and delicate masterpieces of Irish art; in huts in this rath, men like Amargin made things like the Tara brooch. A bronze penannular brooch, half finished, was among the finds and was dated to 5th-6th century. An enormous number of little crucibles, some complete, some broken, were found and stone and clay moulds for casting metal. Then the pottery fragments included those of amphorae, whose type indicates direct trade links with continental Europe. They were probably used in the import of wine and oil. The amphorae themselves were mass-produced in the Eastern Mediterranean area.

Young Finbar was brought up at a place called Achad Durbcon in the same area, not actually at Garranes, according to the 'Lives'. His formal education and training for the priesthood may also belong to West Cork, though the monastic settlements to which he went are usually identified with Kilmacahill near Gowran, Co. Kilkenny and with Coolcaskin and Aghaboe. He returned to Cork and settled at Loch Irce or Erc. This first monastery is not mentioned by the Latin accounts; it seems quite certainly to have been at Gougane Barra. Here the Lee takes origin from a corrie lake high in the west Cork mountains, and it is here that present day devotion to the saint is concentrated. Finbar perhaps started as a lone hermit, but disciples soon gathered round him. In the Irish 'Life' there is a long litany of these saints, and their subsequent churches, which need not be taken too literally, but probably does record many of the churches that were later subject to the jurisdiction of the successor of Finbar.

Finbar did not remain permanently up in the mountains. He made other foundations in West Cork, known today by the placename Kilbarry, and eventually arrived at the mouth of the Lee where it flows into the deep sea inlet of Cork harbour. It was then a marsh, Corcach Mhor Mumhan, the great marsh of Munster, with an intricate pattern of streamlets intersecting marshy ground. Somewhere in that morass, Finbar found a dry ridge—probably where the present Protestant cathedral now stands, the site on which the old cathedral and round tower once stood. Other people, however, have argued for the rocky bluff of Gill Abbey. Again, many monks and students gathered round Finbar and the schools of Cork became famous. It is said that Finbar chose Olan of Aghabulloge in the west, towards Macroom, to be his confessor; there is still local devotion to Olan there and his well is visited on September 5th, Olan's feast day.

It was in the west, in the country between Kilcrea and the river Lee that Finbar died, when on a visit to the little monastery of Cill na Cluaine, often wrongly identified with Cloyne. His body was brought back to Cork for burial.

Gougane Barra is the great centre of modern devotion to the saint. On the Sunday following his feast day, an enormous crowd gathers to walk in the procession from the main road cross below, up to the chapel on the island, where the Rosary is recited, a sermon preached and Benediction given. The island, on which Finbar probably had a hermitage, is reached by a causeway, at the head of which is a holy well. There are no ancient remains on the island, the oldest building being the crude ruins of a Penal days chapel; there is a modern oratory in the style of Cormac's Chapel. The traditional " round " is very long, and its details are noted on a slab at the entry to the enclosure in which the Stations of the Cross are erected. It would appear that Finbar's actual monastery was on the level, fertile land, at the foot of the lake which would provide ample room for such an establishment, and that the island was an occasional retreat for prayer.

The Dominicans of Cork possess a monstrance made in 1669 on which an engraving of Finbar, with the old cathedral and round tower in the background, is the oldest surviving representation of him.

Under the shortened form, Barr, Finbar was greatly venerated in the Scottish Hebrides and on the mainland. Dornoch in Sutherland used to have a fair on his day, September 25. The island of Barra in the Outer Hebrides is named after him; the ruined chapels of Kilbarr (Cill Bharr) are at the north of the island, beside the famous Cockle Strand and looking over the sound to Eriskay and the mountains of South Uist. Martin Martin, writing about 1695, mentioned the presence of " St. Barr's wooden image standing on the altar, covered with linen in the form of a shirt; all (the islanders') greatest asseverations are by this saint. . . . All the inhabitants observe the anniversary of St. Barr; it is performed riding on horseback, and the solemnity is concluded by three turns round St. Barr's church ". This cavalcade was still going on in 1840 when the New Statistical Account was prepared, each man with his wife or lass mounted behind him. The statue however has long since vanished. From Kilbarr comes the only rune inscribed stone to be found so far in the Hebrides, with the rune on one face and a Celtic cross on the other. Barra, of course, is one of the Catholic islands of Scotland. It is possible that Finbar could have visited it in person, or again the devotion may have been taken there by wandering Corkmen.

P. Grosjean, S.J.: " Les Vies de S. Finnbarr de Cork, de S. Finnbarr d'Ecosse et de S. Mac Cuilinn de Lusk." Analecta Bollandiana, t. 69, (1951), pp. 324-347. Summarised in English in J.C.H.A.S., July/Dec., 1953, pp. 47-54.

T. A. Lunham: The Life of St. Finbarre. (The Latin Life translated and annotated). J.C.H.A.S., July/Sept., 1906, pp. 105-120.

P. Stanton: *The Irish Life of Finbar*. J.C.H.A.S., 1893, pp. 61-9 and 87-94.

C. J. F. MacCarthy: *St. Finbar and His Monastery*. Series of articles in vols. for 1935, 1936 and 1937 of J.C.H.A.S. *St. Finnbarr of Cork,* and *The Celtic Monastery of Cork,* in the same Society's Cork City number, Jan./June, 1943.

Ristéard O Foghludha: *Footprints of Finbar*. I.E.R., Sept., 1950, pp. 242-50. A careful identification of the placenames in the *Lives*.

Seán P. O Ríordáin: *The Excavation of a large earthen ring fort at Garranes, Co. Cork*. P.R.I.A., vol. 47 C (1942), pp. 77-150.

D. D. C. Pochin Mould. *The Pilgrimage to Gougane Barra*. J.C.H.A.S., Jan./Dec. 1962

FINDCHU (FANAHAN) OF BRIGOWN

November 25

Findchu or Finnchu, " White Hound ", popularly known as Fanahan, is still the object of very considerable local devotion at Mitchelstown in north Cork. His monastery was Brí Gobann—Smith's Town, Brigown, on the outskirts of the town; the site is marked by an ancient ruined church, the round tower fell in 1720. Not far off is a holy well set on a little tree grown islet circled by a streamlet in the fields outside Mitchelstown. The people make a novena of visits to this well on the days leading up to the feast day; when there are special Masses in Mitchelstown church and a large crowd, old and young, visits the well, often in rain, padding through the mud.

Brigown was one of the great monasteries of Munster, but very little is known of its founder. He is said to have been son of an Ulster chieftain, his parents living in exile in Munster when he was born. Their home was Rath Uí Chuile (Rathealy) in the Fermoy area. Dogs were held in honour in ancient Ireland, and there was nothing derogatory in christening the child, Fionn Cú. He is said to have been baptised at Emly and to have studied at Bangor, but chronological considerations rule out his having any contact, as the " Life " claims, with the founders of these monasteries. He came south from Bangor and settled at Brigown, then called Fan Muilt—the Wethers' Slope. Settlement on this excellent land by the monks met with local opposition but eventually the king of Munster consented to rent the land to Findchu for an anker of wine and a measure of malt for each of the 9 bailies of the monastery. The wine would be imported from abroad. Findchu's establishing a number of metal workers at the monastery is supposed to have resulted in the name being changed to Brí Gobann. Findchu died of the plague in 664 or say the Annals of Inisfallen in 655.

The surviving ' Life ', a late 11th or even 12th century composition, in the " Book of Lismore " may best be described as highly recommended bedtime reading for a small boy. It is not impossible that, as has been suggested, it is a skit on the more extravagant sort of hagiography. Findchu is represented as a kind of cross between a fire breathing dragon and a supernatural hero, a warrior saint, whose victories, of course, result in the side for which he fought, having to pay large and permanent tributes to Brigown. We must assume that Findchu did perhaps play a large part in local political life, and that the important monastery founded by him had later wide influence and extensive claims.

The *aisdre* (bell ringer and door keeper) O Fingin, of Brigown is mentioned in an account of the topography of ancient Fermoy contained in the " Book of Lismore ". Brigown would seem to have had therefore a hereditary door keeper and bell ringer for its round tower. In 1750, Smith, in his account of Cork, mentions the saint's crozier, Baculus Finechani, which used to be kept at Brigown and on which the local people used to make their oaths.

P. Power: *Crichad an Chaoilli*. The topography of ancient Fermoy. Cork, 1932. pp. 24-26, 31, 87-89.

FINIAN OF CLONARD

December 12

Tor óir úas cech lermaig,
gébaid coir frim anmain,
Findén find, frém inmain,
Clúana Iraird adbail.

A tower of gold over every sea-plain:
he will give a hand to (help) my soul,
Findian the fair, a lovable root, of vast Clonard.

(Martyrology of Oengus)

" One may say that the second part of the religious history of Ireland begins quite definitely with the foundation of Clonard in 520 ". (Georges Cerbelaud-Salagnac in " The Miracle of Ireland ".) Finnio moccu Telduib, Finian, Finnian, Fionain, stands at the very start of the great monastic expansion in Ireland, a man not unjustly named "Tutor of the Saints of Ireland", a most attractive personality in his own right, as well.

The earliest account of Finian is the Irish 'Life' written by a Leinsterman in Leinster, using written and oral traditions both from Clonard and Aghowle. This text may go back to a 9th or 10th century original. The Latin accounts, apparently composed under Anglo-Norman influences, are much less informative and composed largely of the stock incidents of hagiography.

Finian was born in Leinster, and made his early studies with a certain Forthcern, probably of Cell Fortcheirn in Uí Drona (Idrone barony, Carlow). He is then said to have made three foundations of his own, all within five miles of this place, Ros Cuire (Rossacurra), Drum Fiaid (Drumfea) and Magh Glas (Kilmaglush). Then he crossed to Wales for further study and experience. In Wales, he is said to have gone to Sts. David, Gildas and Cathmael (Cadoc) and to have stayed at Cell Muine (St. David's). Personal contact with David (q.v.) depends on what chronology one accepts for the Welsh saint; certainly Finian gained experience of monastic life as it was known in Wales, and came back to head its expansion in Ireland. Already it would seem Enda had established a large monastery on Aran, but Clonard, placed in the very heart of Ireland, was an even more influential and vital centre.

Finian returned to Ireland, with, according to one account, some British followers, and settled first at Achadh Abhall (Aghowle in south-west Wicklow) on a site given him by Muredach king of Leinster. Here survives a ruined church and a high cross, plain and massive, of granite, standing 11 ft. high. Nearby was a cell on the flank of the mountain of Condal. Finian later moved on, visiting Kildare (which would come to have close relations with Clonard) but first making another foundation at Mugna Sulcain. After visiting Kildare, he founded Ard Relec across the Boyne, and finally came to Ross Findchuill, his great centre of Clúain Iráird (Erard's Meadow), Clonard.

Clonard is rather more than 3 miles east of Kinnegad on the main Dublin—Athlone—Galway road. Over a hundred years ago the site was still marked by ruined churches and a round tower, all of which have now completely disappeared. It is level country, smiling sunlit fields, this Clonard, and it is easy to see how it could have accommodated and fed large numbers of students. Three thousand is the number of Finian's disciples given in the ' Lives ', and quite possibly that is not too extravagant if we take it for the total number of students and monks over the whole period at Clonard. It is easy to visualise the scattered, hutted, settlement on these plains against the background of the stories of Colmcille building his cell, and Ciaran of Clonmacnois bringing his cow.

Tradition, with a liking for the number twelve and for bringing every great saint into contact with every other great saint, has listed the " Twelve Apostles of Ireland " trained by Finian at Clonard. Some, like Ciaran of Saighir, of course, lived much earlier. The traditional list runs—Ciaran of Saighir, Ciaran of Clonmacnois, Colmcille, Brendan of Birr, Brendan of Clonfert, Colum of Tir da Glas, Molaise of Devenish, Cainnech, Ruadan of Lorrha, Mobi of Glasnevin, Sínell of Cleenish (Fermanagh), Ninnid of Inismacsaint, Lough Erne. Some of these were really students of Clonard, what the list stands for is the formative influence that Clonard had on Irish monasticism. Finian in his own training would have combined the home traditions with those of Wales. Out of that impulse came the great monasteries of Ireland and their apostolic expansion overseas. Nor, of course, should the monastic influence of Scotland be forgotten, from Ninian's Candida Casa and through men like the other Finian, of Moville, who had studied there.

Finian appears to have been an attractive teacher, quickly appreciative of his students' abilities. (Cf. the story of Ciaran of Clonmacnois and the gospel book.) Moreover he seems to have gone out of his way to equip his students when they left. For " no one of those three thousands went from him without a crozier, or a gospel, or some well-known sign; and round those reliquaries they built their churches and their monasteries afterwards ", as the account in the Book of Lismore puts it.

Finian is said to have lived normally on barley bread and water (like David of Wales) but on Sundays and holydays, he took wheaten bread, broiled salmon and a cup of clear mead or ale. He died in 549 (Annals Ulster) or perhaps a year or so later, of, it is recorded, the plague.

Finian's name seems to have been first written Uindio or Uennio, whence Columban's spelling Vennianus, and the Vinniaus of the Penitential. Columban in one of his letters to the Pope (no. 1 in the recent critical edition) refers to " Vennianus " who is identified with Finian of Clonard. Asking Gregory the Great about what should be done with monks who leave their monasteries without permission, either to relapse or live as hermits in the desert, Columban says that " Finian asked the writer Gildas about them, who returned a most elegant reply, but yet anxiety increases with desire of further information ".

Columban's " Penitential " is largely based on Finian's, and thus the Clonard monastery and its abbot was to have European influence. The " Penitential " of Finian is the oldest surviving Penitential (handbook for confessors), it would have been written between, say, 525 and 549. Finian would have been able to draw on Welsh sources as well as Irish ones, he also made use of material from Jerome and Cassian, but by and large, the book seems an original composition. He divided it into two sections, one dealing with the sins of clerics and the other with those of laymen.

Here is an extract from Finian's Penitential : —

" If a cleric is wrathful or envious or backbiting, gloomy or greedy, great and capital sins are these; and they slay the soul and cast it down to the depth of hell. But there is this penance for them until they are plucked forth and eradicated from our hearts; through the help of the Lord and through our own zeal and activity let us seek the mercy of the Lord and victory in these things; and we shall continue in weeping and tears day and night so long as these things are turned over in our hearts. But by contraries, as we have said, let us make haste to cure contraries and to cleanse away the faults from our hearts and introduce virtues in their places. Patience must arise from wrathfulness; kindliness, or the love of God and of our neighbour, for envy; for detraction, restraint of heart and tongue; for dejection, spiritual joy; for greed, liberality; as says Scripture, ' The anger of man worketh not the justice of God ', and envy is judged as leprosy by the law. Detraction is anathematized in the Scriptures; ' He that detracteth his brother ' shall be cast out of the land of the living. Gloom devours or consumes the soul. Covetousness is ' the root of all evil ' as the Apostle says."

(From the translation of the whole text of Finian's Penitential, by John T. McNeill and Helena Gamer in *Mediaeval Handbooks of Penance,* Columbia University, 1938).

The relics of Finian were enshrined at Clonard and the Annals record their violation in 887.

There is a late 13th or early 14th century Office for St. Finian's feast, belonging to the Anglo-Norman period and their interest in him and other eminent Irish saints. The miracles mentioned in the antiphons refer to some incidents not known from other sources, and the material does not seem to be based on any of our surviving ' Lives '. The antiphons include some pleasant, if not particularly original titles for Finian, teacher of Ireland, treasure of Clonard, leader of Meath, father and mirror of monks and light of Clonard.

Kathleen W. Hughes: *St. Finnian of Clonard,* summary of thesis in *Bulletin of the Institute of Historical Research,* vol. 25, May, 1952, pp. 76-78. *The Cult of St. Finnian of Clonard from the 8th to the 11th century,* Irish Historical Studies, March, 1954, pp. 13-27. *The Historical Value of the Lives of St. Finnian of Clonard.* The English Historical Review, vol. 69, no. 272, July, 1954, pp. 353-72. *The Offices of St. Finnian of Clonard and St. Ciaran of Duleek,* Analecta Bollandiana, t. 73, (1955), pp. 343-372, and in the same publication, t. 75, (1957), pp. 337-339, *Additional Note on the Office of St. Finnian of Clonard.*

P. Grosjean, S.J.: *Mention de St. Finnian de Cluain Iraird dans un martyrology visigotique du debut du ix siecle.* Analecta Bollandiana, t. 72, (1954), pp. 347-352. This Spanish martyrology notes Finian at December 12th; it was compiled c. 800 and definitely before 812.

A St. Finian, possibly Finian of Clonard, is one of the saints whose protective girdle (crios) is invoked. Thus Galway and West Munster still invoke " Crios Fionnain " in traditional prayer, whilst an 11th or 12 century lorica prayer from the *Codex Regularum* at Klosterneuburg near Vienna, asks " May Fionnán's crios protect me ".

FINIAN OF MOVILLE
September 10

Clí dergóir co nglaini,
cor-recht tar sál sidi,
súi diand Ériu inmall,
Findbarr Maige Bili.

A kingpost of red gold with purity,
over the swelling (?) sea (he came) with law,
a sage for whom Ireland is sad,
Findbarr of Mag Bili.

(Martyrology of Oengus)

Finian or Findbarr—he was fair haired—of Moville (Magh Bile, plain of the aged tree) was one of the outstanding scholars of 6th century Ireland, to judge by the references to him. Oengus (c. 800) applies the same word, *súi,* sage, alike to Finian and to St. Jerome. Finian came of the royal house of the Dal Fiatach of the district now represented by Down and Antrim. He crossed to Scotland to St. Ninian's famous monastery of Candida Casa, Whithorn or, as often termed in Irish records, Rosnat (little headland). The abbot at this period was a Briton named Mugint. It is possible that Finian worked for some time in Scotland, following up the east coast route north from Whithorn. Some of the Scottish churches named from a St. Finian may relate to Finian of Moville. Thus Kirkgunzeon in Kirkcudbright is supposed to contain the Welsh form of the name Finian. He may also be the saint of Inchinnan.

The very beautiful, scripture inspired hymn of Mugint in the " Irish Liber Hymnorum ", invoking the mercy and forgiveness of God, has in a Preface a curious story about Finian's stay at Candida Casa. These Prefaces are later than the hymns, and represent 10th century traditions. They are not to be taken as historical fact but may contain genuine information. Thus the Mugint story is of interest for its account of women studying at the monastic schools, to which there are some references in Ireland as well, and for its statement that Finian was at Whithorn. The story is that there was a king's daughter, Drustic, a student with Mugint, who fell in love with another student, Rioc. She tried to bribe Finian with all the books Mugint had written, to assist the affair; Finian however sent a certain Talmach disguised as Rioc to Drustic one night. There was naturally a dispute over the paternity of the child, Lonan of Treoit, when it was born, and Mugint determined to be revenged on Finian. Accordingly he sent a man to the church to knock down the first to enter for the night office, normally Finian. In point of fact, that night, Mugint arrived first and got the blow, and wrote the hymn!

Candida Casa claimed to be modelled on St. Martin's famous monastery, and Finian would have there come into contact with the full stream of western monasticism. He returned to Ireland, to his own country and founded Moville at the head of Strangford Lough in Co. Down. This was perhaps between the years 540 and 555. The place became a famous centre of learning, and Colmcille is claimed as one of its students. Adamnan tells two stories about Colmcille and Finian of Moville; how when Colmcille was a student at Moville and still a deacon, " learning the wisdom of Holy Writ " with Finian, the supply of wine came to an end and Colmcille changed water into wine for the Mass (Bk. II, ch. 1). The second story (Bk. III, ch. 4) tells of Colmcille visiting Finian, by then a very old man, just before he set off for Scotland. Finian saw an angel walking with Colmcille and said to his monks, " Look now and you'll see Colmcille coming, who has deserved to have an angel of heaven as companion on his journey ". But Moville may have been founded too late to have Colmcille a student there.

The scrappy references to Finian all bear out the idea that he was regarded as a scholar of high repute, and it is quite possible that he did go abroad and bring back one of the first copies of St. Jerome's translation of scripture to Ireland. But the story of his wrath over Colmcille's copying of this text without permission, must, as I have argued in the account of Colmcille, be rejected. The evidence is not there to prove the story, which is from a late source, and the early, reliable Adamnan would, in his two stories about Finian and Colmcille, seem to indicate a life-long friendship between them.

Finian died in 579 (Annals of Ulster) or perhaps a little earlier, for the Annals of Inisfallen put his death at 576.

The site of Moville abbey lies about a mile to the east of Newtownards. There is the ruin of a 15th century church and the old grave slabs include a series of Anglo-Norman ones. But some are earlier, going back to 900, of which the best known is that inscribed OR DO DERTREND, a prayer for Dertrend. Dertrend has not been identified. The Annals record the obits of a number of the abbots of Moville who succeeded Finian; the place eventually became a house of Canons Regular of St. Augustine.

The beautiful Latin hymn in honour of St. Michael the Archangel, " In Trinitate spes mea fixa non in omine ", was the work of Colman Mac Mur-chon, an abbot of Moville who died in 736.

See also COLMCILLE, NINIAN.
O. Davies: *Movilla Abbey*. Ulster Journal of Archaeology, vol. 8, (1945), pp. 33-38. Description of the ruins and cross slabs.

FINTAN OF CLONENAGH
February 17

" The monks of Fintan Mac Úi Echach; they fed on nothing but herbs of the earth and water. There is not room to enumerate them because of their multitude. Eight Fintans among them."

(*Litany of Irish Saints*)

Fintan was a common enough name as may be judged from the above lines from one of the old Irish litanies of Irish saints. There are a number of Fintans listed as saints, 22 in the Martyrology of Donegal, but there is also the possibility that some may be duplications of the same individual. Fintoc is a variant spelling, whence the Scots name M'Lintock (Mac Gille Fhionntaig—son of the servant of Fintan).

Fintan of Clonenagh was born in Leinster, baptised and later educated by a holy man of Cluain mac Trein—perhaps Ross mac Trein, modern New Ross. Later he went to St. Colum of Terryglass, with whom he was associated in making his own great foundation at Clonenagh.

Clonenagh is yet another of the great early monastic houses that cluster round the Slieve Bloom mountains. It is east of the hills, on the Mountrath-Port Laoighise road, about 2 miles from Mountrath. When O'Hanlon visited the ruined church and graveyard there in the August of 1856, he was told that the place was called the " Seven Churches of Clonenagh " (the number always ascribed to such sites!) and further that the local people could still point out the sites, at Clonenagh, and the two that were some little distance from it.

Fintan's rule at Clonenagh was renowned for its austerity, and one may be reminded of St. David's title of the " Waterman ". In general Ireland did not follow so hard a régime, and the ' Life ' of Fintan includes a story of a deputation of Irish saints, headed by Cainnech coming to urge Fintan to moderate it. Fintan would not do so for himself but did agree to relax the rule for the rest of the community. They are said to have done all the work on their land by hand and owned no domestic animals, not even a cow. Neither milk nor butter was allowed in the monastery. The gloss in the Martyrology of Oengus quotes a little couplet thereon :—

> Generous Fintan never ate anything during his time
> except bread of woody barley and clayey water of clay.

Fintan is said to have obtained the release of young Cormac, son of Diarmaid, king of Ui Cennselach, who had been taken prisoner by another Leinster kinglet, Colum son of Cormac. Cormac ruled his kingdom till old age, when he became a monk of Bangor.

One story about Fintan concerns a man called Fergne, son of Cobthick, before whom Fintan knelt in the road as he drove by in his chariot. The confused layman asked the reason, and Fintan said he would not have done so had he not seen him among the angel choirs. Fintan went on to ask him to change his habit and become a monk. Fergne said he had twelve sons and seven daughters and a beloved wife; he could not leave them. But the end of the story was that he could not settle down again to the domestic round and did in fact leave all to join Fintan.

The same story is told of Fintan as of Colman Elo, of his picking out a future monk from a party of soldiers passing along the road. Another story relates to the problem that Columban wrote about among other items, to Pope Gregory the Great, the monk that left his monastery without permission. This monk of Clonenagh went off to Britain via Bangor. Another monk, his bosom friend, eventually asked permission to go into exile after him, lest he died of the sorrow of separation from his friend. Fintan told him not to worry, for the wanderer would be back that very day, having tired of his travelling.

Fintan died at Clonenagh (Cluain Ednech) in 603. His successor was another Fintan, Fintan Maeldub, who according to the Four Masters ruled till his death in 623.

FINTAN OF RHEINAU

November 15

Fintan or Findan, the hermit of Rheinau, was born in Leinster. Captured and carried off by the Vikings to the Orkneys, he managed to escape, spending two years as a follower of a bishop in Scotland. Then he set off for Rome in fulfilment of a vow to visit the tombs of the apostles. Returning from Rome, he came to the island of Rheinau in the Rhine near Schaffhausen. Here he joined a community already in existence there, apparently of hermits. After a few years Fintan himself became a hermit and spent the last 22 years of his life in that fashion at Rheinau. He died in 878; devotion to him is still alive in that part of Europe.

Fintan seems to have probably owned a sacramentary (Mass book) still in existence (Zurich Kantonsbibl. 30). It was however a continental, not an Irish, manuscript, compiled around the year 800, of the liturgical family known as " Gelasian of the 8th century ". Fintan probably was responsible for a calendar going with it, which may have originated from Nivelles and contains Irish saints, including Patrick, Brigit, Colmcille and Aidan of Lindisfarne.

Fintan's ' Life ' was written fairly soon after his death. It contains some extracts from a monastic rule, and the first, so far known, mention of the term Ceili Dé—Culdee. It says:—" Abstinence by day and night: you must not eat until the Céle Dé eats before you, or a man under religious rules." The ' Life ' also contains some old Irish phrases.

Vita Fintani. Scriptores rerum Merovingicarum, vol. 15, pp. 503-506.

FINTAN (MUNNU) OF TAGHMON

October 21

Anbreo co mbruth athre Fintan fírór promthae, macc Telcháin trén trednach cathmíl credlach crochthae.	A splendid flame with the Father's fervour, Fintan, true gold proven! Telchan's son, brave, abstinent, A battle soldier, trustful crucified.

(Martyrology of Oengus)

Fintán Mocumoie, son of Talchan, of Tech Munnu (Munnu's house, Taghmon, Wexford) died in 635. A friend and junior contemporary of Colmcille, he worked both in Ireland and Scotland; we are fortunate in that not only is he mentioned in some detail by Adamnan but the actual Latin ' Life ' of Munnu does tell a coherent story rather than retail a string of stock miracles.

His name is variously spelled, Fintan, Finten, Finntainn; Munnu, his usual Scottish appellation, is from the affectionate form, Mo Findu, my Fintan.

The long standing friendship between Munnu and Colmcille suggests that the story of the older man prophesying the little boy's future greatness may be less groundless than most of such tales. Young Munnu used to herd his father's flocks on the hill and discovered nearby, at Achud Broan (or Achad Bidam), the cell of a priest named Grellan. So young Munnu introduced himself so as to learn his letters and about the monastic life. His father, Talchan (Tulchan),who came of the stock of the famous Niall of the Nine Hostages, discovering this neglect of the flocks, complained that they would all be eaten by wolves. Munnu's mother, Fedelm, defended the lad, nothing had been lost so far, and later Talchan watching, saw two wolves come out and herd the flock like sheepdogs!

This was in Westmeath, and one day Comgall of Bangor came into the district. Munnu at once joined Comgall's party. As they went along, young Munnu grew thirsty and asked for a drink, for it was a hot, sunny day, when they halted to recite Terce at Áth Férne— probably a ford on the Brosna in Westmeath. Comgall put him off till the next halt and the same thing happened at each pause for the successive canonical hours, Sext at Glassa Assail, None at Commar dá glas—by Drumcree. Finally they got to evening and Vespers, and not surprisingly their fasting earned a miraculous meal!

From Comgall's monastery of Bangor, young Munnu next went to one of Colmcille's, Ceall Mor Dithraimh, the great church in the desert, Kilmore, Roscommon. Then he went to Sinell's Cleenish on Lough Erne. Of the three monasteries, the rule and personality of Colmcille seems to have attracted him most, for he decided to go to Iona to remain there permanently. Here Adamnan (Bk. I, ch. 2) tells in detail what took place. Before leaving Ireland, Munnu met another holy man named Colum Crag, who informed him that Colmcille had just died (June 9, 597). Baithene had succeeded as abbot, and Munnu decided he would go on with his plan of going to Iona. When he arrived and sought admission to the monastery, Baithene told him that Colmcille had said just before he died, that Munnu would come seeking admission but was not to be received. For, said Colmcille, Munnu is not to be a monk of any abbot but an abbot himself, and left directions that he was to return to Leinster, to a site near the sea, and that there he would lead numberless souls to Christ.

Adamnan's source for this story is a monk of Munnu's named Oisseneous, who had it from Munnu himself. Adamnan says that Munnu was held in high repute in all the Irish churches, he had kept purity of mind and body from his youth up and was devoted to the study of divine things.

Munnu, however, did work in Scotland, where there are a number of churches of his, and there was once a live devotion to him in that country. There is Cill Mhunna (Kilmun) on Loch Séanta (Holy Loch) in Cowal, as well as two other Kilmuns, one near Inveraray, and one on Loch Avich. All these lie on the route from Ireland to Iona. Nor is it a long sail from Iona to the sea loch at the foot of Glencoe, Loch Leven of Ballachulish. Here is an island of Fintan, Eilean Mhunna, with a ruined church. At the head of Loch Eck is Inver-

chapel, at which a document of 1497 listing land there includes a
reference to Pordewry " with the staff of St. Munde called in Gaelic
Deowray ". This word, *deoradh*, pilgrim, seems to refer to the practice of carrying the relic of a saint round his *parouchia*, for veneration
and collection of dues. Later the word was transferred to the person
who actually kept the relic, whence the surname Dewar. St. Munn's
fair was held at Earls Ruthven in Forfar. It is worth noting how
these Fintan churches are set along the route from Ireland up the
west Highlands, partly over land and partly by sea. Up the Firth of
Clyde, after the sea crossing, to Holy Loch, then cross country by the
glen in which lies Loch Eck, to the sea again at Loch Fyne and
Inveraray. Then over the ridge to Loch Awe and across that to Loch
Avich, and then by land to the sea once more in the Loch Melfort
area.

Munnu returned to Ireland. The first foundation is probably simply
a legend, for it is the island called Coirmrighi at Ath Cain (Fair Ford)
which Munnu leaves because he is annoyed with the sound of cries
from hell. Then later on, Ath Cain appears as Colmcille's settlement
on the Land of Promise. There was a Briton, a skilled carpenter, who
worked for the Taghmon monks and lived in a hermitage of his own
near them. To this very probable story, Taghmon is near enough to
Britain, is added the strange one of Munnu visiting the Briton and
the latter noticing the wet sand on Munnu's shoes as he sat by the
fire. Munnu is got to admit where he picked it up, a visit paid by
himself, Colmcille, Brendan and Cainnech to the Land of Promise;
Munnu brought back sand to hallow Taghmon graveyard.

So Munnu went on over Ireland and came to Eily in Munster,
settling at Teach Telli, Tehelly near Durrow. However, he gave up
this place to a virgin named Emer, who came with five companions
seeking a site. He left her the whole establishment with its furnish-
ings, going off with his party and a wagon drawn by two oxen
carrying only their immediate needs, their liturgical books, and the
chrismales used for carrying the Blessed Sacrament. He told Emer
however that the place would not bear her name but that of Telli,
son of Segene who would come to live there later.

So he came into Leinster and into Wexford, where he halted at the
Height of the Wild Geese, Ard Crema in the Bargy district near the
sea. It was a cell with monks of Comgall's and the man in charge of
them, Aedh Gobbain, was going off on pilgrimage. He asked Munnu
to take charge for him. However, when Comgall died, in the first

years of the 7th century, difficulties arose. The story has it that a deputation of Bangor monks arrived at Ard Crema and gave Munnu three choices, to go to Bangor and be abbot there, which he refused to do; to head Ard Crema but as a subject of Bangor, again he refused. For said he, Colmcille would not have me as a monk and I will not be subject to any abbot now but God. The third choice, which he took, was to leave altogether.

The story says that angels showed Taghmon to him, his final settlement, and that he marked out the bounds with crosses, which was very likely the usual routine. Taghmon was originally Achad Liathdrom, the field of the grey ridge, and it belonged to Dimma, son of Aedh, who gave Munnu a grant of the land.

Fintan's blessing of a monk's heart was said to banish all vices for life. If Munnu spoke roughly to a guest, he would not eat till he had made friends again, for he used to say, " Just now I was the (carnal) son of Talcharn; now I am the (spiritual) son of God ". In his old age, he suffered from leprosy, or some skin disease which passed for that complaint.

He is also recorded attending a Council at Magh Ailbe on the borders of Carlow and Kildare over the question of the date of Easter. Munnu defended the old use against Laserian of Leighlin for the new. This may have been in c. 630. Munnu, says the legend, wanted a contest of working miracles with Laserian, throwing books containing the old and new calculations in the fire to see which burned, raising men from the dead. Laserian refused this as unfair. For said Laserian, " If you, Fintan, told Slieve Margy over there to move to Magh Ailbe, and Magh Ailbe over to where Slieve Margy is, God would do it for you ".

J.R.S.A.I., vol. 35, (1905), p. 269 has a description and photograph of the massive, but incomplete granite cross in Taghmon churchyard.

FLANNAN OF KILLALOE

December 18

Not very much is known about St. Flannan. There are two versions of his life, the longer is a rather formal composition apparently by a foreigner living at Killaloe in the 12th century. This writer's main objective seems to have been to praise his patrons, the O Briains of Thomond. He did not know Ireland very intimately.

Killaloe, Cell da Lua, is placed where the expanse of Lough Derg of Shannon narrows to the outlet of the great river through the circling hills down to the sea at Limerick. It seems to have been the foundation of a St. Mo Lua or Da Lua, in the 6th century. Flannan belongs to the 7th century, the ' Life ' follows the usual hagiographical device of making Molua hand over his monastery to the saintly young Flannan. More probably Flannan simply succeeded to the abbacy in the ordinary way.

Flannan came of the royal house of the Dál Cais, his father, Torlough, being king of Thomond. Much of the ' Life ' is concerned with the career of this devout king, who retired in his old age to Lismore to become a monk there. Torlough's son, Flannan, studied first with a holy man called Blathmet, then entered Molua's monastery at Killaloe.

He had a great reputation as a preacher. The ' Life ' records an incident on the Isle of Man; there was a church of his at Inishlannaun in Lough Corrib as well as on Inishbofin; but the most famous place connected with his name are the Flannan Islands in the Outer Hebrides. It is not certain however whether the Scottish Flannan is the same as the Flannan of Killaloe; the name (from *flann,* red) is not unique, and it could be there was a second eminent saint called Flannan. The Scottish Flannan very certainly was an eminent man, who left a vivid memory behind him, which in course of time mingled with a most extraordinary set of customs and taboos observed by those who visited the Flannan Islands.

These islets lie far out to the west, off Lewis and Harris. On one of them, on which stands the lighthouse, is a rather curious cluster of stone huts, called the Bothies of the Clan Macphail, and some way off a chapel, built in drystone. It is a rough structure, of uncertain date, the inside measurements being 5 ft. × 7¾ ft. Martin Martin in his " Description of the Western Islands of Scotland " (c. 1695) tells how the Lewismen used to go to the Flannan Islands to take birds, eggs, down, feathers and quills. The remote islands and the tricky seas probably helped the growth of curious customs, certain actions that must be observed, certain words that must not be spoken. They thanked God for their safe arrival immediately they got there. They prayed too morning and evening at the chapel. " I asked one of them," wrote Martin, " if he prayed at home as often, and as fervently as he did when in the Flannan Islands, and he plainly confessed to me that he did not: adding further, that these remote islands were places of inherent sanctity; and that there was none ever yet landed in them but found himself more disposed to devotion there, than anywhere else ".

It is perhaps worth quoting too the account by John Morisone of Lewis, written in the period 1678-88. " There are seven Islands 15 Myles Westward from the Lews, called the Isles of Sant Flannan, lying closs together, wherin there is a cheaple, where Sant Flandan himself lived ane heremit. To those in the summertyme some countriemen goes; and bringeth home great store of seafowls and feathers. The way they kill the fowls is, one goeth and taketh a road (rod) 10 or 12 foot long, and setts his back to a rock or craig, and as the fouls flieth by, he smiteth them continuallie, and he has ane other attending to catch all that falls to the ground; for the fouls flee there so thick that those who are beneath them cannot see the firmament. Those isles are not inhabited but containeth a quantitie of wilde sheep verie fatt and weel fleeced. When the people goe there, they use everie two men to be Comerads. They hold it a breach of the sanctitie of the place (for they count it holier than anie other) if any man take a drink of water unknown to his comerade or eat ane egg or legg of ane foull, yea take a snuff of tobacco. It is for certaintie that upon a tyme a countriefellow being sent there and left in it, be reason he could not be keept from theft and robberie and so on a time the fire went out with him, without which he could not live, and so despaired of lyfe and since he saw that there was no remead, he betook him to pray both to God and the Sainct of the Island as they term'd it, and by night being fallen in a deep sleep, he sees a man come to him well clade saying aryse, betake thee unto the Altar and there thou shall find a peate in fyre, for the Lord hath heard thy prayer. So he arose and accordingly found the fyre, which he preserved untill he was taken home, and henceforth he proved as honest a man as was in the countrie."

That account from the " Description of the Lewis by John Morisone Indweller there " (MacFarlane's Geographical Collections, Scottish History Society, 1907) recalls many miracle stories in the 'Lives' of the saints, where fire is miraculously obtained. These tales have meaning, for we forget how before matches, making fire might be difficult work, and the exile on Flannan's predicament was not by any means an isolated event. Again the " fire houses " of certain Irish monasteries, like Inismurray and Brigit's Kildare, may simply have been to preserve the " stock " as it were, of fire, and were built in stone as an elementary fire precaution in a monastery largely constructed of inflammable materials.

At Killaloe, the cathedral includes a fine Romanesque doorway; alongside is the stone built oratory of Flannan with its steeply pitched roof. Beside the modern Catholic church, the oratory of Molua was re-erected, having been removed before Friar's Island, where it originally stood, was submerged in the Shannon hydro-electric scheme. Killaloe also has a 13th century wooden figure of St. Molua.

The 12th century ' Life ' is interesting in its account of the relics of Flannan then venerated in Killaloe; his shrine ornamented with gold and silver, gold too on the shrines of his gospel book, bell and crozier. The author tells how thieves stole the crozier for the gold, how the actual staff was recovered and regilded, then how it was recovered after having been accidentally let fall into the water— presumably Lough Derg.

Life of St. Flannan. English translation by S. Malone. Dublin, 1902.
H. G. Leask. *The Church of St. Lua or Molua, Friar's Island, near Killaloe.* J.R.S.A.I., vol. 60, (1930), pp. 130-136.

FRIDIAN (FREDIANO/FRIGIDIAN) OF LUCCA

March 20

Fridian of Lucca, whose existence is testified to by St. Gregory the Great recording a miracle of his in the " Dialogues ", was probably a bishop of Lucca in the third century. This fact, which emerges from a study of the oldest lists of bishops of Lucca, disposes of his supposed Irish origin, for it is far too early for wandering Irishmen to be available for election to Italian sees. Nor is the associated St. Silao of Irish origin. Dr. John Hennig summed up the Fridian question :— " The tradition of St. Frediano is the classical example of the Hibernisation of a continental patron-saint. The tradition of St. Silao is an original and free creation ".

Antonio Pedemonte: *S. Frediano.* Bolletino storico Lucchese ix (1937), and in the same publication for 1938 *L'Antico catalogo dei vescovi di Lucca.*

J. Hennig: *A Note on the Traditions of St. Frediano and St. Silao of Lucca.* Mediaeval Studies, 1951, pp. 234-242.

FRIDOLIN

March 6

Fridolin's supposed Irish origin is yet another tribute to Ireland's reputation for sanctity. He seems to have been French, but his wandering career to have suggested the idea of an Irishman! Fridolin who founded the monastery of Sackingen in Baden on the Upper Rhine was the object of very widespread devotion in southern Germany, Austria and Switzerland, and a special patron of cattle and horses. The whole 'Life' by a monk of Sackingen named Balther is quite unreliable.

FURSA

January 16

Go raibh cuing dhlí Dé ar an ngualainn seo,
    fiosrú an Spioraid Naoimh go dtí an ceann so,
    comhartha Chríost san éadan so,
    éisteacht an Spioraid Naoimh sna cluasa so,
    boltanú an Spioraid Naoimh san tsróin seo,
    ionann's ag muintir Neimhe an fhéachaint sna suile seo,
    ionann's ag muintir Neimhe an comhrá sna beola so,
    saothar Eaglais Dé sna lámha so,
    leas Dé agus na comharsan sna cosa so,
    ait do Dhia an croí seo,
    le Dia Athair uile an duine seo.

(Prayer of St. Fursa)

The lines quoted above are a version in modern Irish of the Middle Irish prayer of St. Fursa (printed in Archiv. f. Celt. Lex. 3/232 by Kuno Meyer). The text as we have it would go back to the 11th century but its form and spirit suggest a much older original, and it could, like the Breastplate for Patrick, reflect something of the spirit

and outlook of the saint to whom it is attributed. An English
version runs:—

> May the yoke of the Law of God be on this shoulder,
>   the coming of the Holy Spirit on this head,
>   the sign of Christ on this forehead,
>   the hearing of the Holy Spirit in these ears,
>   the smelling of the Holy Spirit in this nose,
>   the vision that the People of Heaven have in these eyes,
>   the speech of the People of Heaven in this mouth,
>   the work of the Church of God in these hands,
>   the good of God and of the neighbour in these feet,
>
> May God be dwelling in this heart
>   and this man belong entirely to God the Father.

St. Fursa (Fursae/Fursu/Fursey) was one of the most important of
the Irish saints who travelled to Europe, not so much for his actual
work there, but for the extent of his subsequent cult and the way in
which the monasteries with which he was connected became centres
of Irish influence abroad. Peronne, *Perrona Scottorum* (of the Irish),
where Fursa was buried, was in fact staffed by Irish monks. Again
Fursa is important in the history of visions of the next world, for the
one he experienced, is the earliest to be recorded so far as our surviving
texts go.

In most cases, an Irishman who worked overseas was not so well
known back in Ireland, Fursa is an exception to the rule, with his
name, and that of his brother, Foillan, in the Tallaght Martyrologies.
Then too he is the only Irish saint who worked on the continent to
whose Irish connections, mediaeval Irish sources make reference, the
only one to have an Irish vernacular version of his life compiled.
Naturally though, the bulk of devotion and of writing about Fursa is
continental. He has attained wide fame too since Bede, who was
greatly intrigued by his visions, gave a fairly detailed account of him.

It is certain that Fursa was Irish, but nothing else is known of his
Irish background or connections. Bede sums up all we know:—"there
came out of Ireland a holy man called Fursa, renowned both for his
words and actions, and remarkable for singular virtues, being desirous
to live a stranger for our Lord, wherever an opportunity should
offer ". Coming to Britain and the country of the East Saxons, Fursa
was received by the king, Sigebert, with joy. The king gave the Irish
monks a site on which to settle, in a wood, near the sea, at an old

fortress called Cnobheresburg (modern Burgh Castle in Suffolk). Fursa it appears had already made a foundation in Ireland but left it to avoid the crowds who came to visit him there. In England, he again took up the apostolate and converted numbers of pagans as well as working for the existing Christian population. It would appear that he came into East Anglia somewhere between 630/1 and 634. In 635, Sigebert was killed when king Penda of the Mercians attacked the East Angles. Both the unsettled conditions that followed, and his personal longing for solitude, helped make Fursa decide to go further afield, to seek a hermitage on the continent. Leaving his brother Foillan (Faelán) in charge of Cnobheresburg, together with two other Irish priests, Gobban and Dicuil, Fursa crossed the English Channel in 644 or 5, perhaps as early as 640. Just as he had approached a royal court in England, so he now did in Neustria. Here he found a patron in its mayor, Erchinoald, who helped him settle at Lagny on the Marne. Fursa died on 16 January of 649 or 650, at Mezerolles, when he was travelling in that part of Gaul. Erchinoald had the body translated to Peronne, which became the great centre of devotion to Fursa, as well as an Irish monastery of note.

Fursa had another brother called Ultan, both he and Foillan (Faelan/Feuillan) eventually followed Fursa to the continent. Foillan arrived soon after Fursa's death, he arrived in Peronne in 650 and went on to make a fresh foundation at Fosse. Fosse near Namur had close links with Nivelles, a convent founded by Ita, widow of Pippin the Elder, in 640. Irish monks were the spiritual directors of this group of nuns which included St. Gertrude, Ita's daughter. Ita, in fact, was the donor of Fosse to Foillan, and since she died on 8th May 652, he must have made the foundation before that date. Foillan was killed by brigands on 31 October 655, when on a visitation of the whole Irish *parouchia* including Peronne and Lagny. He was attacked in the Forêt Charbonnière near Strépy, not very far from Nivelles. Later on, this place would be the site of a Premonstratensian foundation (Roeulx, 1125) but in Foillan's time it was marked by a wooden church and a graveyard. His body was not recovered until the following January 16th, it was taken first to Nivelles and then back to Fosse.

Ultan, who died 1 May, 686, was present when St. Gertrude died on St. Patrick's day 659. He became abbot of Peronne; his successor, Cellan (d. 706) is the author of a poem on St. Patrick for an inscription in the chapel of the saint. Peronne of the Irish, which the Four Masters called " Cathair Fursa in France " had an unbroken succession of Irish abbots at least till 774. It may in fact have remained wholly Irish till it was ravaged by the Norse in 880. Fosse and the " cell " of Mezerolles were also manned by Irishmen. The whole group, Fursa's incorrupt body forming the centre of devotion at Peronne, with Nivelles, was a regular line of communication between Ireland and the continent. It seems that the earliest, or one of the earliest, layers of continental devotion to Irish saints, came from these houses. Fursa, Dr. L. Bieler believes, actually took out with him copies of St. Patrick's works. The first record of the feast of Patrick being kept on March 17th, and the first Irish text which mentions Patrick's stay in Gaul, both come from Peronne. The liturgical material from Nivelles indicates links both with Ireland and Wurzburg, and it is of interest that a 15th century Nivelles ms. has a rite for the visitation of the sick showing affinity to the Irish one of the 8th-11th centuries.

Fursa and his brothers, as well as Cellan, all appear in a litany from a 9th century ms. of Fribourg-en-Brisgau, a liturgical book once used at Basle though not originally written for that church. The litanies show links with Ireland, northern France, Belgium and Wurzburg; the Irish saints commemorated are:—Kilian, Columban, Columba (Colmcille), Patrick, Comgall, Cainnech, Ciaran of Clonmacnois, Brendan of Clonfert, Finian of Clonard, Fursa, Ultan, Foillan, Cellan, Brigit, Ita and Darerca (Monenna).

Fursa's visions took place in East Anglia during an illness he had there. He saw a vision of heaven and heard its chants of praise. As the Irish version of the vision puts it, he heard " the chanting of the angels of heaven and he beheld them before him. And this is what they were chanting, Ibunt sancti de virtute in virtutem, ' the saints shall advance from virtue to virtue '. And this also they were saying, Videbitor Deus deorum in Sion, ' The God of gods will be seen on Mount Sion ' ". He also saw a vision of hell. The angels carried him up to a great height and looking back he saw four fires that he was told would burn up the world. They were the fire of falsehood (when we do not carry out our baptismal vows to renounce the devil and his works); the fire of covetousness (looking for the goods of this world rather than the next); the fire of discord (when we offend our neighbours over anything or nothing); and the fire of iniquity (when we think it no shame to rob or cheat the weak). Fursa was afraid he would be burned by these fires but the angel told him that the fire he had not kindled would not harm him. He did, however, get a burn the mark of which remained for life, when the devils flung a man being tormented in the fire at him. Fursa had received this man's garment when he died, and to that extent had got the benefit of his sinful life! At least so argued the devils but the angels drove them back saying Fursa had not done so through greed. Bede says he had the story of these visions from a still living but very old brother of his monastery who had had them from another sincere man who had known Fursa and heard him tell of them. Even in the cold of winter, Fursa, though thinly clad, would break into a hot sweat when he told of his experience.

In the Middle Ages, the cult of Fursa was spread all over Belgium and France but is now chiefly concentrated in the diocese of Amiens and in southern Belgium. He is invoked for the protection of cattle. The cult of Foillan and Ultan is proper to Belgium; Foillan's relics being still venerated at Fosse, where, as at Aix-la-Chapelle, he is patron of a confraternity of riflemen, who hold a procession to avert plague. Columban as well as Foillan was a saint invoked against plague in the Middle Ages.

Dr. J. Hennig has traced the development of the continental literary legend of Irish saints, and shown that it has three stages, each of which is exemplified in the hagiography of Fursa. The first stage is the direct historical record, containing little reference to the Ireland from which the saint came. In Fursa's case, this is represented by the first ' Life ' from which Bede seems to have worked, and the references to Fursa in the first ' Life ' of St. Gertrude of Nivelles. The 9th century " Virtutes Fursaei " says no more of his origins than that he came from " de ultramarinis partibus ".

But later the legend is elaborated. 12th century writers on the continent added their impression of what Ireland was like, thus Arnulph's account of this period adds the names of Irish kings, placenames and incidents, some real, some fictitious. It is a little like the Ireland of American song writers; we may compare the " Rathmat " given as the name of Fursa's Irish monastery with another but modern invention, Glockamaura, both intended to sound like Irish names.

Finally this much more detailed legend receives further elaboration from writers with little interest in or fresh information about Ireland. That this later writing on Fursa should connect him with Brendan of Clonfert is not an historical statement of reality, but it does show that continental writers knew of other Irish saints, and did have a quite true idea of how the Irish mission abroad was based on the Irish monasteries and saints at home.

Vita prima Sancti Fursei in vol. iv, Scriptores rerum Merovingicarum. Bede's version, including the Visions (which the editor omits from the above text) in Book 3, ch. 19 of his History.

Betha Fursa. The Life in Irish, edited and translated by Whitley Stokes in Revue Celtique 25, (1904), pp. 385-404.

J. Hennig: *The Irish Background of St. Fursey.* I.E.R., Jan., 1952, pp. 18-28. *Irish Saints in the Liturgical and Artistic Tradition of Central Europe.* I.E.R., March, 1943, pp. 181-192.

P. Grosjean, S.J.: 1. Le Souvenir de S. Kilian a Nivelles. 2. Chronologie de S. Feuillan. 3. Où fut assassiné S. Feuillan? 4. Les compagnons de martyre de S. Feuillan. 5. Les saints irlandais dans les litanies de Pontifical carolingien de Fribourg-en-Brisgau. Analecta Bollandiana, t. 75, (1957), pp. 337-339. Deals with the whole chronology of Fursa and Foillan. Review and summary by Kathleen Hughes in *Irish Historical Studies,* March, 1960, pp. 61-64.

Kuno Meyer on the poem on St. Patrick from Peronne in Eriu, vol. 5, (1911), p. 110.

GALL

October 16

Deus, qui gentes nostras per beatum Gallum Abbatem ad agnitionem verae fidei perduxisti; concede nobis in eiusdem fidei professione inviolabilem firmitatem; ut cum ipso praemia consequamur aeterna.

(God, who brought our race knowledge of the true Faith by means of Abbot Gall; grant we remain unshaken in its profession; that we attain eternal rewards with him).

(Collect. Proper for the feast of St. Gall in St. Gallen diocese)

There is that about St. Gall that makes one feel him one of the most attractive of Irish saints; it is thus doubly unfortunate that the surviving ' Lives ' are not reliable. He was one of Jonas' sources for information about Columban, and is mentioned in the latter's biography, but only briefly. The primitive *Vita S. Galli* was written *c.* 712; a second *Vita* was composed by Wettinus, master of the monastic school at Reichenau; a third by Walafrid Strabo. Wettinus, who died in 824, wrote his book at the request of Gozbert, abbot of St. Gallen from 816 to 837. Gozbert was still alive when Walafrid wrote the third account; Walafrid was a graduate of Reichenau and died at the age of about 40 in 849. Walafrid's account is divided into two books, one about Gall's career, based on the earlier accounts; the other of miracles attributed to Gall's intercession after his death. The latter have a very marked tendency to tell of the awful retribution that will befall anyone who does any harm to the monastery of St. Gall!

There is also a genealogy of St. Gall in a 9th century ms.; this claims he was of royal descent and that his father's name was Kethernach and his grandfather, Unichun. It says that, like Columban, he was a Leinsterman. The genealogy spells Gall's own name Gallech or Callehc, the latter with an obvious transposition of its final letters. Perhaps Gall's name was *Callech,* cognate with O. Irish *Cailech* and modern Irish *Coileach,* a cock, in Latin, Gallus. But it may mean Gall's family had Gaulish origins.

Gall entered the monastery of Bangor and was one of those who set off with St. Columban for continental Europe. Thus, so far as the main events and places go, Gall's story is the same as that of Columban's for they remained together the whole time. Gall was big and tall (here there is the evidence of the size of the saint's bones when the shrine was rifled at the Reformation in 1529), and he was a good preacher with some knowledge of foreign languages. He was also interested in catching fish. It is a fishing story that Jonas tells in his ' Life ' of Columban, one which (as fishermen will) " Gall himself often told me ".

It was at Luxeuil and Columban and Gall had gone off together into a desert place some way from the monastery. Columban told Gall to go to a certain place in the River Breuchin to fish for them both. Gall, for some reason of his own, decided to try his skill on the Lignon instead. He was using a net, with which he tried to enclose a large shoal of fish but without catching any of them. Columban was somewhat irritated by the return of the fishless Gall, when it transpired that the latter had not followed out his instructions. He sent Gall back to the Breuchin, where Gall netted so many fish that he could hardly cope with them.

The account of St. Gall adds details which are lacking from Jonas, but which are in the main outline likely enough. It tells how the party crossed the Rhine and came to the castle of Turégum (Zurich). Then they followed the lake shore to Tuccinia (Tuggen). Here they halted and tried to preach to the local pagans; Gall set fire to some wooden idols, with the natural result that they were violently expelled from the district.

However there were some Christians among the pagans of this mountain country that was to become Switzerland. Columban's party went on over hill and through forest, and came to Boden lake and a walled village called Arbona (Arbon). Here a saintly priest, Willimar, made them welcome and in response to Columban's enquiry, showed them a good place to settle in the district of Pergentia (Bregenz). Experience had taught caution and the Irish did not start idol smashing quite so immediately. Gall, however, eventually thought it safe to do so again and he also broke a container holding 500 measures of beer dedicated to Woden. Jonas, our more authentic source, says it was Columban who spilled the beer—by merely breathing on it, but that only 20 measures were involved. About half the population were favourable to the monks, but the rest gained the ear of the pagan Duke of Alemannia, Cunzo, who ordered them to leave. Columban then set off across the Alps for Italy. Jonas' version of the reason Columban went on is that the quarrel between Theuderic and Theudebert was then at its height and news had come that Theuderic had just defeated Theudebert. Jonas says nothing at all of the story told in the ' Lives ' of St. Gall of a quarrel between Gall and Columban at this point.

Gall was ill with fever and was unable to start with the others for Italy. Columban, giving him permission to stay behind, felt however that he was malingering, and forbade him to say Mass till after Columban's death. Columban's personality, as it comes across in his writings, does not favour the truth of such an action, nor does it seem at all probable that two men who had gone through so much together already, would be likely to have that kind of a quarrel. It seems much better to discard this whole story as a legend (perhaps invented to explain the very Irish veneration of the crozier sent as a dying gift by Columban to Gall), and take Jonas' account as it stands. Columban went on to Italy because of the increasing danger to him from recent political events; Gall was less in the public eye and might safely remain behind and try and continue the work initiated by Columban in the area.

The *Vitae* of St. Gall however preserve a very attractive and picturesque account of how Gall found and settled in the hermitage that would eventually become the famous monastery of St. Gallen. Tended in his sickness by the priest Willimar and two of his clerics, Maginold and Theodore, Gall as soon as he was well enough, asked for a place for a hermitage. Hiltibold, a deacon of Willimar's household, was a keen sportsman and knew of a likely place but he warned the would-be hermit of the savage scenery, the rocks and the mountains and the wild beasts that lived amongst them. Not only harmless creatures but wolves, boars and bears. Hiltibold guided Gall into the hills, having instructed him to bring a supply of food and the smallest of his fishing nets. Gall set off fasting, determined not to eat till God had shown the place where he would settle. So they came to the bouldery mountain torrent of the Steinach, and here Gall, catching his foot in some brambles, took it as a sign they should halt. Here was the chosen place, he cut a couple of hazel branches and set up a rough cross; on it he hung the satchel he had brought with relics of Sts. Mary, Maurice and Desiderius. They lit a fire, but Hiltibold was more than alarmed when a bear came lumbering out of the wood towards them. " Bear," said Gall, " I order you in the name of Jesus Christ, to go back and bring us out wood for the fire." The bear returned with a log; in art, from this story, Gall is shown with a bear carrying a log in its paws.

The story goes on with the ejection of demons that lived in the place, and how Gall fasted three days whilst Hiltibold went back to Willimar to report progress. After his fast was over, Gall too came back and when he was at a meal with the others, Hiltibold said of a sudden to Willimar, " If the bear were here, Gall would likely give him something to eat!"

Gall constructed a hermitage and an oratory at his chosen site, and eventually was joined there by twelve monks. Here too he received miraculous knowledge of Columban's death, for whom he then celebrated Mass, as well as prudently sending messengers to Bobbio for confirmation of the news. Columban's bachall, crozier, was sent as a dying gift by the saint to Gall, a token of forgiveness according to the legend of the quarrel, and became a famous relic of St. Gallen.

St. Gall was greatly venerated in his own lifetime in the area, and Walafrid has a long account of how he was persuaded to come and cure Fridiburga, daughter of a local duke, who appears to have been an epileptic.

Gall died when on a visit to Willimar, aged, it is said, 90, in about the year 630. His body was taken back to the hermitage for burial.

The place continued as such, with pilgrims coming to visit the saint's tomb, for a long time. It was raided and plundered on two occasions. A fully organised monastery only seems to date from 719, when Othmar became custodian of the shrine. Round him, a community grew rapidly and he enlarged and added to the buildings. Othmar adopted the Benedictine rule in 747. From then, till its suppression in 1805, the great abbey of St. Gallen had a distinguished history and gathered a great library, a large part of which (despite the depredations of time and unscrupulous borrowers!) yet remains in St. Gallen. It includes valuable early printed books as well as manuscripts. Whilst St. Gallen was never an Irish monastery, it had many Irish links, its great Irish saint, the Irish who came to visit it on pilgrimage or join the community. Irish mss. are among those of its library. The Irish glosses on a copy of Priscian are well known, for example the little sketch of the scribe working at his copying :—

A hedge of trees surrounds me : a blackbird's lay sings to me—
    praise I will not hide—
above my booklet the lined one, the trilling of the birds sings to me.
In a grey mantle, the cuckoo's beautiful chant sings to me from the
    tops of bushes :
May the Lord protect me from Doom. I write well under the
    greenwood !

See also COLUMBAN, COMGALL.

Vita Galli Confessoris Triplex including *Vitae Galli Vetustissimae Fragmentum*, ed. B. Krusch in Mon. Ger. Hist., Scriptores Rerum Merovingicarum iv, pp. 228-337.

Vita St. Galli, ed. Meyer von Knonau, Mittheilungen zur vaterländischen Geschichte. v. xii (1869).

The 'Life' is given in abbreviated translation in English by Gonzague de Reynold, *St. Columban, St. Gall and the Formation of Switzerland* in *The Miracle of Ireland*, Dublin, 1959, pp. 79-91.

The Life of St. Gall. Translation by Maud Joynt of Walafrid Strabo's *Life*. Notes include a sequence in honour of St. Gall by Notker and a hymn by Ratpert for his feast. London, 1927.

J. M. Clark : *The Abbey of St. Gall as a centre of literature and art.* Cambridge, 1926.

J. Hennig : *The Liturgical Veneration of Irish Saints in Switzerland.* pp. 23-32. Iris Hibernia, 1957.

Sankt Gallus Gedenkbuch. Ed. J. Duft. St. Gallen, 1952.

J. Duft and P. Meyer : *The Irish Miniatures in the Abbey Library of St. Gall.* Berne and New York, 1954.

GERALD OF MAYO

March 13

Three thousands and three hundreds with Gerald the bishop and fifty saints of Luigne of Connacht, who occupied Mag Eo of the Saxons.
(from the first Litany of Irish saints in the
Book of Leinster)

Seven monks of Egypt in Disert Uilaig.
The foreigners in Saillide; the foreigners in Mag Salach.
The Saxons in Rigair.
The Saxons in Cluain Mucceda.
Fifty men of the Britons with the son of Moinan in Land Léri.
(Invocations from the second Litany)

These invocations from two old Litanies of Irish saints give an idea of the little colonies of incomers who came to live in the " island of saints ". St. Gerald of Mayo is the most famous name among them. Mayo, Magh eo na Sacsan, was founded by Colman of Lindisfarne when the Irish and English monks did not agree on Inishbofin. St. Gerald died in 732, " ponifex of Mayo of the Saxons ". Unfortunately the surviving Latin ' Life ' of Gerald is a mixture of historical error, chronological impossibility and wonder stories. All that is certain is that Gerald was a prominent figure among the English monks who came to settle in Ireland in the wake of Colman of Lindisfarne's return to this country.

When Bede wrote, Mayo was large and " still possessed by English inhabitants ". In fact, the name, Mayo of the Saxons, stuck until the 15th century. Alcuin corresponded with the monastery and his letters include one to Leuthfridt, bishop of the monastery of Mayo in Ireland (Ad Leutfredum episcopum coenobii Mugensis in Hibernia) and one to the whole community (Ad Patres Mugensis Ecclesiae). In the latter he urged them to " let their light shine in the midst of a most barbarous people ", and to attend to their studies.

In 786, the Papal Legate reported on two Councils held in England that year. At the first, the bishop of Mayo, Alduulfus Myiensis ecclesiae episcopus, signed sixth in the document issued by the gathering.

Lough Corrib is not far from Mayo and it has an island named

Inchagoill. O'Flaherty's account of Connacht of 1684 has it as the island of the devout foreigner, An Gall Craibhtheach. There are two ruined churches on the island, Teampull Patrick on the highest point, Teampull na Naomh, lower down. The latter has a much weathered but very fine Romanesque door. At St. Patrick's, the graveyard has an interesting pillar stone with inscribed Greek crosses and the name LIE LUGUAEDON MACCIMENUEH or perhaps MAC LIMENUEH, in a very early form of Irish script. The foreigner of the island might have been English, but perhaps more probably, from the use of the word in the litanies quoted above, was of Scandinavian origin.

St. Gerald makes an extraordinary appearance, from the chronological point of view, in a folk tale about the Dominican friars of Urlar! He seems, for whatever reason, perhaps his foreign origin, to have tended to gather legends round his name.

See also COLMAN OF LINDISFARNE, BERCHERT OF TULLYLEASE. Bede. Inishboffin and Mayo foundations. Book IV, ch. 4.

GOBNET OF BALLYVOURNEY

February 11

Mo Gopnat co nglanbail,
im seirc Dé ba hilmain.

My Gobnet with pure goodness,
as to God's love was opulent.
(Martyrology of Oengus)

St. Gobnet is one of the best loved of Irish saints today. Her intercession is widely invoked—and obtained. Her principal site (Ballyvourney, Co. Cork) has been excavated, the finds confirming tradition rather than denying it. Yet only traditions survive of Gobnet's actual history, even her date is vague, and there is now no trace of the ' Life ' Colgan said was extant in South Munster in his time. Gobnet is known and venerated at a number of other old church sites in the south, Dunquin being one of them. At Ballyvourney, February 11th is a parish holiday. There is a special Mass in the parish church, veneration of the mediaeval wooden statue of the saint, and the making of the long traditional " round " at Gobnet's site. In the afternoon, there is Rosary, sermon in Irish, and Benediction in the church. At Whitsunday, a second " pattern " brings a big crowd of outsiders on pilgrimage, coming in many cases quite long distances. There is too a tradition of keeping an over-night vigil in the ruined church. Ballyvourney people, however, make the " round " at all times of the year; one may hardly visit the site without seeing one or more in prayer there. For a very special intention, the " round ", taking about an hour, is made on 21 successive days, concluding by cleaning out the well and going to Mass and Holy Communion. In 1601, the Gobnet devotion was sufficiently famous for Pope Clement VIII to grant an indulgence of ten years and quarantines, to those who visited the parish church of Gobnet on the feast, went to Confession and Communion, and prayed for peace amongst Christian princes, expulsion of heresy and the exaltation of the Church.

The tradition says that Gobnet fled from her home country of Clare to Aran to escape some enemy. There is a church of hers in Inisheer (Inis Thiar) in the Aran islands. An angel appeared to her on these islands and told her that the " place of her resurrection " was not to be there, but where she would find nine white deer grazing. So Gobnet travelled over southern Ireland and her foundations, like Kilgobnet near Dungarvan, are supposed to mark the track of her journey. She saw white deer, three of them, first at Clondrohid in Co. Cork. At Ballymakeera, there were six; crossing the Sullane and going up the hillside with its thickets of coppice wood, she found the nine, on a pleasant spot on the slope. Here was a crystal spring, little plots of quite good land amongst rocky bluffs, an outlook over the Sullane valley to the heathery rise of the Derrynasaggart hills. The idea of wild animals giving a sign to a saint is not confined to the Gobnet legend, St. Brendan of Clonfert is supposed to have told Finan Cam that he would know his chosen spot (Kinnitty) by finding the requisite number of wild pigs on it!

The traditions handed down orally tell of Gobnet's cure of sicknesses, how she cured one of her sick nuns and how she kept the plague out of Ballyvourney. Of how a robber tried to build a castle on a rock across the valley (near the modern Colaiste Iosagain) and how Gobnet destroyed his work as fast as he did it, by casting a stone ball across the glen. This smooth round black ball is now fixed in the wall of the mediaeval ruined church at Ballyvourney and pilgrims venerate it on the " round ". Again, Gobnet whose skill as a bee-keeper has resulted in her representation in art with beeskip and bees, had the inspiration to send her bees after a robber who had " lifted " all the local cattle. Rather unnecessarily the legend makes the bees turn into soldiers before attacking the unfortunate man and forcing him to give up his prey.

Gobnet's spiritual director was a certain St. Abban, whose grave is pointed out in a wood east of Gobnet's convent. Here is a cairn of stones, three ogam stones standing round it, and some rubbed bones kept in a tin box and used for cures. Some people still pay rounds here as well as at St. Gobnet's site. The legend of Abban, constructed out of material about at least two Abbans, makes him give Ballyvourney to Gobnet. But this is in a long list of early churches which Abban is said to have blessed for or given to their founders, and may mean little more than an attempt to exalt Abban above other saints or to establish claims of his monastery over certain territories. It cannot be used to establish Gobnet's date, when the ' Life ' of Abban is itself so confused and uncertain. Nor need we suppose that the Abban of the site near Ballyvourney was the same person as either of the famous Abbans, for the name is not uncommon. Gobnet then has no definite date; she may be 6th century, yet again she could be later.

The excavation of the site in 1951 did not produce any evidence that would date it exactly; equally what was found would fit into the general Gobnet tradition. Clearing a site for the new statue of Gobnet by Seamus Murphy, the overgrown mound known as St. Gobnet's House or Kitchen, revealed itself as a circular stone house. This was on the site of an older rectangular house of wood. In both earlier and later buildings, iron smelting had been carried on. This would not be an unusual activity at a self-supporting Celtic establishment. The finds, such as they were, indicated the keeping of cattle and sheep, the growing of grain, the use of the local hazel nuts for food among other items, a spindle whorl indicated the making of thread for weaving. The tradition connecting the old house with the Gobnet establishment may therefore be quite likely true. The mediaeval church as it now stands includes stones and carved fragments from an earlier 12th century structure. A cross inscribed stone, St. Gobnet's stone, with a cross and the figure of an ecclesiastic, which stands in the valley below, has been put as belonging to the second half of the 7th century. The little wooden statue of Gobnet kept in the parish church is thought to be 13th century. The reputed grave of Gobnet is a large mound in the graveyard at the site. Since the excavation and preservation works on " Gobnet's House ", it is of interest to note how the pilgrims have incorporated the structure into the traditional " round " of prayer, praying inside and outside the house, and making its small domestic well, a second holy well (additional to the fine spring lower down). The round is begun by saying a prayer in Irish to Gobnet:—

> Go mbeannaighe Dia dhuit, a Ghobnait Naofa
> Go mbeannaighe Muire dhuit agus beannaim féin duit;
> Is chughat a thánag a 'gearán mo scéil leat
> A's a d'iarraidh mo leighis ar son Dé ort.

(May God hail you, holy Gobnet. May Mary hail you and I salute you myself. I come to you complaining about my affairs and seeking my cure of you through God).

This prayer is a general formula used quite widely, the name of the saint being inserted according to choice and locality.

J.C.H.A.S.: Jan./June, 1952 issue:—

M. J. O'Kelly: *St. Gobnet's House, Ballyvourney, Co. Cork,* pp. 18-40;
F. Henry: *The Decorated Stones at Ballyvourney, Co. Cork,* pp. 41-42;
D. O hEaluighthe. *St. Gobnet of Ballyvourney,* pp. 43-61.

IBAR (IVOR)

April 23

Lóchet epscoip Ibair	The light of bishop Ibar
asort cenn cech erais,	who has smote heresy's head;
ánbreo úas tuind trilis,	a splendid flame over a sparkling
in hÉrinn Bice behais.	wave,
	In Becc-Eriu, he departed.
	(Martyrology of Oengus)

No ' Life ' of Ibar survives, but he is always coupled with the other pre-Patrician saints, and appears in their ' Lives '. He is said to have been the one who opposed Patrick most of all, on account of his foreign nationality. The Annals of Ulster give the dates 500 and 501 for his death, those of Inisfallen 499. His principal church was on Beggery Island in Wexford Harbour. This is now reclaimed land but was originally a series of marshy islets with tidal inlets between them. It would be an obvious point for early Christian infiltration into Ireland, with sea links with Wales and the continent. It seems to have grown into a sizeable monastery if the Litany of Irish saints is anyway correct in invoking: ' Three fifties of true monks under the yoke of

Bishop Ibar '. Ibar remained the object of a strong local devotion for a long time. Thus in around 1680 people still visited the old church on Beggary Island and claimed cures; a wooden statue of the saint was then preserved in this chapel. It is possible that the stories of the conflict between Patrick and Ibar rest on the fact that the Wexford area was then, as now, *sui generis*, a fertile corner cut off by river and hill from the rest of Ireland to a very large extent. It may have taken time to integrate it into the new nation-wide Church organisation.

ITA (IDE)

January 15

Foráith már ngur ngalar,
carais már tromm tredan,
in grían bán ban Mumam,
Ite Chluana credal.

She succoured many grievous diseases,
She loved many severe fastings,
The white sun of Munster's women,
Ita of Cluain Credal.

(Martyrology of Oengus)

Ita (Ide, or Mo Ide) is a 6th century saint to whom devotion is still very much alive and of whom the ' Life ' builds a quite coherent picture. There are three versions of the ' Life ' which seem to go back to a very early original, and set out clearly the monastic ideal. At the same time, other material and miracles in the text are in a different spirit, glorifying the sept of Uí Conaill Gabra, whose patron Ita was.

Ita was born in the Decies, of a family claiming royal blood. She was very beautiful, so that her family wanted more especially to make a good match for her, but she had set her mind wholly on God. She had a special devotion to the Holy Trinity; thus very early in her career a vision is described in which three precious stones are given to her, to symbolise the coming of the Three Persons of the Trinity to her, her body and soul the temple of God. Her family opposition was eventually overcome and Ita took the veil of the consecrated virgin, vowing virginity to God. We are back at the same early stage of development of religious life as with Brigit. Formal conventual organisation for women was in the making; women like Ita were fairly free to plan their own rule of life, and to organise the community that soon gathered around them.

Ita it would appear had to resist temptations and attacks by the devil as well as from her family. An angel told her after she had made her vow, to leave her home and kindred and go to Uí Conaill and settle under the hills of Sliabh Luachra (Mullaghareirk mountains). If Ita really lived in modern Decies, the Waterford area, she travelled quite a distance to found Cell Ita (Ceall Ide, modern Killeedy). But in her time, people called Deisi were living spread over a larger area, extending further west—the Deise Bec of Co. Limerick. Their centre was Bruff—Brugh na nDéise.

Killeedy is 5 miles south of Newcastle West, in the extreme south of Co. Limerick. Here the level Limerick plains meet the sudden uprise of the mountains to the south, rising to 1341 feet in Mullaghareirk. Killeedy lies on level agricultural land just at the foot of the hills. There is a good spring, now a holy well, at the old church site. Ita refused the offer of a large estate from the king of the Uí Conaill, having the good sense only to ask for enough ground for a garden which would be easily worked and managed, and supply the community with food. It seems to have amounted to about 4 acres.

Many other young women came to join Ita. Some came to be nuns, others for their education. Human nature was the same as ever, the 'Life' tells of one woman who fled the place before her illegitimate baby was born, in the end both she and her grown daughter came back to Ita. From the girls who were simply being educated at Killeedy, Ita is said to have picked a wife for a Connacht man called Beoan, a skilled builder in wood. Ita employed him in this capacity at Killeedy; there follows the miracle of Beoan being killed in a battle when he was called up for military service, and of Ita restoring him to life so that he could beget a child, the future St. Mochoemog.

Ita's most familiar title is " Foster mother of the Saints of Ireland ", and it is therefore noteworthy that the ' Life ' does not describe the small boys, who would become saints, who were sent to be brought up by her. They are mentioned in other ' Lives ' and it would appear fairly certain that she did educate some young boys. " St. Ita loved much fosterage " wrote Cuimin of Connor in a poem about her. Brendan of Clonfert was supposed to be her most famous fosterling, but it is possible they were too near contemporaries for her to have brought him up. Hagiographers were keen to make " their " saint a fosterling of Ita, or to exalt Ita by bringing her into contact with some other famous name. Many religious women would have undertaken the same work at this period.

Ita, according to the 'Life', spent her time mainly at Killeedy; monks, nuns and ordinary folk came in numbers to visit her and ask advice or help. It would appear that the sisters would have such medical skill as then existed to treat the sick.

Ita's own spiritual life was based on penance and asceticism, on vigil, fast and prayer, with the special characteristic of devotion to the Holy Trinity. This, with a vivid sense of the indwelling of the Holy Trinity in the soul, is said to mark a very high level of union with God. Ita's answer to another woman religious, who asked the secret of her being so loved and favoured by God, was to stress continual prayer and contemplation of the Trinity. To do so, meant God was always with Ita; He was the source of all her power. To Brendan, Ita answers in the conventional form of a triad, the three things most displeasing to God:—the face that hates mankind, the will that clings to the love of evil, putting entire trust in riches. The three things most pleasing to God:—the firm belief of a pure heart in God, a simple religious life, liberality with charity.

One of the notes to the Martyrology of Oengus gives the legend of Ita asking for the baby Jesus to nurse, and the same entry gives the Irish lullaby she sang to him. This nursing of the infant Jesus is a common hagiographical theme, one may instance Adamnan being seen with Him, or the very late legend of St. Anthony of Padua. The Ita story cannot be accepted as at all likely to have happened, but it does stand for a symbol of Ita's love of our Lord, and for her work of fostering Him in the persons of her young charges. Robin Flower wrote a fine metrical version of Ita's hymn (p. 56, " The Irish Tradition ", Oxford 1947).

Ita, like other Irish saints, used also to go off at times into a secret hermitage for uninterrupted prayer.

She died at Killeedy in 570 and was buried there. Earlier, on the more material plane, the Annals of Innisfallen note at the year 553 " The battle of Cuilen gained by the Corcu Oche through the prayer of Ite ". In the ' Life ' another victory by the Uí Conaill over much larger hostile forces, is also attributed to Ita's prayers.

Killeedy is also known as Clúain Credal, holy meadow. Not far off is another foundation of Ita's, named from the pet name Mo Ita (Ide) Mide, My Ita, Kilmeedy. There are two Decies churches of Ita

Kilmeedy near Youghal (Cill mo Íde) and Kilmeadan (Cill mo Ídeán), Waterford. Her name is also found in the Westmeath placename, Rosmead, and some Cornish churches were dedicated to her. She was one of the Irish saints known and invoked on the continent in ancient litanies; she is mentioned as well in Alcuin's poem about some Irish saints (Patrick, Ciaran, Columban, Comgall, Adamnan, Brigit, Ita).

After Ita's time, Killeedy seems to have ceased to be a community of women and become one of men. The Vikings plundered it twice. Devotion to Ita is still very much alive in all the district round Killeedy. On the feast day, there are the traditional prayers and rounds at the old church site, and in the parish church, a high Mass with special preacher. It is a local holiday, which if it falls on a Friday, is important enough to be granted a local dispensation from the law of abstinence. It is a day of family reunions and social gatherings in the people's homes. Ita is a common baptismal name in the district.

JARLATH OF TUAM

June 6

Very little is known of St. Jarlath—he is mentioned in the ' Lives ' of other saints and an attempt made to give him a Patrician link by the statement that he was a disciple of Benen. He made a first foundation at Cluain Fois, Cloonfush, about $1\frac{3}{4}$ miles west of Tuam; later he moved to Tuam itself. Jarlath flourished in the 6th century; it is said he taught Brendan of Clonfert and Colman of Cloyne. His holy well half a mile from Tuam drew a large crowd of pilgrims on June 6th, until the 1840's.

Nothing remains of Jarlath's monastic settlement at Tuam, which appears to have been very famous, except for the fine but restored high cross in the market square. A silver or silver gilt shrine of St. Jarlath was kept at a chapel, Teampul na Scrine, at Tuam until its loss in 1830. The Annals mention the violation of the protection of Jarlath's yellow crozier, the Bachall Buidhe, in 1136.

KILIAN OF AÜBIGNY
November 13

Kilian (Chillen is the earliest form of the name) was a contemporary of Fiacre. He had gone on a pilgrimage to Rome and returning, came into contact with St. Faro, bishop of Meaux, who found him a hermitage at Aubigny near Arras. Here Kilian settled down for the rest of his life. Fiacre arrived slightly later, and was in his turn accommodated with a hermitage site by St. Faro.

KILIAN OF WÜRZBURG
July 8

Servi Christi,	Servants of Christ,
Sunt tres iste,	These three
Colonatus et Totnanus	Colonat and Totnan
Et beatus Chilianus.	And holy Kilian.

(from an old sequence for
the feast of Kilian)

At the present time, St. Kilian (Cillian, Killian) is the only Irish saint whose feast is celebrated liturgically in Germany; his Office in the Irish supplement to the Roman breviary the only one (1960) to mention a city in Germany. Originally celebrated throughout western Germany, his feast is now only celebrated in Würzburg—it is actually the feast of the three martyrs, Kilian and his two companions. After Gall, Kilian is the most popular Irish saint's name given to boys on the continent.

St. Kilian was undoubtedly Irish but his place of birth in Ireland and his parents are not known. There is a tradition of the parish of Mullagh in Kilmore diocese, claiming to have been his birthplace; Mullagh used to have a pattern in his honour. Another Irish connection has been thought to be Tuosist in the Beara Peninsula in Kerry, also with a pattern, but it seems more likely that saint there remembered was a St. Coinleán rather than a St. Celléne, whose commemoration was later confused with the Kilian entries in the

Martyrologies. The Kerry saint may be some quite local individual of a similar sounding name.

Kilian with eleven companions left Ireland and arrived at the mouth of the Rhine; perhaps the landfall was Ascaffenburg where there is today a church commemorating their coming. They would, in this case, have sailed up the Rhine and up the Main which flows into it. Würzburg on the Main became Kilian's headquarters in a pagan country. He is regarded as the apostle of Thuringia and Eastern Franconia. He was, it appears, well received and his mission was highly successful. Duke Gozbert who was the ruler of Würzburg was converted from the worship of Diana (or perhaps better, a local goddess identified with her by writers familiar with the classical mythology). After this very satisfactory start to his work, Kilian decided to go to Rome to report and to obtain full papal approval of his work. He is said to have spent two years there; the fact that the visit was to Conon, whose pontificate only lasted from 686-7, fixes Kilian's period very exactly.

Meantime Duke Gozbert had married his brother's widow. When Kilian came back from Rome, he denounced the Duke and the lady, who was not unnaturally highly incensed. She therefore hired two assassins who set on Kilian and two other monks, Colman and Totnan, killing all three. The martyrdom probably took place in 687 or 689. In 752 the relics of the martyrs were solemnly translated to Würzburg cathedral by the Bishop, Burchard, and the spread and development of the cult of Kilian seems to date from this. It is linked too with the development of Würzburg as a cultural and strategic centre at the same period. Probably at the time of the translation of the relics (752) the first account of Kilian's martyrdom was compiled. (The first " Passio Sancti Kiliani ", which was later followed by a second version.) Kilian's importance is realised when he is found, with Boniface, amongst the mainly Roman saints of the calendar of Godescale (probably of 781-3); this calendar in fact places him only second to Boniface in his patronage of the eastern territories of the Franks. An early mention of Kilian from a document of 799, naming a church of Kilian (chirihsahha sancti Kilianes).

The Godescalc calendar simply notes the martyrdom of Kilian and his companions. The " Passio " puts their number at two and gives their names, Colonatus (Colman) and Totnanus (Totnan or Dothan), so that both of them were Irish like Kilian. Kilian's martyrdom was known in Ireland at least at the beginning of the 9th century, for he appears in the Martyrology of Tallaght. But the entry records a different story:—

S. Celiani Scotti martyris cum Sanctis fratribus Aedh ocus Tadg ocus Amarma, conjuge Regis Cothorum truncati a preposito domus regiae in ippodromia Palatii regis.

Here are two Irish monks with quite different names, linked with that of a Gothic queen and killed by the prefect of the royal palace in its hippodrome. It would appear to be an insoluble problem to discover whether the martyrology here combined two different sources, or whether it invented names for the companions of Kilian.

Kilian's head and those of his two companions were enshrined in silver shrines in Würzburg cathedral. In the Middle Ages, the figure of St. Kilian was stamped on the seals and coinage of Würzburg. Since 1926, Würzburg has had an annual mystery play on St. Kilian's life. This is part of the great celebration of his feast, the Kilianifest. In 1952, there were special celebrations for the 12th centenary of the translation of the relics.

In Ireland, the parish church of Mullagh is dedicated to Kilian, and another church at Greystones, Co. Wicklow. This latter was begun in 1866 and put under Kilian's protection to guard the people from the then active Protestant attempts at converting them. The church has a quite attractive figure of Kilian. In America, there are schools and colleges dedicated to Kilian.

There are a number of hymns and folksongs, both in Latin and German, in Kilian's honour, some old, some modern. The oldest German one is the " Ruff ", beginning " Wit ruffen an den thewrei Mann, St. Kilian ". The text of this together with other popular hymn in German and some ancient Latin ones for the feast as well, is give in the Irish Ecclesiastical Record, 1910, Jan/June. vol. 27, pp 655-665 " Hymns and Folksongs in Honour of St. Kilian, St. Colonatus and St. Totnan ".

Herbipolis Jubilans: Würzburg, 1952. Studies on Kilian and Würzburg fc the centenary celebrations.

A. Gwynn, S.J.: *New Light on St. Kilian.* I.E.R., July, 1957, pp. 1-16. *Irelan and Würzburg in the Middle Ages.* Dec., 1952, pp. 401-411.

John Hennig: *Ireland and Germany in the Tradition of St. Kilian.* I.E.R., July 1952, pp. 21-33.

Andreas Bigelmair. *Die Passio des deiligen Kilian und seinar Gefährten.* Wür: burger Diönzesangeschiehisblätter. xiv-xv, pp. 1-25. German translation c the Passio Prima and Passio Secunda. *Die Gründung der Mitteldeutsche Bistümer.* The Irish mission of Kilian. In *Sankt Bonifatius,* 1954, pp. 247-8

LASERIAN (LAISREN)

April 18

Laserian, Laisren, or in the affectionate form, Molaise, of Leighlin, was an important 7th century saint, who worked both in Ireland and Scotland, dying in 639.

The surviving ' Life ' is late and of little historical value. Laisrén moccu Imde seems to have been of royal Ulster stock, but chronological difficulties rule out Cairell, king of Ulster, being his father as is claimed, but he may have been his grandfather. He studied with St. Munnu (Fintan of Taghmon); finally came to Leighlin (Lethglenn, half-glen, a fold in the hills). Here was an established monastery which Laserian took over, the legend makes its previous abbot St. Goban make a gift of it to Molaise.

In his youth, Laserian visited Scotland and was later venerated there. He is the patron of Holy Island, Lamlash Bay, Arran, in the Clyde. This island has a cave of Molaise. The name Lamlash is derived from Eilean M'Laise.

Although Molaise is said to have studied with Fintan Munnu, he opposed him over the question of the new Roman calculations for the date of Easter. Laserian is said to have gone abroad, to Rome, to bring back revised texts of scripture and books on church order and things like the Easter question. Laserian strongly supported the new method of calculating the date of Easter, and Leighlin was a centre promoting its adoption.

There is a story about Molaise of Leighlin in the ' Life ' of St. Magnenn of Kilmainham (Text in O'Grady: Silva Gadelica, I, 37-49: II, 35-49). Magnenn came to Molaise and found him lying crosswise in a hovel with thirty diseases. Molaise explained why he had these numerous complaints:—" I will declare it, holy bishop: my condition is revealed to me as being such that my sinfulness like a flame goes through my body; so then, I want to have my purgatory here and find eternal life on the other side. For, Magnenn, the grain of wheat must be threshed and beaten before it is sown in the earth; so with me before I am laid in the grave. I would have my body threshed with infirmities ". Finally Laserian asked Magnenn to preside at his funeral.

The pattern, centring on the holy well at Leighlin, ceased in 1812, when the parish priest put a stop to it. But the memory of the saint and of the power of the water was still alive, and after a local farmer had received a cure, the devotion was revived. In 1914, the well was restored, solemnly blessed and the ancient cross, a plain stone one, 4½ feet high, re-erected. The well is now once more visited by pilgrims; some traditional stories about Laserian are still remembered in the district.

LIADHAIN (LELIA)

August 11

Liadhain, latinised as Lelia, is the name of several, all obscure, Irish women saints. Ciaran of Saighir's mother was named Liadhain and is said, in old age, to have founded a church near her son's monastery.

The Liadhain who has made an appearance in the Limerick diocesan calendar (and as a result of an error, quite wrongly, for a time in that of Kerry), belongs to Limerick. Her church, Killeely, marked by an old graveyard is ½ mile north west of Thomond Bridge, Limerick city. In the Black Book of Limerick (c. 1200) this church is named Kelliedun, but an alternative reading of the text is Kelliedini. The " Genealogiae Regum et Sanctorum Hiberniae " gives a Liadhain among the Dalcassian saints, whose feast day falls on August 11. She would seem therefore to be the patron of Killeely. She was the daughter of Diarmuid, who was a grandson of the Cairtheann baptised by Patrick at Singland. This genealogy would make both Liadhain of Limerick and Munchin, descendants of a common ancestor, Cas, but not, as is sometimes claimed, brother and sister.

M. Moloney: *Killeely and Kilfinane: Their patrons*. North Munster Antiquarian Journal vol. 1, no. 1, 1936, p. 39.

LIVINUS

November 12

Livinus or Liévin is most probably a doublet of Liafwin. The latter was an Englishman who died in 773. He was the apostle of the Frisians. The alleged ' Life ' of Livinus has been shown to be a fictitious composition written later than 1007 : Kenny commented on it that its " testimony is of more value for the fame of Irish missionaries in the mind of a hagiographer of the 11th century than for the authenticity of an Irish Livinus in the 7th ". The account claims Livinus to have been martyred c. 660, on the continent.

For a discussion of the ideas about Ireland in the composition of such fictitious biographies, the reader is referred to John Hennig's paper on " The Place of the Archdiocese of Dublin in the Hagiographical Tradition of the Continent ", Reportorium Novum, vol. 1, no. 1, 1955. He points out that whilst the material is not historical in regard to the history of the saint, it is of great importance in tracing and understanding continental ideas and information about Ireland.

LORCAN UA TUATHAIL (LAURENCE O'TOOLE)

November 14

Suscitator mortuorum,	Raiser of the dead,
Reparator oculorum,	Restorer of sight,
Emundator leprosorum,	Cleanser of lepers,
Preces nostras suscipe.	Receive our prayers.

(from a hymn in St.
Lorcan's honour)

Lorcan Ua Tuathail (Laurence O'Toole), a contemporary of Thomas à Becket, was archbishop of Dublin during the first Anglo-Norman attack. He stands therefore at the end of the development of a purely Irish, with some Scandinavian admixture, culture. His story forms the natural term to a study of the Celtic saints of Ireland. He was the sort of a man that the reforms with which the names of Cellach and Mael Maedoc are linked, were producing in the Irish Church before the irruption and disruption caused by the invaders. Like Mael Maedoc, he died on the continent and his biographer was a canon of Eu, with little knowledge of Lorcan's Irish background. Native sources on Lorcan's activities are very few, and thus the would-be biographer is left with hardly any information about what he wants to know—the full story of Lorcan's relations with the invaders. The biography is in the ordinary stream of conventional hagiography. On the continent, Lorcan was widely invoked for all manner of help in all difficulties, and against this devotion and the miracle stories, it is hard to realise that the Lorcan the historian looks for was a man who had to negotiate with that same king Henry of England whose actions had led to Thomas à Becket's murder in Canterbury cathedral. The easiest approach to Lorcan's career is perhaps a kind of time chart:—

c. 1123. Lorcan born.

1148. Abbot of Glendalough. 1152 Refuses bishopric thereof.

1152. March 9. Synod of Kells. The four archbishoprics of Armagh, Dublin, Tuam and Cashel established and the pallia conferred.

1162. Lorcan Archbishop of Dublin.

1164. January. In England. The Constitutions of Clarendon. Muirchertach, Lorcan's father, dies.

1166. Diarmait Mac Murchadha, king of Leinster, leaves Ireland to seek allies.

1167. Mac Murchadha returns in August with a small force of Norman, Welsh and Flemish supporters. Further reinforcements came in 1169.

1170. August 23. Arrival of Robert Fitzstephen and Earl Richard Fitzgilbert (Strongbow) in Ireland.

1170. September 21. Fall of Dublin. December 29. Thomas à Becket killed.

1171. May. Death of Mac Murchadha. Synod of Cashel winter 71-72.

1171. October 17. Henry II lands in Ireland. Leaves April 17, 1172.

1175. Treaty of Windsor.

1179. Lorcan goes through England to Rome for the Third Lateran Council.

1180. To England and the Continent, dying at Eu on November 14.

1226. December 11. Lorcan Ua Tuathail canonised.

The political history of the period could be summed up as the jockeying for power and the high kingship of rivals from the different provinces of Ireland, Mac Murchadha's ambitions and efforts ending in his calling in Anglo-Norman help. Yet we would mistake the period to see it as a modern national struggle. Each Norman leader was striking for his own hand. Moreover the feudal system's claims were different from those of a modern conqueror—an Irish king could have acknowledged the English king's overlordship without feeling that there would be any essential change in his own territory and its government.

Lorcan Ua Tuathail came from the province most deeply concerned in the invasion, Leinster. He was of noble blood, for his father, Muirchertach, and some of his other immediate ancestors were local kings. 14 of his ancestors had been kings of Leinster. When Muirchertach died, in 1164, he was described as "lord of Ui Muiredaig and a prince of the Leinsterman in hospitality and valour". Meantime the ruling king of Leinster was Diarmait Mac Murchadha. He and the Ua Tuathail family were on reasonably good terms, he married a daughter of Muirchertach, and he did not interfere with Ua Tuathail's control of Glendalough. Young Lorcan spent a time as hostage with Diarmait and was then, it appears, not too well treated. This ill treatment may have been exaggerated in the telling to some extent; there is, for example, no evidence later on that Diarmait did anything but approve Lorcan's appointment to Dublin as archbishop.

Lorcan next studied at Glendalough and became its abbot at the early age of 25, in 1148. But he refused the bishopric when this became vacant in 1152. That was the year of the Synod of Kells, when the much sought after pallia were eventually conferred on the four archbishops of Ireland, of Armagh, Cashel, Dublin and Tuam.

Ten years later, in 1162, clergy and people of the archdiocese of Dublin chose Lorcan to be the new archbishop. The Primate and the bishops of Kildare and Ferns were probably the prelates who consecrated Lorcan. In Glendalough, he was succeeded by his nephew Thomas—here Mac Murchadha tried to get in a candidate of his own but failed to do so.

It is of interest that Lorcan in Glendalough followed in the track of Coemgen and used to spend Lent in the latter's cave on the crag face of the Upper Lake. Intelligent, ascetic, charitable, that is one's impression of Lorcan. He also followed in the track of Cellach and Mael Maedoc in forwarding the spread of the Augustinian Canons in Ireland, in fact becoming one of them after his move to Dublin.

Meantime, the ard ri, the Ulster Muirchertach Mac Lochlainn, was killed in a revolt against his authority in 1166. This gave the Connacht leader, Ruaidhri Ua Conchobhair, his chance, and he was able to take possession of the high kingship. Mac Lochlainn's fall involved Diarmait Mac Murchadha of Leinster, and the latter fled abroad to seek help where he could. His great ally was Earl Richard Fitzgilbert, the famous " Strongbow " to whom he gave his daughter Eva in marriage and promised the right of succession in Leinster. It is evident that king Henry of England became really afraid that Strongbow and others of his ilk would establish a rival kingdom of their own in Ireland, and it was for this reason, to make certain of their vassalage, not to conquer native Ireland, that he himself came to Ireland in the autumn of 1171.

It is very difficult to trace Lorcan Ua Tuathail in these affairs— he must, as archbishop of Dublin, have been in the very thick of them—he was at the siege of Dublin and a negotiator between the two sides; but we have no information about his real views on the invasion or the details of his work concerning it. The impression is that he worked first for resistance to the invasion but as it gathered strength, he realised that it would be impossible to dislodge the Anglo-Normans and tried to accept and make the best of the resulting situation.

It seems possible that Lorcan may have been a negotiator in that initial treaty of 1169, when Mac Murchadha and his allies had already begun their effort to gain Leinster and extend Mac Murchadha's power. In this treaty, Mac Murchadha was acknowledged as king of Leinster by the ard ri, Ua Conchobhair, in turn he was to acknowledge the latter as high king, and he was to send his allies home to England. Mac Murchadha, in fact, immediately broke his agreement and in August of 1170, his ally Strongbow arrived in Ireland. The latter captured Waterford on 25 August 1170, and next moved against Dublin. Negotiations were begun between the two parties, in which Lorcan, the archbishop, was concerned, and in which Mac Murchadha demanded the city admit his overlordship and give thirty hostages. The Danes refused these terms, and the city fell after an attack on 21 September 1170.

It does not appear that there is a case for supposing that Lorcan was at this time in any way defeatist in outlook; he was concerned in the negotiations over Dublin, but equally he was concerned in working for the effort to recover the city. In May of 1171, Mac Murchadha died, thus leaving Strongbow in sole control of Leinster. The Danish king of Dublin, Hasculf, who had fled in September of the previous year, now returned to the attack with reinforcements which he had gone to collect. His attempt to seize Dublin in May failed, but in June the city was blockaded by sea by a fleet sent from the Isle of Man, and by land by an Irish army. The blockade failed when the besieged were able to make a sortie into the Irish camp and seize supplies, the bulk of the Irish then being absent cutting the harvest which otherwise could have supplied the Normans with food. Lorcan meantime was in Dublin and acted on Strongbow's behalf to negotiate with Ua Conchobhair—the former offered to acknowledge the ard ri, if his kingship of Leinster was also acknowledged. The high king in fact rejected these proposals. We do not know what Lorcan's personal views on the question were, that he was instrumental in the new attack on Dublin being mounted suggests he had not lost all hope of dislodging the invader. That he acted as a negotiator for Strongbow could mean merely that the archbishop was the natural choice in such work, or imply the further conclusion that Lorcan began to think it might be best to make the best of a bad bargain and let Strongbow rule Leinster.

On October 17th, 1171, Henry II arrived in Ireland. He succeeded in getting Strongbow, as well as a number of Irish princes, to do homage to him. It appears however that the leaders of the Church did not make any formal submission to Henry, they regarded this as a matter for the civil authorities. They did inform Rome of the political events in Ireland. During the winter of 1171-2, the period Henry was in Ireland, there was a synod held at Cashel. The papal legate, Christian Ua Conairche, bishop of Lismore, a man who had been a monk of St. Bernard's, presided. The synod proposed to accept the customs of the English church for Ireland—perhaps this means of the universal Church which could be most conveniently copied from England? In September of 1172, the Pope, Alexander III, wrote to the legate and the clergy of Ireland asking them to promote reform and be faithful to the English king, to whom the Pope also wrote asking him to forward reform.

But if Lorcan and other Irish clerics had hoped that the Anglo-Norman invaders could be peacefully integrated into the country and the life of the Church go smoothly forward, it was soon obvious that the very reverse was taking place. Further fighting led in the end to the attempt to stabilise the position by the Treaty of Windsor of 1175. Lorcan was a witness to this Treaty and we may suppose that he was a leading negotiator. It set out to define the Norman held areas of Ireland and to give a feudal organisation to the kingdoms of Meath and Leinster. By now it was obvious that the incomers could not be dislodged. What is striking about Lorcan's position in the tangled affairs of the time is that he seems to have been liked by Irish, Scandinavian and Norman in his diocese. There were no national divisions in the petitions for his canonisation.

The Treaty of Windsor, in which Ruaidhri Ua Conchobhair had acknowledged the overlordship of Henry, did not in fact work. Nor should it be forgotten that Henry had been the author of the Constitutions of Clarendon, in which the king took upon himself a number of quite necessary reforms of the Church—but which belonged to the Church and not to the State to put into motion. Out of that had come the martyrdom of Thomas à Becket, who stood for the freedom of the Church from State control. Over in Ireland, Lorcan seems to have had to try to deal with English clerical place hunters of very dubious morals, and with royal encroachments on powers belonging to the Church. There is a small amount of evidence which suggests that Lorcan was playing a parallel role to Becket in Ireland. Henry apparently as part of his efforts in the way of expiation for the murder in the cathedral, founded a house of Augustinian Canons in Dublin in 1177. Lorcan assisted at this foundation, the Canons belonged to the congregation of St. Victor, this was the first house to be established in Ireland of that particular group of Augustinians. It was in another of the St. Victor Canons' houses, that of Eu in Normandy, that Lorcan died.

At the end of 1178, Alexander III sent special envoys to call the bishops of the Church to a general council, the Third Lateran, which was to meet in Rome in the following Lent—actually from March 5-22nd, 1179. The Irish delegates to the council were Lorcan of Dublin, Cadhla Ua Dubhthaig (Catholicus) of Tuam, Brictius of Limerick, Constantine Ua Briain of Killaloe, Augustin Ua Sealbhaigh of Waterford and Felix of Lismore (Felim). Nobody went from Armagh and it may be that the king would only allow those bishops who were ' collaborators ' to go. They had to travel via England and see the king, to whom they were forced to promise to do nothing in Rome against the interests of the English king and the English state.

In Rome they must have given the Pope a full account of the political position in Ireland and of its effects on the Church. The bishop of Lismore seems to have continued as papal legate until this year; now the Pope appointed Lorcan in his stead. From the Pope, Lorcan got two important bulls, one dated 20 April 1179 guaranteed to Lorcan and his successors in Dublin, papal protection for all the rights of his church and of the five suffragan sees of Glendalough, Kildare, Ferns, Leighlin and Ossory. The other, of 13 May 1179, gave similar protection for the bishop of Glendalough, Malchus. It would seem that there was pressure being put by the king on the Church in Ireland as he had attempted in England, and in fact, some twenty years after Lorcan's death, the Anglo-Normans did succeed in abolishing the separate diocese of Glendalough.

Lorcan was back in Dublin in the summer of 1179. Later that year a synod met at Clonfert, at which he was present. Legislation was passed against the continued abuse of lay control of church appointments, seven so-called bishops, actually laymen, were deposed from their sees. Legislation was also passed against the ordination of the sons of bishops and priests.

During the winter of 1179-80, the archbishop of Armagh, Gilla-in-Choimhdebh Ua Carain, died. Lorcan must have been concerned with the appointment, in January 1180, of his successor, Tomaltach Ua Conchobhair. This choice was right out of the ordinary list of candidates for a northern archbishopric, for Tomaltach was a nephew of the reigning ard ri and grandson of a former one. It is possible that this was all a part of what appears to have been Lorcan's policy, of accepting the Norman invasion since nothing could be done to get them out, but also of trying to maintain the rights of the high king. It is possible that the north did not approve of this new archbishop from Connacht and that they therefore did not record Lorcan's death in the Annals of Ulster, a kind of silent disapproval of the man's policies. This same winter, the last Lorcan was to know in Ireland, was a hard one and he exerted himself as well on relief works.

In 1180 a quarrel broke out between Henry and Ruaidhri Ua Conchobhair. Lorcan, again acting as peace maker, went to England, but this seems only to have been cover for more vital matters. It was not, apparently, as so often stated, Ruaidhri's son that he took with him as a hostage, but his own nephew. The main affair was between Lorcan and the king. The latter resented the papal bulls Lorcan had obtained. Indeed the king's policy toward the Church was well shown by his action in the Dublin archdiocese after Lorcan's death, first seizing on its temporalities for himself for a whole year and then forcing a man of his choice on the diocese, John Comin. Sometime early in 1180, Lorcan met a very angry Henry in England. Whatever happened between the two men, the king had the ports closed against Lorcan getting back to Ireland. The King left Portsmouth for

Normandy on April 15th. Lorcan eventually set out to follow him. It is even uncertain whether he did manage to see the king on the continent, or whether, as the story is usually told, he took ill and died at the Augustinian Canons' house of Eu on his way to the king. He died on November 14th, 1180. It is possible, if he had not in fact seen the king earlier, that if he had gone on, he might have met a similar fate to Becket's. For there are some brief but significant phrases used of Lorcan. Abbot Hughes of Eu, in a letter to Innocent II, said that Lorcan had died " with us an exile and outcast for the liberty of the Church ". Marianus, bishop of Cork, in his testimony urging Lorcan's canonisation, wrote that he had been sent into exile on account of English persecution. This reads very much like the Becket affair.

The various letters sent to Rome urging Lorcan's canonisation are of extreme interest, in that they record an immediate and widespread cult (as with Becket earlier on) covering all Ireland. Abroad at Eu, where he died, a similar and very extensive devotion sprang into being. The bishops who bore testimony to Lorcan's holiness were both Irish and Anglo-Norman, and one of them, the already mentioned John Comin, on a visit to Eu had actually seen a man cured at Lorcan's tomb. This man had been deaf and dumb for fifteen years.

Although the petitions for canonisation followed quickly on Lorcan's death, various delays intervened, and the actual canonisation did not come till 1226. Early on, it seems that the Canons of Eu had both accounts of Lorcan's Irish miracles and of his career brought out from Ireland; the surviving *Vita Sancti Laurentii* seems to have been written just after the canonisation. Its author was a French canon of Eu, most probably Jean Halgrinus of Abbeville, later to be archbishop of Besançon.

Charles Plummer: *Vie et miracles de S. Laurent, archevêque de Dublin.* Analecta Bollandiana, t. 33 (1914), pp. 121-186. Critical edition of the *Vita Sancti Laurentii.*

J. Ryan, S.J.: *The Ancestry of St. Laurence O'Toole.* Reportorium Novum, vol. i, 1955, pp. 64-75.

J. F. O'Doherty: *St. Laurence O Toole and the Anglo-Norman Invasion.* I.E.R., I. November, 1937, pp. 459-477. II. December, 1937, pp. 600-625. III. February, 1938, pp. 131-146.

A. Gwynn, S.J.: *St. Laurence O'Toole as Legate in Ireland* (1179-80). Analecta Bollandiana, t. 68 (1950), pp. 223-240.

Myles V. Ronan: *St. Laurentius, Archbishop of Dublin. Original Testimonies for Canonisation.* I.E.R., I. April, 1926, pp. 347-364. This paper prints the testimony of John Comin of Dublin, Eugene of Armagh, Albin of Ferns and Marianus of Cork.

II, September, 1926, pp. 247-256. The second paper continues the series and includes the testimony of the Archbishop of Rouen and the Abbot of Eu. Also material about the translation of the relics.

III. November, 1926, pp. 467-480. Further testimonies, and text of the Office for St. Lorcan, part of the extensive liturgical material relating to him, originating, of course, from Eu in Normandy.

IV. December, 1926, pp. 596-612. *Lessons, Hymns, Litanies and Prayers.* Continues the printing of extracts from the liturgy for the feast and its octave. Includes also a litany in honour of Lorcan and a set of prayers to ask his help for the remission of sins, for a good life, a happy death, for cures, for deliverance from troubles, from plague, for peace in time of war.

P. J. Dunning: *The Arroasian Order in Mediaeval Ireland.* Irish Historical Studies. September, 1945, pp. 297-315.

It is of bibliographical interest that Fr. O'Hanlon began his work of writing and publishing the *Lives of the Irish Saints* by bringing out a separate *Life of St. Laurence O Toole* in 1857. In this he included a prospectus of his proposed 12 volume work on the saints.

MACARTAN

March 24

Aedh Macartan, the son of Caerthen, appears to belong to a very early generation of Irish saints—he is in fact said to have been placed in Clogher by St. Patrick. It may be supposed that he was one of the earlier outstanding saints but the fragmentary 'Lives' give little certain information about him. O'Hanlon recorded (at August 15th) that his grave in Clogher was for long pointed out and venerated, and that people used to take earth from it as a relic.

It is curious that, apart from a late mediaeval Office of St. Patrick, the only liturgical Office to survive from an Irish source is one of St. Macartan. All the other surviving old Offices of Irish saints are from continental sources.

" The Great Shrine of St. MacCarthinn " intended to contain relics including a fragment of the True Cross, is identified with the still extant " Domnach Airgid ". This seems to have been originally a simple wooden box. It was covered with metal plates as early as the 7th or 8th centuries, further decorations being added as time went on. In later times, it contained a gospel but was not intended originally as a book shrine. Other relics connected with Clogher (Co. Tyrone) are two high crosses at the place itself, and the 13th century processional Cross of Clogher.

E. C. R. Armstrong and H. J. Lawlor: *The Domnach Airgid.* P.R.I.A., 34 C (1917-19), pp. 96-126.

MAC NISSE (MACANISIUS)

September 3

Oengus Mac Nisi (Mac Nisse), also known as Coeman Breac, died early in the 6th century. Patrick, it is claimed, baptised him, the Tripartite Life describes young Mac Nisse as reading his psalms with Patrick. Mac Nisse was named from his mother, Cnes or Ness, his father's name was Forbrecc.

It would seem that he belongs to the early, and little recorded, group of Irish saints. Men like Mac Nisse were the first fruits of the Patrician mission. He chose himself a hermitage on the Kells water (which later grew into Kells monastery), the Desert of Connor, and later seems to have become bishop of his own clan in that area. A cross shaft with sculptured panels survives at Connor (Co. Antrim). But very little else is certainly known, the ' Life ' is late, probably compiled after the Anglo-Norman invasion, though it may include older traditional material. It makes Mac Nisse prophesy the foundation of Colman's Lann Ela, which may be intended to give a historical basis and reason for the subsequent close relations that existed between that monastery and Connor. A suggestion of what Connor itself became comes from Oengus, who speaks in his Martyrology of ' Macc nisse co mílib, ó Chonderib máraib '; Macnisse with thousands, from great Connor.'

G. R. Burck: *The High Cross of Connor, Co. Antrim.* Ulster Journ. Arch., 1903, p. 41.

MAEDOC (AEDAN/EDAN/MOEDHOG/MOGUE)

January 31

Maedoc of Ferns died in 626. His name is found in a variety of forms; he was baptised Aed, and then his fosterers, a family of Ua Dubthaig (O'Duffy), his nurturers " openly gave him through love and affection an eke-name, calling him habitually ' my little Hugh ' (mo Aodh óg), so that the name Maedoc stuck to him as a surname to the exclusion of other names " (Irish Life. II in Plummer). Thus the name is found as Maedoc, Moedhóg, Moeog, anglicised Mogue, and from the original Aedh, as Aedan and Edan. The name is far from being uncommon and a number of other Irish saints bore it, thus the Maedoc of Cill Mhaodhain (Kilmodan) in Glendaruel, Cowal, Scotland, is probably the saint of March 23rd, that Oengus styles " my Maedoc, Alba's diadem ". The name is also found in Welsh place names—Llawhaden at Nolton, Haroldston West and Solfach in Pembrokeshire, Llanmadog in Gower, Capel Madog in the Elan valley, Radnor. As the ' Lives ' bring Maedoc of Ferns into contact with David of Wales, most probably chronologically incorrect if we accept an early date for David's death, it is quite likely that he did visit Wales, David's name standing as a kind of symbol for his so doing. Wales and Wexford are near enough and the Welsh names may relate to Maedoc of Ferns.

There are a number of ' Lives ' of Maedoc in Latin and Irish, but they tell little about the saint himself, though a great deal about customs, traditions and the monastic claims of the time when they were compiled, long after Maedoc's death. Ferns and Taghmon, both in Wexford, were rival monasteries, each backed by the local ruler, and the Maedoc ' Lives ' are concerned to exalt Ferns. All the ' Lives ' except one suppose Maedoc buried at Ferns. The exception is a long account in Irish (II in Plummer's edition), which seems to be derived from two sources, one southern (Ferns) and one northern (Rossinver). This states explicitly that Maedoc was buried at Rossinver. It does not seem possible to accept O'Hanlon's way out of the difficulty by making Maccoige, son of Eochaidh (January 5th), the saint of Rossinver. Maedoc appears definitely as its patron.

Maedoc belonged to Connacht—as that province was then known—the boundaries have changed a little with time, and his father Setna (Sedna) was descended from Conn of the Hundred Battles. His mother's was Eithne. One version makes Maedoc's parents go to Drumlane to pray for a son to be born to them, others make Drumlane a fresh foundation of Maedoc's. He was, anyway, born on Inis Breachmhaigh (Braighwee, St. Mogue's Island), an island in Templeport Lough, Co. Cavan. Here still survive the foundations of a church (late 15th early 16th century in date), together with some carved stones and old querns in the graveyard. It appears that this church was once the principal one of Magh Sleacht—the district in which it is; a mainland church at Templeport was founded c. 1400, but that on the island still continued to exist as well.

Templeport Lough is north of the main road from Ballinamore to

Ballyconnell, south of Slieve Rushen. Rossinver lies north-west from it, at the head of Lough Melvin in Co. Leitrim, and the saint's northern birthplace would seem to bear out the claim that Rossinver was a personal foundation. The 'Lives' bring Maedoc into contact with Molaise of Devenish, and a sign from heaven that one was to go north, the other south. This is chronologically impossible, but it may be based on some friendly contacts between Rossinver and Devenish and the fixing of their respective territories. Devenish lies north from Maedoc's home country. Meantime Drumlane, Druim Lethan, the Broad Ridge, lies in Co. Cavan, between Killashandra and Belturbet, in that country of a network of small lakes and little ridges. The long Irish 'Life' claims it as a personal foundation and gives it precedence even over Ferns.

Maedoc's father was an important man, and his standing resulted in his son being given as hostage to the high king, Ainmire, when the latter came to take hostages of the Úi Briuin, Maedoc's clan. The Annals of Ulster put Ainmire's death in 568, Clonmacnois in 569. Maedoc must have been very young at the time, if he was a hostage of Ainmire's. He seemed so striking a youth that the king offered to let him go, Maedoc refused until he had also granted the release of all the other hostages.

The long Irish 'Life' gives a verse to help one remember Maedoc's churches:—

Aird-chealla Maodhócc íattso:
Druim Lethan ocus Férna,
Ocus Ros Inbhir oghdha,
Nemh da gach áon onórfa.

The high churches of Maedoc are these,
Drumlane and Ferns
And virginal Rossinver,
Heaven to every one who shall honour them.

The same source gives an account of Maedoc laying out Drumlane, of interest in that it gives an impression of what an Irish monastery was like:—

"Maedoc blessed and permanently established the place, arranged its ramparts and fair cemeteries, measured and marked out its temple and fair churches, fashioned and fairly constructed the caps and columns (?) of its round towers, with stone and timber and implements, visited its houses and buildings, ordered its seniors and congregations, ordained and set in honour its clerics and mass priests, its work-people and servitors, its students and men of learning, to sow belief and devotion, to chant psalms and psalters, to celebrate the divine canonical hours, to give refection to guests and destitute (travelling) companies, and strangers, to the weak and feeble, and to all others who were in need, both in state and church. He bequeathed to the place grace of clergy and coarbs, grace of prosperity and abundance, grace of welcome and entertainment for ever, according to the proverb, " the welcome of Erin is Drumlane "."

Ferns—Ferna Mor Maedoc—lies far south in Leinster in Wexford. It is in good agricultural country where the Wicklow mountains peter out in the south, and is on the road between Enniscorthy and Gorey. West of it rise the Blackstairs mountains. Brandub, son of Eochaid, king of Leinster, in somewhat repentant mood, is supposed to have given the site to Maedoc. Brandub was killed early in the 7th century, the Annals give various dates, 601 (Four Masters), 604 (Ulster), 605 (Tighernach). He is said to have reigned 30 years and to have been buried at Ferns.

At Ferns today, the road dips down to the stream in the hollow of the little hills. On the slope to one side is a ruined church of small size, nave and chancel separated by a round arch; on the opposite rise of ground, over toward the castle, is the ruined Augustinian priory incorporating a curious round tower and with a series of graceful lancet windows to light the choir. The Protestant church close by it is built along the fragmentary outlines of the cathedral chancel; three plain crosses of Wicklow granite stand in its grounds and a cross shaft with a complex zig-zag design is alleged to mark the grave of Diarmait Mac Murchadha. A graveslab with the figure of an ecclesiastic on it, preserved inside the Protestant church, is supposed to represent Maedoc. His holy well, Tobar Maedhog, lies beside the stream in the valley between the two church sites. The massive cover of the well has an inscription saying it was erected in 1847 and that it incorporates stones from Clones and Ferns cathedrals. It says that the well was blessed by St. Moling (d. 697) in honour of S. Aedan Maedhog (d. 632). This is evidently based on the story in the ' Lives ' that Moling as a youth came into contact with Maedoc and was picked out by the latter to succeed him as bishop and abbot of Ferns. But it would seem to be a chronological impossibility.

At Rossinver there is a ruined church and another holy well of Maedoc.

The ' Lives ' give some interesting little details of life in telling of Maedoc's miracles. Thus Maedoc plants fruit trees, apples and nuts, in the monastery garden; his helper gives him instead slips of beeches and alders, which of course later miraculously bear fruit. Or we see the heavy ox team in full course, with its primitive plough. Maedoc a hundred miles from Ferns sees the ploughman fall between share and coulter as the team is turning from one furrow to another. Maedoc raises his hand, the oxen stop dead and the man is saved from injury. There is also an amusing story of a party of scroungers who hide their good clothes and come begging to Maedoc. One version makes Maedoc, knowing what they have done, find their cache and simply give them their own clothes back; in another he gives them to more deserving beggars, so that the tricksters depart with neither clothes nor alms.

The long Irish 'Life' gives a little panegyric of Maedoc, a build-up with some truth in it, of the idea of an Irish saint, wonder worker, ascetic, generous to those in need:—

"Maedoc the marvellous of the mighty deeds was seven full years fasting in Drumlane, without milk or ale, without flesh or kitchen, but only a little bit of barley bread and a drink of water from one evening to another, and a little drink of milk every third Sunday, lying on the bare ground or a stone full hard, without any covering or clothing except the skins of wild, untamed animals, continually reciting his psalms and psalters, and praying zealously to God on Lec na Némhann; for he used to recite thrice fifty psalms every day on cold clammy stones, or the bare, clean-swept floor; and seven psalters with fifty psalms in each psalter; and he never rejected the face of any man in the world in respect of food or drink or clothing, if only he saw that there was need of them."

The accounts commit many chronological impossibilities in their effort to bring Maedoc into contact with other famous saints, and to give historical basis to the monasteries' later claims of tribute. The relics of Maedoc were to be turned against the sun against both those who refused to pay up and " on the family of Maedoc, unless they demand this tribute every year ". A cursing stone like those of Inismurray is described in the long Irish 'Life':—

"There is a stone of Maedoc in the place (Cella Becca, Killybeg, Co. Fermanagh) on which he left as one of its virtues, that whoever shall do wrong or injustice to the erenaghs or tenants of this church, shall not be alive at the end of a year, if this stone be turned widdershins against him."

The relics, which the 'Life' above quoted makes Maedoc bequeath personally to his different monasteries, are of special interest in that some of them still exist. Ferns got the staff of Brandub, which had raised the latter to life. The bell of the brooch and the bell of the hours went to Drumlane as well as " my beautiful wonder working reliquary, which travelled with me to every place, in which are relics of the martyr Stephen, and Lawrence and Clement, the ankle of Martin and some of the hair of the Virgin Mary, and many other relics of saints and holy virgins besides which had been divided with variegated arrangement between the *Brec* and the reliquary; and this is why the name *Brec* was given to it, because of the variegated arrangement together of the relics of the saints and virgins which had been united and made fast in it ". Rossinver got the Brec, the white bachall and the Mac Ratha (Son of Grace), a bell. The Bell of the Hours would have been to call the clerics to the church for the Office.

The Brec, Breac Moaedhog, with its satchel for carrying, still survives. The hereditary keepers were the MacGaghran family, later it passed to the parish priest of Drumlane. Oaths used to be sworn on it, whence the saying " as true as if sworn on the Breac ". The parish priest let it out for that purpose on a deposit security of a guinea; in 1846, the ' borrower ' sold it in Dublin. It is now in the National Museum there. The Clog Mogue, the saint's bell and its shrine, was similarly kept and used for oaths; eventually it was presented to the library of Armagh.

MAEL MAEDOC (MALACHY)

November 3

(THE BACKGROUND TO MAEL MAEDOC'S CAREER WILL BE FOUND UNDER THE ACCOUNT OF HIS PATRON, CELLACH)

Mael Maedoc Ua Morgair (Malachy) was born in 1094, in or near Armagh, where his father, Mughron, was ard fer leginn, professor of the schools there. The family would seem to have been anything but provincial in their outlook; the father Mughron was on a visit to Mungret in Limerick when he died in 1102, and he named one of his sons, 'servant' of the great Leinster saint, Maedoc of Ferns. There were at least three children, Mael Maedoc, Giolla Criost (servant of

Christ, latinised Christian) and a girl of rather more worldly tastes than her two brothers. St. Bernard, Mael Maedoc's friend and biographer, has little use for the unfortunate lass when she used to try and stop her brother burying the dead (" let the dead bury the dead " said she). In fact, St. Bernard says that Mael Maedoc eventually broke off all relations with her; after her death, he has a story of Mael Maedoc offering Mass for the repose of her soul and of successive apparitions of the girl urging him to go on so doing till she got free of purgatory. Giolla Criost and Mael Maedoc, however, were much more alike in character. The Four Masters note at Giolla Criost's death in 1138:—
" Gillachrist Ua Morgair, Bishop of Clogher, a paragon in wisdom and piety, a brilliant lamp that enlightened the laity and clergy by preaching and good deeds; a faithful and diligent servant of the church in general, died and was interred in the Church of St. Peter and Paul at Ard-Macha."

The Four Masters also speak of Mael Maedoc's father as a very learned man " chief lector of Armagh and of all the west of Europe ", but it is the mother's influence that St. Bernard stresses, the boy studying in school but learning piety and wisdom at home. Young Mael Maedoc appears to have been a quiet, studious youth; one hopes that he was not quite the dreadful prig that St. Bernard makes him out to be.

There was in Armagh a certain ascetic and saintly man, Imar Ua h-Aedhacain, who lived alone in the ancient tradition of Irish anchorites. This Imar later appears in the records as abbot of St. Peter and Paul's monastery at Armagh, and he actually died in Rome when on a pilgrimage there in 1134.

Mael Maedoc was 16 or 17 when the great reforming synod of Rath Breasail was held (1111), he may have been aged twenty or a little more when he attached himself to Imar. St. Bernard describes this event as the talk of Armagh; was young Mael Maedoc acting wisely in adopting so ascetic a life and what would be the outcome? Bernard remarks that the people were amazed at Mael Maedoc's virtue in following such a vocation because it was " unusual in a rude people ". There is a much more natural explanation of the excitement, that the people were interested both in religion and in the well-known son of their late famous professor. At least, Mael Maedoc was not for very long a lone disciple, for other Armagh youths soon followed his example. One man who was following Mael Maedoc's progress with interest was the bishop and abbot of Armagh, Cellach, who realised that here was likely material for yet another leader of reform and spiritual renaissance in Ireland. Accordingly he overcame Mael Maedoc's hesitations and pushed on his ordination ahead of the canonical age, deacon c. 1118 and priest the following year, 1119. When Cellach went south on his circuit or visitation of Munster in 1120, young Mael Maedoc was left as his vicar in Armagh. Mael Maedoc set energetically to work to forward Cellach's reforms, the old and long standing problems of marriage probably due to the conflict between the Christian idea of the contract and that of pre-Christian Irish law; in addition the sacraments of confession and confirmation were said to be very usually neglected. There was also a liturgical revival in Armagh, for Mael Maedoc " introduced song into his monastery while as yet no one in the city nor in the whole diocese, either could or would sing " Bernard tells us. This was part of the work of bringing local Irish uses into line with those of the universal Church and Rome, and probably means that Mael Maedoc started a new and Roman version of chant. Bernard's statement is contradictory as it stands, for he adds that Mael Maedoc had learned to sing in his youth in Armagh!

After Cellach returned to Armagh, Mael Maedoc was free to go south to enlarge his own experience by a stay at the famous Munster abbey of Lismore. Only then would he have come into contact with " foreign " influences, up till then his whole formation had been exclusively of Irish origin.

Now in 1121 or 1122 Mael Maedoc came into contact with English Benedictine influences, for Lismore's abbot was an Irishman who had been a monk at Winchester. He was Maol Iosa Ua-Ainmire (Malchus). St. Anselm had consecrated him first bishop of Waterford in 1096; at Rath Breasail he appears as archbishop of Cashel, but in his later years seems to have retired to Lismore—where he died in 1135 at the age of 88. Mael Maedoc spent some two years in Lismore which seems to have been in a most flourishing state, and would there have had opportunity to gain further information on the customs and usages of Rome which Cellach wished to adopt over all Ireland. At the end of this period Mael Maedoc was recalled by Cellach and Imar to the north.

Mael Maedoc was not the only northern visitor in Lismore. The bishop of Down was there, and in fact died in Lismore in 1123. He was bishop Oengus Ua Gormain, and was also comarb of Comgall's foundation of Bangor. The local ruler to whom this comarbship

went on Oengus' death asked Mael Maedoc to take his place; the
latter agreed to accept the ancient monastic site but refused its lands,
an arrangement that led to later difficulties between their holder and
the Bangor monks. It is possible that Oengus followed Mael Maedoc
to Lismore to try to get him to take over Bangor. Mael Maedoc,
anyway, with ten others, probably from Imar's community, set about
rebuilding and restoring Bangor with great energy. But Bangor was
not the only work for which Mael Maedoc was wanted back in the
north. In 1124, Cellach consecrated him bishop of Connor. The diocese
of Connor seems to have been vacant since 1117, and there was
need of an active bishop. In fact, discounting much of Bernard's
French rhetoric, it does seem that the Connor assignment was one of
the toughest jobs of work of all Mael Maedoc's career. Priests were
few, preaching neglected, and the people thoroughly out of the habit
of frequenting the sacraments. Nor, says Bernard, did they give first
fruits or tithes. But they responded quickly enough to the attractive
and saintly young bishop and there was a rapid change for the better.
The previous abbot of Bangor had also been bishop of Down, and it
appears that Mael Maedoc was in charge of this diocese as well as of
neglected Connor.

Very soon however a local war forced Mael Maedoc south again. In
1127, this resulted in the invasion of Bangor by the king of Aileach,
Conchobhair Ua Lochlainn. Mael Maedoc, with a number of his
monks, went to Lismore and there came into friendly contact with
king Cormac Mac Carthaigh (of Cormac's chapel fame) who was then
a refugee, as a result of yet another war of this same year of 1127.
The Four Masters record that : —

1127. " An army was led by Toirdhealbhach Ua Conchobhair (Turloch
O Connor) by sea and land until he reached Corcach-mor (Cork) in
Munster; and he drove Cormac to Lismore and divided Munster into
three parts, and he carried off thirty hostages from Munster.
Donnchadh (Donogh), the son of Mac Carthaigh, was afterwards
expelled into Connacht, with two thousand along with him, by
Cormac Mac Carthaigh, after returning from his pilgrimage; and the
men of Munster turned against Toirdhealbhach."

Cormac, in fact, settled down quietly at Lismore with Mael Maedoc
as his spiritual director and was only with some difficulty persuaded
back to his kingdom : — " Conchubhar and Toirdhealbhach, two sons
of Diarmaid O Brien, went to Lismore and clasped hands with Cormac
Mac Carthaigh, and brought him back to lay life " (Miscellaneous

Annals). When the king did return, he gave Mael Maedoc a site for a monastery of his own, to which Mael Maedoc with 120 followers then went. This " monasterium Ibracense " has been shown by Dean Reidy to have been most probably Ballinskelligs in Kerry, which was for long afterwards a house of Augustinian Canons Regular.

Whilst Mael Maedoc was at Ballinskelligs, Cellach died at Ardpatrick in the April of 1129. He named Mael Maedoc as his successor and sent him his bachall in token thereof. According to Bernard, Mael Maedoc had a curious dream at the time of Cellach's death; of a woman, Cellach's " wife " (diocese) coming to Mael Maedoc and giving him this staff. Mael Maedoc resisted the appointment, he wanted to remain in monastic poverty and peace and he knew the opposition he would have to meet. " You are leading me to death," he said in the end, " but I obey in the hope of martyrdom."

Meantime the ordinary rules of succession had taken their normal course, and Muircheartach was comarb of Patrick. St. Bernard has no word bad enough for this man or the " evil seed " of his family, but when Muircheartach died in 1134 the Four Masters record a different impression:—" Muircheartach, son of Domhnall, son of Amhalghaidh, successor of Patrick, died after the victory of martyrdom and penance on the 17th of September."

In point of fact, the south of Ireland, where the ideas of the reform were more firmly established, seems to have accepted Cellach's nomination of Mael Maedoc as successor. It was in the north that he had to face opposition. The papal legate, Giolla Easpuig (Gilbert) of Limerick, and Maol Iosa Ua-Ainmire (Malchus) of Lismore, urged Mael Maedoc to act and in 1132 he consented, on condition that when Armagh had been regained and the reform fully established, he could retire from the archbishopric. So he went north, leaving the hereditary comarb with the city and the revenues, and starting on his strictly spiritual apostolate outside Armagh. Nor did Muircheartach's death end the affair, for he was followed at once by Niall, son of Aedh, who got possession of the traditional insignia of the comarb, the Staff of Jesus, Patrick's Bell and the Book of Armagh and took these around the country to prove to the people that he was the real successor of Patrick in Armagh. Niall did, in the end, about 1137, abandon the struggle with Mael Maedoc, he died two years later in 1139, " after intense penance " as the Annals have it, taking a rather different view of the man from Bernard for whom he was a devil incarnate.

In the north, Mael Maedoc had, it would seem, the support of a local king, Domhnall Ua Cearbhaill of Oirghialla. As Mael Maedoc had expected, it was a period of some danger, until Niall had finally retired from the fray. At the same period, Giolla Criost, Mael Maedoc's brother, was made bishop of Clogher. Mael Maedoc seems to have been in charge not only of Armagh but in addition Down and Connor. In 1134, he went on the usual circuit (cuairt) of Munster, and arriving at Cashel, would have found the lately consecrated Cormac's Chapel in all the brilliance of fresh cut stone and new paint.

But as soon as matters had been put on a firm and permanent footing, Mael Maedoc carried out his threat of resignation, and betook himself to the diocese of Down, whilst appointing the abbot of Derry, Gille mac Liag (Gelasius) to Armagh. Gille mac Liag took up his appointment without any of the opposition that Mael Maedoc had had to face, and governed Armagh from 1137 until his death in 1175.

In Down, Mael Maedoc's establishment consisted of a " convent of regular clerics ". These would have been following the rule of the Canons Regular of St. Augustine. It is possible that it was Cellach who first introduced the Canons to Ireland, certainly Mael Maedoc encouraged their spread, and they were, in fact, to be found later on, carrying on the work of a great many of the older Irish monastic foundations.

But Mael Maedoc was not left to a life of quiet and contemplation, prayer and poverty, for the crowds, great men and ordinary folk, came flocking round him, merely to see the man as well as to ask his advice and guidance. It is evident that although he was no longer archbishop of Armagh, he was regarded as a key man of the reform. It was, in fact, Mael Maedoc himself who determined to go to Rome, to get official approval of the various reforms, and the official insignia, the pallia, for Ireland's new archbishops of Armagh and Cashel. Ireland was loth to let Mael Maedoc go, more especially as Giolla Criost had only lately died, but when it was agreed to decide the issue by casting lots, the lot fell for him to go.

Accordingly in 1139, Mael Maedoc set out for Rome, travelling from the north of Ireland to Scotland and then going south through England. The party travelled with the poverty that Mael Maedoc always practised, and had but three horses. In York, the prior of the Canons at Kirkham, Waltheof, gave Mael Maedoc his own horse. Waltheof apologised that it was only a pack animal and rough to ride. But Bernard claims that with Mael Maedoc's handling, the animal's performance was entirely changed for the better and it even changed colour, from black to white " till there was scarcely a whiter horse to be found than it "! Perhaps Mael Maedoc groomed the animal more attentively than the English Canons had done; it remained his usual mount to the time of his death.

It was on his road to Rome that Mael Maedoc visited Clairvaux and met St. Bernard. Both were mutually attracted to one another, the ascetic and somewhat extremist Frenchman falling under the spell not only of Irish sanctity but of an Irish smile. " His laughter displayed love or aroused it," Bernard wrote, it was rare, never forced, " it made known the gladness of his heart in such fashion that his face did not lose in grace but gained thereby."

Meantime Mael Maedoc longed to throw up the cares of office and become a monk of Bernard's. He went on to Rome and informed Pope Innocent II that he would like to do this. Innocent refused to contemplate the idea and instead made Mael Maedoc papal legate for Ireland. The Pope approved all the activities and measures of the Irish reformers, but would not at once grant the desired pallia. For that, a request must come from a general synod of the clergy of Ireland, and Mael Maedoc was to go back and summon such a council. Before he left Rome, Innocent gave Mael Maedoc a present of his mitre and the stole and maniple that he had been using when saying Mass.

Whilst a number of the Irish monasteries, like Lismore, were in a flourishing condition, the Irish obviously wanted to be more fully in the stream of the religious life of Europe by introducing continental Orders as well. Moreover, as the diocesan system in Ireland was increasingly patterned on that elsewhere, and the cities of the Northmen were being integrated into the life of the Irish church, the work of the diocesan clergy became increasingly important. Thus Mael Maedoc was concerned, not only with introducing the Cistercian monks to Ireland, of which Bernard naturally tells a good deal, but also with, possibly, the introduction, and certainly the spread, of the Canons Regular.

On his way back to Ireland from Rome, Mael Maedoc again called at Clairvaux and left some of his companions to be trained there. Out of this came the first Cistercian foundation in Ireland at Mellifont in 1142, and its subsequent rapid spread:— Baltinglass (1151), Bective (1151), Newry (1156-60) and so on. Mael Maedoc was, in doing this, introducing the most active and influential monastic group then to be found in Europe.

But according to an account written in 1179 by Gaultier, abbot of Arrouaise, Mael Maedoc called there as well as to Clairvaux. At the time of his visit, the abbot was the saintly Gervase. Unlike Bernard, Gervase has left no account of what his impressions of the Irish bishop were. But as at Clairvaux, Mael Maedoc made a study of the Canons' rule and left some of his party there for further training. This Congregation of Arrouaise was one of the most important of the several groups of Augustinian Canons. They combined the monastic ideal of prayer and contemplation with active apostolic and diocesan work. Ireland would eventually have 26 cathedral churches in the care of these Canons Regular. They already had houses in England, one of which was at Carlisle through which Mael Maedoc would have passed.

" The introduction of the Arroasian Order into Ireland and Mael Maedoc's connection with this work testifies to the earnestness of the Irish reformers and indicates that the Irish reform movement did not lag behind the continental one. It helps considerably to counteract the unjust attacks upon clerical morality and ecclesiastical discipline made by Giraldus and the apologists of the Norman invasion " (P. J. Dunning, " Irish Historical Studies," Sept. 1945).

Mael Maedoc was at Clairvaux in the period July/August of 1140 and back at Bangor late in 1140, following the same route as that by which he had come. In Scotland he met King David and worked a cure of his young son, Henry, then at the point of death. If the Cistercian monks were new to Ireland, the Canons, as already suggested, had perhaps a foothold before the Arrouaise visit, if their taking over of Patrick's Purgatory is correctly dated 1139/40.

St. Bernard describes Mael Maedoc's work in Ireland after his return from Rome, how he went about reviving and restoring the old, introducing the new. Like the friars who would come later, he was a preacher who normally went on foot, he and his companions. " That was the apostolic rule," says Bernard, " and it is the more to be admired in Malachy because it is too rare in others. The true successor of the Apostles assuredly is he who does such things."

The same year that Cormac's Chapel was built, king Cormac Mac Carthaigh had refounded St. Finbar's abbey in Cork. This was 1134. St. Bernard describes how Cork was without a bishop and agreement on whom to elect could not be reached. Mael Maedoc arrived in the city and picked " a certain poor man whom he knew to be holy ", a man moreover who was not from the Cork district. This individual seems almost certainly to have been Giolla Aodh Ua Múighin (d. 1173) from whom Cork's Gill Abbey took its name. It was probably at this same time that Mael Maedoc brought the Augustinian Canons to the cathedral of Cork, though the history of its Chapter can only be traced back to 1175.

St. Bernard tells how at Armagh " with one of his fellow bishops, he rose in the night and began to go round the memorials of the saints, of which are many in the cemetery of St. Patrick ". A bright light over one of the altars convinced Mael Maedoc of the holiness of the person buried there; the interest of the story is rather in this account of a " round " of a cemetery recalling present custom on Irish traditional pilgrimages.

Finally, in 1148, the official synod was called to ask for the pallia for the archbishops, and Mael Maedoc again set out for Rome by the Scottish/English route. Pope Eugene III, a Cistercian late of Bernard's monastery, was then in France and Mael Maedoc hoped to overtake him there. However, the king of England, Stephen, was engaged in a quarrel with the Pope and considerably delayed the Irish party's Channel crossing. When they did eventually get over, the Pope was back in Rome. In October, Mael Maedoc halted at Clairvaux. After a little time, he was down with fever. It did not seem serious but Mael Maedoc knew that it was. He died in Bernard's arms on November 2nd, 1148. As for the request for the pallia, this was to be granted but they were not conferred until the 1152 Synod of Kells, when four, not two archbishoprics were created, Armagh, Cashel, Dublin and Tuam.

Mael Maedoc made an enormous impression on St. Bernard, who was only too eager to respond to the request of an Irish Cistercian, Abbot Congan, to write his friend's 'Life'. There also survive two sermons of Bernard's on Mael Maedoc, one probably delivered on the day of his death, the other for an anniversary, perhaps the Month's Mind, perhaps the next anniversary in the November of 1149. There are three short letters of Bernard's to Mael Maedoc, dealing with the new Cistercian foundations in Ireland; one of these, perhaps written in 1141, thanks Mael Maedoc for sending a stick " to support my weak body ". One wonders if it was an Irish blackthorn. In Mael Maedoc, Bernard not only recognized a saint, but a man who lived the answer to Bernard's own problem—the smooth synthesis of the active and contemplative vocations. Of Mael Maedoc, he wrote, when you saw him plunged into affairs, you thought he " was born only for his country; if you had seen him alone, living on his own, you would have thought he had lived only in God, and for Him ".

See also CELLACH.

St. Bernard's Life of St. Malachy of Armagh. Translated and edited by H. J. Lawlor together with the two sermons and letters. London, 1920.

H. J. Lawlor: *Notes on St. Bernard's Life of St. Malachy and his two sermons on the Passing of St. Malachy,* (with suggested chronology and itineraries), P.R.I.A., vol. 35 C. (1918-20), pp. 230-264.

A. Gwynn: *St. Malachy of Armagh.* I.E.R., November, 1948, pp. 961-978, February, 1949, pp. 134-148, April, 1949, pp. 317-331.

P. J. Dunning: *The Arroasian Order in Medieval Ireland.* Irish Historical Studies. September, 1945, pp. 297-315.

T. J. Walsh and Denis O Sullivan: *St. Malachy, the Gill Abbey of Cork and the Rule of Arrouaise.* J.C.H.A.S., July/Dec, 1949, pp. 41-60.

Jean Leclercq: *Documents on the Cult of St. Malachy.* Seanchas Ardmacha. Vol. 3, no. 2. 1959.

MAELRUAIN OF TALLAGHT

July 7

Mael Rúain iarna goiri	Maelruain after his pious service,
Grían már desmaig Midi,	the great sun on Meath's south plain,
Occa lecht co nglaini	
Icthair cnet cech cridi.	at his grave with purity is healed the sigh of every heart.

(Martyrology of Oengus)

St. Maelruain, who died July 7th, 792, is the best known name of the Céili Dé reform of the 8th-9th centuries. He founded the monastery of Tallaght on the foothills of the Wicklow mountains, south of Dublin, probably on August 10th, 774. The site was given to him by the king of Leinster, Cellach mac Dunchada. The latter died in 776 and was buried at Tallaght. Maelruain had been taught by Ferdacrich, the abbot of Dairinis, an islet in the Blackwater near Youghal. It appears that Maelruain eventually became a bishop as well as being abbot of Tallaght.

Much nonsense has been written about the name Céili Dé, anglicised Culdee. The movement began as one of reform towards the end of the 8th century, there was then obviously a fresh upsurge of religious and ascetical life. Céili Dé material speaks of the " old churches " and their laxer customs as against the poverty and austerity of the new foundations and their monks. Monasteries of Céili Dé, and those in sympathy with the movement, seem to be related to the development of the art of the high crosses. It was a movement that involved not only a renewal and increase of religious life but of intellectual and artistic activity as well. Obits of scribes and anchorites become numerous in the Annals—Ireland had well organised scriptoria by the first half of the 8th century in monasteries mostly sited on the great sea and land routes, for their scribes were in the same kind of work as a modern publishing house and by no means all the manuscripts were intended for use at home. Efforts have been made to try and link the scribes and anchorites and Céili Dé together, as part of one movement, but as Kathleen Hughes has recently pointed out, the distribution of scriptoria (marked by obits of the head scribe) and of anchorite-Céili Dé centres is by no means identical. Again, the use of the word " anchorite " does not mean hermit in our modern sense in every case. " In Irish and Irish Latin documents, the word interpreted *anchorite* does not seem to have the strict meaning attached to it in continental sources. In Irish sources it seems to be frequently synonymous with monk, especially with monks living in community, but in remote and secluded places and islands. Hence it does not often indicate a solitary hermit." (Felim O Briain, O.F.M., unpublished papers on St. Brigit). Thus the well-known 9th century lyric in Irish, called the Hermit's Song, is of a community of " six pairs beside myself " (13) living in a solitary place in a wood by a stream, and chanting the Office together in their little church.

One of the first references in a surviving text to the Céili Dé seems to be that in the ' Life ' of Fintan of Rheinau (q.v.). The name is usually taken as equivalent to the Latin, *servus Dei*, servant of God, but *ceile* also means husband/wife (no English equivalent, except perhaps ' mate ', often translated by the dreadful latinism ' spouse ') and friend. "The husband of every faithful soul is God, because it is united with him by faith," wrote St. Gregory the Great, expressing the Church's widespread and ancient use of the marriage symbol for the union of love between a man and God. The originally secular love poetry of the Song of Songs has been adopted by the Church to express this spiritual love. The Céili Dé made their own and original use of that same Song of Songs. " When a man was at the point of death, or immediately after his soul departed, the *Canticum Salomonis* was sung over him. The reason of this practice was that in that canticle is signified the union of the Church with every Christian soul " (Teaching of Maelruain).

But as time went on, Céili Dé and Culdee changed, as words will, their meaning and one finds the term applied to secular priests living in community; even, by the Four Masters, as late as 1595, to the Dominicans of Sligo.

A large number of Irish monasteries were associated with the original Céili Dé movement. Dublitir's Finglas, north of Dublin, was another important centre in the same part of the country as Tallaght. The earliest reference to Finglas is in 763 and the place lasted at least a hundred years. There appear to have been convents for women religious near both Finglas and Tallaght. Both places were cut short in their expansion by the Viking attacks.

The Book of Leinster contains two lists of the *Oentu Maelruain* which appear to be quite historical in content. An *oentu* implies a close relationship between a saint and another person or community.

The movement itself seems to have come from the south and spread north, up the river Barrow and west of the Wicklow hills towards Tallaght, and also up Shannon. It was connected with Dairinis on the Blackwater near Lismore and Ferdacrich (Fer dá Chrích) its abbot who died in 747; with Clonenagh on the Nore whence came St. Oengus of the famous Felire; with Castledermot, founded by a Diarmait who died 823; and with Kilcullen of Dalbach. It was also associated with Terryglass and perhaps with Lorrha, on the Shannon —Maelruain's name suggests a devotion to Ruadhan of Lorrha. At Finglas (Finn-glas) were bishop Caencomrac (d. 791) and Dublitir (Dub-littir), who died in 796. Elair (d. 807) was at the head of a group of hermits on Monahincha, the island in Lough Cre at Roscrea. Rahan, of which nothing is recorded after Mo-Chuta's expulsion, reappears with the Ui Suanaig, one abbot and the other an anchorite, both flourished in the first half of the 8th century. Fothad na Canoine of Rathan in Donegal, died 819, has been suggested as author of the Rule of Mo-Chuta. Our versions of the Irish ' Rules ' go back to just this period but they may embody earlier material. It is evident from the references that Maelruain's Rule was a written document.

Mention of Rahan recalls nearby Lann Ela of Colman; according to the genealogies, Maelruain himself was descended from Colman Ela's grandfather, Mochta: Maelruain m Colmain m Seanaigh m Edhnigh m Mochtae. Maelruain's successor at Tallaght was a bishop Echaidh, who died 812.

Dr. F. Henry has described St. Moling of St. Mullins on the Barrow as the " familiar pet saint " of the Céili Dé. St. Mullins and Ullard on the Barrow seem to have been older centres sympathetic to the new movement, so also the Columban group of houses. Iona had a Céili Dé community. All these places, St. Mullins, Ullard, Castledermot, Moone of Colmcille, Kilcullen, are connected with the development of the figured crosses. The earliest pillars and slabs had shown the cross, sometimes with geometrical decorations, sometimes with figures, but now a new development took place. The cross broke free of the slab, shaped it, instead of being cut on a rough *gallan* or slab or pillar. The whole face of the cross was divided into panels and each had its own design, intended to tell a story, the sort of thing that could stand as illustration to an outdoor sermon. The centre piece on the head of the cross is usually the Crucifixion, one side, and the Last Judgment, the other; but the other panels are chiefly based on two scriptural series, one, the older, about the help of God; the other concerned with the liturgical cycle and the great feasts of the year. Thus some crosses have pictures to illustrate Christmas—Epiphany; others Easter. But the earliest series is that of the help of God. The Jews had had a prayer of this sort for use on fast days, reminding the Lord of past incidents when He had shown His almighty help to His people. St. Cyprian of Antioch at the end of the 2nd century adapted this old prayer to Christian use, adding New Testament miracles to the series. It is still in the litany in the Roman Breviary for a departing soul, in one of its versions. Another, much more poetical one, is the prayer of Oengus to Jesus in his Felire. On the high crosses, the series, more or less worked out, is readily followed—incidents like the Children in the Fiery Furnace and Daniel in the Den of Lions are frequently shown. The cross base at Seir Kieran (Saighir) has perhaps the oldest coherent set, when on one face are shown the Fall, the Three Children, the Sacrifice of Isaac, and Jonas.

From Tallaght itself comes a rather disproportionate amount of our material relating to the early Irish Church. There are the Stowe Missal, the Martyrologies of Tallaght and of Oengus, a document setting out the teaching of Maelruain (Teagasg Maoil Ruain) and a Penitential. In the same Céili Dé connection, there survives also a Rule of the Céili Dé, dated to the 9th century. Thus while we do not have very much ordinary biographical material about Maelruain, his teaching and outlook is well recorded, and something too of the liturgy and customs of the Irish monasteries and churches of his time.

The account of the teaching of Maelruain (Teagasg Maoil Ruain) seems to have been written for the most part between 831, when abbot Diarmait of Iona died and 840 when Maeldithruib, the anchorite of Terryglass, died. For Diarmait is mentioned as dead, and in most of the text, Maeldithruib is obviously a person still alive. Part was written after his death however. The author appears to have been a monk of Tallaght, who most likely knew Maelruain. The account is a collection of material, of Maelruain's teaching and Maeldithruib's, together with extracts from Maelruain's Rule and Penitential and stories of other Céili Dé settlements, from Clonmacnois, Devenish, Monahincha, Iona, Terryglass. Maeldithruib was a monk of Tallaght, who knew Maelruain; he eventually moved to Terryglass.

Maelruain's monks did not eat meat, except wild swine or deer very occasionally. Nor did they drink alcohol in any form. Maelruain is represented preaching total abstinence to Dublitir of Finglas who allowed his monks beer on the great festivals. " As long as I shall give rules," said Maelruain, " and as long as my instructions are observed in this place (Tallaght), the liquor that causes forgetfulness of God shall not be drunk here." " Maelruain was accustomed to allow thick milk mixed with honey on the eves of the chief festivals. . . . They admitted no increase of the bread ration on festivals, but only of drink and condiments and other things generally." The word translated ' condiment ', perhaps better represented by the word ' kitchen ', was fairly far reaching, for it might be fish, cabbage, eggs, apples, of the latter 3 to 4 if large and 5 to 6 if small. It suggests a reasonably well balanced diet. Maelruain taught that even in Lent one should take meat if there was famine in the land and the alternative was starving.

Unlike some Orders of monks, Maelruain's did not sleep in the clothes they wore during the day. " No one administered castigation to himself, but received it from another," this particular penance was forbidden between Christmas and Epiphany (Notluig Stéil—Star Christmas, the two Christmases) and during Paschal time. The custom of standing in water (which has survived in that of wading the stream at the annual pattern at Mothel, Co. Waterford, into our own times) is also mentioned. " It was Colcu's opinion that those who used to stand in water did so for the purpose of crushing and subduing their desires and longings; or else simply as an additional labour of piety."

The Stowe Missal, written either at Tallaght of Lorrha, represents the liturgy of the Mass as then celebrated there and elsewhere in Ireland. There was Mass on Sundays, Thursdays and the great feasts. There are very detailed instructions about Communion, whether in one or both kinds, and how often it should be received. There was a graded frequency of Communion in the Céili Dé Rule, the postulant apparently not receiving It at all at first, then with increasing frequency to once a week as minimum. If a monk missed his Sunday Communion, Maelruain said he must receive at the Thursday Mass, for a whole week was too long to go without Communion. Midnight Mass is mentioned as a frequent occurrence, and at it, Communion seems to have been given only under the species of Bread.

Spiritual direction and frequent Confession were also stressed. Maelruain taught that his monks should not put off till Sunday, confession of venial sins, slight offences, murmuring, idle words, but confess them immediately. Maelruain told Maeldithruib that in choosing a confessor one should " seek out the fire that you think will burn you the fiercest ".

" Frequent confession, however, does not profit, if the transgression be also frequent " (Rule of the Céili Dé). There was a certain difficulty in gearing the current heavy penitential discipline to the poor, the elderly and the sick. This problem is discussed both from the confessors' and penitents' angles. The latter are advised not to put off confession on account of being unable to carry out the full penance due. " For once anyone confesses his sins, even if he should not perform in full the penance due, he is on the road in which he may have hope in God that he will be saved."

Maelruain was careful about receiving strangers to spiritual direction, making sure first that they had their previous confessor's permission. So when Maeldithruib came to him, with in fact his confessor, Echtguide's, permission, Maelruain said, " Craftsmen, such as smiths and carpenters, do not like their apprentices to go and seek instruction from another man : why then should your confessor like you to come to me?"

Liturgical prayer patterned day and night. Cross vigil (praying with the arms outstretched in the form of the cross) and genuflection were worked into the rhythm of the chanting of the psalms. " Dublitir's usual vigil was the 150 psalms standing with a genuflection after each. Maelruain said one should chant alternately sitting and standing, so as neither to go to sleep or be tired out." The 118th psalm was specially beloved, the present liturgical reform which has reduced greatly the frequency of its recitation would not have been popular with Irish monks. Many ordinary folk knew it by heart. Thus Muirchertach mac Olcobhair, erenagh of Clonfert, reckoned 12 *Beati* (the 118th psalm) as equivalent to the whole psalter. He advised the use of this equivalent, for there were many monks and penitents who knew the 118th by heart, but not the whole 150 psalms. After each *Beati,* he recited the *Magnificat,* he had learnt this from a Son of Life (Culdee), for " it is right that the work that is made for a king should be gilded and adorned outwardly. And this is the gilding of the work we fashion for God, even the song which the Holy Spirit uttered through the mouth of Mary ".

But it was recommended that one should recite the psalms from the written text when this was available and not from memory. " A Son of Life should always recite his psalms by the psalter. This is what he used to say of this. ' There are three adversaries busy attacking me, my eye, my tongue and my thoughts: the psalter restrains them all '. Howbeit, this is what Maelruain said to Maeldithruib, ' The thought is no less occupied with the meaning when one is reciting the psalm by rote than it is when he is reading it with the psalter '."

Devotion to Our Lady, the angels and the saints was strong. There was a special devotion to Michael the archangel. There was a legend that Maelruain would not take possession of Tamlachtu (Tallaght) until Michael, with whom he had a friendship, should take it. Michael gave Maelruain possession by the ancient custom of sarsine, the handing over of a sod as a symbol of the transfer of ownership. A sod and an epistle came down from heaven to Maelruain, and Tallaght, also, it was said, had relics consecrated to Michael. Legend apart, the records of the customs of Tallaght show this devotion to St. Michael. A hymn to Our Lady was sung in the morning, to Michael last thing at night, and these were called the invocations of Michael's Protection and of Mary's Protection. On Sundays, the hymn of Michael, *Beati,* and *Hymnum Dicat* at mid-day, and the hymn to Mary and the *Beati* in the evening.

The *Hymnum Dicat* is that attributed to St. Hilary, a telling of the gospel story in verse, and is one of those included in the Antiphonary of Bangor. The other two hymns are very probably those two still in existence, very fine examples of Irish hymn writing. The one of St. Michael is very likely Colman Mac Mur-chon's ' *In Trinitate spes mea* '; that to Our Lady Cú-chuimne's ' *Cantemus in omni die* '. Colman died in 731 or 36, Cú-chuimme probably in 747, he appears to have been a monk of Iona. These three hymns then make a nicely balanced little set in honour of Our Lord, Mary and the angels.

It would be impossible to work out in detail the Office as celebrated in Tallaght, for the material we have is in the nature of notes and special customs in a well-known basic formula, the text of which we do not have. The general impression is clear, however, of length and devotion, both in the official liturgy and in private prayer.

" Now Maeldithruib sings between every two psalms of the 150, *Sancte Michael, ora pro nobis, Sancta Maria, ora pro nobis,* adding the saint whose feast falls on that day. When the office of nocturns is over, then Maeldithruib sings *Celebra Juda* (Hymn of Cummean Fota, d. 662) and *Cantemus* and *Averte faciem* (Psalm 50 v. 11) and so forth, and thereafter *Hymnum dicat,* this last in a cross vigil. Then the *Beati* of nocturns, and along with it the *Magnificat.* As to the *Beati* of the refectory, however, the *Magnificat* and *Hymnum* and *Unitas* are sung with it, and *Ego vero orationem* (Psalm 68, v. 14) and so forth. But on Sunday night, the *Beati* is sung twice over. The psalms of prayer are sung on Saturday night and Sunday night at vespers. It is also his custom to recite on Sunday nights a table grace and thanksgiving. Immediately after dinner, he sings *Averte faciem* to a chant; after it a prayer, *Columba sancte, sume nos in gremio, Caritatis tutela tuae sit nobis.* After that, O Stephen, help me! guard with your hand my heart against the snares of death. O Holy Fire, save the household of my dwelling. Let there be no pains or torments, *et reliqua.* Then he crosses himself."

Here is a nicely balanced selection of material in the above set of customs, using the psalms and canticles of the Old Testament over against the story of the New in Hilary's hymn and the *Magnificat* together with prayer to the angels and saints, including Colmcille and Stephen (the first martyr). The *Cantemus* of the series is perhaps not the hymn to Mary but *Cantemus Domino,* one of the Canticles of Moses (Exod. 15, 1-19). (See also Moling and the Book of Mulling).

There was a rather attractive little custom of making a protective lorica or breastplate by turning to the four points of the compass and making the sign of the cross at each. The sign of the cross was called

Luireach chrabhaid according to the Latin fragment of Maelruain's Penitential. After saying the *Pater noster* one stood facing east, hands raised in the ancient position of prayer, said *Deus in adjutorum meum intende. Domine ad adjuvandum me festina.* (God come to my help. Lord hasten to help me). Then they made the sign of the cross, and repeated the formula to the four quarters, first with eyes cast down, then again looking up to heaven.

There is a brief reference to the liturgy of Holy Week. On Maundy Thursday, Maelruain had a sermon preached on Christ and His apostles eating the supper of the Paschal Lamb. This took place at mid-day. Dinner followed; then came the ceremony of the washing of feet. Whilst this took place, the *Beati* was sung. After that there was a sermon on Christ washing the apostles' feet, and then vespers followed immediately.

There was reading at mealtimes, from the gospel, working straight through, Matthew in the spring and so on, a book to every quarter. As well, monastic rules and the lives of the saints were read. The reader took his meal first; the monks were questioned next day to see if they had been listening to what had been read. There was a very lengthy grace before meals, to which the monks were summoned by the ringing of a bell or a knife handle banged against a dish cover.

" Some persons aver that the small delicate diet is safer and better for the soul than the large coarse diet." " Do not eat till you are hungry; do not sleep till you are ready for it; speak to nobody without cause."

Meantime the long liturgy and private devotions did not fill the whole day, there was work to be done on the land to maintain the monks, as well as study, copying of texts and preaching. " Three profitable things in the day: prayer, labour and study: or it may be, teaching or writing or sewing clothes, or any profitable work that he can do; so that none may be idle, as the Lord has said, ' You shall not appear in My sight empty '." And again from the Rule of the Céili Dé:— " Labour in piety is the most excellent of all labours. The kingdom of heaven is granted to him who directs study, he who studies, and he who supports the student."

" He did not wish anyone to decrease part of his burden, however heavy he might feel it. ' The duty I owe,' said he, ' it is not right for me to seek to put it from me, but it must be paid as a debt due by me.' He used to lighten the burden of the priests whenever he saw that it was a hindrance to them in saying Mass."

Prayer for the dead is mentioned in some detail, the singing of the *Beati* of the refectory standing and then reciting the requiem for the dead also standing. " There is nothing that a man does on behalf of one that dies that does not help him, whether it be vigil or abstinence, or reciting intercessory prayers or aimsgiving or frequent benediction. Maedoc and his monks were a full year on bread and water to obtain the release of the soul of Brandub mac Echach (who had given them Ferns). Sons ought to do penance for the souls of their departed parents, etc."

In the matter of keeping vigils, Tallaght seems to have had a permanent one of sorts, two monks reciting the psalter in the church till Matins began; another two carrying on between Matins and Lauds.

Priests who sinned, no matter how penitent afterwards, should not be made bishops. Mac Oige of Lismore was asked what was the best point in the clerical character. He replied that the best attribute for the clergy was perseverance, that is, constancy, for he had never heard any fault found with this. ' If a man is charitable,' said he, ' people say he is the worse for his charity. If he is humble, they say the same. If he is given to fasting they say the same of him and so on. But I never heard anyone say of another that he was too persevering, or that he was the worse of his perseverance. For,' said he, ' whatever art a man devotes himself to, it is best for him to persevere in it, in order to acquire it, and this is specially the case with piety, if that is what a man devotes himself to.'

The position of the clergy was strongly emphasised. " If anyone will not accept the yoke of a confessor, so that he is not under the authority of God or man, he has no claim to be given communion, nor to have intercession made for him, nor to be buried in God's church; because he has refused to be under God's authority in the churches in the land of Erin. For it is right to show reverence to ordained priests, and to fulfil their behests, just as if they were God's angels among men : seeing that it is through them that the kingdom of heaven is to be won, by means of baptism and communion and intercession, and by the sacrifice of the Body and Blood of Christ, and by preaching of the gospel, and by building up the Church of God, and by unity of law and rule; and this is what is pleasing to God on earth." (Rule of the Céili Dé).

Some internal evidence links the Stowe Missal with Tallaght and dates its compilation to some time between the years 792 and 812. As well as the text of the Mass, it contains excerpts from St. John's gospel, the order of baptism with communion of the newly baptised, the order for the visitation of the sick with extreme unction and communion, a tract on the Mass in Irish and three short spells, also in Irish.

The Mass rite in the Stowe Missal belongs to the older and more elaborate variations of the Latin rite in the West; out of which uniformity and brevity have only grown gradually. Like the Antiphonary of Bangor, it has a long series of Communion antiphons. The fraction of the Host was very elaborate and symbolic in its character— with different arrangements of the broken fragments on different feasts. There is a long string of names of Irish saints in the litany (reduced in the present Roman rite simply to the *Kyrie*) and another lengthy series in the commemoration of saints and dead in the actual Canon.

The tract on the Mass sets out to show how the liturgy symbolises and tells the whole story of man's salvation and connects it with the doctrine of the Mystical Body of Christ. The altar is the symbol of persecution, the chalice on it the Church founded on that persecution and the martyrdoms. The water poured into the chalice (this was prepared at the beginning of the Mass) are the people ' poured ' into the Church; the wine poured on the water, Christ's Godhead assuming His Manhood. Meantime the Host on the altar is symbolic of Christ's Body set in the linen sheet of Mary's womb.

The chalice seems to have been covered by two veils and their gradual removal had a symbolic meaning. Thus fully veiled, up to the epistle, symbolised the law of Nature; then as they were taken away, one by one, the partial revelation of the Old Testament and the Prophets; finally at the offertory, complete unveiling to symbolise the full revelation of the New Testament. After the Consecration, the Host on the paten is Christ's flesh on the tree of the cross; the fraction the breaking of His Body with nails, the coming together of the fragments after the fraction, symbolises the Resurrection. " This is what God deems worthy, the mind to be in the symbols of the Mass, and this be your mind : the portion of the Host you receive to be as it were a member of Christ from His cross, and that there may be a cross of labour on each in his own course, because it unites to the Crucified Body."

Whilst the Stowe Missal shows an extraordinarily full commemoration of the saints at every Mass, it contains no Proper of the Saints. Dr. Hennig has argued that this did not, in fact, exist in Ireland at this time. The liturgy followed the basic cycle (to which present reforms are bringing it back) based on Christmas, Lent and Easter. It is evident that the saints' feast days were known and commemorated but they did not apparently have a specific Office and Proper of the Mass.

The two most ancient Irish Martyrologies also come from Tallaght. The Martyrology of Tallaght is in Latin, with some attractive little Irish notes (e.g., ' On the feast of Ciaran, son of the wright, wild geese come over the cold sea '). It seems to be contemporary with the Stowe Missal—c. 800. It contains a fairly full list of the saints of the Roman calendar, not just the principal ones who only, with a long series of Irish saints, are in the metrical Martyrology of Oengus. In Irish verse, the *Felire Óengusso Céli Dé* represents, according to Dr. Hennig, " the greatest attempt ever made to present the subject matter of the Martyrology in a poetical form ". Oengus mentions the death of the ard ri, Donnchad, in 797; it is said in the Martyrology of Gorman that Oengus used that of Tallaght in making his Felire. The work was begun at Clonenagh and finished at Tallaght—it was complete in 804, when Oengus showed it to Fothad na Canoine.

Although the Felire is worked out day by day, " the full crew of each day ", it was meant to be recited as a whole, the poem is a unit to be said complete in honour of the saints (cf. the story of how Oengus got the idea for it, from an ex-layman's custom of reciting names of the saints each day, *vide* Colman of Cloyne). Thus like the long lists of saints in the Mass book from Tallaght, the Felire stands for a rather different approach to the commemoration of the saints than the present one. Dr. Hennig believes that these early Irish martyrologies with their commemorations of all the saints of different areas, or all the saints of different groups—martyrs, virgins, etc., a feature too of the invocations of the litanies, foreshadowed both the idea of a feast of All Saints, and a certain European consciousness. The Tallaght Martyrology seems to be the first source to show our modern concept of an area called Western Europe. It commemorates all the saints of Europe.

Oengus himself was the son of Oengoba, son of Oiblén. He became a monk at Clonenagh, then came to Tallaght and Maelruain. At first he disguised his abilities and past career, but he was soon found out! Eventually he became an abbot and a bishop and went back to Clonenagh where he died, on a Friday, March 11th. The year could have been 819, 824 or 830. There is a poem about him in the Leabhar

Breac—" 'Tis in Cluain Eidnech he was reared: in Cluain Eidnech he was buried: in Cluain Eidnech of many crosses he studied his psalms at first ". A later prologue to the Felire says that at a certain hermitage Oengus had, he used to say 50 psalms in the river with a withe round his neck tied to a tree, 50 under the tree and 50 in his cell.

Oengus calls himself *bochtán* (pauper) and *in pauperám trúagsa* (this wretched beggar). The title Culdee, now linked to his name and his Felire, seems only to have been added in the 17th century.

Between Oengus and Maelruain there was a deep and lasting friendship. In the epilogue to the Felire, Oengus wrote:—
" May the full blessing of this King with his beautiful hosts be over your assemblies on Maelruain before all other men!
May my tutor bring me to Christ, dear beyond affection, by his pure blessing, with its heart's desire!"

Extracts from Oengus' great work decorate the present book; they are brief, formal, stylised, but at the same time definitely intended to catch the outstanding characteristic of the saint to which they refer.

At Tallaght today little now remains except the site on which the Protestant church stands, to mark Maelruain's monastery. Here is preserved a large trough, cut from granite, and named Moll Rooney's Lossit. Tradition said it was used for washing pilgrims' feet; others have supposed it a baptismal font; the present writer suspects it a trough for watering animals, or some other such domestic purpose. Once several stone crosses stood in the graveyard, now only a base and a fragment survive. The present church, built in 1829, was partly constructed from material from an older building, of which the tower survives. Under this old, mediaeval church, were found the foundations of a still earlier one, of uncut stones. Church and tower stand in the middle of a raised earthwork.

Until the Dominicans came to Tallaght in 1856, Maelruain's day still had its traditional pattern. A garland was carried in procession from house to house, accompanied by a fiddler or a piper. At each house, the inmates were asked to come out and dance a jig. A collection was taken up and spent on drinking at the day's end. This colourful, if somewhat riotous, affair, which did also involve genuine prayer and devotion to Maelruain, was most unhappily suppressed by the Dominicans, who thus signally failed to grasp a unique opportunity, to preserve, direct and purify, an ancient Irish devotion to one of the country's most outstanding saints.

A late 14th or 15th century wooden figure of St. Maelruain is preserved at Crossbeg near Enniscorthy.

E. J. Gwynn and W. J. Purton: *The Monastery of Tallaght.* P.R.I.A., 29 c. (1911), pp. 115-179.

E. Gwynn: *The Rule of Tallaght.* Hermathena. no. 44. 2nd supplemental volume. Dublin, 1927.

Canice Mooney, O.F.M.: *Paenitentiarium S. Maoil-Ruain, Abbatis Tamhlachta.* Celtica, vol. II (1954), pp. 297-304. This is a Latin fragment. The Irish Penitential of Maelruain is edited in Eriu, vol. VII, the only Penitential known to survive in Irish.

The Martyrology of Tallaght. H.B.S., London, 1931.

Félire Oengusso Céli Dé. H.B.S., London, 1905.

The Stowe Missal. H.B.S., London, 1906.

P. Grosjean, S.J.: *Le Martyrology de Tallaght.* Analecta Bollandiana, t. 51, (1933), pp. 117-130, an informative review of the H.B.S. edition above mentioned. Discusses the problem of Donnan of Eigg.

Brendan O Dwyer, O.Carm.: *Literary and Historical Aspects of the Culdee Movement in Ireland (750-1150).* Unpublished Ph.D. Thesis, Dublin, 1951.

John Hennig: *The Felire Oengusso and the Martyrologium Wandalberti.* Mediaeval Studies, 1954, pp. 219-226. *The Irish Counterparts of the Anglo-Saxon Menologium,* Mediaeval Studies, 1952, pp. 98-100. *Britain's Place in the Early Irish Martyrologies.* Medium Aevum 26, 1957, pp. 17-24. *Appellations of Saints in Early Irish Martyrologies,* Mediaeval Studies, 1957, pp. 227-233. *Studies in the Tradition of the Martyrologium Hieronymianum in Ireland.* Studia Patristica, vol. I, Berlin 1957, pp. 104-111. *A Feast of all the Saints of Ireland.* Speculum. Jan., 1946, pp. 49-66. *The Place of the Fathers in Early Irish Devotional Literature.* I.E.R., October. 1955, pp. 226-234.

MAELRUBHA (MALRUBIUS)

April 21

I n-Albain co nglaini	Into Scotland with purity,
iar lécud cech subai,	after leaving every happiness,
luid úainn cona mathair	our brother Maelrubha went
ar mbráthair Mael-rubai.	from us with his mother.

(Martyrology of Oengus)

Next to Colmcille, the cult and reputation of Maelrubha of Applecross was the most widespread and honoured in Scotland. Maelrubha, like Moluag and Columban, was a monk of Bangor, though never, as sometimes claimed, abbot there. He was born January 3rd, 642;

his father was Elganach, and Maelrubha himself 8th in descent from Niall of the Nine Hostages. His mother, Subtan or Suaibsech, was related to Comgall of Bangor's family. Maelrubha's father was of the Cinel Eoghain of Tir-Eoghain (Tyrone) and Inis-Eoghain (Inishowen).

When he was 29, in 671, Maelrubha left for the Scottish mission. In 673, he made his great foundation at Applecross in Wester Ross. There he died, at the age of 80, in 722. His name, in a variety of forms, is stamped over the face of Scotland in placenames. It is probably true that many are personal foundations, that the man's apostolate and that of his monks did cover a very extensive area of the mainland and the western isles. His cult was to be found all over Scotland and Presbyterianism found it very hard to eliminate it. (For a map of Maelrubha's churches, see Douglas Simpson " The Celtic Church in Scotland ", p. 73).

Maelrubha died peacefully at Applecross on April 21st in 722, the legend of his martyrdom by Norse raiders seems to be due to a confusion of his name with that of the martyr Rufus of Capua.

Applecross is a beautiful and sheltered bay, ringed by red sandstone mountains, with an outlook to Raasay and the hills of Skye. Placenames suggest Maelrubha worked up the west coast of Scotland to this place and out from it over the islands. The short route from Bangor to Scotland is across the North Channel to Kintyre. There is a Kilmarow (Cill Ma-Ruibhe) in Kintyre and across on the island of Islay, Kilarrow (Cill á Rubha). On the mainland, heading north, are other churches of Maelrubha, Strathlachlan and Dunstaffnage among them, Tobermory on the island of Mull is very likely Maelrubha's well. There is a Cill ma Ruibhe in Arisaig. Naturally enough, with its closeness to Applecross, there are a number of places connected with the saint in Skye, Kilmarie (Cill Ma Ruibhe), Aiseag Ma Ruibhe (Maelrubha's ferry) and so on. There is also a site of his in Harris, and Harris men have the Gaelic exclamation, ' Ma-Ruibhe!'. On the northern mainland, Loch Maree and Eilean Ma Ruibhe are the best known places connected with him. Loch Maree is correctly Loch Ma Ruibhe. Maelrubha is said to have had a hermitage on one of its islands; here even Queen Victoria added her coin to those visitors stuck in the trunk of the saint's tree! Lunatics were taken there for a cure, to drink of the saint's well and then be towed three times sunwise round the island behind a boat. This treatment was successful as late as 1868.

Following the mountain passes in from Applecross to the east coast, there are a further series of churches connected with the saint. Lairg is one of them, Contin another. Both had fairs connected with the saint, Lairg, St. Murie's Fair, Contin, Feil Maree on the last Wednesday in August—it was eventually transferred to Dingwall and only discontinued in 1880. Lairg has another island site of Maelrubha, Eilean Ma Ruibhe in Loch Shin. A different variation on the name, Maelrubha (servant or lad of the headland) gave the name of a fair once held in Keith (Banffshire):— Summareve's Fair (Saunct Ma Reve). Other sites are at Forres, Rafford, Forduce, Kinnell, Amulree (Ath Maol Ruibhe—Maelrubha's ford) and Crail; all strung out along the east coast of Scotland.

Although the Applecross monastery was raided by the Vikings soon enough, it continued some sort of an existence and was one of the great sanctuaries of the north. In Gaelic, it is A'Chomraich, the Sanctuary. The east coast had a similar sanctuary, of St. Duthac, at Tain. Stone crosses, later to be smashed by Presbyterian enthusiasts, marked the boundaries of the termon of Applecross. At Applecross today the site of the saint's grave is still pointed out—to take earth from it is supposed to bring one safely back to Applecross. There are also a few carved slabs, some in the Presbyterian church, and one tall cross in the graveyard which is said to have marked the grave of the second abbot, Ruaridh Mor MacAogan.

To Applecross came pilgrims to make rounds at the chapels and crosses as they still do in Ireland, and it took time for the Presbytery of Inverness and Dingwall to end their devotion. The Presbytery reports tell what went on (Printed by the Scottish History Society, Edinburgh 1896:— " Reports of the Inverness and Dingwall Presbytery, 1643-1688 "). Meeting at Applecross on 5th September, 1656:—

" The said day the Pbríe of Dingwall, according to the appoynment of Synode for searcheing and censureing such principalls and superstitious practizes as sould be discovered thaire, haveing mett at Appilcross, and finding amongst wyr abominable and heathinishe practizes that the people in that place were accustomed to sacrifice bulls at certaine tyme wppon the 25th of August, wc. day is dedicate as they coneave to St. Mourie, as they call him, and that thair wer frequent approaches to some ruinous chappells and circulateing of them, and that future events in reference especiallie to lyf and death in taking of jurneys was expect to be manifested by a holl of a round stone, qrein they tryed the entreing of thair heade, wc. if could doe, to witt, be able to put in thaire heade, they expect thair returneing to that place, and faileing, they conceaved it ominous; and withall thair adoreing of wells, and other superstitious monuments and stones tedious to rehearse, have appoynted as follows:— That quhosoever sall be found to commit such abominations; especiallie sacrifices of ony kind or at ony tyme, sall publickly appeire and be rebuked in sackcloath sex severall lords dayis in sex severall churches, viz. Lochcarron, Appilcross, Contane, Fotterlie, Dingwell and last in Garloch paroch church."

Pilgrims coming from a distance were also to be tracked down:— " Appoynts Mr. Allexr. McKenzie to inform the Presbiterie of any strangers that resorts to theas feilds as formerlie they have to thair former heathinishe practizes, that a course may be takin for thair restraint". A letter, of 6th August, 1678, from the minister of Gairloch, reported that a certain Hector MacKenzie and his sons had sacrificed a bull on Maelrubha's island in Loch Maree, for the recovery of his wife who had been sick. This Loch Maree devotion had been under discussion earlier, September 9th, 1656, and the people's hope of a cure for " theas poore ones quho are called Mourie his derilans " (Gaelic, *deireoil*, afflicted. " The Lord hath comforted his people, and will have mercy on his poor ones " Isaias, ch. 49)). The Presbytery tried to keep a check on those who had boats on Loch Maree and took pilgrims to the island.

Thus Maelrubha's intercession was sought for both mental and physical illness. The Presbytery reports simply record a traditional pattern, prayer at church and cross, a few curious customs (we may match the hole for the head, with the crawling under Declan's stone at Ardmore, or through the window of the old church at Kilmalkedar in Kerry, for example), and a festival meal. It is very doubtful whether, even neglected as they were, the people of Applecross really sacrificed a bull to Maelrubha. It is much more probable that we are dealing with a feast day meal of roast or boiled beef. Different feasts had special food, St. Michael's day had its lamb (as also Easter) and its special cakes. Pancakes were made for the eve of St. Brigit's day. At Christmas we have adopted a special menu of turkey and plum pudding. Presbyterianism made a great effort to stamp out all such heathenish, papistical practices, even to sending inspectors out on Christmas day to see nobody was quietly eating a Christmas dinner.

See also COMGALL, MOLUAG.

William Reeves: *St. Maelrubha: His History and Churches*. Proc. Society of Antiquaries of Scotland. Vol. III (1857-60), pp. 258-296.

MEL (MAOL)

February 6

Virtually nothing is known of Mel or Maol (bald/tonsured). He is supposed to have been a disciple of Patrick, indeed to have been a Briton who came over with the saint's mission. He is also said to have given the veil of the consecrated virgin to Brigit. Tirechan's account of Patrick says that Patrick " came through the River Inny into the two Teathbhas, and he ordained Mel a bishop and he founded the church of Bili (prob. Brí Léith, the hill beside Ardagh)." The Tripartite Life says Patrick went " into southern Teffia, where stands Ardachad . . . and there he left Bishop Mel and Bishop Melchus his brother ". Mel and Melchus are likely one and the same person, two forms of the one name. All we can say with certainty is that Mel was one of the earliest Irish saints, and that his work was centred on Ardagh and district. The Annals of Ulster put his death in 488, the Four Masters 487. The crozier of St. Mel is preserved in Longford.

Maire MacDermot: *The Crosses of St. Dympna and St. Mel and 10th century Irish metal work*. P.R.I.A., 58 C (1957), pp. 167-195.

MOBI

October 12

St. Mobi or Mobhi, of Glasnevin, was the son of Beonaigh and of the Fotharta people. It seems he was christened Berchen and nick-named Mobi. He had the facial deformation known as " clár ainech ", flat-faced, so often mentioned in the ' Lives ' of Irish saints. He is supposed to have been a student of Finian of Clonard before he made his own foundation at Glasnevin, now part of north Dublin. Colmcille was a student here, and Mobi is said to have had some 50 students at this time. He is also said to have been a poet. Then came bubonic plague, the school dispersed and Mobi took the disease and died. The annals of Inisfallen record in 544, " The first mortality, which is called ' blefed ' in which Mo Bí Chláraibech fell asleep "; the Annals of Ulster put his death a year later. There is a holy well of Mobi at

Grange, Glasnevin, but today no devotions at it though the water is sometimes taken for the cure of warts, toothache and sore throat.

Mobi's girdle was quite possibly enshrined and kept as a relic at one time. (One surviving belt shrine is known, that found in a bog at Moylough, Sligo, in 1943). " MoBhi's girdle, it was not rushes around wool; it was never opened around satiety; it was never closed around lies ", according to a verse in the ' Liber Hymnorum '. The references to these wonder working belts suggest they were worn as a protection in some cases, in others resorted to as a remedy for concupiscence. (For a description of the Moylough shrine, and extracts from the ' Lives ' of the saints about wonder working belts see M. Duignan. " The Moylough (Co. Sligo) and other Irish Belt-Reliquaries", Journal Galway Arch. & Hist. Soc. vol. 24, 1951 pp. 83-94). Furthermore there exists a lorica form of prayer called a Crios :—that of Finian (Clonard), the Crios Fionnáin, also includes the lines, " I am under (the protection of) MoBhi's cochall (cowl)". The protective nature of saints' cowls can also be illustrated with stories from the ' Lives.'

MOCHAOI OF NENDRUM

June 23

Very little is known of Mochaoi of Nendrum, the modern Mahee island on Strangford Lough. He is said by the Tripartite Life to have been a young swineherd converted and ordained by Patrick. A tradition makes him the first man of the saints of Ireland to whom Patrick gave a gospel and crozier. " Mo-Choe of Naendruim " died in 498 according to the Annals of Inisfallen, those of Ulster give the dates 497 and 499. Thus he could easily have belonged to the group of Patrick's converts. One of Mochaoi's own students is said to have been Colman of Dromore; later under Abbot Caylan, Finian of Moville is said to have spent some time at Nendrum. A number of the names of the abbots of Nendrum have been recorded, among them is Cronan Beg, a bishop, died 642, one of those addressed in the letter from the Pope about the date of Easter which is quoted by Bede. The last entry in the Annals is " Sedna O Deman, abbot of Nendrum, was burned in his own house " in 974. The place, on its islet in Strangford Lough, was of course, in the very path and track of the Northmen, a fragment of a Norse runic slab was found on the site. Much later, the English founded a Benedictine house there but its life was very short—only till c. 1204. The place then became a parish church, the last reference to it as such being in 1450.

Nendrum was excavated in the years 1922/23/24 and the result provides much useful information about the Celtic monasteries. The place itself is attractive, one of a number of low, ridge backed islets on the gleaming sea lough, each ringed with yellow seaweed at low tide, approached today by roads carried on causeways. Attempts have been made to pick out a skyline showing nine ridges; it is however possible that the real name was Aendrum, one ridge, which is much more in character with the island.

There are three massive, concentric, dry stone, cashel walls at the monastic site. They enclose over 6 acres, the outside one being a third of a mile in circumference, the innermost enclosure is just under an acre. H. C. Lawlor in his account of the excavation thought it was a pre-Christian cashel donated to the Church, later he was inclined to change his mind when he realised that the hill with the three concentric walls of the Patrician site at Armagh was virgin when Patrick took it (p. 192 in " Ulster: Its Archaeology & Antiquities "). The Nendrum cashel walls stand on earlier buildings, these crude structures may represent the beginning of the monastery rather than pagan homes. Prof. O'Kelly's excavation on Church Island, Valencia Harbour, showed that the monastic settlement there had begun with small and simple buildings, later the cashel was built as the place expanded (P.R.I.A. 59C (1958), pp 57-136). Later still, the importance of the cashel walls diminished and the space between the middle and inner ones was levelled to make a terrace on which paved paths and buildings were set. There were two boat quays, and two wells.

Church and round tower (marked now by a mere stump) stood in the inmost cashel (as does the little chapel on Árd Óilean of St. Fechin, where there are also three cashel walls). There was a paved path up to the church. Large circular huts occupied the middle enclosure and here was also the rectangular school house. It had been thatched and had been destroyed by fire. Like Tassach's Raholp and Ninian's Candida Casa, the stones of its walls were cemented with hard clay not mortar. In it were found some 30 tablets of slate or stone, marked with lettering and Celtic ornament. It is evident that they were used in teaching, the instructor tracing an example which the students then copied on their " slates ". The iron styles for so doing were also found, and one for use with waxed tablets. Short knife blades were probably meant for carving bone and wood.

Pottery was also made there—the monastic character of the site is shown in that all the finger prints on the ware are male! Other finds including animal bones, sea shells, oysters, limpets, the kitchen midden piles of the place; quern stones, iron slag, a bronze ingot, worked flints, quartz strike-a-lights, a stone pestle and fragments of ironstone —the ore being broken up on the spot small enough for smelting. A bronze book clasp, bronze pins and a highly ornamented penannular brooch also came to light; perhaps the most extraordinary find, however, was the monastic bell, wrought iron dipped in bronze, which was discovered in the stones of the outer cashel wall. It may have been hidden there when the Northmen attacked. To them have also been attributed the common graves with bones of men, women and children, which look like the result of a massacre. But one must remember that the bell could have been dug up by some local farmer and pushed into the wall out of his hand but where he could find it again. Prof. Estyn Evans has remarked that old walls are often treasure houses for things dug up in the adjacent fields. From the later period of occupation comes a slate clock face, 24 hours in two twelves in Roman figures. It may have been worked by water or by sand. As well, a number of ancient cross fragments, carved stones and a sundial, of various dates, were unearthed. Only one metal cooking vessel was found, an iron saucepan or frying pan.

Careful preservation and restoration work was done on the site, so that the visitor today gains a clear impression of it and the discoveries.

H. C. Lawlor: *The Monastery of St. Mochaoi of Nendrum.* Belfast, 1925. A full account of the excavation, giving as well all the known references to Nendrum.

MOCHUA OF TIMAHOE

December 24

The short Latin ' Life ' of Mochua is evidently intended chiefly to exalt Mochua at the expense of other Irish saints:—Colman Elo's pride in his wisdom is punished by loss of memory, Munnu with leprosy, the humble Mochua cures them. Mochua came from Achonry district in Connacht. His father's name was Lonan. Mochua was a late vocation, a famous warrior who became a monk in the prime of life. He is said to have made foundations in both Scotland and Ireland, the last being Derinish in Cavan where he died, in 657 or 8. His principal foundation and church however was Timahoe (Tech Mochua, Mochua's house) in Laois. This is on the road from Port Laoise to Castlecomer, five miles due south of the Rock of Dunamase, and nine miles west south west of Athy. It is an attractive spot, tucked in beside a stream among little hills. A very fine round tower survives there, the only one that has an elaborately carved Romanesque doorway.

There are said to be 59 saints recorded bearing the name Mochua, but some may be simply duplications of the same person. Mochua of Timahoe should not be confused with Mochua or Cronan of Balla in Mayo, whose feast day is March 30th. Mochua of Balla died in 694, so the claim that he was fostered by Comgall of Bangor is manifestly false.

The Annals, at 1069, mention a shrine called the Caimmin (a crozier one supposes, the crooked one) being carried away from Timahoe by O'More, who was later killed " in revenge for Fintan, Mochua and Colman ".

H. S. Crawford: *The Round Tower and Castle of Timahoe*. J.R.S.A.I., vol. 54, (1924), pp. 31-45.

MOLAGGA

January 20

Molagga, the saint of the very interesting Labbamolagga near Mitchelstown in north Cork, was born of poor parents, who were, however, of noble descent. He was, the story goes, a child of prayer and of old age, modern tradition puts his birthplace at Shanballymore. A miracle ascribed to him, raising the wife of the king of Munster, Cathal, to life after she had died in childbed, helps fix the saint's period. Cathal died in 640, so Molagga would be early 7th century.

He made his first monastic foundation at Tulach Mhin, identified by Canon Power with " an almost forgotten cillin on the summit of

Bawnanooneeny hill ", that is mid-way between two other north Cork foundations of his, Labbamolagga and Ahacross.

Labbamolagga in the fertile country between the Galtees and Bally-houras, is 4 miles north west of Mitchelstown. The larger of the two churches, and latest in date, may be the *Eidhnéan* of Molagga or on its site, the ivy covered church. The earlier and smaller Labbamolagga (Molagga's bed or grave) is a small oratory with antae; its west door built of three great slabs, two uprights and a lintel. The saint was buried inside this small 13 ft. 1 in. x 9 ft. 5 in. church. On its altar used to be preserved two stone objects rather like candle-sticks; one survives in the safe keeping of the Presentation Convent, Mitchelstown, with the erroneous title of " St. Fanahan's Candle-stick ". Canon Power showed that it came originally from the cillin of Bawnanooneeny.

There used to be a pattern on Molagga's day.

On the Cork coast is Timoleague, Molagga's house, a sea inlet now dominated by the beautiful Franciscan ruins on the old church site. Nothing remains of the earlier Celtic foundation.

Patrick Power: *Crichad an Chaoilli* (The Topography of Ancient Fermoy), Cork, 1932, pp. 26, 84-85, 95. With a photograph of the " candlestick ".
St. Molagga's Church, townland of Labbamolaga Middle, Co. Cork. Description and plans in 77th Annual Report of the Commissioners of Public Works in Ireland, 1908-9. The same Report has an account of the Franciscan ruin at Timoleague.

MOLAISE OF DEVENISH

September 12

Molaise, Mo Laisse is the pet name form of Lasren, or Laissren, of Devenish (Damh Inis, Ox island) in Lough Erne. Lasren moccu Mechtai was son of Nadfraech, of royal Ulster stock; his mother Monoa came of the royal line of Tara. Born at Airud Bhairr, baptised by Bishop Eochaidh, Molaise studied with Finian of Clonard, and then went north to make his own foundation on the island in Lough Erne. He died in 564 or 571. Unfortunately neither the Latin nor Irish ' Lives ' tell much more of this important saint than stock miracle stories. On his island site, he may well, of course, have prayed standing in the water as they claim! It is of interest that he is recorded as author, or rather according to the Irish ' Life ', copyist, of a road book, " a book of ways ". He meets a company of clerics who are travelling along with a very good road book to help them find their way; he asks to copy it, neither he nor they have a pen but a quill conveniently falls to his hand from some birds flying overhead.

Molaise too is said to have brought a load of soil from Rome to hallow Devenish, and many relics including some of Peter, Paul, Laurence, Clement, Stephen, a lock of Mary's hair and an ankle bone of Martin, some of these he gave to Maedoc of Ferns for the Breac, Maedoc's reliquary. It is therefore of interest that a hip roofed shrine was found in Lower Lough Erne in 1891. Again Molaise is supposed to have brought from Rome a gospel and bell (which, of course, he got miraculously there!) and also to have there transcribed " all that was needed of (canonical) law and rule, and of all knowledge, such as was not before in Ireland " (Irish Life). The shrine of Molaise's gospels (Soiscél Molaise) still exists. It was made at Cennfaelad's order, who was abbot of Devenish from 1001-1025.

In the Irish ' Liber Hymnorum ' there is an amusing little jingling alphabetical poem in praise of Molaise, each line with a virtue and beginning with a different letter of the alphabet—" D octor aeclesias-ticus ", " L ucerna erit in tota M acculasrius Hibernia " and so on, up to his exaltation in heaven. Its Latin indicates it is of later date than most of the material in this collection of hymns.

The remains on the island of Devenish, Lough Erne (Co. Fer-managh) are of very considerable interest and extent. They consist of the ruins of St. Molaise's ' house '; of Teampull Mor, Molaise's church, 11th-12th century Romanesque work; the ruins of the abbey of the Canons Regular of St. Augustine; a sculptured cross, some half dozen cross slabs, and a very fine round tower.

Molaise's house, an early oratory of the type of Colmcille's ' house ' at Kells or Coemgen's ' kitchen ' at Glendalough, was intact until the site was deliberately used as a quarry in the period 1797 to 1806. A study of what is left of the building shows that it had carved pilasters at each outside corner (after the style of Temple-na-hoe at Ardfert, Kerry) whilst the door, with its inclined jambs, was rather like those found at Aghowle, Banagher and Maghera. Size and steep pitched roof put it amongst the early oratories; on the other hand the art of the pilasters resembles that of the chancel arch at Rahan, and the roof seems to have been constructed like that of Cormac's chapel, an inner roof, then a space between that and the outer roof.

Until the 19th century, there was a pattern on Molaise's day at his well on Devenish.

S. H. O Grady: *Silva Gadelica*. London, 1892. I pp. 17-37. II pp. 18-34. *Irish Life of Molaise.*

A Preliminary Survey of the Ancient Monuments of Northern Ireland. Belfast, 1940, gives details of the Devenish remains.

D. Lowry-Corry: *St. Molaise's House at Devenish, Lough Erne and its Sculptured Stones*. J.R.S.A.I., vol. 66 (1936), pp. 270-284. Full photographic record of the oratory, early drawings before destruction, discussion of the nature of the building.

J. E. McKenna: *Devenish*. (History, antiquities, traditions) Dublin, 1931, (2nd edition).

MOLAISE OF INISMURRAY

August 12

Whilst St. Muredach (q.v.) is the founder saint of the very well preserved and interesting monastic site on Inismurray off the Sligo coast, its most well-known and beloved saint was Molaise, a different person from Molaise of Devenish. A little wooden figure of the saint was long venerated in the oratory in Inismurray cashel, it was removed to the National Museum in Dublin when the island was evacuated. It is of 15th century date. The Tallaght Martyrology names Molaise as Molaise mac Deglain. Nothing seems known about him. Tradition makes him, or Molaise of Devenish, Colmcille's confessor.

Catriona MacLeod: *Some Mediaeval Wooden Figure Sculptures in Ireland. Statues of Irish Saints*. J.R.S.A.I., 76 (1946), pp. 155-170.

MOLING

June 17

In doss óir ós chríchaib,
in grían an úas túathaib,
congreit ríg, bale bráthair,
cain míl, Moling Lúachair.

The golden bush over borders,
The splendid sun over tribes,
a high champion of the
    (heavenly) king,
Strong kinsman, a fair soldier,
Moling of Luachar.
    (Martyrology of Oengus).

Moling, founder of St. Mullins on the Barrow, was one of the outstanding 7th century saints. His fame extended all over Ireland though naturally enough it was especially concentrated in Leinster. He seems to have been a special favourite patron saint with the Culdees (see Maelruain of Tallaght). He is said to have obtained the remission of the hated bóroma tribute for the Leinstermen. He died in 692 or 697.

The ' Lives ' tell very little real history about St. Moling, The Irish version, which is different from the Latin, has a background of 11th-12th century date, the Latin account has been shown to be not earlier than the mid-12th century. One pleasant theme of Irish hagiography is that the accidents of birth or parentage are no hindrance to the grace of God. This is the theme of the Moling legend. He was the son of a wright named Faelan who lived in eastern Cennselach near the sea; his mother Emnat being the sister of Faelan's wife. Emnat intended to kill her child as soon as it was born but a pigeon flew in her face repeatedly so that she could not lay hands on it, until such time as a party of clerics arrived, who rescued the child, baptised and reared him. The legend thus explains the name they gave the child, Tarchell (from the ' surrounding ' of the pigeon), or Dairchell. The lad is said to have been very active and athletic and an old woman who saw him spring across a stream gave him the nickname by which he would always be known:—" Well has Moling the scholar leaped in Luachair ", said she.

Moling is said to have studied at Ferns, though he cannot have come into contact with its founder saint, Maedoc. Then he went to the River Barrow and founded St. Mullins. He is said to have also spent a period ruling Glendalough and later to have been bishop of Ferns.

St. Mullins, Tech Moling, was originally known as Achadh Cainnich or as the badger wood, Ross Broc. It is said that Moling revived an earlier and deserted foundation made there by Brendan of Clonfert. The place is on the River Barrow, one of the great waterways of Ireland. Between New Ross and Graiguenamanagh, the broad river, still feeling the pull of the tide, flows in a deep trench. West of it, heathery Brandon Hill rises to 1,694 feet; east, St. Mullins is placed on a grassy shelf above the river. Here Moling is said to have run a free ferry across the river (the ferry became a permanent feature on the river here, but no longer free of charge!), and here a large monastery grew up. Like Mochuta at Lismore, Moling is said to have had a little private hermitage some way off from the main monastery on the river bank. The best known story of Moling is of his cutting the mill stream for the monastic mill, working alone, and taking no drink nor wash from the water all the time he was labouring at it. The mill stream, a mile in length, and the mill, were solemnly blessed by Moling when finished. The wading, against the current, of the mill stream became part of the pilgrimage of St. Mullins.

The stories in the 'Lives' about Moling are very obviously constructed with the background of the Barrow valley in mind. Thus there is a miraculous flood to bring down timber from the woods flanking the river, a miraculous shifting of a rock out of the roadway and the mending of a large slab intended for a sundial when it fell off the cart on which it was being brought to the monastery. Or the amusing tale of the woman who brought her dead child to Moling, who refused to touch it as he did not want the reputation of raising people to life. The woman therefore flung the child at Moling, who started back and let it fall into the river. However the mere touch of the saint revived him, in fact, did more, taught him to swim, which he had never learned! Moling then fished him out of the Barrow and gave him to his mother.

Moling's kindness extended to animals as well as to men. He feeds a pack of hungry hounds with bread and butter, keeps a pet fox of which various foxy stories are related, entertains a pack of foxes at Ferns. Neither man nor dog hurt the foxes for they all knew they were going to Moling at Ferns. Moling meantime warned his monks to prepare for guests who'd never known hospitality before, never stayed amongst men. When the foxes arrived, Moling told them he would soon leave this city and go to his own place, and foxes and men grieved, for they knew he spoke of his approaching death.

The legend makes Moling extract the remission of the bóroma tribute by a trick. Pursued after this was found out, he and his monks sought safety by reciting a litany of Irish saints, beginning with Brigit and ending with Our Lady. It is of interest that just such a litany, in lorica form, in Irish, still survives, which would be the kind of thing Moling used. It begins 'I place myself under the protection, of Mary the pure virgin, of Brigit, bright and glowing' and so on for a long list of Irish virgin saints. The local version of how Moling tricked the high king, as told in the 1880's, is amusing enough to quote:—a courtier had been listening to the conversation between king and saint. When the saint had gone " he up an' asked the King did he know what he was after promising that little grey headed ould man? ' Begor I'm not rightly sure,' says the King, ' for he had such quare ould Irish I could hardly understand him '. (You see, 'twas something like broken English). ' Well,' says the courtier, ' you're after promising him not to ask the tax until the day after the day of judgment ' ' ".

Another well-known story of Moling, which is found in the notes and glosses on the Martyrology of Oengus, is of how the devil came to him and pretended to be Christ. Moling would not believe him, for he was dressed as a prince, and Christ, said Moling, always came to the Céili Dé as a sick man or a leper. The devil asked Moling for a blessing, or " the full of a curse," both of which were refused. Moling then sang a song describing sanctity and contrasting it with the character of those who would not serve God. The first verse runs : —

> " He is pure gold, he is a heaven round the sun,
> He is a vessel of silver, full of wine,
> He is an angel, he is wisdom of saints,
> Everyone who does the will of the King ".

At St. Mullins today are the ruins of four churches, a little oratory and the stump of a round tower, all contained within a circular enclosure. From this site, steps go down to the small tributary stream below, the holy well, the site of the saint's mill with its old millstone. The pilgrimage still takes place, with the recitation of the Rosary in the graveyard and visits to the well, but no longer on the immense scale of days gone by. Thus the Franciscan John Clyn of Kilkenny, tells how the pilgrims gathered there in 1348, when the Black Death was raging in Ireland. " This year, and chiefly in the months of September and October, great numbers of bishops and prelates, ecclesiastical and religious, peers and others, and in general people of both sexes, flocked together by troops to the pilgrimage and wading of the water at Thath-Molingis insomuch that many thousands might be seen there together for many days; some came on the score of devotion, but the greatest part for fear of the pestilence." The full " round " of the traditional pilgrimage included wading up the mill stream.

From St. Mullins also comes the Book of Mulling and its shrine. It is a text of the gospels, dated from the writing to the 9th century, though the colophon, perhaps copied from an older text, attributes it to Moling himself. Of great interest in this old manuscript is a diagram which seems to be a plan of the monastery of St. Mullins, giving the positions of its crosses. Crosses set about the monastic precincts, to make the boundaries of its lands, or to mark places where some special incident had happened, are frequently mentioned in the 'Lives'; a good number still stand on the actual sites. The Book of Mulling diagram shows the circular *lios* of the monastery and outside it two rings of four crosses each, the crosses of the four evangelists on the outside ring and of the four great prophets on the inside. This arrangement links directly with Colga Ó Duinechda's famous " Broom of Devotion " in which he invokes:—

I beseech with you, holy Jesus, your four Evangelists who wrote your divine gospel, Matthew, Mark, Luke, John.
I beseech with you, your four chief prophets who foretold your Incarnation, Daniel and Jeremias and Isaias and Ezechiel.

Reading anti-clockwise, the St. Mullin's crosses followed the same sequence as this prayer. Colga died in 796. There are also shown a group of crosses inside the *lios*, one being of Christ and the apostles. This cross actually still stands at St. Mullins, with a crude bold carving of Our Lord and the Apostles in Wicklow granite. It faced the entry—for Christ said He was the door of the sheepfold.

Another page of the Book of Mulling, which has become almost unreadable, was reconstructed by H. J. Lawlor, who was able to show that it consisted of a short, as he termed it, " liturgical fragment ". In it, the concluding verses of several well-known hymns were said, the part in this case substituting for the whole. (There are stories of a saint putting the blessing and value of saying a hymn on its final verses, when people complained of its excessive length!) The formula in the Book of Mulling began with the Magnificat, then something not yet deciphered, then the last three verses of Colmcille's ' Noli Pater ', a reading from St. Matthew v, the last three stanzas of Secundinus ' Audite Omnes ', with two others supplementary thereto, the last three of Cummean Fota's ' Celebra Juda ', an antiphon, " Exaudi ", the last three stanzas of Hilary's ' Hymnum dicat ', with antiphon ' Unitas in Trinitate ', the Apostles' Creed, the Pater Noster and possibly a collect, ' Ascendat oratio '.

H. J. Lawlor described the above as a liturgical fragment, or a daily service. But it bears much more the character of a private devotion or of a little set of prayers tacked onto the main Office as part of a monastery's special customs. We may conclude that this is what it was, for it bears a strong family resemblance to the similar set of hymns and prayers, using some of the same material, which is set out in the account of the teaching of Maelruain. In this, the passage begins. " When the Office of nocturns is over, then Maeldithruib sings *Celebra Juda*" etc. St. Mullins and Tallaght would then appear to have followed Matins with this little set of *preces*. (See Maelruain).

H. J. Lawlor: *Chapters on the Book of Mulling.* Edinburgh, 1897.
Whitley Stokes: *The Birth and Life of St. Moling.* Irish text and translation, *Revue Celtique*, 27, (1906), pp. 257-312.
S. H. O'Grady: *Silva Gadelica.* I. pp. 359-390. II, 401-424. From the Book of Leinster. A whole history of the Bóroma tribute from its origins, to Moling's intervention and its remission.
P. O'L (eary): *The Ancient Life of Saint Moling.* Dublin, 1887. This tiny booklet is of interest for the notes on the translation of the *Life* giving some local customs and traditions as they were current in the 1880's. A sample has been quoted above in connection with the tribute.

MOLUA OF CLONFERTMULLOE

August 4

Bid fáilid iar ríchtu,	Blithe will he be after arriving
frimm is mór a doche,	in heaven),
in nóebgerat rígdae,	great is my confidence in him,
mo Lua Macc oche.	the holy, royal champion,
	my Lua MacOche.
	(Martyrology of Oengus)

Molua of Cluain Ferta Molua (Clonfertmulloe, Laois, south of the Slieve Blooms) and of Druim Sneachta (Drumsnat, Co. Monaghan) was born c. 554, died 606 or 609. His ' Life ', of which three versions survive, does attempt real characterisation of Molua and tells a definite story about him as well as giving some intimate details of Irish life. He was a Munster man, son of Carthach and Sochla, youngest of their three sons. He used to herd the family cattle and frequent the cell of the seven sons of Coelboth, priests all of them. Then St. Comgall came into the district and was so impressed by young Molua that he asked to have him to instruct.

Molua was so quick and intelligent that Comgall warned him of the dangers of intellectual pride. But Molua answered that no harm nor sin could come to him if he had God always in his mind. And Comgall agreed that Molua's faith was so strong that it would be by his good understanding he would gain eternal life.

To a certain extent, one suspects that such a tale is meant to exalt

Molua at the expense of Comgall but Molua's statement about the place of reason in life does reflect the real outlook of the Irish saints. There are a whole series of charming boyhood miracles and of others about monastic life with Comgall told in the ' Life '. One refers to the Easter vigil. Comgall was celebrating the vigil Mass, and young Molua dropped off to sleep holding his lighted candle which fell into the font of blessed water. Molua woke at the splash and picked up the thoroughly wetted candle, which, of course, miraculously relit.

There is another story of how when Comgall's confessor died, Comgall blessed the students' eyes and they saw themselves all headless. For a man, Comgall taught, without a soul-friend, spiritual director, is like a man without a head. Molua said someone should hold up the gospel till Comgall got a confessor out of it. Molua held up the book and then Comgall took him for his confessor. Molua is also represented in the notes in the Martyrology of Oengus as confessor of David, Cóemóc, and Maedoc. It does seem that Molua laid special stress on the need for frequent confession. A story, found in slightly different versions in the different recensions of the ' Life ', gives his teaching. One version says there was a layman staying at Molua's monastery who would not go to confession. One day, travelling with Molua, he was surprised when the saint knelt at a cross by the roadside and said he had sinned by not making his daily confession. The man said surely it was enough to ask God direct for forgiveness. Molua said no, for the sure way to forgiveness was by confession and that just as the floor should be brushed every day, so the soul be cleansed by daily confession.

After Molua had been ordained, Comgall told him to go and make his own foundation. With a party of monks from Bangor, Molua went first to Druim Sneachta in Monaghan. He is also said to have visited Clonard, before returning to Munster and making his principal foundation at Clonfertmulloe—one of the great series of important monasteries that circle the Slieve Bloom foothills. The founding party is represented travelling along with their five cows. Molua is represented as travelling fairly widely over Munster and going far south into Decies and east into Leinster.

Molua is represented as knowing of Gregory the Great's election as Pope, and as sending a copy of his monastic rule to Gregory by the hand of abbot (or bishop) Dagan. Gregory highly approved of Molua's Rule. Molua's Rule divided the day into three parts, for prayer, for study and for manual labour. Molua's dying instructions to his monks are interesting. They were told to take good care of their land, so as to have enough to live on, for on this depends monastic stability and good religious life. And the end of religious life is eternal life. He stressed also the need to be hospitable, to receive travellers in the name of Christ.

Drumsnat, about five miles west of Monaghan, and Clonfertmulloe (Kyle) close to Borris in Ossory, are marked by ancient graveyards. The bell shrine and part of the bell of Molua are still extant, it used to be used for swearing oaths on. Considerable devotion to Molua exists in the Kilmallock area, where a fortnight is devoted to making "rounds" at the well of Molua at Martinstown east of Kilmallock, Co. Limerick. The adjacent graveyard is also visited. The first fortnight of August, ending with the 15th, is the period of making the "round". In 1950, fairly large scale restoration and improvement work was done by Muintir na Tire on the well and its approaches.

MOLUAG OF LISMORE

June 25

Moluag is the same name as Molua, both being the affectionate form of Lugaid, my Lugaid, Luag, Mo-Luóc. Moluag of Lismore, Scotland, was born in the north of Ireland, perhaps about 530. He is identified with St. Bernard's *Luanus*. Bernard in his account of Mael Maedoc, says of the monastery of Bangor, that one of its sons, Luanus, had alone founded a hundred monasteries. This, somewhat exaggerated statement, could be fitted to the very numerous churches of Moluag in Scotland. Moluag, " the pure and brilliant, the gracious and decorous ", then, it appears, after studying at Bangor, left for Scotland and made his principal foundation on the island of Lismore in 562. Tradition represents him and Colmcille racing for this fertile island in the mouth of the Great Glen, and Moluag winning. Perhaps there was indeed rivalry between the two men. In the end, it was not Colmcille's Iona that became the seat of the bishop of the Isles but Moluag's Lismore.

Lismore is well placed in Loch Linnhe for travel across Scotland to the east via the Great Glen, and for the sea routes about the Isles and back to Ireland. It is a limestone island, very green and fertile with little grey outcrops of rock here and there. As with Mo Chuta at Lismore, there is a story about the placename, that Colmcille jeered at the small foundations and enclosing lios of the new foundation. " Call that a *lios mor* (large enclosure)," said he. " Not only *lios mor* but *lios thorrach* (a pregnant enclosure)" answered Moluag. And indeed Moluag's name is broadcast over Scotland in old church sites. A number may be personal foundations. He died at Ardclach in Nairn on June 25, 592, and was buried at Rosemarkie in the Black Isle—though Lismore also claims his body. At Rosemarkie, the saint's reputed grave is marked by a noble standing cross slab carved with all the elaborate skill of Pictish art.

On Lismore the site of Moluag's foundation is marked by the Protestant church which incorporates the chancel of the old cathedral of the bishop of the Isles. The bishop's castle, at Achadun, also on the island, still stands in massive ruin. The Moluag church sites are strung out along the route from Bangor to Lismore (a map, p. 7, of these is given by Dr. Douglas Simpson in his " The Celtic Church in Scotland "), reaching north into Skye and the Outer Isles, and then in eastern Scotland, reached via the Great Glen, at Strathpeffer, Rosemarkie, Mortlach, Clatt, Clova, Tarland, etc. The Gaelic names are Cill Mo Luáig, Moluag's church, the most common placename; Dabhach Mo Luáig (Davoch, an area of land), Strathpeffer; Croit Mo-Luáig (croft, small farm), at Ballaggan on Loch Ness; Port Mo-Lúaig (harbour) on Raasay. Alyth had a fair of ' Molouach ', Clatt celebrated " St. Molloch's " fair. Around 1200, in Aberdeen, the personal name Gillemelooc (servant of Moluag) occurs. The use of Luke as a baptismal name in the areas of Moluag's churches, would also seem to derive from the saint's name.

Devotion to him seems to have been extremely strong. In the north of the island of Lewis in the Outer Isles is Teampull Mo Luigh, Moluag's church, a place still marked by its ancient (restored) church. Like Maelrubha, Moluag was invoked for the cure of insanity. At the Lewis church, the patient was walked seven times round the old church, given a drink from nearby St. Ronan's well and tied to the altar overnight. If he slept, a cure was looked for. This custom persisted into the 19th century. An Englishman, Captain Dymes, who visited Lewis in 1630, describes the gatherings in Moluag's honour then. There were two " pattern " days, Candlemas (February 2) and All Hallows (November 1). There was eating, drinking and dancing, as well as a procession with lights and an all night vigil in the church. The minister was at the time trying to stop the affair. Dymes wrote that : —

The Lewis people were " most especially devoted to one of thaire Sts. called St. Mallonuy, whose Chappell is seated in the north part of the Ile, whome they have in great veneration to this daie and keepe the Chappell in good repair. This St. was for cure of all thaire wounds and soares and therefore those that were not able to come vnto the Chappell in person they were wont to cut out the proporcion of thaire lame armes or legges in wood with the forme of thaire sores and wounds thereof and send them to the St. where I have seen them lyinge vpon the Altar in the Chappell. Within the Chappell there is a Sanctum Sanctorum wch is soe holy in theire estimation that not anie of their woemen are suffered to enter therein. Anie woman with child dareth not to enter within the doores of the Chappell, but there are certaine places without where they goe to their devotions ".

The sending of votive models of cured arm or limb is a very ancient custom, still to be seen in certain countries of which Italy is one. Lewis seems, if the good Captain did not misunderstand, to have used these models in place of the modern written petition so commonly sent (with an offering) to shrines of particular saints.

Moluag's croizer is still in existence—the *Bachuill Mor*. Long preserved at Bachuil in Lismore by its hereditary keepers, a family of Livingstones, it was given to the Duke of Argyll when the last of the Livingstone family died. The crozier is blackthorn enshrined in gilt copper. It used to be carried into battle by the men of Lorne, as likewise the Cathach by the O'Donnells. Moluag's bell was also on the island of Lismore till the 16th century and then disappeared. It has been suggested that it may be the enshrined bell which was found near Kirkmichael Glassary in 1814.

MONENNA (DARERCA)

July 6

Moninne in tslébe
Cuilinn ba cáin áge,
gabais búaid, gell glaine,
siur Maire máre.

Moninne of the mountain of
    Cuilenn was a fair pillar:
she gained a triumph, a hostage
    of purity,
a kinswoman of great Mary.
        (Martyrology of Oengus)

Darerca or Monenna of Slieve Gullion in Ulster is one of the early and important pioneers of religious life for women in Ireland. It is

necessary to disentangle her career from the story told by he
biographer Conchubranus. He wrote between 1000 and 1050 and mad
a kind of amalgam of material from a brief early 'Life' of the Iris
Monenna, with that of Modwenna (Monenna) fl. 650-700 of Burton
on-Trent and Scotland, and with material from the 'Lives' of othe
Irish saints. The short account in the Codex Salmanticensis, 'Vit
Sanctae Darercae seu Monynnae' seems nearest the ancient, now lost
original account. It takes the story of the convent to its fourth
abbess, Derlaisre (d. 600) and was probably compiled during th
period of her successor, Cron, who governed Killeevy from 600 to 624

The girl's name seems to have been Darerca, Monenna being
later addition. There is a tale of a dumb poet recovering his speech
by Darerca's intercession, his first words were 'nin nin', so the sain
was called Mo Ninne! She is also known as Sarbile; her local nam
on Slieve Gullion, is St. Bline. The account evidently tries to brin;
Monenna into contact with other eminent saints, making her receiv
the veil from Patrick, visit Brigit and found a religious settlement nea
Ibar.

What would appear to emerge is a quite probable story of an earl
religious foundress like Brigit. A priest living near her parent
instructed her in the religious life. Eight virgins and a widow with
baby joined her. Monenna fostered this child, Luger, who later becam
a bishop. She and her community left her calf country for a mor
distant site (allegedly with Ibar) for they found themselves too much
subject to interruption at home. The community grew and eventuall
they moved again, to Slieve Gullion. Here their site is low down on
the foot of the mountain (summit, 1,893 ft.), Sliabh Cuilinn (mountai
of holly). The place is called Killeevy—Cill Slaibhe Cuillean (th
initial s is elided, and the final Cuillean dropped in the modern place
name). There are here two old churches built east end onto west wal
of each other. The eastern church is 13th or 14th century, its eas
window is decorated outside with two human heads. The west one
which is the older, has a Romanesque window and is dated to 11-12th
century, but its west door is perhaps part of a still older, even 9th
century, structure. Its lintel is a single mass of granite, 6 ft. long, broa
in proportion, estimated to weigh ten tons. There was a round towe
on the south side of the older church. The place suffered fairl
frequent raiding in its later days from the Northmen based on Carling
ford Lough.

Monenna's community feared want for themselves from her excessive charity to strangers. In fact, they seem at times to have come near starvation. They had cattle on the hill, a calf carried off by a wolf came home safe. A sister had a solitary hermitage to which food was sent daily. One day a robber intercepted it, but he and his companions got lost and in the end had to yield up their prey.

Monenna is called a daughter of John the Baptist or of Elias in her mountainside search for perfection. The whole community set themselves to imitate the life of the early desert fathers with prayer, fast and vigil. Monenna sent one of the community, Brignat, over to Rosnat —Ninian's Candida Casa—to gain additional knowledge of monastic life. But she herself, it seems certain, never crossed to Scotland.

The account in the Codex Salmanticensis goes on to list Darerca's successors, Bia, Indiu, Derlaisre. It tells also of the miraculous getting of a suitable piece of timber, perhaps for the roof ridge, for a new wooden church that was being built by the sisters. Finian of Moville is described as a visitor—turning water into wine. Monenna's own death took place in 517 or 518, the foundation of Killeevy would therefore belong to the second half of the 5th century.

Darerca of Valentia island (March 22nd) is a different person from Darerca of Slieve Gullion. Perhaps she too was a very early saint. Nothing is known of her, the statement she was Patrick's sister being manifestly false.

M. Esposito: *Conchubrani Vita Sanctae Monennae.* P.R.I.A., 28 C (1910), pp. 202-246. With two alphabetical Latin hymns and a short poem in her honour. Further mss. are listed by the same author in *Hermathena,* vol. 50, pp. 145-51.
The Sources of Conchubranus' Life of St. Monenna. English Historical Review, vol. 35 (1920), pp. 71-78.

MUNCHIN

January 2

All that is really known of Munchin of Limerick (Manchén, Mainchin) is summed up by Mgr. Moloney—" Mainchine was connected with Cineal Sedna and in the 7th century a ruling prince bestowed on him the Island of Limerick ".

The saint is only known from the Dalcassian genealogies, the oldest of which says he was descended from Setna, son of Cas, and that

Ferdomnach (whose country was between the Shannon fords and the Cratloe hills and Cullane lakes) granted Inis Sibtonn (Ibton, in the tidal marshes at Limerick) to Mainchine Luimnich. Munchin's own people may have lived in the Lahinch-Ennistymon area where a parish and old graveyard preserve the name, Kilmanaheen. The Shannon island at Limerick is near to the mainland church sites of Liadain (Killeely) and of Feidelm (Killalee), aunt of Ferdomnach. In return for this Inis Ibton, Munchin is said to have given Ferdomnach, " the blessing of honour and chieftaincy and hence he exercised supremacy over the Dal Cais ". Ferdomnach flourished at the end of the 7th century. There seems to be no evidence of Limerick having a traditional feast in honour of Munchin.

M. Moloney: *Limerick's Patron.* North Munster Antiquarian Journal, vol. 7, (1957), pp. 11-14.

MUREDACH

August 12

Muredach, of the race of Niall of the Nine Hostages, is patron, probably founder, of Killala. Two contradictory dates are linked with his name and virtually nothing else. One makes him a convert of Patrick and Killala a Patrician foundation. The other makes him meet Colmcille at Ballysodare after Drumceatt. The placename Kilmurray, seems usually to mean the church of Muredach, but not necessarily the Killala one.

It is likely that the Killala Muredach is founder and patron of the great monastery on the island of Inismurray off the Sligo coast. The saint chiefly honoured there by the people in recent times, was the equally enigmatic Molaisse, whose feast day is also August 12th. The Inismurray remains are still very complete, the immense cashel wall of stone, perhaps a secular fort donated to the saint, the series of churches, including a little stone oratory, the beehive cells and the ' Altars ' (one with the famous cursing stones) and in addition a very interesting series of cross inscribed slabs. Some of these are set up in the cashel, others outside, some of them mark the ' stations ' of the traditional pilgrimage which made a circuit of the whole island. The Inismurray remains are the most complete Irish example of an early Irish monastery on a large and fertile (till the soil had all been stripped for fuel by the people) island, just as Skellig Michael represents the most complete island hermitage.

W. F. Wakeman: *Survey of the Antiquarian Remains on the Island of Inismurray*. R.S.A.I., extra volume for 1892.

NATHY

August 9

I nAchud cháin clantair Nathí credal cruimther, Nathy the pious priest is buried in Ached Cain, Oengus wrote in his Felire. Nathy is said to have been born in Connacht, in the barony of Leyny in Sligo and to have made a foundation at Achonry. Here many students gathered round him, among them Fechin of Fore. Attracta is also brought into contact with him, but virtually nothing more is known about the saint. The Fechin contact, if correct, would date Nathy to late 6th, early 7th century.

NESSAN

July 25

" Nessan the deacon " as he is always called, was founder of the famous monastery of Mungret (Mungairit) near Limerick. His death is placed in 551. Nothing else seems to be known about him.

NINIAN

September 16

Deus, qui populos Pictorum et Britonum per doctrinam sancti Niniani Episcopi et Confessoris tui ad tuae fidei notitiam convertisti; concede propitius; ut, cuius eruditione veritatis tuae luce perfundimur, eius intercessione caelestis vitae gaudia consequamur. Per Dominum etc.

(God who brought knowledge of your faith to the Pictish and British peoples by the teaching of St. Ninian, bishop and confessor, grant, by his intercession, whose teaching made the light of truth shine on us, that we may reach to the joy of life in heaven).

(Collect for the Mass of St. Ninian in Scotland)

The biographer of St. Ninian, who may well have been the first apostle of what is now Scotland, is faced by a whole series of questions and controversies. The one date in Ninian's 'Life' is hotly denied as a later and fabulous addition. How far is the reliable Bede reliable in the matter of geography, of geography of a country he neither knew, nor it would appear, particularly liked? Who were the Picts and what was the southernmost boundary of their territory? The whole problem is further queered by the attempt to read into it answers to later religious controversy, to show the early church of southern Scotland as independent of Rome and Ninian's supposed visit there a mere trick of Roman hagiographers.

First of all, certain facts of the geography of Scotland need to be stressed. Its great mountain backbone runs from north to south, the Ridge of Scotland (Alba), Drum Albyn. It is crossed by a number of mountain passes, which take the traveller from east to west, in particular the NE-SW trough of the Great Glen, Glen Mor na h-Alba. Drum Albyn sends out a massive shoulder or spur eastward in central Scotland, the ridge called the Mounth (incorrectly known today by the ghost word, Grampian, a scribal error in copying Mons Graupius). The Mounth however does not reach right to the east coast. There is a lowland coastal plain which extends the length of Scotland, from the Border country, across the Midland Valley and right up to Caithness. Meantime the country is separated from England by the lower and less rugged mountains of the Southern Uplands, extending east-west across the country but again crossed by passes. Scotland's basic partition has never been between north and south, but between highland and lowland, between the men of the plains of the east and the south and the men of the mountains and the islands.

Bede states that Colmcille converted the northern Picts, Ninian the southern. Present day geography would make the Mounth the divide between southern and northern Picts. But Bede's reliability should not be pushed to the length of infallibility. It is quite possible he had in mind Ptolemy's geography, which canted Scotland over on its axis relative to England, to make northern really western, and southern really eastern. That Bede was not sure about the geography of Scotland seems very probable from Adamnan, who tells of Colmcille working in western Dalriadian territory, west of Drum Albyn. True, he visited Brude, got a safe conduct, as well, for Cormac Ui Liathain to go to the Orkneys, but he does not appear in Adamnan as apostle of the whole north. Thus it is quite possible to argue that Bede meant to indicate Colmcille's territory as west of Drum Albyn and Ninian's as east of it.

Who indeed were the Picts? Perhaps they were originally no single nation or race, but settlers of different races who eventually were welded into a kingdom. There is some very slender evidence to suggest that Scotland had two languages before the Irish came to Dalriada, one of some very early settlers, which was not Celtic at all; the other a form of P-Celtic which had closer links with Gaul than with adjacent Britain, and Brittonic. The present tendency seems to be to suppose that the Picts and their kingdom never came south of the Forth-Clyde line, the Midland Valley. Ninian belonged to the country south of that, south-west Scotland, which had British inhabitants. Patrick, in his Letter to the Soldiers of Coroticus, calls them allies of the " Scots and the apostate Picts " (socii Scottorum atque Pictorum). This suggests that some early, pre-Patrician, missionary work had been done north of the Forth-Clyde line.

Ninian, or to use the native British form, Nynnyaw, has no anywhere near contemporary biographer. There is an 8th century poem on his miracles (Miracula Nynie Episcopi). Then there is the 12th century ' Life ' by Ailred of Rievaulx. Ailred makes the conventional claim of rewriting older material more stylishly, and it is probable enough that the poem and the 12th century ' Life ' use common sources. Ailred says that Ninian went abroad to study, that he went to Rome, that he visited Martin of Tours, returned to south-west Scotland, to Whithorn and began to build a church there. Whilst this work was going on, news came of Martin's death; the Whithorn church was dedicated to Martin. Martin died in 397. This would date Ninian, but the 8th century poem makes no mention of a visit to Martin. Negative evidence is never entirely satisfactory, a poem about miracles is, strictly speaking, about miracles, and a visit to Martin of Tours is not in itself a miraculous occurrence! On the other hand, the Roman visit is a common stock item of hagiography. Are we then to conclude with a number of authorities that Ninian is lost in the darkness of time?

Or dare we accept that Ninian was in Whithorn, Candida Casa, around 397, and that the thin line of old dedications to Ninian that runs right up the east coast of Scotland, Dunnottar, Methlick, Navidale, and another in the Great Glen on Loch Ness, suggests the first Christian penetration of Scotland?

Martin too is a vital link in the development of monasticism in the west. His monastery took the ideals of the desert fathers and combined them with that of the apostolate; Martin was the apostle of the French countryside. If Candida Casa, Whithorn, or Rosnat as the Irish sources call it, had close links with Martin, it was a line by which Martin's teaching could reach Ireland, for Irish students are mentioned studying there. One was Finian of Moville; earlier, Darerca or Monenna of Slieve Gullion sent one of her nuns to Rosnat to gain further knowledge of monastic observance.

Thus Ninian may be the first apostle of Scotland, and he may be an important link in the spread and development of monasticism in both Scotland and Ireland. In point of fact, he could perfectly well have visited Europe, perhaps not go so far south as Rome, but at least come under Martin's influence in Gaul. A little later, Patrick would take the same route. The tradition of Ireland's pre-Patrician saints involves a visit to " Rome ", that is to continental sources of Christianity before beginning their home apostolate. Thus, though often enough the visit " to Rome " may mean exactly nothing, in other cases it may involve a very genuine bit of tradition. Again, the cult of Martin became so widespread that a hagiographer would try to bring his hero into contact with Martin (thus Patrick is represented as related by blood to Martin). But again, there were genuine personal contacts with Martin. For Ninian, the present evidence seems insufficient to decide one way or another with any finality, the present writer is inclined to accept the contact with Martin and a very early apostolate up the east coast plains of Scotland.

The Whithorn remains are of extreme interest. There are two sites, at Whithorn town itself, and then on the Isle of Whithorn, a windswept headland on the northern shore of the Solway Firth. In 1949, excavations revealed the surviving walls of Ninian's " Candida Casa ", the White House. It is now up against the east wall of the ruined priory of the Premonstratensian Canons, so that its west wall is lost. It is built of local rock, shale and slate split along their bedding planes and not dressed square, set in greenish clay. That is an early form of building, using clay, not mortar; it is found in the ancient church of Raholp (see Asicus) and the school house at Nendrum (see Mochaoi) both in northern Ireland. Again, the building has some affinities with the ancient ruined chapel on the Garvellach islands in the Firth of Lorne (see Colmcille). Some of the original white finish (a coarse cream mortar) which gave the place its name was found still sticking to the outside of these old walls. On the ' isle ' site, there is the shell of a 13th century church; very probably Ninian sought out this spot as a hermitage for occasional retreat. Whithorn too has a very interesting series of inscribed stones, bearing the Chi-Rho monogram, early crosses, and inscriptions in the rough Latin one would expect of a partially Romanised North Britain. The impression one gains from them is of an ancient and early centre of Christianity. The oldest is thought to be the Latinus stone, in translation:— " We praise you Lord. Latinus aged 35 years and his daughter aged 5 years. Here the descendants of Barrovad made a monument " (to them). Another early stone, bearing a Greek cross in a circle is inscribed " The stone of a servant of St. Peter the Apostle." This ancient stone even has been hauled into the field of religious controversy and writers have attempted to post-date it so as to make it the work of much later " Romanising " influences!

Ninian's name became in vernacular Scots, Ringan and in Gaelic, Truinnean. Thus ' church of Ninian ' is Teampull an Truinnein in Gaelic. In Galloway and Ayrshire, Killantringan is formed from Cill an Truinnein. Norse has Rinan, and it seems probable that Rinansey, now North Ronaldsay in the Orkneys, is Ninian's Isle. Churches of Ninian are numerous in Scotland and are, of course, in very many cases, later dedications. In mediaeval times, Whithorn continued to be a famous place of pilgrimage of southern Scotland.

(The following sources give the known facts, such as they are, for Ninian. Several of them carry as well a certain religious bias for which the reader should make due allowance).

W. Douglas Simpson: *St. Ninian and the Origins of the Christian Church in Scotland*. Edinburgh, 1940.

Whithorn Volume (Dumfries, 1950) of the Dunfriesshire and Galloway Natural History and Antiquarian Society. Includes the account of the excavations at Candida Casa made by C. A. Ralegh Radford in 1949.

Wilhelm Levison. *An Eighth Century Poem on St. Ninian*. Antiquity 14, (September, 1940), pp. 280-291.

P. Grosjean, S.J.: *Les Pictes Apostats dans l'Epitre de S. Patrice*. Analecta Bollandiana t. 76, (1958), pp. 354-378.

Alan Orr Anderson. *Ninian and the Southern Picts*. Scottish Historical Review, April, 1948, pp. 25-47.

The Problem of the Picts. (Edinburgh, 1955). Symposium edited by F. T. Wainwright.

ORAN (ODRÁN/ODHRÁN/OTTERAN)

October 27

Several Irish saints, of none of whom any real historical record survives, have been named Oran (Odrán). In the Náemsenchas in the Book of Ballymote is recorded the pedigree of : —

> Odrán Iea chrábhaidh chruaidh
> mac Aingein co mórbuaidh,
> maic Boguine in gaisgidh ghér
> maic Conaill Gulbain maic Néill.

(Oran of Iona, of severe piety, son of triumphant Aingen, son of Boguine of keen valour, son of Conall Gulban, son of Niall—of the nine hostages). ' Odrán sab sóer snámach ', Oran, strong, noble and bouyant, is noted in the Martyrology of Oengus at October 27. The gloss thereon at once introduces the complexity of any study of the St. Orans, noting that the saint of October 27 could be from Tech Airennain in Meath, from Letracha Odrain in Munster or from Relic Odrain in Colmcille's Iona, " or he is in Gair maic Moga, i.e., an island in Corco-Duibne, and by swimming he went into it ". It is generally accepted that the patron of Waterford is the Oran (or in the Scandinavian form of the name, Otteran) of Iona and Reilig Oran; however an old ' Ordo Divini Officii Recitandi ' of 1761, edited by Peter Purcell, P.P. of St. John's Waterford 1759—67, gives an utterly different account. Purcell's story, known from no other source, says Otteran was an 8th century bishop who died as a martyr in Suevia (Suabia) where he had gone as a missionary.

Scottish writers have taken Oran of Iona to be Oran of Leitrioch Odráin, Letteragh, Co. Tipperary, whose death is recorded by the Four Masters in 548. This would make Oran's church the first foundation on Iona, as the veneration in which it was held suggests it very likely was. But the genealogies contradict such an identification, for Oran of Iona is the person cited above, a great grandson, like Colmcille, of Conall Gulban. Oran of Letteragh, whose day according to the Martyrology of Tallaght is October 2nd, is listed among the saints of the Slechta Conaire Meic Modha Lamha : Odhrain m Meic Craith m Trochaill m Easamain m Doighre m Nuaidhaid neimhnigh. It seems that this Oran founded Letteragh monastery and died and was buried at it. Other Orans were a brother of Ciaran of Clonmacnois and in the legend of Patrick, the saint's charioteer (19 February).

Oran of Iona evidently worked and was the object of devotion over an area of the western isles. There are for example the following sites of his:— Kiloran on Colonsay, Claodh Odhrain at Kirkapoll, Tiree and Tiroran on Loch Scridain in Mull. The legend of Oran as the first of Colmcille's monks to die on Iona, a kind of propitiatory human sacrifice, may be dismissed at once. Adamnan says definitely the first monk to die on Iona, well after the foundation had been made, was Brito (or a Briton) (Bk. III, ch. 6). Much more probably this legend was made up to try to make Colmcille the sole saint and founder of Iona whilst explaining the veneration given to Oran there. Very likely Oran was a slightly older contemporary of Colmcille's, who founded the first church on the Island. At least, Reilig Oran marked today by its ruined Romanesque chapel, was the most hallowed ground in Iona and its great burial place. Here, where many of their grave slabs still lie, were buried chiefs of the western isles, some of the early kings of Dalriada, and also it appears Scandinavian chiefs and some Irish princes. (Whence the story of the graves of the kings of Scotland, Ireland and Norway, which were once marked there by inscriptions as Sir Donald Munro, High Dean of the Isles, described after his visit of 1549).

Some accounts connect this Iona Oran also with the Oran of Tigh Erennain in Meath. It was probably because the Iona graveyard was so famous and that Scandinavian leaders had chosen it for their burial place, that the Ostmen of Waterford picked on Oran for the patron of their city. This must be about the first occasion that a saint, unconnected with a particular district was chosen for its patron, in Ireland. Oran's connection with Waterford would date from 1096, when the Danes got their first bishop.

The legend of the death of Oran, as told by Manus O Donnell in his ' Life of Colmcille ' makes the latter tell Oran, " I will give you the Kingdom of God, and moreover I grant you this, that whoever makes a request at my tomb or my resting place, shall not get it until he first makes prayer to you ". Dean Munro's account tells the same story, that Reilig Oran was the most holy site on Iona. Having listed the kings and chiefs buried there, he says it was " because this sanctuarey wes wont to be the sepulture of the best men of all the iles, and als of our kings, as we have said; becaus it was the maist honorable and ancient place that was in Scotland in thair days, as we reid ".

PATRICK

March 17

Lassar gréne áne,	The flame of a splendid sun,
apstal Hérenn hóge,	The apostle of virginal Ireland,
Pátraic co méit míle,	may Patrick with many thousands,
rop dítiu ar tróge.	be the shelter of our wretchedness.

(Martyrology of Oengus)

' Patraic apstol Herend, cend creitme na nGóidel,' Patrick, apostle of Ireland, head of the belief of the Gaels, as he is styled in the Martyrology of Gorman (compiled between 1166 and 1174), is a person of whom we know, as it were, everything and nothing. From the man's own writings, whose authenticity is now unchallenged, we have a complete picture of the saint, the sort of person he was, a summary of his life and achievement. But Patrick gives no dates, nor any names to which dates could be attached. His biographers' work only dates from the 7th century, they drew on earlier, now lost, biographies and on living tradition, but in them legendary material is mingled with the basic facts. Patrician chronology remains a source of lively controversy. " All difficulties concerning Patrick hinge upon his chronology," says Professor James Carney (Radio Éireann Thomas Davis lectures). In the same series of talks, Fr. John Ryan, S.J., remarked that we have " St. Patrick's own word for it that he suffered grievously from the scholars of his day. He has been suffering at the hands of scholars ever since."

It is my personal view that fewer difficulties arise from accepting the traditional dates for Patrick, one Patrick and not two, with his arrival in Ireland about 432 and his death in 461 on March 17th. But since the other theories have much to be said for them, it is essential to make a sharp distinction between what Patrick tells us himself, and what we know, or think we know, from other sources.

St. Patrick. From his own account of himself.

The two main Patrician documents are the saint's " Letter to the Soldiers of Coroticus " and the " Confession ". The first was written after a raiding British prince had pounced on a number of Patrick's newly baptised Irish converts, killing some and carrying off the rest.

It is probably earlier than the " Confession " which is a defence of Patrick's whole work and mission. There survive as well some " Sayings " of Patrick, and the Canons issued in the name of the bishops Patrick, Auxilius and Iserninus. These Canons are obviously those of a young and growing missionary church operating in a still partly pagan country. There is no reason why they should not go back to Patrick's time.

Patrick the man and the saint comes clearly through to us in his urgent and moving account of himself. " Although I am imperfect in many things, I never the less wish that my brethren and kinsmen should know what sort of a person I am, so that they may understand my heart's desire " (Confession). And Patrick is eminently successful in conveying " what sort of person " he was.

He tells us that his father was a deacon named Calpornius, and his grandfather a priest, Potitus. (Married clergy were not unusual in the early Church, had not St. Peter been married? any more than they are now in the Eastern Churches). Patrick's father owned a country house near a place, whose identity is now lost though claimed for many places, called Bannavem Taburniae. It was near the sea and the Irish Channel, for it was from this country house that Patrick aged about 16, with many thousands of others, was carried off into slavery by a party of Irish raiders.

Patrick had never taken study, or his religion, seriously. Now he tells us that he spent six years tending sheep in Ireland and in the solitude of the Irish hillsides and the Irish woods, "the love of God and His fear came to me more and more, and my faith was strengthened ". He would say a hundred prayers in the day " and almost as many in the night . . . and I used to get up for prayer before daylight, through snow, through frost, through rain, and I felt no harm, and there was no sloth in me—as I now see, because the spirit within me was then fervent ".

Then one night he had a dream and heard a voice telling him he would soon go to his own country. Soon after, the voice told him, " See, your ship is ready ". It was 200 miles away, at a place Patrick had never before visited, but he got there and found the ship ready to sail. Patrick offered to pay for his passage; the captain refused. Then as Patrick was going back to the house where he was staying, a sailor shouted to him to come back. They agreed to take him in spite of the fact that Patrick would not go through the pagan ritual of friendship of sucking their breasts. Three days at sea brought them to land but one deserted and desolate. They and their cargo of Irish wolfhounds were dying of hunger as they crossed this devastated countryside. The sailors asked Patrick, if his God was all powerful, to pray for help. He did so, and a herd of pigs appeared on the road, which they killed, feeding themselves and the dogs. They also came on some wild honey but Patrick would not touch it because they had offered it first to their gods before eating it.

" That same night ", Patrick asleep was attacked by the devil, who fell on him like a large rock. Patrick called on Helias and woke, seeing the sun rising in the sky, a symbol of the light of Christ falling on him. The Church had shifted the idea of sun worship to that of the true Sun, the Sun of Justice, Christ, and Patrick's cry seems a direct reference to this. At the end of his " Confession " he wrote, " For this sun, which we see rises daily for us because He commands so, but it will never reign nor will its splendour last. . . . We, who believe in, and worship the true sun—Christ. . . ."

Patrick makes a reference to having fallen into captivity again, " after many years ". The main story goes on to describe their travelling for 28 days through the desert country and having no food left when they did come to inhabited land. " After a few years," Patrick was back with his people in Britain who wanted him to stay permanently with them. But Patrick had a vision in the night of a man called Victoricus coming from Ireland with many letters. And reading one of them, Patrick thought he heard the Voice of the Irish, those beside the Wood of Voclut near the Western Sea, and that they called him to come and walk amongst them once more.

" And I was quite broken in heart, and could read no further, and so I woke up. Thanks be to God, after many years the Lord gave to them according to their cry."

Ireland is unique in having first kidnapped her national apostle, and Patrick remained a Briton at heart. He not only describes himself as unlearned, feeling always the result of his neglected education, the stone lifted up from the mud and set on top of the wall, but he is also the reluctant apostle:— " I did not go to Ireland of my own accord, not until I had nearly perished " (Confession). " Did I come to Ireland without God, or according to the flesh ? Who compelled me? I am bound by the Spirit not to see any of my kinsfolk. Is it of my own doing that I have holy mercy on the people who once took me captive and made away with the servants and maids of my father's house?" (Letter).

" Thus I am a servant in Christ to a foreign nation for the unspeakable glory of life everlasting which is in Christ Jesus Our Lord " (Letter). Patrick does not tell us much about how he trained or where, for his " laborious episcopate ". He tells in some detail of an attack on his fitness to be a bishop by his seniors. A friend who had told Patrick that he should be a bishop and promised his own support, in fact, at a critical meeting, brought up some sin Patrick had committed in his youth and confided to this friend before Patrick's ordination to the deaconate. Patrick was heartbroken over this action of " my dearest friend "; again he was consoled by a vision in the night.

" Therefore I give Him thanks who has strengthened me in everything, as He did not frustrate the journey upon which I had decided, and the work which I had learned from Christ my Lord; but I rather felt after this no little strength, and my trust was proved right before God and men."

The objections to Patrick being made a bishop were overcome; but it appears he always had to face a current of opposition, his lack of learning, perhaps the very success of his mission, were always being held against him.

Patrick quite definitely represents himself as the apostle of Ireland. Both " Confession " and " Letter " described a pagan country into which Patrick brings the Faith, baptises many thousands, ordains and organises a native clergy. It was dangerous work at times, Patrick mentions " twelve dangers in which my life was at stake—not to mention numerous plots ". That no one should say Patrick was preaching the gospel for gain, he gave back, often to the offence of the donors, all gifts. He refused presents given at baptisms, or from those he ordained priests. On the contrary, " I spent money for you that they might receive me; and I went to you and everywhere for your sake in many dangers, even to the farthest districts, beyond which there lived nobody and where nobody had ever come to baptise, or to ordain clergy, or to confirm the people. With the grace of the Lord, I did everything lovingly and gladly for your salvation ". He goes on to say that he gave presents to local kings, the obvious missionary policy in a country with Ireland's political structure of many small kingships. Even so they wished to be rid of Patrick and to kill him.

Men and women were not only converted but felt a call to the monastic vocation. " Hence, how did it come to pass in Ireland that those who never had a knowledge of God, but until now always worshipped idols and things impure, have now been made a people of the Lord, and are called sons of God, that the sons and daughters of the kings of the Irish are seen to be monks and virgins of Christ?" (Confession).

Patrick stresses that his achievement is not his own, but the grace of God working through " Patrick, a sinner ". " For I am very much God's debtor, who gave me such great grace that many people were reborn in God through me and afterwards confirmed, and that clerics were ordained for them everywhere, for a people just coming to the Faith, whom the Lord took from the utmost parts of the earth." (Confession).

" So, now I command my soul to my faithful God, for whom I am an ambassador in all my wretchedness; but God accepts no person and chose me for this office—to be, although among His least, one of His ministers . . . But what can I say or what can I promise to my Lord, as I can do nothing that He has not given me?" (Confession).

" Wherefore may God never permit to happen to me that I should lose His people which He purchased in the utmost parts of the world. I pray to God to give me perseverance and to deign that I be a faithful witness to Him to the end of my life for God " (Confession).

" Now I have given a simple account to my brethren and fellow servants who have believed me because of what I said and still say in order to strengthen and confirm your Faith. Would that you, too, would strive for greater things and do better! This will be my glory, for a wise son is the glory of his father " (Confession).

This is the voice of the real St. Patrick. His Latin is not the Latin of a trained writer, rather we hear the spoken word, the awkwardnesses and uncertainties of the written text would disappear with the inflections of the man's voice. He was obviously a popular and convincing speaker. His native language would have been a Welsh (Brittonic) form of Celtic, and he would have had to learn Irish, which belongs to the other group of Celtic languages. Père Grosjean has suggested that part of the form of Patrick's writing may be due to his preaching, at least for part of his time, in Ireland through an interpreter. Although Patrick harps so much on his lack of learning, he means specialist and scholarly learning. He had made sufficient studies abroad for his work as priest and later bishop. He was obviously soaked in the scriptures, their language is his own. He seems to have been familiar both with Jerome's Vulgate text and some of the earlier Latin versions as well—he used the old Latin version for the

Old Testament, the Vulgate for the Acts and a mixture for the rest of the New Testament. The story of his stay at the island of Lerins seems ruled out by the fact that his scripture versions are not the text then used at that monastery.

St. Patrick from other sources.

Tírechán's account of St. Patrick, a survey of the churches founded by the saint, was perhaps written c. 670, if by the " recent mortalities " is meant the plague of 664-8. Tírechán seems to have been a native of Tirawley and was a follower of Bishop Ultan of Ardbreccan in Meath. Muirchú moccu Machtheni, the other early biographer of Patrick, appears to have belonged to the church of Slebte in Leinster. He was commissioned to write a ' Life ' of Patrick by Bishop Aed of Slebte—who died in 700. Both accounts are based on earlier material, both written and traditional. Colmcille is said to have been the first person to collect the miracles of Patrick. Tírechán says he used a book about Patrick belonging to Bishop Ultan as one of his sources.

From these two accounts and other traditions and later accounts as well, we can sift out some further information about Patrick. That his full name was Magonus Sucatus Patricius, and that his mother was called Concessa. That he studied at Auxerre in Gaul, attracted to this place by the fame of its bishop, Germanus, the man who had been sent as papal legate to Britain about the Pelagian heresy in that country. His place of captivity in Ireland is named, Sliab Mis (Slemish), Co. Antrim, and his master, a druid or learned man called Miliuc maccu Boin. The Wood of Voclut has been identified with a site near Killala, Co. Mayo, though what Patrick had to do in particular with this place remains unknown. We do not know from what port he left for the continent, but the devastation he found there may have been the result of the Vandal onslaught, which began on the night of New Year, 406-407. This would put Patrick in Gaul in the year 407, and his birth around 385.

Prosper of Aquitaine's Latin *Chronicon* notes that in the year 431, " To the Irish believing in Christ, Palladius, ordained by Pope Celestine, is sent as their first bishop ". The Irish Annals put Patrick's arrival in 432. The traditional version of what these two dates mean, the *Chronicon* is a reliable, contemporary record, is that Palladius' mission failed, and that Patrick's followed at once. It could tie up with what Patrick says about the arguments over his fitness for being consecrated a bishop.

The traditional accounts make Patrick land at Saul (Sabhal) in the north of Ireland and work south. The Annals of Ulster put the foundation of Armagh in 444, and there seems sufficient reason to accept this date and that Armagh is a Patrician foundation. The " pre-Patrician " saints of the south who had already established the Faith to some extent there, might well be left to get on with the job whilst Patrick went into virgin country in the north. His own account quoted above, of baptising etc. in country in which nobody had yet gone to do so, rather implies that in other parts of Ireland, nearer to continental contacts, such preaching and baptising had been done.

In 441, the Irish Annals note that Patrick was given " approval in the Catholic Faith " by the newly elected Pope Leo I. There is no evidence that Patrick went personally to Rome on this occasion, but some official report on progress in Ireland may have been forwarded then. Other helpers were sent to him, Secundinus (whose name is preserved in that of the hamlet of Dunshaughlin) came in 439, died in 447. It seems certain enough that he is the author of the famous Latin hymn in praise of Patrick, *Audite omnes*. Another incomer was Auxilius (d. 459), a third Iserninus (d. 468). These three bishops appear to have come from Gaul to Patrick together. Patrick, Auxilius and Iserninus are the bishops by whose authority the Armagh Canons were issued. They give some intimate details of the young Irish Church. Among them is the regulation that baptism is only to be given after the forty days fast:— that is at Easter, after the final instructions as well as the fast of Lent, the ancient custom of the whole Church. Patrick, in his " Letter " describes the newly baptised who were killed or carried off as wearing the white garments, which the neophytes assumed after the Easter baptism and wore all Easter week (whence our name for Low Sunday, Dominica in albis, when the baptismal robes were taken off).

Other men came to help from Britain and most important, there were the Irish themselves. Benen was one of the first followers of Patrick, but soon there were very many, enough to provide the bulk of the clerics needed for the growing Church.

The traditionally accepted date for Patrick's death is March 17th 461. He may have died at Saul, but it may be safer to say that we do not know where he died.

What Patrick did in Ireland is well symbolised by the story of his lighting the Easter fire on Slane Hill, bringing the light of Christ into the darkness of Ireland. The story however is not historically true, a later composition which could not be correct, for the ceremony of the Paschal Fire only goes back to around the 8th century. The ceremony of the Paschal Candle is, of course, much more ancient and important and was well known in Italy, Gaul and Spain in the 6th century.

The story of Patrick's Lenten fast on the mountain of Croagh Patrick (2,510 ft.) on Clew Bay in Mayo, may very well be true. His " Confession " tells of how he had prayed on the hillsides and he may have continued to find them suitable places for prayer. It is now the great mountain top pilgrimage of Ireland. Patrick's Purgatory, in Lough Derg, Donegal, appears to have no connection whatever with Patrick. Patrick's crozier, the Bachall Jesu, survived until it was publicly burned at the Reformation. His bell and its shrine still exist; there are also the shrines of Patrick's hand, jaw, thumb and tooth. The ancient Irish lorica, St. Patrick's Breastplate, cannot be proved to be the saint's own composition, though its spirit is in tune with that of the author of the " Confession " and " Letter ".

Patrick aroused and held the love and devotion of the Irish people. As Dom Louis Gougand put it:—" For having annexed Ireland to the kingdom of God, amid so many sufferings and tribulations, with unrivalled Christian heroism, his people have honoured and blessed him throughout the ages, as has been the case with no other national apostle."

A full Patrician bibliography would be immense, ranging from the arguments over Patrician chronology and the possible existence of two Patricks, to the numerous popular biographies of the saint. The present work does not seem to be the place to discuss the chronological question in detail and the views of the different scholars who have specialised thereon, nor the thesis of the Two Patricks. The following books and papers give the Patrician sources, an account of the present state of the question and further references to the other numerous studies.

Ludwig Bieler, (editor): *Liber Epistolarum Sancti Patricii Episcopi*. I. Introduction and Text. II. Commentary. Dublin, 1952. (Translator and annotator). *The Works of St. Patrick. St. Secundinus Hymn on St. Patrick. The Lorica.* Vol. 17 in Ancient Christian Writers series. London, 1953. (Author). *The Life and Legend of St. Patrick.* Dublin, 1949.
James Carney: *The Problem of St. Patrick.* Dublin, 1961.
Christine Mohrmann: *The Latin of Saint Patrick.* Dublin, 1961.
Saint Patrick. Radio Eireann Thomas Davis lectures. Dublin, 1958. In which a group of scholars put forward their differing views.
Francis Shaw, S.J.: *The Myth of the Second Patrick.* Studies, Spring 1961, pp. 5-27.
Tomás O Fiaich: *St. Patrick and Armagh.* I.E.R., March, 1959, pp. 153-170.
St. Patrick and Armagh, symposium in Seanchas Ardmhacha, vol. 2, no. 1, 1956.
Seanchas Ardmhacha, special issue, *The Patrician Year,* 1961-62.

RUADHAN

April 15

Lorrha (Lothra) in north Tipperary was one of the most important monastic centres in Munster. Unfortunately we know very little indeed of its founder, Ruadhan (died 584). The surviving ' Lives ' are later and are mainly concerned with the entirely legendary tale of the cursing of Tara and with magical themes like the wonder tree of Lorrha.

Lorrha is one of the many early monastic foundations made along the great highway of the Shannon. It lies immediately to the east of the head of Lough Derg of the Shannon, four miles east, that is, of Portumna. The place itself is in a hollow, but the land is dry and suitable for farming, rising above the marsh and bog of the surrounding plains. The importance of the place is shown by its surviving series of ruins. The Celtic foundation of Ruadhan is marked by an ancient oratory built onto the Protestant church with some broken cross shafts and bases near by. One, of 8th century date, shows a procession of horsemen and horses. There are also the ruined mediaeval parish church; the ruin of the Augustinian foundation of Fons Vivus, and the church, still massive in its decay, of the 1269 Dominican foundation under the invocation of St. Peter Martyr.

Ruadhan himself is said to have been son of Fergus Bern, son of Dera Dubh, of the race of the kings of Munster. He is said to have studied at Clonard and after his ordination there, to have made a foundation of his own in Ara mac ua Neitt in Muscraighe Tire. This district lies to the north-east of Lough Derg of Shannon. From there he moved to Lorrha. The Irish version of his ' Life ' makes a wild boar (of which Ruadhan was considerably afraid) give up its lair in a hollow tree to the saint at Lorrha.

It has been suggested from some passages in the accounts of Finian of Clonard and of Ruadhan that there were at various times disputes and negotiations between Lorrha and the other great Irish monasteries. Brendan of Clonfert has to give up a site on Tulach Brendan as being too close to Lorrha! There is the story of the deputation from the saints of Ireland to make Ruadhan and his monks abandon their life of idleness, for they were able to live entirely on the sap of the magic tree! But this story, with its corollary of monks deserting to Lorrha from other Irish monasteries, is simply one lifted out of pre-Christian mythology and tales of magic.

Tara does not seem to have been abandoned till mid-7th century;

the story of its cursing is a myth. The account, as given in the ' Lives ' of Ruadhan, does contain two little bits of interesting information. It brings vividly to one's mind the Irish homesteads, the raths with their narrow, roofed entries:— for the high king's envoy would not walk through them politely but carried his spear athwart so that the rath wall had to be pulled down to let him in. Again, when Aed Guaire, king of Ui Maine, killed the envoy for this conduct, Ruadhan hid him in an underground chamber under the floor of an oratory at Poll Ruadain (Pollrone, Kilkenny). In answer to the king's questioning of the saint of the whereabouts of Aed, Ruadhan avoids telling a lie or telling where the man is, by saying, " I don't know, unless he be under your feet ". This story is of interest as a literary reference to the souterrains so commonly found in Irish raths and at some ancient Irish church sites.

Another tale makes Ruadhan a friend of Colman Elo. A hind comes each evening to Lorrha to be milked for Ruadhan, and then runs to Lann Eala for a morning milking for Colman! Another of the legends makes Ruadhan a friend of Aed mac Bricc. But very little indeed emerges about the real saint Ruadhan. It seems possible that St. Maelruain (' servant of Ruadhan ') had some connection with Lorrha. Yet it is always difficult to be sure why a child should be given a particular name, Maelruain does not necessarily mean a live devotion to Ruadhan in the child's family:— just so a child may be christened Michael in honour of the archangel, or equally on account of his Uncle Mick!

Ruadhan's hand, enshrined in silver, was preserved at Lorrha until the Reformation period, when it was lost.

RUMOLD (ROMBAUT)

July 3

Rumold (Rombaut, Rombaud) apostle of Malines, where his relics are still preserved, lived as a hermit in that part of Belgium. He was murdered c. 775. His supposed Irish origin is yet another tribute to Ireland's reputation as an island of saints. The earliest surviving ' Life ' of Rumold, by Thierry of S. Trond, itself as late as c. 1100, makes no mention of an Irish origin for Rumold.

For the development of the legend of an Irish origin for these continental saints, and the significance of the legend itself, see J. Hennig. *The Place of the Archdiocese of Dublin in the Hagiographical Tradition of the Continent.* Reportorium Novum. Vol. 1, no. 1, 1955, pp. 45-63.

RUPERT (RUDBERT)

March 27 (29)

Another saint of alleged Irish origin, most probably French, is Rupert (Rudbert/Ruperteach), bishop of Worms and apostle of Bavaria. He died c. 710. He appears, however, to have been a friend and patron of Irishmen in Europe. Ferghil of Salzburg built that city's cathedral in Rupert's honour, the latter was in fact founder of Salzburg.

SAMTHANN

December 19

Frimm anmain rop fáilid,
co naidbli a slógaid,
cain glanmann Dé dúilig,
Samthann Clúana Brónaig!

Blithe unto my soul,
with the vastness of her host,
be the fair manna of elemental God,
Samthann of Cluain Bronaig!
(Martyrology of Oengus)

Cluain Bronaig, Clonbroney, Co. Longford, lies off the main road from Granard to Longford, about five miles WSW of Granard. Its patron, Samthann, died in 739. She is the latest in date of the Irish saints included in the Stowe Missal litany, and she and Maelruain the two latest in the list in the Canon (diptychs) in the same Mass liturgy. Her cult spread early abroad, where it seems to have been introduced at Salzburg by St. Ferghil (q.v.)

It is evident that Samthann was one of the great women saints of Ireland, but the surviving Latin ' Life ' is late and includes a good deal of conventional material—multiplying food, releasing captives, with other stories belonging to the cult of the saint in later times. Thus it tells how the old bent stick, the bachall of the saint, was miraculously straightened to allow its enshrinement at the order of king Niall son of Ferghal (Niall Frossach, king from 763 to 778). On the other hand it also includes some sayings of the saint which seem likely enough to be genuine.

Samthann's father was named Diamran, her mother Columba, she came of Ultonian stock, and was fostered by the king of Cairbre Gabhra, Cridan. The consummation of a " made match " was miraculously prevented and Samthann went her own way to become a nun. She went first to St. Cognat at Ernaide (Urney—oratory—south-west of Strabane on the borders of Donegal and Tyrone). From there she moved to Clonbroney. This is claimed a Patrician foundation, the ' Life ' represents it as given to Samthann by a different and still living founder, St. Fuinech (December 11th).

Some little bits of local colour emerge from the account; how the wooden oratory was built and of its shifting when the monastery was being enlarged. Probably belonging to the period after Samthann's death is the account of the prioress, Nathea, travelling into Connacht to get pinewood for their building. Samthann first appears to Nathea in sleep telling her where to find suitable timber; then to the owner of the woods. Striking him with her bachall, Samthann forced him not only to donate the timber but to provide transport for it back to Clonbroney!

One story of the release of captives relates to a " rex Kennedus ", perhaps Cinaed son of Irgalach (d. 728). Two formulas for their release are given. One, reminding of St. Ita's devotion to the Blessed Trinity, would seem to apply to a period when Samthann was alive. Kennedus' captive, Fallamain, is sent a message that he be freed from his chains in the name of the Holy Trinity and is to go in safety to Samthann, handmaid of the Trinity. The other formula, used by Nathea when she leads a party to obtain the release of a hostage from a king of Tethbha, is to tell the captive to be free of his chains and come to them " in the name of Our Lord Jesus Christ and holy Samthann His handmaid ".

Samthann's sayings are of some interest. A certain monk asked in what attitude one should pray, lying, standing, sitting. He got the obvious retort that prayer should be made in every position. A teacher, named Daircellach or Taircellach, comes to Samthann and tells her he is going to give up study so as to have more time for prayer. Samthann answers that he will never be able to form and fix his mind and pray, if he neglects the study of spiritual things. He then says he wants to go abroad on pilgrimage, and Samthann answers that God is near to all who call on Him, one can reach the kingdom of heaven without crossing the sea.

She is also represented as a lover of poverty, the community did not keep more than six cows, and she refused to accept large estates as gifts. On her death, the ard ri, Aedh Allan, made a poem in her honour. Of the records of subsequent abbesses of Clonbroney, the last to be recorded died in 1163, " Caillech Domhnaill, the daughter of Naoneanaigh, abbess of Clonbroney and coarb of Samthann ".

J. J. MacNamee: *History of the Diocese of Ardagh.* (Dublin, 1954), pp. 86-93, 579. Aedh Allan's poem and the subsequent history of Clonbroney are included in this account.

SENACH

Senach was a very common name, saints bearing it are commemorated in the Martyrologies at January 10, February, 11, May 11, June 22, August 21 (abbot Clonard), September 10, November 2 and 10. Very little seems known of any of them and I have not been able to discover anything about the Senach of the very interesting remains on Oilean t-Seanaig in the Magharee Islands, Co. Kerry. Here enclosed by a massive cashel wall survive a group of beehive huts, two stone oratories, one partly ruined by the encroaching sea, and a plain high cross. An underground passage leads from one of the beehive cells to a chamber in the cashel wall.

One tradition makes Senach a brother (? in religion, monk) of Senan of Scattery. It is, of course, possible that the Magharee Islands were connected with Senan's monasteries; equally, they might have links with those of Brendan of Clonfert. A Senach, abbot of Brendan's Clonfert, died in 604. That Senach was a fairly early saint and the Magharee foundation an old one, seems indicated by the discovery of the beautiful early cross pillar at the old graveyard at Kilshannig on the mainland opposite the island.

Account of the remains on Magharees in the R.S.A.I. handbook of 1905, *Guide to the northern, western and southern islands and coasts of Ireland.*

F. Henry: *Early Christian Slabs and Pillar Stones in the West of Ireland.* J.R.S.A.I., 1937. Vol. 67, pp. 265-279.

SENAN

March 8

Senan of Inis Cathaigh (Scattery Island) off Kilrush in the mouth of the Shannon, is a saint still honoured by the last of the islanders and by the people of the adjacent mainland. Scattery, a sizeable, fertile island, became an important monastery. Yet certain information about Senan is rather sparse. He is said to have died on March 8th, 544. A Metrical ' Life ' in Latin survives as well as a prose ' Life ' in Latin and another in Irish (in the Book of Lismore). These give different pedigrees for the saint, the Irish version making him son of Gerrgenn, the metrical, son of Ercan and the Latin prose ' Life '' of Ergind. However, there is a real Senan at the back of the conflicting traditions and the wonder tales told of him.

He was born near Kilrush, Co. Clare, at Magh Lacha, now Moylough. Here " rounds " are still made by the local people at graveyard and holy well on March 8th and June 29th.

It seems that Senan's family had two farms, one at Moylough and the other at a spot called Tracht Termainn, perhaps summer grazing, shieling or booley. There is a pleasant account of their seasonal comings and goings between these two places and of Senan being sent ahead to ready the place for the family's arrival. A version of the Colman MacDuach story of the flying dinner is here introduced, when Senan, failing to get ahead and make preparations, brings farm buildings and plenishings flying through the air !

Senan does not seem to have originally intended to be a monk. He is said to have gone, unwillingly though, by the " violent force of the Prince ", on a raid of his own Corco Baiscinn people into Corcomruadh (Corcomroe). Here he went to sleep in a barn and was left behind, however the Corcomruadh folk let him go free. Later on, he was one evening driving his father's cattle from Irrus to Magh Lacha, and coming to Dún Mechair, asked a night's shelter and was refused. Here on the north shore of the Shannon, the sea runs inland in places, and it seems Senan, in the dusk, tried to cross one such inlet. Suddenly he, waiting the ebb, saw the strand clear before him, he drove the cattle across but as he lifted his feet over high tide mark on the further shore, he heard the wave striking his heels. This was Senan's road to Damascus. " Sufficient for me is the length of time I have been at this layman's work," said he, and broke his spear to make a cross of it.

Senan studied first with a certain Cassidan in Irrus, then with Notál at Cell Manach Droichit, which has been identified with Kilnamanagh in Kilkenny. The 'Lives' list various foundations which Senan then made after leaving Notál. Iniscarra on the Lee, a little way up river from Cork city, is one of the best known. However, he returned to his home country on Shannon side and to its numerous islands. Where Fergus meets Shannon, he founded a monastery on Inis Mor, most probably Canon Island. At the end of the 12th century, Donal Mor O Brien of Limerick, " restored " the monastery there by making a foundation of Augustinian canons. As well as the beautiful and very complete remains of their house and church on Canon Island, there is also an older cashel wall. Before Senan landed on Inis Mor, a contrary wind swept him onto Inis Tuaiscirt, most probably another Shannon island, not the one of that name in the Blasket group. He also made a foundation on Inis Caerach Céoil, Mutton Island, off the Clare coast north of Kilkee, which still has a ruined church dedicated to Senan. His name is associated with the ruined beehive oratory and cell on the stack of rock off the cliffs just south of Kilkee. The Bishop's Rock was most probably in Senan's time not an island, but a headland fort, on which a little church was placed. Later cliff erosion cut through the neck of the headland and made the place an island.

His principal monastery however was on Inis Cathaigh (Scattery Island), the low green island about a mile off the coast from Kilrush. The Cata is, in the legend, a monster which Senan must first expel before taking over the island, a theme found in other 'Lives' of Irish saints. The legend in the Senan version is attractive in the way it brings Senan into contact with the archangel Raphael. Raphael tells Senan that God put the beast on the island to keep it free from any human sin, until Senan should be ready to take the place. Together, saint and angel survey the property from the highest point of the island, the Angel's Height (Ard/Cnoc an Aingil), and go sunwise around the island to bless it. (The sunwise, right handed round, at tide mark, is part of the traditional pilgrimage on Scattery). Later, there was a drought, and the legend tells of the angel coming to point out to Senan at night where to dig for a new well. Senan dug with a holly stick, " as Senan dug, the angel cleansed ". Seanan left the stick in the ground when the work was finished, by morning it was a full grown tree! It is also said that the local king, Mac Tail, objected to

Senan taking the island and unsuccessfully tried to dislodge him therefrom.

Another amusing tale, it is no more, is of the virgin Canair who wanted to be buried on Scattery. Senan would allow no woman on his property. Canair argued with him. " Christ is no worse than you are. Christ came to redeem women just as much as men. He suffered just as much for the sake of women as of men. Women gave service and help to Christ and to His apostles. Women enter the kingdom of heaven just as often as do men. Why then, should not women land on your island?" Senan relented, allowed Canair to land, and later be buried on Scattery.

The island today is dotted with the grey ruins of the churches which later formed part of this important monastery. Teampall na Marbh, so called from being the present and only burial place, is close to the landing place. The building is not earlier than the 14th century. Inland a little are the remains of the cathedral (Ard Eaglais) and an oratory alongside it, together with the magnificent round tower, complete and the tallest remaining in Ireland. The cathedral is thought to be of 9th or early 10th century date, the oratory probably 11th century. Higher up the slope of the island is Senan's well and church, Teampall Senan. It is here the saint is buried. There is an inscribed slab too:—OR DO MOENACH AITE MOGROIN, Pray for Moenach, tutor of Mogran. Finally on the very height of the island with a wonderful outlook up and down Shannon are the scanty remains of the Angel's Church, a building striking even in its present ruin for the way enormous undressed boulders were incorporated into the lower courses of its wall. The traditional pilgrimage, till lately made by the islanders, is a circuit, barefoot, of the whole island, and then five rounds at all the churches and the well.

From Scattery, Senan also worked on the Kerry side of the Shannon. The common Kerry Christian name of Synan represents Senan.

The shrine of Senan's bell was bought in London in 1921, for £1,300 and presented to the Royal Irish Academy by the purchaser, Mr. G. W. Panter.

P. Grosjean, S.J.: *Trois Pièces sur S. Senan.* Analecta Bollandiana, t. 66 (1948), pp. 199-230.

For the remains on the island, R.S.A.I., *Guide to the Northern, Western and Southern islands and coasts of Ireland.* Dublin, 1905.

Colman of Cloyne is claimed to have been the author of the metrical life of Senan.

SINACH MAC DARA

September 28

Sinach (Sionach) Mac Dara, of the island of Cruach Mac Dara in southern Connemara, off the coast west of Carna, is one of many Irish saints to whom a very strong local devotion has persisted, but nothing is known of the man himself. A pilgrimage, in Connemara hookers, goes out to the island on July 16th and a regatta held at the same time; the saint is also honoured on his proper feast day. Sinach Mac Dara may have lived in the 6th century. On the island is the much photographed and almost complete massive stone oratory. With its projecting antae and steeply pitched roof and high gables, it has been suggested that it represents a wooden building translated into stone! Here too is a holy well, a series of crosses and " altars ", at which rounds are made, and as well, what appear to be the foundations of beehive cells. A wooden figure of the saint, now lost, was once preserved in the chapel. The elaborately carved gable finial of the chapel, of imported blue limestone, was found in 1884.

Sailing ships used to salute the island and the saint by dipping their sails as they passed it. To omit this salute was held unlucky and traditions tell of the fate that overtook the skippers who neglected to carry it out. Mac Dara is invoked in traditional prayers. From Aran comes this one:—

Aingil Dé d'ár gcoimhdeacht	Angel of God protecting us, and
'S d'ár sábháilt arís go faoithin,	saving us again till night,
Ar choimrí Dé agus Muire,	Under the protection of God and
Mhic Duagh agus Mhic Dara,	Mary,
Agus Cholmcille,	Mac Duagh and Mac Dara,
Arís go faoithin.	And of Colmcille,
	Until night.

F. J. Biggar: *Cruach MacDara, off the coast of Connemara; with a notice of its Church, Crosses and Antiquities.* J.R.S.A.I., vol. 26, (1896), pp. 101-112.

TIGERNACH

April 4 (5)

Cain Tigernach credal
ar Chríst cech mbáis breuis,
asa mbrucht srúaim sois,
Clúana álne hEuis.

Sing pious Tigernach,
for Christ's sake he conquered
every lust,
Out of whom burst a stream
of knowledge,
of beautiful Clúain Euis.
(Martyrology of Oengus).

Of Tigernach of Clones, whose death is placed in 549 or 550, very little is recorded. He was, it appears, the illegitimate child of Derfraich, one of three young women being fostered by king Echachus (Eochaid) of Oriel. His father was a Leinsterman named Cairbre. The child is said to have been taken to Kildare, to Brigit and Conleth for baptism; later to have been carried off by pirates to Britain. In that country he studied at Whithorn. Then he returned to Ireland and made his principal foundation at Clones, Co. Monaghan. In his old age, he is said to have gone blind. Eogan of Ardstraw (q.v.) is supposed to have been his great friend, indeed the two are said to have been carried off together to Britain. Hymns for Vespers and Matins on Tigernach's feast day, have been preserved with the Latin ' Life ' of the saint. A round tower and a high cross still survive at Clones.

Spiritalis tritici semen erogavit
Dogmatizans populis culpas relaxavit,
Sua dans pauperibus, se Deo donavit.
(from the hymn for Vespers).

APPENDIX

Stowe Missal : The Litany

Peccavimus, domine, Peccavimus parce peccatis nostris et salva nos qui gubernasti Noe super undas dilui, exaudi nos et Ionam diabiso (de abysso) verbo revocasti, libera nos qui Petro mergenti manum porrexisti auxiliare nobis Christi fili de ficisti mirabili domini cum patribus nostris et nostris propitiare temporibus, emite manum tuam de alto libera nos Christe, audi nos Christ, audi nos Christi, audi nos, cyrie elezion.

Sancta Maria   ora pro nobis
Sancte Petri
Sancte Pauli
    Anrias (Andreas)
    Iacobi
    Bartholemai
    Tomae
    Mathei
    Jacobe
    Tathei   (Matthia)
    Madiani (Thaddaee)
    Lucae
    Stefane
    Martini
    Hironime
    Augustine
    Grigorii
    Hilari
    Patricii
    Ailbei
    Finnio
    Finnio
    Ciarani
    Ciarani
    Brendini
    Brendini

Columba
Columba
Comgilli
Cainnichi
Findbarri
Nessani
Factni
Lugidi
Lacteni
Ruadani
Carthegi
Coemgeni

Mochonne
Sancta Brigta
    Ita
    Scetha
    Sinecha
    Samdine

Omnes sancti orate pro nobis
Propitius esto parce nobis
Domine propitius esto libera nos
    Domine
ab omni malo libera nos Domine
Per crucem tuam libera nos
    Domine.

LITANIES OF THE SAINTS

In Irish, from the 12th century Book of Leinster.

LITANY OF IRISH SAINTS—1

Seven hundred and seventeen holy bishops of the people of the grace of the Lord in Corcach Mór with Bairre and Nessen, quorum nomina scripta sunt in celis.

Hos omnes invoco in auxilium meum

Seven fifties of holy bishops with three hundred priests, whom Patrick ordained with three hundred alphabets (which he wrote) when consecrating churches, whereof was said:

> Seven fifties of holy reverend bishops
> Did the venerable one ordain,
> With three hundred virgin priests
> On whom he conferred orders.
>
> Three hundred alphabets he wrote,
> Sweet was the good fortune of his hands,
> Three hundred fair churches he left,
> He raised them from the ground.

Hos omnes invoco in auxilium meum

Three fifties of holy bishops in Ailén arda Nemid;

Hos omnes invoco in auxilium meum

Seven fifties of holy bishops, seven fifties of priests, seven fifties of deacons, seven fifties of subdeacons, seven fifties of exorcists, seven fifties of lectors, seven fifties of door-keepers, with all holy monks (endowed) with the grace of God at Loch Irci in the borders of Muscraigie and Ui Eachach Cruada, ut dicitur:

> The commemoration of Loch Irci
> Wherein is a little bell melodious;
> Many as leaves on branches,
> Are the Saints that are therein.

Hos omnes invoco in auxilium meum

Forty saints in Glen da Loch with Coemgen, noble priest; with Mochoe of Aired; with Maelanfis; Mochua of Cluain Dolcain; Morioc of Inis bó finne; Affinis (a Frank) priest; Cellach, a Saxon and arch-deacon; Dagan (of Inber Daile); Moshenoc (of Mugna); Mochonoc (of Gailinne); Moshinu (of Glenn Munare); Mobai (mac hua Allae); Rufin (an anchorite); Mogoroc (of Dergne); Silan (a bishop); Darchell (an abbot); Molibba (son of Araide); Guaire (son of Dall); Glunsalach (of Slíab Fuait); Murdebur (brother of Caeman) sage and scribe; Corconutan (brother of Murdebur); Aedan (brother of Caeman) son of Congnad; Lochan of Cell Escrach; and Enna; Petran (of Cell Lainne); and Menoc, etc.

Hos omnes invoco in auxilium meum

Twenty seven holy bishops in Cell Manach Escrach with Lochan and Enna

Hos omnes invoco in auxilium meum

Ten thousands and nine score hundreds (28,000) of priests in Cluain Mór with Maedoc and Mac ind Eicis (i.e. son of the poet);

Hos omnes invoco in auxilium meum

Three thousands and three hundreds with Gerald the bishop and fifty saints of Luigne of Connaught who occupied Mag Eo of the Saxons;

Hos omnes invoco in auxilium meum

Seventeen holy bishops in Cell Ailech of the Uí Echach; two holy bishops in Daurthech of the Uí Briuin Cualann; seven pilgrims of Imlech Mór;

Hos omnes invoco in auxilium meum

Three fifties of holy bishops and twelve pilgrims with Sinchell the younger the priest; and with Sinchell the elder, the bishop, and the twelve bishops who occupy Cell Achid of Drummfota among the Ui Falge:

Hos omnes invoco in auxilium meum

These are the names of bishops at Cell Achid: Budoci (3), Conoci (3), Morgini (3), Uedgoni (6), Beuani (6), Bibi (6), Glomali (9), Ercocini (9), Grucinni (9), Uennoci (12), Contumani (12), Anoci (12).

The Senchilli (the two Sinchells above mentioned) were Britons from Britain, the Cerrui from Armenia.

LITANY OF THE SAINTS—2

Thrice fifty coracles of Roman pilgrims who landed in Erin with Ele, with Notal, with Neman the venerable, with Corconutain;
>Per Iesum

Three thousand anchorites who assembled with Mumu (? from Munster) for one quest with Bishop Ibar, to whom the angels of God brought the great feast which St. Brigit made to Jesus in her heart;
>Per Iesum

Thrice fifty men of orders, true royal heroes each one of them, of the Gaels, who went on pilgrimage in one company with Abban Mac hUi Chormaic:
>Per Iesum

Thrice fifty other pilgrims who went with Abban to Erin of men of Rome and Letha;
>Per Iesum

Seven hundred true monks who were hidden in Rathen before Mochuta went on his course of exile to Lesmór;
>Per Iesum

Eight hundred men who occupied Lesmór with Mochuta, each third one of them a man of the grace of God;
>Per Iesum

Thrice fifty true monks under the yoke of Bishop Ibar;
>Per Iesum

The monks of Fintan Mac Uí Echach; they fed on nothing but herbs of the earth and water. There is not room to enumerate them because of their multitude. Eight Fintans among them;
>Per Iesum

Four thousand monks with the grace of God under the yoke of Comgall of Benchor;
>Per Iesum

Thrice fifty true martyrs under the yoke of Munnu son of Tulchan, on whom no man may be buried till doom;
>Per Iesum

Thrice fifty true pilgrims across the sea with Buite the bishop, and ten holy virgins with the grace of God;

Per Iesum

The twelve pilgrims who went with Maedoc of Ferns across the sea

Per Iesum

Twelve youths who went to heaven with Molasse without sickness, the reward of their obedience;

Per Iesum

Twelve youths who went with Columcille on pilgrimage to Alba;

Per Iesum

The twelve pilgrims of whom Brendan found one man alive in the Cat's Island;

Per Iesum

Three score men who went with Brendan to seek the land of promise;

Per Iesum

Thrice fifty true monks with the grace of God in Daire Connaid;

Per Iesum

Four and twenty men of Munster who went with Ailbe on the ocean to revisit the land of promise, who are there alive till doom;

Per Iesum

The anchorite whom Brendan found before him in the land of promise, with all the saints who fell in all the islands of the ocean (i.e. the household of Patrick);

Per Iesum

Colman Find (the white) with twelve men in Martra Corthea;

Per Iesum

The Romans in Achad Galmae (in Ui Echach); the Romans in Letair Ecra; the Romani and Cairrsech daughter of Brocan in Cell Achid Dallrach; Cuan the Roman in his church;

Per Iesum

The innocent boys in Cell Ailche, i.e. thrice fifty lads;

Per Iesum

Alfinus, the holy pilgrim, and Mochonoc, and Mochasco, and Anfegen cum sanctis omnibus in Tech na Commairgi;

Per Iesum

The Romans in Cluain Cain Cumni; the pilgrim in Cluain cain Mor;

Per Iesum

The Romans with Aedan in Cluain Dartada;

> Per Iesum

The twelve Dogheads with the two Sinchells in Cell Achid; the dogheaded ones with Manchan of Liath Mór;

> Per Iesum

Seven monks of Egypt in Disert Uilaig;

> Per Iesum

The pilgrim with Mochua son of Luscu in Domnach Resen;

> Per Iesum

The pilgrim in Belach Forcitail;

> Per Iesum

The pilgrim in Cuil Ochtair;

> Per Iesum

The foreigners in Saillide; the foreigners in Mag Salach;

> Per Iesum

The foreigners in Achad Ginain;

> Per Iesum

The Saxons in Rigair;

> Per Iesum

The Saxons in Cluain Mucceda;

> Per Iesum

The pilgrim in Inis Puinc;

> Per Iesum

The twelve pilgrims in Lethglas Mór;

> Per Iesum

The twelve men of the household of Finnia in Ard Brendomnaig

> Per Iesum

Nine times fifty monks under the yoke of Mochoe of Noendruim;

> Per Iesum

Fifty men of the Britons with the son of Moinan in Land Léri;

> Per Iesum

Five pilgrim men in Suide Chail;

> Per Iesum

Thrice fifty pilgrims in Gair Meic Moga;

> Per Iesum

Thrice fifty disciples with Manchan the Master;

> Per Iesum

Twelve men who went with Ailbe to death;

Per Iesum

The three Ui Corras with their seven;

Per Iesum

Twelve men with Morioc (i.e. Mac hUi Laegde) across the sea;

Per Iesum

The twelve boys in Daire Raibne;

Per Iesum

The fifteen men who went with Ciaran of Saighir;

Per Iesum

The folk that went with Patrick to Sliab Arnchin(?);

Per Iesum

Fifty four men who went to martyrdom with Donnan of Egg;

Hos omnes invoco   Per Iesum

(Whilst there is no break in the MS at this point, the litany changes its character and the following section may in fact be a separate composition).

Seven holy bishops of Druim Urchailli; shb ** of Cell Derc Daim; shb of Tulach na nEpscop; shb of Domnach Eochailli; shb of Tulach Olcain; shb in Dart;

Per Iesum

Seven holy bishops of Cell Giallain; shb of Miliuc Fiaich;

Per Iesum

Seven holy bishops of Mag Bolg; shb of Mag Brechmaigi; shb of Druim Dúin;

Per Iesum

Seven holy bishops of Druimm Airbelaig; shb of Raith Cungi; shb in Dairi;

Per Iesum

Seven holy bishops in Imlecha;

Per Iesum

Seven holy bishops in Tamnacha;

Per Iesum

Seven holy bishops of Domnach Ailmaigi; shb of Domnach Iarlainni;

Per Iesum

**Shb:— Seven holy bishops.

Seven holy bishops of Domnach Calliraigi; shb of Domnach Lethan; shb of Domnach Lini; shb of Domnach Mor Chuti; shb of Domnach Maigi Luadat; shb of Domnach Aband Lifi;

Per Iesum

Seven holy bishops of Domnach Mór Maigi Coba; shb of Domnach Mór Damairni; shb of Domnach Mór Findmaige; shb of Domnach Mór Culae; shb of Domnach Mór Alaith; shb of Domnach Mór Tuammae; shb of Domnach Mór Phile;

Per Iesum

Seven holy bishops of Druimm Lethind; shb of Druimm Airmedaig; shb of Raith na nEpscop; shb of Domnach Mór Echraid;

Per Iesum

Seven holy bishops of Cluain Domail with Aedán; shb of Cluain Eithne; shb of Cluain Bainb; shb of Cluain Airthir;

Per Iesum

Seven holy bishops of Rigdond;

Per Iesum

Seven holy bishops of Domnach Fairne; shb of Domnach Ascaid; shb of Domnach Fothirbe; shb of Domnach Tamnaigi Buaidche; shb of Tamnach Fiachrach;

Per Iesum

Seven holy bishops of Coine, shb of Cell Fróich; shb of Druimm Alad; shb of Tuaim Fobair; shb of Cell Tine; shb of Disert na nEpscop; shb of Raith Baruu;

Per Iesum

Seven holy bishops of Magh Itha; shb of Dún Gaimin; shb of Fothairbe Mór; shb of Domnach Cule; shb in Echaired; shb in Troscad; shb of Coilbda;

Per Iesum

Seven holy bishops of Druimm Salaind; shb of Cell Tuaiti; shb of Domnach Mór Maige Femin; shb of Druimm Airthir; shb of Druimm Lias; shb of Cluain Cae; shb of Cluain Find (chaill); shb of Druimm Aiti;

Per Iesum

Seven holy bishops of Cell Cuilind; shb of Cell Belota; shb of Coindera; shb of hI (Iona); shb of Cuil Carech;

Per Iesum

Seven holy bishops of Domnach Mór Áine; shb of Domnach Maige Fane; shb of Domnach Mór Argarui; shb of Domnach Mór Drothir Dremna; shb of Domnach Mór Santlóir; shb of Domnach Mór Assi; shb of Domnach Dromma Cethig;

Per Iesum

Seven holy bishops in Raith Scothgan; shb of Bordgal; shb of Cluain Muccada; shb of Cluain Cain;

Per Iesum

Seven holy bishops of Cell Inbir; shb of Cell in Chluana; shb of Cell Fini; shb of Cathir Suibni; shb of Ard Chluain; shb of Daire;

Per Iesum

Seven holy bishops of Domnach na nEpscop; shb of Tech Lonain; shb in Raith Cind Slebi; shb of Achad Ualind; shb of Achad Nitt; shb of Ross Roichbi;

Per Iesum

Seven holy bishops of Domnach Mór Direthir; shb in Etargabail; shb of Tech Silain; shb in Glenn Moronoc; shb of Tír Cóicfhir;

Per Iesum

Seven holy bishops in Domnach Nachain; shb of Domnach Taulche; shb of Domnach Ualand; shb of Domnach Úa Fithis; shb of Domnach Erobi; shb of Domnach Bernsa; shb of Sen-Domnach;

Per Iesum

Seven holy bishops of Cell Forlochta; shb of Cell Cunid; shb of Cell Culi; shb of Cell Onchon; shb of Cell Aedloga; shb of Cell Raisse; shb of Cell Úa Carthind;

Per Iesum

Seven holy bishops in Uthmana; shb in Ucht Foraid; shb of Raith meic Mella; shb of Achad Glinni; shb of Enach Duin; shb of Tuaimm da Ualand;

Per Iesum

Seven holy bishops of Tulach Labair; shb of Tulach Craebain; shb of Druimm meic Thail; shb of Cúil Ferthigi; shb of Ardachad Brechmaige;

Per Iesum

Seven holy bishops of Raith Epscoip Comraide; shb of Raith Fiachrach; shb of Domnach Achaid Shetna;

Per Iesum

Seven holy bishops of Cluain Emain; shb of Cluain Airthir; shb of Cluain Daim; shb of Cluain Bini; shb of Cluain Rathe; shb of Cluain Talatho;

Per Iesum

Seven holy bishops of Tech na Commairge; shb in Rúscacha; shb of Cell Ard; shb of Cell Garbain; shb of Findglass;

Per Iesum

Seven holy bishops of Tech Áine; shb of Cell Roiss; shb of Cell Iae; shb of Cluain Fota;

Per Iesum

Seven holy bishops of Druimm Druith; shb of Brúcas; shb of Druimm Craebain; shb of Druimm Crema; shb of Carraic Mor;

Per Iesum

Seven holy bishops of Cell Corbran; shb of Cell Bratha; shb in Land Lere; shb of Uinnes Mór; shb of Domnach Cairne;

Per Iesum

Three hundred true monks who occupied Lethglenn, and twelve hundred of the servants of God with Molasse and the two Ernans; and Martin holy bishop of Lethglenn:

Hos omnes invoco in auxilium meum

———

Recite this (to wit) the seven bishops, over water against boils and jaundice, and the plague and every other pestilence. Let the water be applied to the sick man et bene sanat et reliqua. Finit. Amen.

A LIST OF IRISH WOMEN SAINTS FROM A SHORT LITANY IN THE BOOK OF LEINSTER.

(Entitled ' Litany of the Virgins ' in the Henry Bradshaw Society's edition of the Irish Litanies. This, so far as the MS evidence is concerned, is the oldest of the Irish metrical litanies)

> I place myself under the protection,
> Of Mary the pure Virgin,
> Of Brigit, bright and glowing,
> Of Cuach of great purity,
> Of Moninna and Midnat,
> Of Scire, Sinche, and Samchaine,
> Of Caite, Cuach, Coemill,
> Of Craine, Coipp, and Cocnat,
> Of Ness the glorious of Ernaide,
> Of Derbfalen (?) and Becnat,
> Of Ciar and Crone and Caillann,
> Of Lassar, Locha (?) and Luaithrenn,
> Of Rond, of Ronnat, of Rignach,
> Of Sarnat, of Segnat, of Sodelb,
> And of the virgins in one place (i.e., all together)
> North, South, East, West.

A Sermon of an Irish Saint

ST. COLUMBAN: Sermon 13.

We have been talking about the miseries of human life, as we know it each day, and with that, the fear aroused by the prophecies of God. Talking as far as we are able to do so effectively, though some of our listeners may say we talk too much! But it seems worth while to us, rousing, if not other people's sloth, at least our own. Whatever about the very learned, for the likes of us, even a little of knowledge and wisdom is useful. It is wrong to keep quiet about what is harmful. So it seemed better to speak about it, even to speak badly, rather than say nothing. Better too to deal with that subject than with mere trifles or things of no particular use.

So please listen again, for what we have to say further can be of use to you.

We want to talk about that divine fountain from which you may quench the thirst of your souls. Drink, yes, but be yet thirsting for more. For it is the living fountain, the fountain of life, who calls us to himself saying, " Whoso thirsts, come to me and drink ". Understand what it is you drink. Isaias will tell you in the words of the fountain himself, " For, says the Lord, they have abandoned the fountain of living water ". (This text is actually from Jeremias, 2, 13). It is the Lord himself, our God, Jesus Christ, who is the fountain of life and he asks us to come to that fountain that we may drink him. He drinks who loves, who is filled by the word of God, who cares enough, longs enough, who is eaten up with the desire of wisdom. Yes indeed, we, the gentiles, should drink eagerly that which the Jews forsook. Perhaps it was said of us with the gentiles: ' He breaks off in amazement of mind, the heads of the mighty shall be moved, nor do they open their mouths, like a poor man eating in secret ' (Cf. Habacuc, 3, 14). That was written about the perfect, and we too should open the mouth of our inner man for the eating of that bread which came down from heaven. Let us eat fast and eagerly, that no one see us, as if we ate in secret. Therefore let us eat the bread, drink at the fountain; both of them the same Lord Jesus Christ. He says, as it were for our taking, that he is the living bread which gives life to this world, and at the same time explains he is also the fountain, saying, ' Whoever thirsts, come to me and drink '; of which fountain the prophet also said, ' For with you is the fountain of life '.

Look at the source of the fountain, for it and the bread which comes down, have the single source. For our God, the Lord Christ, the only Son, is both bread and fountain, for whom we ought always to hunger. And though we eat him in loving, feast on him in desiring; we must still hunger the more for him. In the same manner with the fountain, we should drink him always in the fulness of love and of longing, enjoying something of his sweetness. For the Lord is sweet and pleasant; so that while we eat and drink him, so we should always continue to hunger and thirst for him for our food and drink cannot ever be exhausted. Though he is eaten, he is not consumed; though he is drunk, he is not lessened. For our bread is eternal and our fountain is perennial and sweet. So then, the prophet says, ' You who thirst, go to the fountain '; the fountain that is for those who thirst, not those who are surfeited. So then, he calls the hungry and the thirsty, whom at another time he had called ' blessed ', to himself, those who have never drunk enough, for the more they drink, the more they thirst.

Yes, indeed we should long for, look for and love the ' fountain of wisdom, the word of God on high ', in which, as the Apostle tells us, ' all the treasures of wisdom and knowledge are hidden '. Those who thirst for it, he calls to drink. If then, you thirst, drink the fountain of life; if you are hungry, eat the bread of life. For they are blessed who hunger for this bread and thirst for this fountain. The more they eat and drink, the more they long to eat and drink. For that is sweet beyond all else, ever eaten and ever drunk, yet always hungered and thirsted for, always tasted and always desired; of which the prophet king said, ' Taste and see how sweet, how lovely is the Lord '. Therefore, let us follow this call by which we are called to the fountain of life by the Life which is the fountain, not only a fountain of living water, but of eternal life, a spring too of light and brightness, for from him comes all these things, wisdom and life and eternal light. The author of life is the fountain of life; the creator of light, the source of light. Therefore turning our backs on the created things of this world, we, like wise and intelligent fish, should seek the fountain of light and life and living water in highest heaven, that there we may drink the living water that springs up to eternal life.

Merciful God, just Lord, I wish that you would let me come to that fountain, and that there, with those of yours who thirst, I might drink of the living stream of the living fountain of the water of life. Then rejoicing in that sweetness, clinging to him on high, I could say, How beautiful is that spring of living water, which never goes dry, water springing up into eternal life. Lord, you yourself are that fountain, always to be longed for, always to be drunk. Lord Christ, give us this water that it may be in us a fountain of living water, springing up into eternal life. Yes, I know I'm asking a lot. But, King of Glory, you know how to give great things and have made great promises. There is nothing that is greater than you, and you have given yourself to us, who gave yourself for us. So we ask that we may know what we love, for we are asking nothing less than yourself to be given to us. For, you are our all, our life, our light, our health, our food, our drink, our God. Our Jesus, inspire our hearts with that breath of your Spirit and wound our souls with your love, so that we all can say in truth, ' Show me he whom my soul has loved; for I am wounded by love '. Lord, I would like those wounds. For blessed indeed is a soul so wounded by love. It will seek the fountain, always drink, yet always thirst, for here to drink is to thirst the more. Thus it will seek in loving whilst it is healed in being wounded. May then the Physician of righteousness and health, our God and Lord Jesus Christ, wound our inmost souls with this healing wound, who is one with the Father and the Holy Spirit, world without end. Amen.

BIBLIOGRAPHY

The sources of information about the Irish saints are very scattered. The two attempts, saying nothing of their critical value or otherwise, at a complete " Acta Sanctorum " for Ireland, of John Colgan and John O'Hanlon, were both cut short, one by the difficulties of the times, the other by death. Again, one must distinguish between hagiography and history. The present work has attempted to keep to the history of the saints, as against the study of the development and interrelations of the legends of the saints. It is true that history may be dug out of hagiography, but many of the studies published on the material relating to the Irish saints are more concerned with the history and development of the literary legend than with the facts with which the present book is concerned.

The Bollandists' *Acta Sanctorum* began publication in 1643, following the order of the calendar, and has now reached the month of November. Here are published, for the Irish saints, such ' Lives ' and critical remarks thereon as were available at the particular period of their publication. From the same source, *Analecta Bollandiana* contains a great deal of information on Irish hagiography in many numbers of its issues.

For Irish saints, *per se*, John Colgan set to work upon his " *Acta Sanctorum veteris et majoris Scotiae seu Hiberniae, sanctorum insulae* ", but only the volume for the first three months of the year reached publication (Louvain 1645). Colgan also produced his " *Triadis Thaumaturgae* " (Louvain 1647) which is concerned solely with Patrick, Colmcille and Brigit.

Much later, John O'Hanlon (1821-1905) attempted an English and popular but fully comprehensive " Lives of the Irish Saints ". Death overtook him when the volume for October was still unfinished. To us, O'Hanlon's uncritical, pious and interminably long-winded accounts are utterly unreadable, but a certain amount of inspired skipping can make available tit-bits not otherwise easy to get:— O'Hanlon's own observations of local customs, or his often excellent footnotes, for example.

The ' Lives ' of Irish saints from the *Codex Salmanticensis* have been published as a single volume:—Edinburgh and London 1888 and again recently in the Bollandists' " Subsidia Hagiographica ". The saints included in the Codex Salmanticensis are:—Brigit, Fursa, Brendan of Clonfert, Ciaran of Clonmacnois, Darerca (Monenna), Finian of Clonard, Tigernach, Colmcille, Fintan of Duleek, Ailbe,

Molua of Clonfertmulloe, Fintan of Clonenagh, Finan of Kinnitty, Ruadhan, Aodh of Killare, Cainnech, Fintan (Munnu), Colman Elo, Colum of Terryglass, Maedoc of Ferns, Abban, Cronan of Roscrea, Mael Maedoc (St. Bernard's account), Lorcan Ua Tuathail, Flannan of Killaloe, Senan, Comgall, Carthach, Laisren of Leighlin, Macartin, Ciaran of Saighir, Moling, Colman of Dromore, Coemgen, Baithene, Dagaeis, Mochti, Eogan of Ardstraw, Macnisse, Cuannath (abbot Lismore) and Mochullus.

Excellent critical editions of both Latin and Irish ' Lives ' of a selection of Irish saints were published by Charles Plummer. The Latin Lives: *Vitae Sanctorum Hiberniae,* Oxford 1900 (no translation) include the following saints: —

Vol. 1. Abban, Aed Mac Bricc, Ailbe, Finbar, Berach, Buite, Brendan of Clonfert, Cainnech, Carthach, Ciaran of Clonmacnois, Ciaran of Saighir, Coemgen, Colman Elo.

Vol. II. Comgall, Cronan, Declan, Enda, Fechin, Finan of Kinnitty, Fintan, Gerald, Ita, Molaisse/Laserian, Maedoc, Mochoemog, Mochua of Tech Mochua, Moling, Molua, Munnu, Ruadhan, Samthann, Tigernach.

Plummer's *Bethada Náem nErenn,* Oxford 1922, two vols., text and English translation, has the Irish ' Lives ' of the following saints: — Abban, Finbar, Berach, Brendan of Clonfert, Ciaran of Saighir, Coemgon, Colman Elo, Maedoc, Mochuta (Carthach), the sons of Ua Suanaig and Ruadhan.

The essential guide to this mountain of legend and molehill of history contained in the ' Lives ' of the Irish saints is James F. Kenney's " The Sources for the Early History of Ireland, Vol. I. Ecclesiastical." Columbia University Press, New York, 1929. Again, the author died before he could bring out his second volume on the secular side of the same period. Kenney lists the manuscripts, printed editions, and articles thereon relating to the saints with which he deals. He thus provides a guide to all the published material up to the 1920's, when he was working on his book.

No comparable guide exists for the period after the 1920's. For the saints from Ireland, or supposedly from Ireland, who worked abroad, much excellent material has been published abroad in a variety of languages and periodicals. For the ordinary English speaking reader this source will normally not be available. Nor perhaps will he be much better placed to dig out the many articles published in English, on the saints, the sites connected with them, the manuscripts and the monuments. Important articles are to be found scattered through the Proceedings of the Royal Irish Academy, the Journal of the Royal

Society of Antiquaries, the numerous local Irish historical and antiquarian societies' publications. The early 19th century Ordnance Survey Letters contain local traditions and accounts of the sites as they then stood:—these are available in typescript copies in certain libraries. Published Diocesan histories, of very varying critical standards, often contain good material on the local saints. Now and again, a locally got-out booklet or guide, may have some stray useful bit of information, though normally their critical standard is very low.

Many excellent summaries and articles on the Celtic saints and the Celtic Church and the early liturgy have been published abroad in the monumental French " Dictionnaires." That currently appearing, " Dictionnaire d'Histoire et de Geographie Ecclesiastiques " is carrying a brief and excellent series of accounts of the Irish saints.

Again, articles of importance appear in periodicals of more general scope like the " Irish Ecclesiastical Record " and " Studies". " Irish Historical Studies " now publishes an annual list of important articles dealing with Irish history that have currently appeared, but it does not include all the material that relates to Irish saints—for example the liturgical studies.

The Irish *Annals,* which have now been edited and translated and published at various intervals, are a much briefer and more sober approach to Irish history than that provided by the ' Lives ' of the saints. The material contained in them has not yet been fully worked over as a source for the early Church history of Ireland. In general reliable, the brief entries and dates given in the different series of Annals, need to be handled with an understanding of the sources. The earliest notices now contained in a single consecutive account originated in much more diverse forms, notes written in calendars, liturgical books, separate fragments, and when these came to be put together into one volume, entries and dates could well be separated or misunderstood. It will have been noted how often in the present text, two different dates for the death of a single saint are quoted from the Annals of Ulster.

The popular and liturgical cult of the saints at home and abroad is a specialised and fascinating field of enquiry. There are very numerous Offices of Irish saints in both manuscript and printed Continental breviaries. Dr. John Hennig seems so far, the only person to have attempted to study and understand the significance of the continental legend, and the liturgical celebrations, connected with Irish saints.

For the mind of the Irish saints, a far better and more certain approach than the ' Lives ' is through the surviving fragments of the liturgy as celebrated in early Ireland, and through surviving prayers and hymns and commentaries. Kenney, in his work cited above, notes details of this material as well as of the " Lives". The Henry Bradshaw Society of London has published a number of early Irish liturgical texts, as well as the Martyrologies of Tallaght, Oengus and Gorman.

In the present book, specific references of importance are listed after the entry for the saint concerned. The collections of ' Lives ' and more general references are listed, however, in the general bibliography. In addition to the sources cited above, the following books and papers should be noted.

Abbreviations:—used here and in the main text:—

P.R.I.A. Proceedings of the Royal Irish Academy.

P.S.A.S. Proceedings of the Society of Antiquaries of Scotland.

J.R.S.A.I. Journal Royal Society of Antiquaries of Ireland.

J.C.H.A.S. Journal Cork Historical and Archaeological Society.

I.E.R. Irish Ecclesiastical Record.

L. Bieler, " Recent Research on Irish Hagiography." Studies 1946 pp. 230-238; 536-544.

E. G. Bowen. " The Settlements of the Celtic Saints in Wales." Cardiff 1954.

F. P. Carey. " O'Hanlon of the ' Irish Saints ' ". I.E.R. September 1955 pp. 145-163.

Alexander Carmichael. " Carmina Gadelica." Edinburgh 1900. A collection of traditional Gaelic hymns and prayers with translations and notes.

Henry S. Crawford. " Descriptive List of Early Cross Slabs and Pillars." J.R.S.A.I. 42 (1912) pp. 217-244: 43 (1913) pp. 151-169; 261-265; 326-334. " Descriptive List of Irish Shrines and Reliquaries " J.R.S.A.I. 53 (1923) pp. 74-93; 151-176.

H. Daniel-Rops. " The Miracle of Ireland." Dublin 1959. " The Church in the Dark Ages," London 1959.

Liam de Paor. "A Survey of Sceilig Mhichil " J.R.S.A.I. 85 (1955) pp. 174-187.

Máire & Liam de Paor. " Early Christian Ireland," London 1958.

Sr. Mary Donatus. " Beasts and Birds in the Lives of the Early Irish Saints." Philadelphia 1934.

Michael Duignan. " Irish Agriculture in Early Historic Times." J.R.S.A.I. 1944. pp. 124-145.

Aloys Fleischmann. " References to Chant in Early Irish MSS " pp. 43-49. Féilscríbhinn Torna, Cork 1947.

Louis Gougaud, O.S.B. " Christianity in Celtic Lands," London 1932. " Gaelic Pioneers of Christianity," Dublin 1923. " Les Saints irlandais hors d'Irlande " Étudiés dans le Culte et dans le devotion traditionnelle. Louvain 1936.

J. Hennig. " Irish Saints in the Liturgical and Artistic Tradition of Central Europe." I.E.R. March 1943, pp. 181-192. " Studies in the Liturgy of the Early Irish Church." I.E.R. 1951 April, pp. 318-333. And very many other papers in different publications, a number of which are cited at the appropriate entries in this book.

F. Henry. " La Sculpture Irlandaise pendant les douze premiers siècles de l'ère Chrétienne." 2 vols. Paris 1933. " Irish Art in the Early Christian Period " London 1940. " Early Christain Irish Art." Dublin 1954. And a number of papers on specific sites and crosses, including the following surveys:— " Early Christian Slabs and Pillar Stones in the West of Ireland " J.R.S.A.I. 67, pp. 265-279. " Early Monasteries, Beehive Huts, and Drystone Houses in the neighbourhood of Cahirciveen and Waterville, Co. Kerry." P.R.I.A. 58 C 1957. pp. 45-166.

W. P. MacArthur. " The Identification of Some Pestilences recorded in the Irish Annals." Irish Historical Studies, March 1949. pp. 169-188.

Eoin MacNeill. " Phases of Irish History," Dublin 1920. " Celtic Ireland," Dublin 1921. " Early Irish Laws and Institutions," Dublin 1936.

John T. McNeill & Helena M. Gamer. " Medieval Handbooks of Penance." Columbia University Press, 1938. With translations of the principal Penitentials.

G. T. Marcus. " The First Discovery of Iceland." Studies 1955, pp. 315-318.

D. D. C. Pochin Mould. " Ireland of the Saints," London 1953. " Irish Pilgrimage," Dublin 1955. (A study of the Irish pilgrimages). " The Celtic Saints," Dublin 1956. (A study of Celtic spirituality).

Felim O Briain, O.F.M. " The Expansion of Irish Christianity." Irish Historical Studies March 1943, pp. 241-266. September 1944, 131-163. " Irish Missionaries and Mediaeval Church Reform " pp. 228-254, Miscellanea Historica Alberti de Meyer. Louvain 1946. " The Blessed Eucharist in Irish Liturgy and History." pp. 216-245. Studia Eucharistica. Antwerp 1946. " Irish Hagiography: Historiography and Method," pp. 119-131, Measgra Mhichil Uí Chléirigh. Dublin 1944. " Miracles in the Lives of the Irish Saints." I.E.R. November 1945, pp. 331-342. " Saga Themes in Irish Hagiography " pp. 33-42. Féilscríbhinn Torna, Cork 1947. " The Hagiography of Leinster " pp. 454-462. Féilsgríbhinn Eóin Mhic Neill. Dublin 1940.

C. O Danachair " The Holy Wells of Co. Limerick " J.R.S.A.I. 85

(1955) pp. 193-217. " Of North Kerry," J.R.S.A.I. 88 (1958) pp. 153-163. " Of Corkaguiney, Co. Kerry " J.R.S.A.I. 90 (1960) pp. 67-78. "Of Co. Dublin," pp. 68-87 Reportorium Novum, Vol. 1, No. 1 (1957-8).

The study and careful listing of holy wells is a guide to early monastic sites and to the state of present day devotion to Irish saints. " Bealoideas " contains other papers by various authors on holy wells and associated traditions, etc. e.g., 1933, Carlow; 1934, Tipperary; 1936, Donegal.

Tomas Ó Fiaich: Gaelscrínte I gCéin. Dublin, 1960.

Colm O Lochlainn. " Roadways in Ancient Ireland " pp. 465-474. Féil-sgríbhinn Eóin Mhic Neill, Dublin 1940.

Standish O Grady. Silva Gadelica. 2 vols. London 1892.

P. Power. " The Bounds and Extents of Irish Parishes." Féilscríbhinn Torna, pp. 218-223. Cork 1947.

J. Ryan, S.J. " Irish Monasticism." Dublin 1931.

St. John D. Seymour. " Irish Visions of the Other World ". London 1930.

W. Douglas Simpson. " The Celtic Church in Scotland." Aberdeen 1935.

Whitley Stokes. Editor and translator. " Lives of Saints from the Book of Lismore." Oxford 1890.

Whitley Stokes & John Strachan. " Thesaurus Palaeohibernicus." Vol. II, Cambridge 1903. Includes Irish prayers, hymns and glosses.

Anselmo M. Tommasini. " Irish Saints in Italy." London 1937.

P. Walsh. " The Dating of the Irish Annals." Irish Historical Studies, September 1941 pp. 355-375. " Genealogiae Regum et Sanctorum Hiberniae ". Dublin 1918.

W. J. Watson. " The History of the Celtic Place-Names of Scotland ". Edinburgh and London 1926. (Contains much detailed information about Irish saints in Scotland—church sites, wells, etc).

INDEX

In this index of placenames and personal names, the principal references are given in roman type, the subsidiary ones in italics.

A

Abban, of Ballyvourney, 194: of Killabban, *2*, 14: of Moyarney, *14*
Achonry, *151*, 265
Adamnan (Eunan), 15, *25*, *93*, *198*, *199*
Adamnan's Croft (Scotland), 16
Aengus the Culdee—see Oengus
Aedan of Ferns—see Maedoc
Aed Mac Bricc, 22, *281*
Aed Slane, 23, 86
Aghaboe, 52, *154*, *162*
Aghabulloge, 162
Aghowle, 166
Aidan of Lindisfarne, 5, *25*, *90*, *173*
Ailbe, *2*, 28, *136*, *138*, *140*, *142*
Airbertach mac Coisi-dobrain, lector Ross Carbery, 150
Albert, 30
Alcuin, 155, 156, 191, 199
Aldfrith, king, 15, 18
Alexandria, 19
Amulree (Scotland), 243
Annagh (Co. Kerry), 37
Annegray, 110
Anselm, 65, 221
Aodh mac Bricc—see Aed
Aodh Ua Foirreidh, bishop Armagh, 62
Applecross (Scotland), 241
Aran Islands, *28*, *33*, *72*, *84*, *91*, *95*, 147, *193*
Arculf, bishop, 18
Ardagh, *43*, 245
Ardfert, 37, *251*
Ardmore (Co. Waterford) 138
Árd Óilean (High Island, Connemara) 151, *247*
Ardpatrick, 70, 223
Ardstraw, 149, *289*
Armagh, 5, *32*, 62, *67*, *75*, *206*, *210*, *211*, *219*, *247*, 278

Arnold's Seat, St. (Scotland), 15
Arraglen, 38
Arrouaise, 226
Assicus (Asic/Tassach), 30
Athracht (Attracta), 31, *265*
Aübigny, 200
Auxilius, 32, 273, 278

B

Bachuil (Lismore, Scotland), 261
Baithene, 16, 87, 101, 175
Balla (Co. Mayo), 249
Ballinskelligs, 223
Ballyvourney, *34*, 192
Bamborough (England), 27
Bangor (Ireland), 7, *10*, *11*, 49, *58*, *97*, 107, 125, *164*, *172*, 187, 221, *234*, *238*, *241*, *258*, *259*
Barra (Scottish Hebrides), *39*, 163
Bealin (Co. Westmeath), 74
Bede, 17, 20, 26, 89, 134, 182, 191, *246*, 266
Beggary Island (Co. Wexford), 195
Benedict, 112
Beginish, Valencia, 6
Benen (Benignus), 32, *199*, *278*
Berchert of Tullylease, *4*, 33
Bernard, 220, 259
Bishop's Rock (Co. Clare), 286
Birr, *17*, 35
Bline, (Monenna), 262
Bobbio (Italy), *106*, 123, *129*, *146*, *189*
Boniface (St.) 155, 201
Boniface IV, Pope, 120
Boyndie (Banff, Scotland), 39
Braighwee (St. Mogue's Island), 215
Brendan of Birr, 35, *167*
Brendan of Clonfert, *12*, 36, *84*, *99*, *107*, *147*, *158*, *167*, *171*, *184*, *193*, *197*, *199*, *253*, *280*, *281*
Breuil, 156

Brian Boru, 51, 65, 150
Brigit (Brigid), 41, 51, 145, 146, 156, 159, 173, 179, 184, 244, 254, 262, 289
Brigown (Co. Cork), 164
Bristol, 39
Brittany, 39
Broccán Clóín, 44
Brude, king, 56, 97, 127
Bruges, 45
Buite (Boecius) of Monasterboice, 48
Burgh Castle (Suffolk, England), 183
Bute (Scotland), 39

C

Cadoc, 53
Cadroe, 64
Caencomrac, bishop, 230
Caher Island (Connemara), 90
Caimin of Inis Cealtra, 50
Cainnech (Canice), 39, 52, 86, 97, 107, 127, 133, 167, 172, 176, 184
Canair, 287
Candida Casa (Whithorn, Scotland), 3, 31, 98, 148, 149, 167, 170, 247, 263, 267, 289
Canice—see Cainnech
Canon Island (Shannon), 286
Canterbury, 65, 70
Cape Clear (Co. Cork), 76
Capel Colman (Wales), 85
Capel Madog (Wales) 215
Carbuddo (Scotland), 48
Carthach (Carthage/Mo Chuta, Mo Chuda), 57, 86, 230, 253, 259
Cashel (Co. Tipperary), 28, 30, 140, 148, 158, 224, 226; Synod of Cashel, 6, 67, 85, 206
Castle Bernard (near Kinnitty), 158
Castledermot (Co. Kildare), 230, 231
Cathal (Cataldus) of Taranto, 61
Caylan of Nendrum, 85, 246
Ceannaille (Burren, Co. Clare), 91
Cellach mac Aodh (Celsus), 60, 62, 205, 220
Cellan of Peronne, 183, 184
Celsus—see Cellach
Christian Ua Conairche, bishop of Lismore and papal legate, 209
Church Island (Lough Currane, Co. Kerry), 158
Church Island (Valencia, Co. Kerry), 247

Ciaran (Kyran) of Clonmacnois, 71, 142, 147, 156, 167, 184, 239, 271
Ciaran (Kieran) of Saighir, 2, 53, 76, 138, 167, 204
Cill Bhrianainn (Scotland), 39
Cill Mo-Luaig (Scotland), 260
Clairvaux, 225
Cleenish (Lough Erne), 107, 175
Cloghane (Co. Kerry), 38
Clogher, 213, 220, 224
Clonard, 15, 35, 37, 53, 68, 72, 94, 107, 137, 158, 165, 245, 250, 258, 280, 284
Clonbroney (Co. Longford), 282
Clonenagh, 50, 126, 171: 230, 239
Clones, 289
Clonfert, 35, 36, 234, 284. Synod at, 211
Clonfertmulloe, 257
Clonmacnois, 5, 6, 23, 27, 51, 71, 87, 133, 232
Clontarf, battle of, 5
Cloyne, 84
Coemgen (Kevin) of Glendalough, 14, 79, 149, 207
Cogitosus, 44
Coinleán of Tuosist (Co. Kerry), 200
Colman of Cloyne, 84, 199, 239
Colman of Dromore, 85, 246
Colman Elo, 58, 80, 173, 230, 248, 281
Colman of Lindisfarne, 4, 27, 89, 191
Colman MacDuach, 91, 288
Colman Mac Murchon, 11, 171, 235
Colman Mac Ui Cluasaig, 44
Colmcille (Columba), 3, 4, 7, 15, 20, 25, 35, 39, 46, 48, 53, 86, 93, 107, 127, 147, 156, 160, 167, 170, 173, 174, 184, 235, 245, 256, 259, 264, 266, 270, 277, 288
Colmonell (Ayr, Scotland), 88
Columba—see Colmcille
Columban (Columbanus), 3, 4, 7, 10, 13, 105, 128, 130, 156, 167, 173, 184, 185, 186. Sermon of, 300
Colum Mac Crimthainn, 50, 167, 172
Comgall, 10, 39, 54, 56, 58, 97, 107, 125, 175, 184, 242, 257
Cong, 6, 65, 81, 151
Conleth (Conlaid/Conlaed) 44, 132, 289
Connor, 85, 86, 214, 222
Constantinople, 18, 20

Coolavin, 31
Cooldrevny, battle at, 95
Corcumruadh (Co. Clare), 29, 92
Cork, 65, 160, 212, 222, 226
Cormac MacCarthaigh, king, 222, 226
Cormac Ua Liathain, 39, 99, 267
Critan, hermit, 128
Croagh Patrick, 82, 279
Croit Mo Luáig (Scotland), 260
Cronan of Roscrea, 132
Cruach MacDara, 33, 288
Cu-Chuimne, 11, 235
Cummean Fota, 235, 256
Cuthbert, 27, 134

D

Dalbach of Kilcullen, 230
Dabhach Mo Luáig (Scotland), 260
Dairinis (near Lismore, Ireland), 230
Damhnat of Tedavnet, 146
Darerca—see Monenna
Darerca of Valentia, 263
David, 31, 135, 139, 166, 215, 258
Declan, 2, 135, 137, 159
Derry, 93, 224
Devenish, 22, 216, 232, 250
Diarmaid/Dermot, 142
Diarmait of Castledermot, 230
Diarmait of Iona, 232
Diarmait Mac Murchadha, king of
    Leinster, 206, 217
Dimma MacNathi, Book of, 133
Donard (Domangort), 143
Donat (Donatus) of Fiesole, 143
Donnan of Eigg, 241
Dornoch, 163
Down, 222, 224
Downpatrick, 42
Dromore, 85
Drumahose (Co. Derry), 54
Drumceatt, Convention of, 4, 98, 127
Drumlane, 215
Drumsnat (Co. Monaghan), 257
Dublin, 5, 66, 67, 70, 205, 227
Dublitir, 230, 232, 233
Dunadd (Scotland), 97
Dun Cethirn, battle of, 127
Dunlichity (Inverness, Scotland), 160
Dunshaughlin, 278
Durrow, 88, 93
Duthac, 243
Dympna of Gheel, 146

E

Edan—see Maedoc
Eilean Fhionain (Loch Shiel, Scotland)
    160
Eilean Ma-Ruibhe (Scotland), Loch
    Maree, 242: Loch Shin, 243
Eilean Mhunna (Loch Leven,
    Scotland), 175
Elair of Monahincha, 230
Elphin, 30
Ely Island (Lough Erne), 126
Emly, 28, 159, 164
Enda, (Eanna), 3, 28, 33, 73, 84, 147,
    166
Eogan (Eugene), 80, 149, 289
Erc, 37
Eu (Normandy), 206
Eunan—see Adamnan

F

Fachtna (Fachanan), 149
Faha (Mount Brandon, Co. Kerry),
    38
Faithlenn, 159
Fanahan—see Findchu
Farne Island, 134
Faro, 157, 200
Faughart, 42
Fechin, 151, 265
Felim, 154
Ferdacrich of Dairinis, 228
Ferghil (Virgil/Virgilius), 154, 282
Ferns, 214, 253
Fiacre of Breuil, 156, 200
Fiacre of Ullard, 128, 156
Fiesole, 143
Finan Cam, 158, 193
Finan Lobur, 159
Finbar of Cork, 136, 150, 160
Findchu (Fanahan), 164
Finglas, 230, 232
Finian of Clonard, 3, 53, 73, 94, 107,
    137, 158, 165, 184, 245, 246, 280
Finian of Moville, 25, 85, 94, 126, 127,
    169, 246, 263, 268
Fintan of Clonenagh, 126, 171
Fintan (Findan) of Rheinau, 173, 229
Fintan (Munnu) of Taghmon, 20, 174,
    203, 248
Flann of Monasterboice, 49, 63
Flannan of Killaloe, 177

Flannan Islands, 178
Foillan (Faelan/Feuillan), 182, 185
Fontaines, 110
Fore (Co. Westmeath), 151
Fosse (Belgium), 183
Fothad na Canoine, 230, 239
Friars Island (Shannon/Killaloe), 180
Fridian (Frediano/Frigidian) of Lucca, 180
Fridolin, 181
Fursa (Fursey), 40, 181

G

Gall, 3, 106, 108, 119, 186, 200
Garranes (Rath Raithleann, Co. Cork), 161
Gartan (Co. Donegal), 94
Garvellach Islands (Scotland: ? Adamnan's Hinba), 39, 55, 97, 269
Gelasius—see Gille Mac Liag
Gemman, 94
George, 20
Gerald of Mayo, 4, 33, 90, 191
Gertrude of Nivelles, 183
Gervase of Arrouaise, 226
Gheel, 146
Gilbert—see Giolla Easpuig
Gille Mac Liag (Gelasius), 224
Giolla Aodh Ua Múighin, 227
Giolla Christ Ua Morgair, 220, 224
Giolla Easpuig of Limerick (Gilbert), 68, 223
Glasnevin, 53, 94, 245
Glencolumcille (Co. Donegal), 95
Glendalough, 5, 14, 79, 206, 211, 251, 253
Glenfinnan (Scotland), 160
Glen Lyon (Scotland), 16
Glen Urquhart (Scotland), 16, 100
Gobnet, 192
Gougane Barra, 161
Gregory the Great, 114, 180, 258
Gregory VII, Pope, 66
Guaire, king of Connacht, 50, 91, 152

H

Hare Island (Lough Ree), 74
Hartlepool, 27, 90

High Island—see Árd Óilean
Hinba, 39, 55, 97, 99, 127: and see Garvellach Islands
Hollywood (Wicklow Mountains), 80
Hugh Mac Bricc—see Aed Mac Bricc

I

Ibar (Ivor), 2, 14, 28, 138, 140, 195, 262
Iceland, 4, 40
Imar Ua h-Aedhacain, 220
Inchagoill (Lough Corrib), 192
Inchcleraun (Lough Ree), 142
Inchinnan (Scotland), 170
Inchkenneth (Inner Hebrides), 54
Inchmahome (Lake of Menteith, Scotland), 85
Iniscarra (Co. Cork), 286
Inis Cealtra (Lough Derg of Shannon), 50, 84, 144
Inisdadroum (Fergus River), 39
Inisfallen, 28, 158
Inisfallen (Ireland's Eye), 160
Inisglora (Co. Mayo), 39
Inishboffin (Connemara), 90, 178, 191: (Lough Ree), 20
Inishlannaun (Lough Corrib), 178
Inishmore (Aran Islands), 33, 91, 148
Inismacsaint (Lough Erne), 72
Inismurray (Co. Sligo), 5, 23, 179, 218, 252, 264
Inis na mBeo (Island of the Living, Monahincha), 82
Inis Tuaisceart (Blasket Islands), 38
Inverchapel (Scotland), 175
Inverness, 56
Iona, 5, 11, 15, 25, 36, 54, 75, 87, 90, 93, 127, 156, 175, 231, 232, 259, 270
Ireland's Eye—see Inisfallen
Iserninus, 273, 278
Ita (Ide), 37, 39, 150, 156, 184, 196, 283

J

Jarlath, 37, 84, 199
Jarrow (England), 5
Jerusalem, 18
Jonas, 106, 128, 186

K

Kells, 5, 69, 93, 251: Synod of, 67, 206, 227
Kenneth—see Cainnech
Kevin—see Coemgen
Kieran—see Ciaran of Saighir
Kilarrow (Islay, Scotland), 242
Kilbarry and Kilbarr, 162, 163
Kilberrihert, 34
Kilbride, 45
Kilchennich (Scotland), 55
Kilchenzie (Scotland), 55
Kilcolmanel (Knapdale, Scotland), 88
Kilcullen (Co. Kildare), 230, 231
Kildare, 5, 41, 132, 166, 179, 289
Kilennan (Islay, Scotland), 160
Kilgobnet, 193
Kilian of Aübigny, 157, 200
Kilian of Würzburg, 200
Kilkenny, 53
Killabban, 14
Killala, 264, 277
Killalee, 264
Killaloe, 159, 177, 210
Killantringan (Scotland), 269
Killaraght, 31
Killare, 23
Killeedy, 37, 197
Killeely, 204, 264
Killeevy, 262
Kilmachalmaig (Bute, Scotland), 85
Kilmaclenine (Co. Cork), 84
Kilmacreehy (Co. Clare), 50
Kilmacduagh, 91
Kilmacrenan (Co. Donegal), 94
Kilmainham, 203
Kilmalkedar, 38, 244
Kilmanaheen, 264
Kilmarie (Skye, Scotland), 242
Kilmarow (Kintyre, Scotland), 242
Kilmeadan (Co. Waterford), 199
Kilmeedy, 198
Kilmodan (Glendaruel, Cowal, Scotland), 215
Kilmore, 154
Kilmore (Co. Roscommon), 175
Kilmun (Scotland), 175
Kilmurray, 264
Kilnamanagh (Tallaght), 80, 83, 149
Kiloran (Colonsay, Scotland), 271
Kiltallagh, 58
Kilshannig (Co. Kerry), 284

Kinnitty, 158, 193
Kirkbuddo (Scotland), 48
Kirkcowan (Scotland), 149
Kirkcudbright, 24
Kirkgunzeon (Kirkcudbright, Scotland), 170
Kirkmabrick (Wigtown, Scotland), 24
Kirkmadrine (Scotland), 38
Kyran—see Ciaran of Clonmacnois

L

Labbamolagga, 249
Lagan Choinnich (Scotland), 55
Lagny, 183
Lambay Island, 5
Lamlash (Arran, Scotland), 203
Lanfranc, 65
Laserian (Laisren), 177, 203
Laserian of Devenish—see Molaise
Leighlin, 203
Lelia—see Liadhain
Lérins, 112, 277
Lesmahagow (Scotland), 154
Letteragh (Co. Tipperary), 270
Liadhain (Lelia), 204
Limerick, 5, 204, 210, 263
Lindisfarne, 5, 26, 34, 89, 191
Lisbon, 45
Lismore (Ireland), 5, 57, 70, 178, 209, 210, 221, 230, 237, 259
Lismore (Scotland), 259
Livinus, 204
Llandaf (Wales), 48
Llangolman (Wales), 85
Llanffinan (Anglesey, Wales), 160
Llanmadog (Wales), 215
Llansantffraid (Wales), 45
Llawhaden (Wales), 215
Loch Maree (Scotland), 242
Lorcan Ua Tuathail, 6, 9, 82, 205
Lorrha, 230, 233, 280
Lough Currane (Co. Kerry), 158
Loughrea, 25
Lough Ree, 22, 31
Lucca, 180
Luxeuil, 110, 187
Lynally, 58, 86, 214, 230, 281

M

Macartan, 213

Mac Caille, 43
Maccoige, 215
Mac Creiche, 50
Mac Nisse, 214
MacRegnol of Birr, gospel book of, 36
Maedoc (Aedan/Mogue) of Ferns, *136*, 214, *219*, 237, *251*, *258*
Maeldithruib, 232
Mael Maedoc (Malachy), 6, 9, 63, *103*, *205*, 219
Maelruain of Tallaght, 5, 7, *10*, 228, *257*, *281*, *282*
Maelrubha (Malrubius), 241, *260*
Magharee !slands, 284
Maghera, 143
Magnenn, 203
Malachy—see Mael Maedoc
Maol Iosa Ua Ainmire (Malchus), 221, 223
Maolmuire Ó Dunáin, 6, 68
Martin of Tours, *3*, *112*, *115*, 267
Martinstown (near Kilmallock), 259
Mayo, *33*, 90, 191
Mel (Maol), *43*, 245
Mellifont, 225
Melrose, 27, 90, 134
Michael (archangel), 11, 51, 171, 234, 244
Milan, 120, 129
Mitchelstown, 164
Mobi, *53*, *94*, *167*, 245
Mochamnoc of Inis Cealtra, 84
Mochaoi of Nendrum, 246
Mochoemog, 197
Mochua of Balla, 249
Mochua of Timahoe, 248
Mo Chuda (Mo Chuta)—see Carthach
Modomnoc, 136, 159
Modwenna, 262
Mogue—see Maedoc
Molagga, 249
Molaise of Devenish, *22*, *167*, *216*, 250
Molaise of Leighlin—see Laserian
Molaise of Inismurray, 252, *264*
Moling, *217*, 231, 235, 252
Molua of Clonfertmulloe, 257
Mo Lua of Killaloe, 178, 180
Moluag of Lismore (Scotland), *3*, 97, *127*, 259
Monahincha (Island of the Living/Inis na mBeo), *54*, *82*, 133, *230*, 232
Monasterboice, *6*, 48, *61*, 75

Monasterevin, 42, 45
Monenna (Darerca), *184*, 261, *268*
Moone (Co. Kildare), 95, 231
Mothel (Co. Waterford), 232
Mount Brandon (Co. Kerry), 38: (near Bristol), 39
Moville, *11*, 25, *94*, *126*, *127*, 169
Moyarney (Co. Wexford), 14
Moylough (near Kilrush), 285
Mugint, 170
Muirchertach Ua Briain, high king, 66
Muirchú moccu Machtheni, 277
Muiredach of Monasterboice, 48
Mullagh (in diocese of Kilmore), 200
Munchin, *204*, 263
Mungret, *219*, 265
Munnu—see Fintan Munnu of Taghmon
Muredach, *252*, 264
Mutton Island (Co. Clare) 286

N

Nathy, *151*, 265
Nechtan's Mere, 15
Nechtan Morbet, king, 48
Nendrum, *31*, *85*, 246, *268*
Nessan, 265
New Ross, 172
Nigg (Kincardine, Scotland), 157
Ninian, *3*, *94*, *98*, *148*, *167*, *170*, *263*, 265
Ninnid, 72, 73, 167
Nivelles (Belgium), *173*, 183

O

Oengus (Aengus) the Culdee, *85*, *230*, 239
Oengus Ua Gormain, abbot Bangor, 221
Olan of Aghabulloge, 162
Omey Island (Connemara), 152
Oran (Odran/Odhran/Otteran), *98*, 270
Orkney, 39
Oswald, king, 25
Oswin, king, 26
Otteran—see Oran
Oughtmama (Burren, Co. Clare,) 92

P

Palladius, 2, 277
Patrick, 2, 7, 12, 28, 30, 32, 42, 46, 64, 74, 88, 138, 156, 173, 183, 184, 195, 214, 245, 246, 262, 264, 268, 271, 272
Patrick's Purgatory (Lough Derg, Donegal), 82, 226, 279
Peronne, 182
Piacenza, 146
Port Mo Luáig (Raasay, Scotland), 260

R

Racoon (near Ballintra), 31
Rahan, 58, 86, 230, 251
Raholp (Co. Down), 30, 247, 268
Rahugh (Co. Westmeath), 23
Raphoe, 16, 17
Rathan (Co. Donegal), 230
Rathan—alternative spelling of Rahan
Rath Breasail, synod of, 67, 220
Rathlin O Byrne Island, 31
Ratisbon, 30
Reichenau, 53, 187
Reilig Oran (Iona) 98, 271
Rheinau, 173, 229
Rinansey (Orkney), 269
Rioc, 22
Rome, 82, 106, 224, 268: Irish monastery at, 65, 67
Roscrea, 132
Rosemarkie (Black Isle, Scotland), 260
Rosmead (Co. Westmeath), 199
Rosnat—see Candida Casa
Ross Carbery, 149
Rossinver, 215
Ruadhan, 167, 230, 280
Rumold (Rombaut), 281
Rupert (Rudbert), 155, 282

S

Saighir, 53, 76, 231
St. Andrews, 55
St. Davids, 135, 166
St. Gallen (Switzerland), 46, 186
St. Kilda, 39
St. Mullins, 231, 252

St. Ronan's Well (Lewis, Outer Hebrides), 260
St. Vigeans (Scotland), 154
Salzburg, 154, 282
Samthann, 156, 282
Sarbile (Monenna), 262
Saul, 278
Scattery Island, 72, 133, 150, 285
Sean Ross (near Roscrea), 133
Secundinus, 32, 256, 278
Senach, 284
Senan, 73, 84, 142, 284, 285
Shetland, 39
Silao, 180
Sinach Mac Dara, 33, 288
Sinell, 107, 167, 175
Sinlan of Bangor, 49
Skellig Michael, 159, 265: Ballin-skelligs, 223
Slane Hill, 278
Slemish, 277
Slieve Donard, 143
Slieve Gullion, 261
Slieve League, 22, 23, 31
Stellan of Inis Cealtra, 50
Swords, 95, 159

T

Taghmon, 174, 215
Tallaght, 5, 7, 10, 20, 80, 228, 257
Tara, 280
Taranto, 61
Tassach, 30
Tedavnet, 146
Tehelly, 176
Teilo, 48
Teltown, synod at, 35
Temple Benen (Aran Islands), 33
Templeport Lough (Co. Cavan), 215
Teampull an Truinnein (Scotland), 269
Teampull Mo Luigh (Lewis, Scotland), 260
Terryglass, 50, 172, 230, 232
Tigernach, 149, 289
Timahoe, 249
Timoleague, 250
Tírechán, 277
Tiree (Inner Hebrides, Scotland), 99, 127, 271
Tiroran (Mull, Scotland), 271

Tobar Maedog, 217
Tobar na Molt (Wether's Well, Co. Kerry), 37
Tobar olla Bhreanain (Valencia), 39
Toberaraght, 32
Tobermory (Mull), 242
Toirdelbach Ua Briain, high king, 66
ToorWell (Co. Waterford), 141
Tory Island, 95
Tuam, 37, 67, 84, 199, 206, 227
Tullylease (Co. Cork), 33
Tuosist (Co. Kerry), 200

U

Ua Suanaig of Rahan, 230
Uinmeras (Co. Kildare), 42
Ullard, 128, 156, 231
Ultan, 183, 184

Ultan of Ard Breccan, 47, 277
Urney, 283

V

Valencia, 6, 38, 247, 263
Virgil/Virgilius—see Ferghil

W

Wales, 2, 39, 45, 47, 48, 53, 85, 86, 9
135, 139, 166, 195, 215
Waterford, 5, 66, 69, 208, 210, 22
270
Wether's Well—see Tobar na Molt
Whitby, synod of, 4, 27, 89
Whithorn (Scotland), 3, 38, 267—se
Candida Casa
Würzburg, 200